12/11

HOBOPHOBIA:
THE POLITICS OF FEAR

by BILL BOUDIER

Editors: Michelle B. Raley, Sarah Driffill and Eileen Wilson
Formatting and Design: Michelle B. Raley

Consultant: Denise Sewart

Published by Bonita and Riverside Press
Roseville, California
2017

www.rosevillehobophobia.com
www.hobophobiathebook.com

ISBN: 9780692678374
Library of Congress 2016937872

Contents

Definition of the Word "Hobophobia"

(noun) fear of hobos or homeless persons

http://nws.merriam-webster.com/opendictionary/
newword_search.php.

Submitted by: J.C. Moore from Pennsylvania on
Aug. 14, 2008 15:02

Origin of the Word "Hobophobia"
Hobophobia – 1992:

"...Cormack and other St. Rose officials lament a new strain of
discrimination – "hobo-phobia."
Sacramento Bee Placer Neighbors,
November 19th, 1992

"Hobophobic (Scared of Bums)" – 1995*

American punk rock band NOFX

Hobo – I'm hobophobic so what AH AH AH
Scared of bums
Not just because they stink bad
Not just because they're crackers
From drinking too much Lysol
Let them be
Just don't get ------n' near me
Scared of bums AH AH AH AH
Infested with microscopic bugs
Endocrine systematic Doo Doo
Why don't they get a job?
Let them be
Scared of bums AH AH AH

*Track 1, "Heavy Petting Zoo," Recorded October 1995, *Epitaph*
Records, Razors Edge Studios and Fat Planet 1996©
2013 Anti, Inc. ISRC: USEP40310301

This Book Is Dedicated

To the homeless men and women who have found themselves living on the streets of our community over the years and who may have been subjected to unnecessary force, bullying and violence at the hands of both private citizens and public officials.

To those who fear seeking aid in shelter programs because they imagine it is more dangerous than living on our streets, like Erica and Melinda.

To those who have died on our streets, like Juan Lara and Big Mike.

To those who were once productive citizens of Roseville, but who could see no rational alternative to homelessness as they slowly descended into the hell of schizophrenic hallucinations and delusions, eventually disappearing into custodial care, like Neal.

May Providence protect and console them. They are children of God, just like you and me.

"Don't forget to show hospitality to strangers, for in doing so, some have entertained angels without knowing it."
Hebrews 13:2 (63 AD) World English Bible Version

Acknowledgements

I'm very grateful to the people who have blessed my life by bringing me to the place where I could write this book, especially my parents Ed and Evelyn Boudier, the De La Salle Christian Brothers, Father Michael Cormack, James H. Bush, Sherry Schiele and Annette Boudier.

These kind and caring people have helped me become ever more aware of the needs of the homeless men and women I have encountered.

To each of them, I am very indebted for their encouragement, good example and generous hearts. I am thankful for their gifts of compassion and understanding from which I have learned.

I am very grateful to Denise Sewart and Mike Miller for their help and partnership with me in forming The Gathering Inn.

To Denise for creating, developing and implementing the program name, trade style and logo, and for her dedication of time and energy to the marketing effort and the formation of The Board of Directors;

To Mike for creating, developing and implementing the business plan, personnel policies and operational procedures, as well as for his dedication of time and energy to the management of the program;

And to both of them for their steadfast support and welcomed good counsel during the program's infancy.

I am very grateful for the financial support and caring example of Eileen and Leo French, whose generosity made the dream of The Gathering Inn year-round shelter program come true.

_____

Preface

As I began planning to write this book in 2011, I pulled out five old file boxes jam-packed with notes and records on Roseville's politics of homelessness going back to the community's beginnings. Getting reacquainted with the material I had accumulated over the last thirty-plus years took some time, leading me to reconsider whether I wanted to dedicate myself to telling this story as it needed to be told.

I had forgotten many of the incidents that popped up from the dusted-off pages. After reading them, I discovered that there were stories within those stories, so many so that it reminded me of opening a Russian stacking doll, only to find a smaller one inside, and then a smaller one inside of that one, followed by an even tinier version hidden within it.

Ultimately, I realized that the only way to weave all of these bits of history into a meaningful narrative was to organize them into what was essentially a journal. That seemed like the best tool to help the reader navigate through the sea of events that make up the history of Roseville's politics of homelessness.

The genesis of my drive to tell this story can be found within an incident that happened in 1987, when my local government began pushing me to discriminate against a class of people based on who they were and how they looked.

There are all kinds of human discrimination, often based on "phobias". Some might seem more important than others: racial (xenophobia) sexual (genophobia) and ageism (gerontophobia) among them. Probably, the degree of importance is in the eye of the beholder, most likely whether or not he or she has been discriminated against.

The kind of discrimination I'm writing about is different. It's discrimination that stems from "hobophobia", the dislike or even hatred of homeless people, especially homeless single men.

When Roseville tried to stop me and the organization I represented from providing hot meals to these people, even though they were peaceful and cooperative, a struggle ensued. It took twenty years to resolve it, and only after a full array of services for these folks had been developed by the community's churches and nonprofit providers.

This is the story of that struggle as it evolved within the larger history of Roseville's endemic aversion to homeless single men.

Introduction

The reaction was less than encouraging nearly every time I mentioned to my friends, and even some family members, that I was writing a book about "hobophobia". Even after I pointed out that it would be focused on their home town, the up-and-coming California city of Roseville, there was a reticence to engage. Each reply was different, but all had a similar ring: "Who cares?" or "So what?"

Their indifference caught me off guard. But I was determined to tell a story that was emblematic of how homeless single adults had been treated across the nation until recently, when their plight became a social justice issue. In my community, the memory of its own hobophobic conduct proved to be very short lived. And what was left of that memory was more the fluff of nostalgia than the hardness of reality.

How could this be? Homelessness in Roseville had been a hot topic of conversation from the 1980s and into the early years of the new millennium. It had drawn the attention of not only our local newspapers, but also of the print and TV media of Sacramento and Los Angeles. Roseville's response to the issue was infamous: City government organized political attacks on the grassroots efforts of citizens to aid homeless persons in the community, adding more fuel to the fire.

The ability of a collective conscience to expunge the abuse it has inflicted on others for decades is stunning and is what allows local governments, to this day, to be less than resolute in helping solve the injustices heaped on their needy populations.

One facet of this book is my recounting of a lifelong experience of engaging with people who are homeless, trying to help them deal with their struggles and demons. I credit my parents for this gift. They taught me by word and example to respect everyone and to always be ready to provide a helping hand.

As for my encounters with the politics of homelessness in Roseville, I have been able to describe, by using the files that I have kept over the years, not only what I sensed was in the hearts of people on both sides of the issue, but also to accurately report what their words and actions were during those times, rather than what they might now wish they had either said or done.

_____

**BIBLIOGRAPHY AND SOURCES OF INFORMATION
ARE LISTED BY CHAPTER NUMBER
ON PAGES 419 THROUGH 436.**

The materials listed, with the exception of emails, St. Vincent de Paul minutes, cited published books and personal appointment books are in the possession of and the property of the Roseville, California, Public Library's Local History Collection.

Chapter 1:
Where the Roads of Times Past Lead Us
(1857–1983)

The sunless sky was as dull and dark as gray could get; the frigid air went right through my winter coat. I was just a kid, nine years old. It was 1950 and Thanksgiving time in Sacramento, California. Winter's usual cold, wet and overcast weather made it a typical gloomy day for the season.

My parents were taking my little brother Johnny and me to a place just a few miles from our nice warm house, to somewhere that would make me feel like I had just landed on another planet. It was a lonely looking place on the northern outskirts of the city that I had seen from a distance along the road many times before as my Pop and I drove to our North Natomas ranch.

This day would be different. We weren't just driving by. No, we were headed into the middle of it. It would be up close and scary. The place was a triangular patch of land overgrown with wild blackberries and laden with small piles of rusty tin cans. It was located where the Garden Highway, Northgate Boulevard and the Arden-Garden Connector now come together.

We were going to drive into a shantytown where homeless squatters lived, Sacramento's last "Hooverville", a remnant of the Great Depression of the 1930s. The fifty or so shacks were built of everything from discarded sheet metal and wooden shipping crates to pieces of used lumber and plain old canvas.

As we pulled off of the paved road and onto the rutted trail, I could see that Johnny was looking as anxious as I felt inside. But deep down, we knew that Ma & Pop had only our best interest at heart. They had shown us when we left home that the trunk of the car was filled with groceries the four of us were going to give to a "poor family". I was about to have an experience that would change me for the rest of my days.

When Pop pulled to a spot with no potholes, the four of us got out of our Buick and walked to the rear of the car. Pop opened the trunk and handed Johnny and me two small boxes of groceries.

Ma said, "Now you boys are to pick out any house, knock on the door and give them the boxes. Be sure to say 'Happy Thanksgiving.'" It

1

only took us a minute to make a choice – the shanty closest to the car. That way we could see Ma and Pop, and they could keep an eye on us.

The tin chimney jutting from the left side of the windowless shack was puffing out small curls of smoke. Johnny and I cautiously approached the door with our boxes of groceries. I timidly knocked, and in a matter of seconds, it creaked open just far enough for a pair of eyes shrouded in darkness to peer out. A woman's weak voice asked, "Yes? What do you want?"

I nervously stretched out my arms toward her showing her my box of groceries. The door quickly opened all the way, and we saw what she was hiding – three little children clinging to her skirt.

As soon as Johnny and I handed her the boxes and blurted out the obligatory "Happy Thanksgiving," we spun around and made a break for the car. We didn't get far. We ran smack into both of our parents who had the rest of the food from the car loaded in their arms. They both were beaming as they turned us back toward the shack and walked us to the open door, giving the woman all that they carried.

Before Ma or Pop could utter a word, the lady graciously smiled and said "Thank you and Happy Thanksgiving!" After a few words of friendship and best wishes, it was over. The woman and her children waved goodbye, the door closed and we were back in our warm Buick, headed for our Land Park home.

Our parents taught us many lessons that day: First, with plenty comes responsibility; second, it makes you feel warm inside to help others; third, respect everyone; and most importantly, given a little kindness, even the most desperate souls can find California to be their land of opportunity.

California has always been known as a modern Eden. It is a place so rich that John Steinbeck in his award winning literary masterpiece, *The Grapes of Wrath*, called it "the land of milk and honey."

His 1939 novel set in the Depression told the story of the Joad family who symbolized the tens of thousands of flat broke refugees who fled the Dust Bowl of the Midwest and headed for California in search of food and jobs. Many Californians quickly labeled them "Okies" and drove them out of their towns, unless there was some farmer or other employer who would put them to work at substandard wages.

But the story of the Okies is one of endurance and eventual success, because no matter how anyone gets to California, the place has always offered a unique promise for those seeking a better life. With the state's abundance of natural beauty, wonder and wealth at hand, it has been proven true that when Californians share these gifts by welcoming and respecting even the poorest outsider of good will, the bounty of this place continues to grow.

Some California towns have been slow to embrace this understanding, in particular railroad towns which are often impacted by homeless people, especially homeless single men who have arrived on freight trains. One such place in the center of the state, Roseville, was afflicted with a particularly deep aversion to these people for most of its one hundred fifty year history. The malady quickly festered into more of a scorn bordering on hatred – what I call "hobophobia". Its origin sprang from the coming of the railroads, but was fed by the anger and fear that poured out of the experiences of railroad workers and into the homes, businesses and public institutions of the town.

1857:

Several years before Roseville was founded, Colonel Charles L. Wilson, a successful builder of San Francisco's transportation infrastructure, came onto the scene, bringing the new age of railroad technology with him. His Sacramento Valley Rail Road Company, which ran from Sacramento to Folsom, began buying up land to extend his line north to Marysville and beyond. The route would operate as the "California Central Rail Road," with the new tracks passing through a farm that would become the original town site of Roseville: the three hundred seventy-five acre homestead of Tobias S. and Eleanor Grider, located about eighteen miles northeast of Sacramento. In October of that year, the railroad bought a strip of land ninety-nine feet wide through the Grider property, with additional room for a terminal, all for the price of one dollar.

November 1859:

Two land speculators, Tabb Mitchell and George Anderson bought balance of the Grider farm for the bargain price of one thousand five hundred dollars.

October 1861:

California Central rail service began from Folsom to the stop known as "Grider's" and on to Lincoln. Soon after, new public maps pinpointed that the California Central and the planned transcontinental Central Pacific Rail Road would intersect at Grider's. The maps labeled the crossroads as "Junction."

June 1863:
Mitchell and Anderson sold a right-of-way through their property to the Central Pacific Rail Road.

October 25, 1863:
The two men unloaded the remainder of the land for two thousand five hundred dollars to O. D. (Orville Dewey) Lambard, a self-confident thirty-four-year-old Sacramento businessman who envisioned a bustling town rising up around busy rail yards at the Junction.

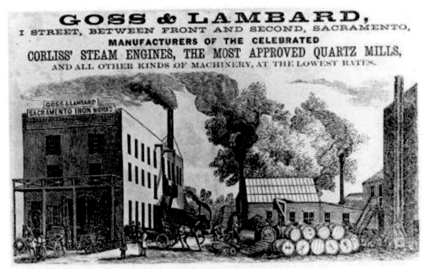

Goss & Lambard Sacramento Iron Works
Internet Image

But Lambard was likely unaware of recent railroad developments that Mitchell and Anderson probably had in their "hip pocket." Through their newspaper contacts, they must have learned that the Central Pacific Railroad would make Rocklin its division headquarters, rather than anywhere near the Junction.

April 6, 1864:
Following the arrival of the Central Pacific Railroad's locomotive "Governor Stanford" from Sacramento, directly linking the Junction with the state's capital city, the stop still didn't seem to hold much promise. Unfortunately for Lambard, "the Junction" remained not much more

than a spot on a map.

Then, nineteen days later, the Central Pacific began operating scheduled trains from Sacramento that pulled into the Junction before going on to the end of the line. All that could be counted on as commerce was the loading or unloading of a few passengers, a smattering of mail, a little freight and some farm produce and livestock.

The new route took at least twelve miles off the journey on the "old" California Central, making the thirty-one mile route via Folsom obsolete. In just a few short months, the California Central would fall on hard times, and Colonel Wilson would find himself in a financial pickle.

August 13, 1864:

Lambard put a name to the new town he envisioned when he filed his "Plan of the Town of Roseville at the Junction of the Central Pacific and Cal. Central R.R." with the Placer County Recorder.

The plan was bare bones. Just five streets were labeled – Pacific, Atlantic, Washington, Vernon and Lincoln Streets. But the town had a name that stuck. It was a small place populated with a few folks.

November 1864:

O.D. must have thought his dreams were finally coming true when Roseville earned a mention in a newspaper. The hamlet's name appeared in print for the first time when the press reported that forty-six men in and around Roseville voted in the presidential election, twenty-nine for Republican Abe Lincoln and seventeen for Democratic nominee General George McClellan.

1869:

Wilson's California Central assets were gobbled up by the Central Pacific. The tracks between Roseville and Folsom were ripped up. The remainder of the California Central line to Lincoln, Marysville and points north terminated into the east-west Central Pacific route at Roseville, which became the transfer point for train passengers and freight coming and going to all destinations far north.

1871:

Roseville's real estate market soured. When Lambard finally realized that he had a turkey on his hands, he disposed of the balance of his Roseville holdings to G.T.M. Davis and retreated to Sacramento. Local land prices remained depressed for years.

The village survived, serving local ranchers and the few residents. There wasn't much in the area to attract new settlers, but a few enterprises including a blacksmith's shop, a freight and passenger depot and a general store with a post office managed to hold on. The majority of rail passengers who got off at the station were just transferring to another line.

While they waited for their connections, they could take advantage of the amenities of either the Roseville Hotel operated by Daniel Neff or William Thomas' hotel, located above his general store.

Roseville Hotel proprietor Daniel Neff
Courtesy City of Roseville

1873:

Like the passenger trains, the freights also brought travelers to Roseville – free riders. The strangers were euphemistically known as "transients," many of whom were Civil War veterans. When the Long Depression began that year, many men who had fallen on hard times took to the rails, wandering the country in search of a fresh start. They found themselves lumped together with other freight riders regarded as troublemakers, bums, tramps and hobos.

The free riders were forced off the trains by rail workers and company police when the freights stopped at Roseville to switch cars from one route to the other. Like the passenger car patrons, the men had to wait for a train going their way, requiring them to improvise as they attended to their normal bodily functions of sleeping, eating and relieving themselves. There were no facilities or services for them. Some of the men sought out odd jobs to earn a little money for food and tobacco. If they had to, they would rummage through trash cans for a meal or steal what they could in order to eat, then relieve themselves

William Thomas' General Store and Hotel
Courtesy City of Roseville

wherever they found the "right spot," all of which enraged the locals. At sundown most of the men migrated to camps along the public creeks close to the tracks, where they could keep an eye open for departing trains or could party before bedding down for the night.

August 4, 1894:

The Placer Herald reported that "The Deputy Constable and U.S. Soldiers rounded up 27 (tramps) Monday night. They filled the prison and a boxcar. Justice Tuppitt gave them three hours to leave town." With the then population of about two hundred fifty, that meant there was more than one homeless person for every ten residents.

November 1897:

A news article detailed still more trouble. The paper noted "it was rumored" that the local icehouse was destroyed in a fire set by a "band of hobos" who broke in to keep warm. Residents threatened to take matters into their own hands by organizing a vigilante committee if the constable didn't do a better job of corralling the men. The locals were frantic for a solution.

1906:

Roseville's fortunes took a turn for the better, and Lambard's vision of a bustling town finally blossomed. Southern Pacific Railroad (SP) the successor to the Central Pacific, moved its division operations from Rocklin to Roseville. SP was set to expand its switching yards and build a new roundhouse to better manage the phenomenal growth in freight traffic and to handle the addition of the new Pacific Fruit Express business.

News of Southern Pacific's decision to shift operations to Roseville began what was called the "Big Move." Not only did the railroad relocate its division headquarters, but some of its employees also literally towed their houses the four miles to Roseville, using steam tractors or teams of mules and horses.

Relocating the railroad facilities and developing the necessary improvements took two years. The town's population grew tenfold to two thousand six hundred eight by 1910. Roseville was transformed into an economically vibrant little community, complete with a major industrial base.

Sadly, some residents and business people reacted angrily when they realized that the increased railroad activity would bring more transients. Any outsider would have seen it as just a side effect of progress. However, for the locals, the presence of a few more drifters seemed so threatening and overpowering that the hobos became objects of hatred and derision, rather than as an expected part of daily life that needed to be better managed. Hobophobia embedded itself into Roseville society and politics.

Families of railroad workers heard tales of run-ins that occurred on the job between some of the free riders and the working men. There were endless stories of how the hobos drank, cursed at the workers and threatened them with knives or other weapons. Then there was the evidence: litter of every type left in the open boxcars that the yard crews had to clean up. At a minimum, the riders were regarded as a nuisance. In the worst case, they were seen as a threat to life and limb.

Some merchants felt that having a down-on-his-luck traveler just saunter past their shops hurt the business climate. Women with children crossed the street to avoid eye contact with them. Little kids playing in neighborhoods were prepped by their parents to drop everything and run for safety if they saw a transient coming toward them.

Local law enforcement made it a top priority to harass the men, destroying their camps, taking their personal belongings and running them out of town or back onto railroad property.

Roseville's commercial and cultural life remained dominated by the railroad yards well into the twentieth century. It included deeply rooted economic and social structures, as well as a status system that provided stability for residents and businesses alike.

The community literally grew up around the rail yards. Streets of modest homes were constructed along both sides of the complex where trains were broken up and reassembled for different destinations. The yards were open for business 24/7.

Almost everyone who lived in Roseville was connected to the railroad in one way or another. In its prime, SP could claim that at least twenty percent of Roseville residents worked for the railroad. If a man was not employed by the railroad, he probably worked in a business that depended on paychecks from the rail yards for its bread and butter. All this affirmed that Southern Pacific was the lifeblood of the town.

The coming of the modern age was significant for Roseville not only because of the railroad expansion, but also because the automobile emerged as part of American life. Dirt and gravel roads leading to and from Roseville were paved and transformed into highways. Roseville found itself joined to the outside world by two new major arteries in addition to the Southern Pacific: the coast-to-coast US Route 40 and the north-south US Route 99E.

Highway traffic through town grew to be a significant part of local commerce. Roseville became a transportation hub: a layover for train passengers, highway travelers and truck drivers. Local retailers whose shops lined the two highways depended heavily on travelers who stopped for food, shelter, fuel and mechanical needs, and sometimes even bought new cars and trucks.

The 1950s:

Roseville took its first steps away from its reliance on the railroad during with the development of three new projects: the construction of the first major residential subdivision, Sierra Gardens by local investor John Piches, the building of the Community Hospital on Sunrise Avenue in 1955 and the completion of the new Interstate 80 Freeway in 1956.

Both Sierra Gardens and the hospital were geographically unique to Roseville because I-80 separated them from the older parts of town, the railroad and the transportation corridors that were US 40 and US 99E. New and old Roseville were directly connected by just a single overcrossing of I-80 at Douglas Boulevard.

Outsiders working in Sacramento were attracted to Sierra Gardens because of Roseville's quality of life: publicly owned utilities, great schools and parks, a community-owned hospital, a large pool of physicians and easy access to the freeway. There also were Roseville residents who moved into the new area from original parts of town to escape the noise and endemic hubbub of the rail yards.

February 23, 1966:

Roseville had nearly doubled in size since 1950, and its future remained filled with promise. It was during this wave of growth in the community that Annette, my wife at the time, and I bought a stake in Roseville's future. We purchased the Fosters Freeze Drive-in Restaurant business on Vernon Street next to the Tower Theater from Victor and Olive Styles, who wanted to retire.

When we arrived in Roseville, we encountered something unexpected and even "foreign": the town's insular inter-connectedness. Newcomers were regarded as outsiders until it was determined that they fit the narrow spectrum that reflected how the citizens of Roseville saw things.

The local population was largely made up of blue collar union workers. The folks who controlled the local levers of power were good-hearted people, but very cautious about welcoming newbies from different social, economic or ethnic backgrounds.

Community standards were consistently and effectively enforced and appearances meant everything. Annette and I felt fortunate that we passed the test and were very happy with our decision to invest in Roseville. We were the new energetic owners of an established business on the main street. Our children, Paul and Michelle, were loved by our customers and were thought of as regular members of the crew. As cute towheaded tykes, they would clean tables and socialize with guests.

Our store was a hit. I was invited to join the Lions Club and the Chamber of Commerce. Local politicians and businessmen like Mayor George Buljan, Paul Wagner and the manager of the JC Penney store, Bob Smith, would stop in for lunch. And their employees, along with those of Bud's Cleaners, Bank of America, Citizens Bank, Lenzi's TV and Appliance, Miller's Furniture and Appliance, J&J Body Shop and Caddel Chevrolet all got their noon meal from our Fosters Freeze on a regular basis. We were very happy with our decision to invest in Roseville's future promise.

Paul Boudier and postal workers on afternoon break, 1972
Boudier Collection

As I became acquainted around town, I found that some residents and merchants reacted to sighting a "hobo" with an unusual amount of fear and distrust. The presence of the guys off the rails didn't bother me. I was raised around them. My dad often hired men who had come into town by rail. Most were extremely hard workers.

Once a person learned to distinguish between a man who wanted to work and one who just wanted a handout, there was no need to respond irrationally. Pop taught me how to see the difference. The simple test was to look at a man's hands. Calluses said a lot about a fella.

I saw the men differently than old-time Rosevillians. Most travelers who asked for help at the Fosters Freeze were sober and wanted to

11

work in exchange for a meal. The men were never a threat to our business. If they were panhandling or were intoxicated, I encouraged them to move on in a hurry. I don't recall one instance when I called for the police regarding a transient. For rowdy teenagers, yes! But not for any adult.

I always had some small outside job for a man who wanted work. Often a guy would have a trade that we could put to use. Sometimes the building exterior needed a paint touch up, the parking lot had to be swept or it was time for the trash cans to be emptied and washed. No one was ever turned away.

When customers noticed a stranger working outside, they usually seemed amazed and pleased. It was good business to provide a sober man with a meal; and it was the right thing to do, especially when I knew I had been very fortunate.

1971:

The year was a tough one for most downtown retailers. They were dealt a blow when the brand new Sunrise Mall in neighboring Citrus Heights opened its doors. Citrus Heights residents no longer had to come to Roseville to shop, and Roseville residents had easy access to a modern mall just minutes away on the newly improved Sunrise Boulevard. Who needed old downtown Roseville?

The majority of Vernon Street businesses either moved to another area or went under. JC Penney's closed and consolidated with its new superstore in Sunrise Mall. Paul Wagner's Richardson's Menswear relocated closer to the freeway in Roseville Square, and the Pacific Gas and Electric office moved to Harding Boulevard. One by one, other stores closed: Taylor's Red & White Grocery, Wolf & Royer Hardware, Lloyd's Hardware and Huskinson's Pharmacy. The economic center of town started to shift toward the freeway.

1972:

Because we couldn't afford to move our business, we tried a different approach. With the help of Mike Royer and Gene Garbolino of Citizens Bank, and our landlord Al Moore of San Jose, we were able to purchase the Fosters Freeze real estate in March.

A month later, we began expanding and modernizing our building. A dining room was added and a mansard roof and a few other architectural treatments were installed to dress up the exterior. The transformation took three months but was completed just in time for the summer rush. Our sales tripled!

In the larger economic picture, railroad passenger traffic dwindled to a trickle. In February 1973, after SP determined there was no longer a need for a passenger station in Roseville, the building was demolished.

Michelle and Bill Boudier changing signs, summer 1974
Boudier Collection

Money continued to drain out of downtown, severely crippling Roseville's old city core. All of the auto and truck traffic that had crawled through town on Highway 40 now zipped up and down I-80.

Our success was an aberration. The exodus of businesses from Vernon Street continued. The new car dealerships, once confined to small locations, saw the future and decided to move to sites where they could spread out their inventory and be more accessible to buyers. Saugstad Ford, Frank Andrews Lincoln-Mercury, Reliable Pontiac-Cadillac and Caddel Chevrolet abandoned downtown and moved to larger and better locations.

We were looking beyond Roseville, too. To diversify into other investments, we needed to strengthen our financial position by generating cash. The first asset to go was the Roseville Fosters Freeze real estate, which was sold to Lenford and Hattie Retzer of Lodi, with the agreement that either we or successive operating business owners would lease it from them.

1976:

Following the summer rush, sales at our remodeled Fosters Freeze had peaked, making the business ripe for selling. When we put the operation on the market, Kerry Kassis of Sacramento snapped it up. The escrow closed on January 2, 1976. That left us with one remaining property in old Roseville: our retail buildings at 514-520 Vernon Street, which we sold later that year.

We were able to get out of downtown just in time. As the late seventies arrived, the Roseville Theater had closed and the Tower was holding on by a thread.

The early 1980s:

By this time the Tower was boarded up, too. The service stations that had dotted at least one corner on nearly every block of Riverside Avenue and Vernon Street had been shut, and most were torn down. The rest of Vernon was a nearly abandoned business district, pockmarked by empty storefronts with doorways littered with pieces of old newspaper, dirt and dried up leaves. Riverside and Atlantic were close behind, with all their ticky-tacky used car lots and old storefronts. The blocks that once made up a bustling commercial downtown were depressing to see.

If John Steinbeck had walked down Old Roseville's Vernon Street, there was a good chance he would have felt that he was in Oklahoma during the tough times. From the appearance of the buildings, Steinbeck could have concluded the whole town was in a state of decline.

The only enterprises keeping Vernon Street afloat were the four "anchors": city government offices, Citizens Bank of Roseville, Roseville Telephone Company and Elbe and Wilma Miller. City government was determined to keep its headquarters on Vernon and to revitalize the corridor. Citizens Bank held fast to its branch at the corner of Lincoln and Vernon, and continued to serve businesses and residents throughout Roseville. Roseville Telephone obviously wanted its namesake to do well; and Elbe and Wilma Miller's furniture and appliance store was the lone thriving major retailer. I think that if any of the four had left, the whole place could have been dedicated as a slum.

1982:

It had only been six years since we had sold the Roseville Fosters Freeze when I decided to retire from business. I was just forty-one. A mild heart attack was the all the signal I needed to change my lifestyle. Annette and I realized we had been successful enough that we didn't have to worry about putting bread on the table if we led a modest lifestyle for the balance of our days.

We sold our business holdings, put our large home in Fair Oaks on the market, and looked to purchase a smaller place in Roseville.

Part of changing my lifestyle was to take a fresh stab at being an active Catholic. I had attended Catholic schools growing up and wanted to find a deeper purpose for my life, so I started attending St. Rose Church in Roseville, where I met Father Mike Cormack, the best friend I ever had.

It was important to Annette and me that our new home be in one of Roseville's older neighborhoods, preferably close to St. Rose. We both wanted to commit time and energy to some kind of work that involved the faith. I had heard of the Catholic diaconate program for married men who felt called to ordained ministry in the Church. It definitely interested us. We purchased a brand new home across the way from the St. Rose parish center.

Most new homes and businesses were being built in "New Roseville" to the east and the west of downtown. The larger community was booming. Roseville was emerging as a bright economic center in its own right. Unfortunately, the five blocks of old downtown looked grim, seemingly stuck in the past and forgotten.

As the city continued to grow, with a population of over twenty-four thousand in 1980, the politicians were laser-focused on building services to attract more middle-class families, while economic conditions worsened in the older areas. If you were a poor resident down to your last dollar and in need of essentials such as food or help with rent, all you could do was turn to your neighbor, a friend, a relative, the church down the street or the Police Benevolent Fund, and hope for the best. If you were a homeless family, your only choice was to stay on the lookout for a helping hand.

The transients were worse off than ever. They became an easy political target to blame for the loss of old Roseville business income, store vacancies and declining property values. This economic decline led to increased fear and dislike of the men, which local politicians capitalized on, by either acknowledging their own fear or taking advantage of the fear of others for their own political gain.

Since Roseville had no organized services for homeless folks – no food, shelter, showers, clothing, regular non-emergency medical help or Salvation Army, they were considered lucky if they got free rides to Sacramento, courtesy of Placer County,.

If you were a transient, you were probably plumb out of luck.

Chapter 2:
It Started with a Conversation
(Jun. 1983–Dec. 1983)

June 1983:

When a medical doctor and a priest got together for dinner in Roseville on a June evening, something totally unforeseen occurred. As Dr. Tom Stanko shared his concern with Father Mike Cormack about how some folks in Roseville found themselves short on food at the end of the month or unable to pay their rent and utility bills, the two resolved that something had to be done.

Father Mike Cormack
Boudier Collection

Doctor Tom Stanko, MD
Courtesy Dr. Stank

Within a few days after that June dinner, Father Mike and Dr. Stanko asked me to help organize a service group to address the unmet needs they saw. A growing and dynamic Roseville lacked an organization that could operate in a proactive mode, not dependent on just government funding, bureaucratic oversight and seasonal customs, such as Christmas baskets, to get the job done. The community needed an organization that was on the job every day, year-round.

But, where to start?

The three of us agreed that a local St. Vincent de Paul Society group would be the best way to begin the effort. I had been involved with the agency as a teenager, and Father Mike was very familiar with its principles and objectives. Its charter was loose enough to give us the flexibility we wanted to develop an operation that could best serve the basic needs of our community.

We scheduled an organizational meeting for August 22nd in the St. Rose Parish Center, inviting anyone interested to attend. Joe Laharty and Art Guerrero of the Sacramento District Council of St. Vincent de Paul were asked to be there to tell the group about the Society's work.

August 22, 1983:

Father Mike Cormack, Dr. Stanko, Bob and Nadine Baggarley, Annette Boudier, Peggy Carey, Jessie Chambers, Paula Chappie, Deane Conard, Paul Croisetiere, Winnie and Andy Lavigne, Martha Luke, RoseRita Ponzo, John Roe, Russ and Marilyn Sisley, Joe Sovey and yours truly were at the meeting.

It was the consensus of the group that Placer County government was not meeting the needs of Roseville's low-income folks with such basic services as housing assistance, emergency food and medical care. Doling out county welfare payments, food stamps and minimal non-emergency medical aid was not enough. One excuse the county had was that it was formally classified as "rural" even though its southern boundary was less than twenty miles from the state capitol building. Another factor which made it difficult for Rosevillians to access county services was that county staff was concentrated in north Auburn, over twenty miles from Roseville, the county's population and economic center. It was difficult and expensive for many of our residents to make the trip "up the hill," especially if they had small children in tow.

Roseville city government at the time viewed social services, even low-income housing, as being outside of its purview. Government policies and budgeting practices seemed locked into the status quo.

The new St. Vincent's group voted that night to move ahead with organizing to help needy persons in our community avoid the despair of abandonment when they fell on hard times, coming up short on food, clothing, rent or money for utilities. We would try to improve their quality of life in simple but significant ways. We formally launched the St. Vincent de Paul Society, St. Rose Conference, and agreed that it was not a matter of whether we would move ahead with our plan, but only a question of how many of us there would be to initiate our endeavor. Everyone voiced support for making sure the organization got off to a good start.

It was typical for a St. Vincent de Paul conference to use the parish office or a room on parish grounds as home base. But, in this case, I asked the conference members to be open to a location on a major street in Roseville to "advertise" that services were available for those in need. I assured members that the cost would not be a problem. Annette and I had agreed to buy the necessary property. We committed to donate it rent-free for St. Vincent's use until the charity was well on its feet. All that we expected was that the organization would take care of the property — maintain it in good condition and cover the cost of taxes and insurance.

Father Mike followed up with a generous guarantee that the parish would help the new organization with financial support. Everyone was fired up and agreed to the plan.

After the meeting, I started looking for the ideal spot "to open for business." As fate would have it, the perfect building for our project soon turned up for sale. It was at the corner of Riverside Avenue and Bonita Street, smack dab on a major transportation corridor — right where we were needed. According to the 1980 census, the area was one of the poorest in Roseville, a place where an operation like the one we planned would do the most good. I put in an offer on the property right away.

September 14, 1983:

Before the purchase escrow closed on the building, I made sure that city utilities were connected to the property and that St. Vincent's had a business license from the City of Roseville to operate "Charitable Services" at the site.

By obtaining the license ahead of time and ensuring the utilities were on, we could not be stopped by the city apparatus, which might try to interfere with opening such an activity on a highly traveled street like Riverside. In fact, the city license clerk went over and above what she usually did to issue a business license. She proactively obtained an emergency clearance form from the planning department on our behalf, avoiding our plans being scrutinized by city staff.

September 27, 1983:

The purchase of the retail building at 141 A & B Riverside & 105 Bonita was a done-deal, and the site was given over for St. Vincent's use, with the space divided to accommodate four activities:

- The thrift store at 141A;
- The office at 141B to help people with their personal needs such as rent, utility assistance, clothing, furniture and appliances such as refrigerators;
- The Dining Room at 105 Bonita; and
- The Food Locker at the same address.

As we got ready to open the Dining Room and the Food Locker, we tried to anticipate what some of our day-to-day problems might be. The biggest risk we saw was that because the site was within pistol shot of the rail yards and a few blocks from Vernon Street, which was becoming an economic backwater, a free dining room would attract transients. With the community's inbred hobophobia always ready to break out like the pox, the opposition to providing free meals to "bums" might become overwhelming. A meal program that was organized and ongoing could be regarded by local residents, business people and politicians as a threat to the community's stability. They most likely would decry the regular meals, seeing them as a magnet drawing the singles to Roseville from across the country.

We knew better. The railroad caused the city's transient problem to begin with, by dumping the men here. The right thing for us to do was to help them. If they were cared for, everyone's quality of life would improve.

Getting the Dining Room and the Food Locker ready to open was less complex than we thought. Dan Delaney, who had recently started the Loaves and Fishes meal program in Sacramento, had warned us of how his group was hassled by area businesses and the city just months before when Loaves and Fishes opened. We expected to have to jump through all kinds of bureaucratic hoops, too. But Roseville did not have ordinances or regulations to restrict operating a food locker or a free dining room. It was full steam ahead to open as soon as possible.

November 15, 1983:

The members got together to consider temporary policies and procedures, focusing on the meal program. I provided a couple of guiding principles. First, the facility would be known as "the Dining Room" because it was intended to be a place where folks could have a meal with a sense of dignity and comfort. It was not a "soup kitchen."

And second, the food served would be known as "dinner" to remind volunteers that the meals were to be complete and prepared for "sit-down consumption." The goal was to provide nutritious, well-balanced, wholesome and appetizing meals. What patrons were served might be the only healthy, hot food they would have all day.

Right off, some members who had family that worked for the railroad were afraid that even though the Dining Room was opening to serve local residents, transients and local homeless folks would show up, too. And that would be trouble!

I told the group that based on my experience, we wouldn't have any problem when they showed up. As long as the men and women were sober and cooperative, we should take the chance and welcome them like anyone else. I went on to remind them that discriminating against anyone for any reason would be violating our religious values. After some discussion, the group decided to give the policy a try.

Winter 1983:

When word spread around town that St. Vincent's was going to open a center on Riverside at Bonita, many good folks from a variety of faiths and service groups wanted to join. The first was Jim Bush Sr. from the Methodist Church, one of the finest men I have ever known.

Bush and his pastor, Reverend Lee Backman, showed up one day at our building to volunteer their help while I was working in the store, getting it ready for opening day. I heard a loud banging on the locked glass door. It was gentle Jim's thunderous knock.

When I first saw him, he had his hands on either side of his face trying to look through the glass. As soon as I could unlock the door and swing it open, he jumped in and introduced himself and Backman. Next, he said they wanted to help get the meal program going.

I couldn't believe my ears. What a relief! I remain thankful to this day that the two men showed up when they did. Bush and I became true partners in the Dining Room endeavor.

By the end of December, the Thrift Store and Office were open and the Dining Room and Food Locker were ready to begin operation. Al Foley did most of the carpentry, including building the Dining Room cabinets. Jerry Risse gave us a good deal on the new tub enclosure for our shower program.

With the Food Locker stocked with donated groceries, and the Dining Room featuring a new four burner stove from Sears and the old parish house refrigerator, along with two new large wooden picnic tables for seating, we were set to open!

Jim Bush: "I do pots and pans by the hundreds!"
Courtesy Roseville Press Tribune

Chapter 3:
"And away we go!"*
(Jan. 1984–Mar. 1987)
*Jackie Gleason, 1956

January 1984:

In the beginning, the Food Locker and the Dining Room operated only one day a week. On the very first day the Dining Room was open, twenty-four people, including some homeless men, were served. Of the twenty-four, seven or eight were residents of the Barker Hotel, the main low-income hotel in town about a mile away. All showed up hungry and left stuffed after enjoying a home-cooked Italian meal. The chefs of the day were Jeanette and Evo Pieracci, with executive chef Deane Conard looking on.

By the end of January, a noon meal and bagged groceries were available three days a week – Thursdays, Fridays and Saturdays. We were amazed at how everything was falling into place.

The next big event of that month was the purchase of the property next to the Dining Room, the 1920s Festersen Home at 111 Bonita. Annette and I turned it over to St. Rose Church's Youth Ministry for use as an after-school center for the teens of the parish.

February 1984:

At our monthly meeting, Dining Room chairperson Deane Conard said that over five hundred hot meals were served in January. Food Locker chairperson Jessie Chambers reported that groceries for more than two thousand meals were provided through her ministry. Right away, we knew we were needed. There were hungry people in Roseville.

Both programs were intended to help local residents who occasionally ran short of food, often at the end of the month. However, as we predicted at our planning meeting, many of those in town who were homeless, some of them transients, showed up for the meals too.

The opening of the Dining Room program was "a step up" for Roseville. After the program began, the police reported that calls concerning people scrounging food from dumpsters and garbage cans decreased.

23

On the management side, Jessie Chambers recommended limiting our Food Locker services to local residents because they could store food safely and cook it in a sanitary way. The team agreed. The team also concurred that the Dining Room policy was working well and should remain the same: Everyone was welcome unless he or she was disruptive or "under the influence."

There was a sense of wonder that the food and volunteer support needed to provide Dining Room meals three days a week was always there. Every time we thought we had come up short, more food and helping hands showed up. We had made a leap of faith, pure and simple.

With all of the excitement, executive chef and chief Dining Room volunteer Deane Conard was feeling a bit overwhelmed. When I told him we were ready to open the Dining Room on additional days, Conard admitted he needed help to get the job done.

Spring 1984:

Right on cue, what I regard as a couple of small miracles occurred. Two incredible people arrived on the scene to get us over the hump. The first was Yvonne Schliekelman who, to Conard's relief, took on the day-to-day operations of the Dining Room.

Schliekelman and her volunteers dished up noon meals Tuesday through Saturday. She was there every day, planning menus, organizing volunteers and, with the help of her husband Keith, turning out a noon dinner that was not only nutritious, but "homemade delicious."

The second miracle was the arrival of Bob Letskus. Letskus and I first met in at Sacramento's Loaves and Fishes, where he worked for Dan Delany as a manager. I needed someone just like him with a strong spirit of charity and compassion to keep things running smoothly among volunteers and clients at St. Vincent's in Roseville. Letskus had been a Marine and then a Trappist monk. He had arrived in Sacramento just a few months earlier to help Delany with starting Loaves and Fishes.

Then one day, he turned up in Roseville and said he would like to help me. I told him I was delighted he was here, but reminded him that I never asked him to leave Loaves and Fishes. He said he knew that I could use some help, and then told me he believed he had a "calling" to move on to Roseville.

April 16, 1984:

Harry Crabb became Mayor of Roseville for the second time.

May 1, 1984:
Annette and I acquired the building at 139 Riverside. The property was completely refurbished as an expanded office and food locker with an apartment in the rear for Letskus. In the former Food Locker area, a wall came down and seating was added for the Dining Room. The thrift store at 141 Riverside took over the former office space.

June 1984:
The meal service had expanded to five days a week. About two thousand hot meals were being served per month, and the bathroom shower was available to the men before meals. The guys stood in line for up to two hours just for the chance to get cleaned up and into fresh clothes.

June 31, 1984:
Bishop Quinn of the Catholic Diocese of Sacramento, who had taken a special interest in the work we were doing, came Roseville to lead our dedication ceremony.

Fall 1984:
As summer passed and the weather cooled, some Dining Room volunteers worried that those who were waiting outside for the meal were getting cold. They suggested that we give them coffee.

The suggestion made Letskus, Bush and me edgy because the folks were lining up at the Dining Room door too early in the morning, some before 8 a.m. just so they could get a shower. Others simply had nothing else to do. Eventually, many of the early birds got restless and began to roam the sidewalks or snooze against the upholstery shop building across Bonita Street.

Steve Scott, the shop's owner, and his employees were upset. They pleaded with me to get the guys back to our side of the street. Moving the men just those forty-plus feet to the St. Vincent's property was like herding cats! As soon as we moved one group off of the upholstery shop's sidewalk, another bunch started to settle in.

Letskus, Bush and I were concerned that the situation might get out of hand, with tempers and words flying between the upholstery shop employees and the guys. We began encouraging the ones who didn't want a shower to come back at mealtime.

November 28, 1984:

We voted on the coffee issue at our membership meeting. The group realized that making the waiting crowd more comfortable would only aggravate the situation. A vote was taken to keep things as they were, and not to give out hot coffee. It passed without a hitch. A notice was posted on the Dining Room bulletin board, and the issue was closed.

It was still difficult for the good-hearted volunteers who just wanted to keep everyone warm to understand that giving the clients hot coffee would make the situation worse.

Winter of 1984:

The Roseville Ministerial Association started a new movement to help homeless people. In the past, the Association had been very low-key. Its main work had been to function as a support group for the ministers and to organize community worship services on special days, such as Good Friday and Easter Sunday. Members met monthly for breakfast and fellowship with a "program and guest speaker presentation" on a topic of interest. I always looked forward to the get-togethers.

The Association also maintained a "Benevolent Fund" that was collected to be used for helping needy people, both travelers and local residents. The group had entrusted the Police Department to administer the monies.

The consciences of some of the Ministerial Association members were stirred by the activities at St. Vincent's, making them realize that there was much more charitable work that could be done by the religious community. They collectively decided to discuss how to make services for the needy more accessible and how churches could step up aid to the poor folks in town.

Police Chief Jim Hall was invited to come to one of the meetings as a guest speaker to share how he was using the Benevolent Fund monies. We knew there were lots of homeless people in town, but could not understand why the Benevolent Fund always had a comfortable balance.

December 12, 1984:

Chief Hall met with the ministers for breakfast at the Heritage Coffee Shop. He didn't mince any words, saying that his department would not support any activities that encouraged homeless people "to hang around Roseville." His policy was to limit help to local families when they had nowhere else to turn, meaning he would not even consider helping single persons or out-of-towners.

Hall went on to say that many local folks temporarily in need of help would not go to the police for financial assistance. He made it clear that he believed the chronic poor and needy should be moved out of town and affirmed that single men should not be helped at all.

After the Chief left, the group formed an ad hoc committee to gather information on community resources already available to help needy people. The ministers also wanted to come up with a better way to utilize the Benevolent Fund for the community. They were ready to end the Police Department policy of just sitting on the money.

January 1985:

The Ministerial Association members reviewed the ad hoc committee report and decided to form a new branch of service for the needy, dubbing it "Community Ministries," headed by Jim Bush, with oversight by a committee of ministers. The organization would coordinate charity work in the name of the local churches and relieve Jim Hall's Police Department of its Benevolent Fund responsibilities.

Forming this new Community Ministries Committee represented a paradigm shift for the ministers, away from just sponsoring devotional events and toward a commitment to works of mercy.

They also decided to back St. Vincent's policy of welcoming transients to meals, even though it meant that it would most likely be met with a "push back" from the larger community at some point.

February 1985:

Bush reported to his Community Ministries Committee that the Dining Room served up to one hundred fifty people a day, many of them transients. The new group quickly decided to move into action by getting involved in social outreach. Using Bush's plan as a blueprint, the members voted to support St. Vincent's Dining Room efforts to open seven days a week. That decision was followed by a commitment to fund a Community Ministries office where members of the public needing help could make contact.

Soon after, Community Ministries opened an office in donated space in the evangelical church building at Bonita and Clinton Streets. Marlene Friend was hired as Director. The Ministerial Association agreed to underwrite Community Ministries' expenses up to five hundred dollars per month for the first year, with the balance of its funding needing to come from private donations.

Although the new residents flocking to Roseville had brought the city's population to nearly thirty thousand, the old guard remained in control. Rumors spread among the old-timers that the community was split over the scope and effect of providing free meals to homeless people. Some folks welcomed the hot meal program as a sign of progress and change, while others, especially people along the old Highway 40-99E corridor, reacted negatively.

The dissenters began grousing that helping transients and other homeless folks represented a threat to the community's way of life and to their material well-being. Some merchants and residents claimed the Dining Room was hurting the value of their businesses and homes.

August 14, 1985:

The Roseville City Council, led by Mayor Harry Crabb, started to push back against our efforts after he received complaints from downtown and Riverside business interests about the growing numbers of transients over the previous two years.

Crabb championed an emergency ordinance that beefed up city laws on loitering and panhandling. But the law missed the mark, dealing with the symptoms, rather than the real causes:

- Southern Pacific Railroad's financial problems and the subsequent cutbacks among railroad security personnel, especially company police. With such lax security on the line, more freeloaders were able to jump on for the ride, only to be chased off railroad property when the trains pulled into Roseville.
- the city's old downtown business core, which was dying of old age, a casualty of economic neglect.

The Council members held a lengthy conversation with Chief Hall and other "good ole boys" about the ordinance. The chief said, "We want to get a different kind of message out on the rails – and that is if you stay here, you'll get locked up." He concluded, "If we let the transients know we have a new law like this, then they may not be as likely to stay here."

The *Press Tribune* reported that during the confab before the vote on the ordinance, "Mayor Harry Crabb said he recognized the danger of transients while (he was) walking one night along Dry Creek. 'I was surprised by the number of transients who were passing through, sleeping there and building fires,' he said."

The ordinance passed. Eventually the Dining Room was framed as the patsy for the city's worsening transient issues, even though the railroad and its impending economic death were at the center of the problem. But the rail company remained big, politically powerful and was headquartered far away in San Francisco. On the other hand, St. Vincent's was little, easy to pick on and close by, just five blocks from City Hall. Whatever the future held, our group remained resolved to provide meals to homeless men and women.

Unfortunately for St. Vincent's, the Council's action occurred about the same time that the hot meal program was operating near its peak. The Dining Room had served dinner to one hundred sixty-five people in just one afternoon the month before.

August 20, 1985:

The *Press Tribune* editorialized about the new ordinance: "It's easy to decry anti-hobo ordinances as attempts to legislate against the poor, but Roseville's new law does no such thing. It merely protects the community from idle transients who can effectively erode our quality of life."

What the *Tribune* was talking about was not the reality of a booming and forward-looking Roseville with issues that faced a rapidly growing city, but a throwback to "the old days," a fabrication of the imagination that Roseville was more like "Mayberry," Andy Griffith's mythical town where the bucolic existence of white middle-class folks went on without the intrusion of any reality. The paper just parroted the Council line and missed the truth. Hobophobia was alive and well.

Despite concerns from neighboring businesses and the city's new "anti-transient ordinance," the First United Methodist Church and St. Vincent's went ahead with plans for a noon meal at the Dining Room on Mondays.

September 23, 1985:

On the first Monday that the Dining Room opened for a noon meal, ninety-five people were served. Bush was so jazzed that he suggested expanding the meal program to Sundays by recruiting other Protestant churches to participate. He even volunteered to oversee the Sunday meals, assuring that Letskus and I would have the day off.

October 23, 1985:

Bush announced that St. John's Episcopal Church and Bethel Lutheran Church had stepped up to help the Methodist volunteers on Mondays.

November 12, 1985:

In city elections, Alan Pineschi received the most votes to take over as mayor from Harry Crabb. Jim Ross, in the second spot, became mayor pro tem. Phil Ozenick gained a seat when he came in third.

The *Press Tribune*, in a feature story, also reported on the decision by the Methodist Church to extend the hot meal program at the Dining Room to every Monday. Bush and his pastor, Rev. Virginia Pearson, told the newspaper that they decided to help St. Vincent's expand the meal program by one day a week because, as the *Press Tribune* stated in the lead, "Hunger is not confined to a five-days week even though few food programs operate on a seven-day basis."

Bush said, "(Preparing the meals is) rewarding to me. The people are friendly and they're very appreciative." He concluded with a laugh, "I do pots and pans by the hundreds!"

Winter 1985:

It wasn't long before Bush and Pearson began recruiting more churches so that a hot Sunday meal could be provided at the Dining Room. Soon, they had seven congregations signed up. This commitment meant that for the first time in Roseville, free meals were available for hungry people every day of the week.

An average of one hundred and as many as two hundred ten people were served daily during the hour and a half the facility was open.

The Methodist and Episcopalian congregations served on Monday and Tuesday, and Pentecostals took on another day of the week. Among the groups who cooked the midday Sunday meal were the Seventh Day Adventists, the Jewish Congregation Bet Haverim of Orangevale and Bethel Lutheran Church – all working in harmony, assuring no one would go hungry in our city. When the Adventists began volunteering, they told me, "Now our sisters and brothers can enjoy their Sunday Sabbath in peace. We'll make sure a great meal is served."

It didn't take long for people from nearly a dozen different faiths to become involved in this "Catholic" organization. By providing a place for this new charitable work, the Roseville St. Vincent de Paul Society became a catalyst for a small but significant social change, with the buildings at Riverside and Bonita at the center. There seemed to be a passion among the volunteers to share their bounty with folks who might go hungry if the Dining Room wasn't open. The noon meal program developed into not only a beacon of hope for needy people, but also a symbol of ecumenical harmony.

But trouble was brewing for the Dining Room. I had received more feedback from area businesses and the police that the clients were causing problems. Chief Hall and some of the business owners I knew claimed that transient clients were hanging around on Riverside Avenue, running off their customers. They asserted the problem was caused by St. Vincent's Dining Room, seeming to forget that it was Southern Pacific and its cops who had given transients a free pass to town.

These men and women, like everyone else in our city, needed to eat, whether from out of trash cans, begging or being given a meal by the Dining Room.

In an immediate attempt to cut down on complaints, Letskus, Bush and I began to require those who were waiting for showers and meals stay on St. Vincent's property and then leave as soon as possible. It was tough to keep them from wandering to the opposite side of Bonita Street because it provided some protection from the elements and we had no place for them to sit.

We also routinely walked around our half of the block to roust anyone loitering, sending them on to the Dining Room if they wanted to eat or telling them to shove off if they didn't. Our bigger problem was that clients continued to show up when we were closed.

Another setback for old Roseville came when the Highway 65 bypass opened, offering a shortcut around what had been the Highway 99E route through downtown Roseville. The remaining business owners along the old corridor were hit in the gut again. When they looked for someone to lay their troubles on, they picked on the transients.

Early 1986:

By this time, most of the major religious congregations, some service clubs and a few businesses like Placer Title Company joined up to provide crews for St. Vincent's meal program. I think that most of this new interest in serving in the Dining Room was attributable to the leadership of the city's pastors, who were in sync with one another and preached the Social Gospel, making it relevant to their members.

Reverends Virginia Pearson of the Methodist Church, Tim Gentry of the West Roseville Baptist Church, Tim Brooks of Hillcrest Alliance Church, Roy Herndon of the First Baptist Church and Mike Cormack of St. Rose Church made for a formidable force for good in the community.

April 16, 1986:

Virginia Greenwald, an outreach worker from Lutheran Church of the Resurrection in Granite Bay, hosted a meeting to introduce a new shelter program to serve homeless families, Project Home. Greenwald invited community activists to explore starting a local version of Sacramento's Project Home.

Sherry Schiele of St. Vincent's, staff members from Placer County and the City of Roseville and a group of pastors accepted Greenwald's invitation. The meeting at the Lutheran church marked the birth of the first viable and continuously operating transitional housing program for homeless families in Placer County.

The Project Home six-week shelter program provided temporary living accommodations, counseling and rehabilitation services to homeless families. At the end of the six weeks, a family was "adopted" by a church. Church members then mentored the family and helped secure permanent housing and, if needed, gave a hand with rent, security deposits and finding employment.

May 29, 1986:

The building at 137 Riverside Avenue was purchased and added to the St. Vincent's complex. After it was refurbished, it became the new home of the Food Locker, freeing up space at 139 Riverside for additional administrative staff members, including those from Project Home.

July 1986:

Project Home, managed by Schiele, began working directly with St. Vincent's. Two people who were among Project Home's first supporters were Eileen and Leo French. The couple anonymously donated two thousand one hundred dollars to help the operation pay for an estimated six months of apartment rent for a homeless family.

September 1986:

When Alan Pineschi was appointed to the bench, Jim Ross became Roseville's mayor and Phil Ozenick was bumped up to mayor pro tem.

October 1986:
St. Vincent's formally shifted its own homeless families program over to Project Home.

Fall 1986:
The city put a law on the books prohibiting camping on public property.

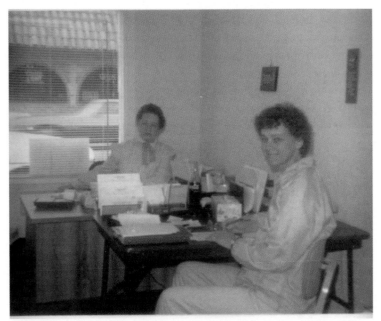

Winnie Lavigne (L) and Sherry Schiele (R) at the SVDP office
Boudier Collection

March 1987:
Four new efforts to help homeless people sprang up in Placer County:

1. Roseville's Community Ministries branched out to coordinate not only with St. Vincent's, but also with the Placer County Concilio to jointly administer an emergency shelter motel voucher program. With this new program, anyone in the general homeless population could be eligible for emergency shelter aid, a concept previously unheard of in this town.

2. As part of a plan to help low-income persons avoid homelessness, Placer County's Office of Community Services

applied for a one hundred thousand dollar state grant to start a loan program for rent deposits.

3. The Placer Coalition on Housing and Homelessness was formed. One of its first goals was to determine how many homeless persons there were in Roseville and in the county.

4. Project Home received a ten thousand dollar grant from the Lutheran Brotherhood.

The grant was used to house two families in a duplex at 224-226 Grape Street that Project Home was renting from St. Rose parishioner Sandy Becker. Becker had offered to sell the duplex to Project Home at the discounted price of seventy thousand dollars in memory of her recently deceased father who had directed her to use part of his estate to help homeless persons.

There was one problem prohibiting Project Home from completing the purchase: The agency was not incorporated. To get over that hurdle, Becker granted Project Home a no-cost option to buy the property, with Project Home agreeing to pay one thousand dollars total per month rent for the two units in the interim.

Chapter 4:
A Rocky Ride for the Dining Room
(Apr. 1987–Oct. 1987)

April 3, 1987:

Jim Ross resigned as mayor as he prepared to move out of the area for business reasons. Phil Ozenick, next on the totem pole, became mayor.

As Roseville prepared to launch its downtown redevelopment project, the St. Vincent's meal and shower programs were seen as major obstacles to the effort's success. City politicians and staff, as well as some of our neighbors, were convinced that these services were "magnets," drawing homeless men and women to Roseville from as far away as New York City just for a free meal, a shower and clean clothes.

June 26, 1987:

The uninterrupted expansion of St. Vincent's came to an abrupt halt when, from out of the blue, city planning staff members Jean Chaney and Chris Burrows showed up at St. Vincent's office. They said they came by to inspect the St. Rose youth ministry house at 111 Bonita.

The two also quizzed St. Vincent's staffer Sherry Schiele about the use of each of the other buildings in the complex, even though her written report indicated Cheney and Burrows were focused on parking and permit issues surrounding the little house.

It was curious that they were primarily interested in the youth ministry house. There was nothing significant about the building other than it was part of the property on which St. Vincent's was located. For the previous three years, it had been a safe place for teens to socialize,

June 30, 1987:

We received a formal notification from Chaney that claimed the house had been "improperly" converted from residential use to commercial use in 1984, requiring a site review. It also said we were to submit an application to initiate the process no later than July 17th, as required by the municipal code.

A site review meant that the property could be subject to two public hearings, the first before a city planning panel and a possible second with the City Council. The site review as a public hearing process would require that we notify all property owners within three hundred feet of the house about the hearing.

July 2, 1987:

I called Chaney to inform her that if the city chose to go after the charity, it was not just me they would have to deal with. They would be attacking St. Rose Church. The church, under my agreement with the parish, was responsible for the buildings in the complex while St. Vincent's or the parish used them. The pastor of St. Rose, Father Mike, needed to be involved in all the discussions and correspondence.

As we talked, I avoided mentioning the site review. Instead, I told her that the Sisters of Mercy were making plans to open a clinic at St. Vincent's. Chaney circled right back to the site review and said the clinic permit could be handled at the same time as the 111 Bonita site review was processed.

I told her we had a business license for all the addresses and didn't need any additional permits.

She asked that Father Mike and I come into her office for a meeting. We set an appointment.

July 6, 1987:

Father Mike and I met with Chaney in the City Planning Department conference room at 1 p.m. She started with, "Do you have any questions about my letter, or are you ready to submit an application for the site review?"

I replied that St. Rose was the responsible party controlling the property and that the church had permission to use it for charitable purposes. So far, the city had not given notice to the church on the matter of the site review.

We gave her a copy of the business license issued by the city, as well as a copy of our 1987 license application listing all of the property addresses at St. Vincent's. I pointed out that the license itself said "charitable services," just as it had since 1983.

At that point, Chaney excused herself and left the room.

She came back a couple of minutes later with John Ford, a senior member of the planning department staff, to "straighten us out." After a quick introduction, he got right to the issue.

He preached the old line that having a license did not excuse us from the site review. He went into the routine that the site review was necessary because the house was being used for the first time for a commercial purpose – not as a residence. Ford went on to explain that the site review matter came to the city's attention when a business in the area complained about the change in use.

He said that a check by the planning department of city utility billing records showed a change in use at 111 Bonita from residential to commercial in 1983. He added that at that time, the planning department had a heavy workload, and this was such a small issue, it was "put on the shelf."

Two of his facts were incorrect:

1. I had purchased the house on Bonita in 1984, not 1983.
2. According to my check of the city's utility records, the house had always been billed as a residence, never as a commercial use. It was the Dining Room that was purchased in 1983 that had been consistently handled as commercial.

If the house was not the issue, was it the Dining Room next door?

I tried to pin Ford down with three questions:

"Is (Police Chief) Jim Hall after us again?

"Three years after I bought the house, are you trying to whip up opposition to the Dining Room with the public hearing process?"

"Or is it both?"

Then Father Mike asked a question: "Is this (the site review for the house) just the tip of the iceberg?"

Ford reluctantly responded with a yes, this was just part of a bigger problem, and maybe it was time it should be addressed. Father Mike posed two more questions to Ford:

1. Why did the youth ministry house need a site review, when a few years earlier, the city had allowed St. Rose to convert part of the convent from the nuns' residence to the school library and meeting rooms with nothing more than a building permit?
2. How were the St. Rose circumstances different from the youth ministry situation?

Ford said he was not prepared to answer any more questions. With that, Father Mike asked for a meeting between the city attorney and the attorney for the church (even though we didn't have one at the time) to determine the legality of the city's demand.

Ford volunteered to ask the city attorney for a legal opinion first and mail it to St. Rose. Then, our attorney could look it over.

Father went on to point out that if the bigger problem was the entire St. Vincent's center, which included the youth ministry site, the city should be cautious about how it proceeded. St. Vincent's work was supported by most local churches and service clubs. At that time, there were about one hundred thirty volunteers from at least eleven churches and clubs who worked in the Dining Room. He also said the Ministerial Association would be asked to get involved and would be watching to see what the city's actions would be.

Ford seemed to sense that public hearings for the little house might actually be more detrimental to the city than to the Dining Room. Was this a public relations nightmare in the making? He suggested the matter be taken directly to the City Council, reminding us that the planning department was just trying to enforce existing law.

As the meeting wound down, we all agreed that the city attorney would be asked for an opinion on whether it was necessary to have a site review on the matter. We told Ford that our attorney would respond on our behalf and we also might ask the Ministerial Association to go to the City Council members – without a site review – to find out who or what was really behind the planning department's actions.

Placer County Environmental Health Department records showed that within an hour after we left the meeting, Chaney had telephoned the agency to request an inspection of St. Vincent's Dining Room. Chaney's call confirmed that the city was not after the youth ministry's use of the little house. The target was the Dining Room.

July 8, 1987:

Chaney left a phone message at the rectory asking me to call her.

Once I reached her, she said that when she checked with a senior planner about the legal opinion, she was told that no legal opinion was needed. We simply needed to apply for the use permit.

I asked her to put that in writing for our phantom attorney.

July 9, 1987:

Another letter from Roseville City Planning arrived, reminding us to submit the application for a site review for 111 Bonita. Still, there was nothing in writing from the city on the Dining Room issue.

That same day, Janette Sanders, the new Dining Room chairperson, received a call from Placer County Environmental Health sanitarian Ralph Echols. He asked her to meet him for a Dining Room inspection. "...a complaint was issued against St. Vincent's."

Sanders' notes state that when she arrived for the meeting, she discovered that "the planning commission from Roseville had called Mr. Echols' office...to issue a complaint." Things were moving too fast. We had to slow them down!

As Father Mike and I thrashed through the problem, we realized that the city didn't want to hurt the activities of the Food Locker or office because they focused on serving local families and households. Messing with those services could backfire on them. They were just after the Dining Room.

So, we felt that there might be protection for the Dining Room if we put the whole St. Vincent's operation on the line and asked for "equal treatment" for of all of St. Vincent's activities. We knew that, technically, the Food Locker was subject to the same city regulations and state health code as the Dining Room. The two should not be treated differently.

July 13, 1987:

We wrote a proposal to city manager Bob Hutchison, asking him to set up meetings for us with each concerned city department to review all of St. Vincent's facilities, not just the Dining Room. Our purpose was to get to the bottom of who at City Hall was behind this push, forcing them to come out of the shadows. We requested the meetings begin after September 1st because of vacations and prior commitments.

We also met with Thom Carmichael, chief sanitarian for Placer County and a long-time St. Rose parishioner who had worked with Father Mike on other community issues. He told us that he was very upset that Chaney had called him personally to ask for an inspection to write up the Dining Room for health code violations. The Dining Room was a project Carmichael believed in. He went on to convey that she had stated that she would like the inspection completed before the "city shuts St. Vincent's down."

Carmichael reminded us that he was obligated to enforce the law. Given the new circumstances, the Dining Room would have to meet code requirements, but he would do all he could to keep the expenses down. Carmichael had Ralph Echols do the inspection only because the city officially asked for it. If it had been an informal complaint, he would not have taken any action.

Carmichael knew we were serious about keeping the Dining Room open. He was ready to help us.

July 14, 1987:

Inspectors from the Roseville Fire Department showed up. After they went through the entire complex, they handed us their report. It was "clean" – no violations. The timing of the visit seemed a little strange in light of what was going on at City Hall.

City manager Hutchison called a few days later, a bit frustrated He didn't understand what his planning department was up to. All he could say is that he would be in touch with us when he got the matter straightened out.

July 24, 1987:

The *Press Tribune* announced that Police Chief Hall was retiring at the close of the year.

July 28, 1987:

Thom Carmichael arranged for John Miners from his office to meet with Father Mike and me to brief us on the inspection process.

July 29, 1987:

Evidence was mounting that Chief Hall planned to go out in a blaze of glory by closing St. Vincent's:

- Jean Chaney told me that Hall had complained to her about St. Vincent's, asking her for enforcement help.
- Sherry Schiele reported that the chief, in a conversation at a charity event at the fairgrounds, told her the city was going to close down the St. Vincent de Paul center or move it out of town.
- My office manager, Winnie Lavigne, informed me her nephew, Roseville police officer Steve Uribe, bragged to her that Chief Hall told his staff that shutting down St. Vincent's before retiring was his top priority.

Word must have gotten back to Hall that I took his remarks seriously. While Ray Daniels and I were having breakfast at the Heritage Coffee Shop, I looked up to see the chief chatting with his buddies in a booth across the room. I caught his eye, and he came over and sat down.

I usually found Hall easy to read. That morning, things were no different. I could see that he had a sheepish "the devil made me do it" smile on his face. As he began talking about St. Vincent's, he fumbled his words, barely able to tell me that the rumor that he wanted to shut down St. Vincent's was not true. Was he feeling guilty?

When I asked him why he said what he did to Schiele last week, he replied that he was kidding her because "she wants to save all those guys." Our mission was a joke to him.

He also clarified that he didn't want to see St. Vincent's moved out of town, but did think it should be relocated somewhere away from Riverside Avenue – over to Old Town, for example, or out by the welfare office on Taylor Road.

Then, he joked that St. Vincent's would be better for Old Town than the "dirty book store" on Main Street, which he was also trying to shutter.

Hall ended on a serious note, promising to help us (rather than force us) to move to another location.

After the chief left, Daniels and I discussed the Dining Room situation. Daniels said he had written a letter about it to the *Press Tribune*.

Daniels' letter showed up in that day's paper.

The same issue of the *Press Tribune* carried an editorial "saluting" Chief Hall for his "effective handling of the homeless problem."

The paper noted that "Despite Roseville being a magnet for transients and the violent crimes that often accompany them...the city has been spared...Credit that to Hall's policy of making sure his officers kept vagrants moving..."

July 30, 1987:

Father Mike called Bob Hutchison to see what he had been able to resolve. Hutchison responded that he had not even looked into the matter. "I misunderstood your intentions. I'll check it out and get back to you soon."

There could be two explanations for Hutchison's answer: either he was being coy, stalling for some advantage, or he wasn't in close contact with his senior staff, like the planning director and the police chief.

Later that day, we got a third letter from the city planning department with a significant new development; now the city didn't want a site review for just the youth ministry building, but also wanted one for the Dining Room. City planning claimed that parking shortages for the Dining Room were now a concern. St. Vincent's didn't have any designated parking, just what was available on the street.

For the city to suggest a parking requirement for a dining room that served people without cars was ridiculous.

July 31, 1987:

Father Mike and I met both Miners and Carmichael at St. Vincent's to discuss in general what changes were necessary to get the Dining

Room to conform to the health code. The remodeling list was extensive, but barebones, as to what we had to do.

Carmichael said that he was going to follow Miners' recommendation to give us as much time as we needed to get the job done, and we could remain open during the remodeling.

While we appreciated the leniency, Father Mike and I told them we wanted to bring the issue to a close as soon as possible so that the environmental health department would not have to be involved with the city. The four of us were satisfied that we had mapped out a good plan. Carmichael and Miners looked relieved.

August 3, 1987:

I called Bob Hutchison to see what provoked the city to suggest that the Dining Room needed dedicated parking for its clients. I also asked him about Jim Hall's comments to Schiele at the charity event.

Hutchison sounded frustrated – not with us, but with his staff. He seemed clueless. His words were, "I can't figure out who's upset and who's putting on the heat. I know it's not the Council. They haven't given me any directive to close down St. Vincent de Paul. I'm going to call in Steve Dillon and get to the bottom of this. I'll be in touch."

Steve Dillon was the city planning director at the time. It was hard to believe that Hutchison had not bothered to talk to Dillon about the proposal made in our letter four weeks before.

I decided the most important thing I could do at this point was to continue to stall.

August 5, 1987:

Chaney sent a letter to let us know that the application deadline for the site review hearing for both the youth ministry building and the Dining Room had been extended to August 21st.

August 7, 1987:

I left a phone message for Chaney asking for an appointment. I wanted the chance to informally let the planning department know we were not interested in meeting their deadlines and ultimatums. I felt it was important to keep the city staff guessing.

At 11:45 a.m., Chaney called back and suggested I come to her office to meet with her and her associate "Denny." I replied, "No. I'd like to talk to you one-on-one so we can go over some ideas." It seemed like a good time to begin asking her questions.

"Jean, why do you want to close down St. Vincent's?"

"I don't."

I told her that people in city government had told us otherwise. No response.

I asked, "Jean, why is Roseville city planning trying to slowly wear us down? Do you have a list you're using, going item by item until you guys close the meal program? Like the letter you just sent (saying) for the first time the Dining Room needs a site review."

No reply.

"Why did you call the (County environmental) health department about St. Vincent's when there are lots of public kitchens in town that don't meet code? We were singled out!"

Finally, she shot back, "We're not selectively attacking St. Vincent's. I don't have any personal grudge against you. But the law must be upheld!"

I told her that we had asked Bob Hutchison to set up a meeting so we could work on a compromise to replace the site review and that she should know the Ministerial Association was getting involved too.

Sensing that I had made my point, I reminded Chaney that the two of us could talk about a compromise anytime.

Chaney changed her tone and said the whole process was getting to be very emotional for her.

I thought the conversation was over, but then she blurted out, "No one's filed a formal complaint. There isn't anything in the file that's come from the public."

I took a breath and asked her why this whole thing was being pursued so vigorously.

"Because the department noticed on its own that the law hasn't been strictly followed according to code."

I didn't believe her.

I closed the conversation. Enough pot-stirring for one day. I needed to rally our troops.

My first call was to Rev. Tim Brooks, secretary of the Ministerial Association. I filled him in on what the city was doing to St. Vincent's and asked for the Ministerial Association's help. Brooks agreed. The plan was for me to draft a letter to member churches suggesting how the association would carry out its theme for the coming year, "relating to the community and community leaders."

Once we had something on paper that he could use, he would get the word out to the other churches. I wrote to him on St. Rose letterhead.

"In late June, the City Planning Department began spearheading an attempt to shut down the St. Vincent's facility in its entirety. According to two other governmental sources, the Planning Department has set this as a priority, selectively utilizing governmental codes against St. Vincent's to achieve this end...Therefore I believe that the primary function of the Ministerial Association this year should be to meet this (the city's) challenge with a united front."

Chaney phoned to be sure that I knew the new application deadline. So much for her willingness to talk about a compromise.

August 13, 1987:

I mailed Hutchison a second letter to let him know we were not going to respond to Chaney's demand and that our plans for updating the Dining Room were on hold until his side laid out its agenda. I sent a copy to John Miners of Placer County Environmental Health.

Surprisingly, in the afternoon, Bob Hutchison's response to our July 13th letter showed up in the mail. In it, he politely defended the city's actions and asked us to meet him before the end of the month. He avoided both of our suggestions of meeting with the various individual city departments and having them scrutinize the other charitable activities of St. Vincent's.

There was no doubt left in my mind that the Dining Room was the issue.

I called to tell Hutchison about the letter that I had mailed him that morning and to schedule a time to meet. Father Mike was out of town, but I would mark his calendar, making sure that when he returned from vacation, he could plan to be there along with Jim Bush and me.

Hutchison picked a time that was convenient for the necessary city staff to be there as well.

He also mentioned that there was a property owner on Riverside who he had talked to about "the transient problem." The property owner said other businesspeople didn't want to formally complain because they were "afraid of retaliation from the bums." Hutchison let me know that he was just telling me as a courtesy, and unless the business folks were willing to come forward with a written complaint, he was going to leave it at that.

He felt that all of the drama created by the planning department's handling of the matter up to this point had to end.

A Rocky Ride for the Dining Room

August 18, 1987:

As part of our plan to show the city that the Dining Room was important to local residents, we started a formal one-week survey asking clients where they came from. The information would give us some hard facts to work with.

August 19, 1987:

I called Aldo Pineschi, Sr., a St. Rose parishioner and the campaign director for Councilman John Byouk, to ask for his help on the Dining Room front. His wife, Claire, was a long-time St. Vincent's volunteer.

He offered to check things out with the Council members and city staff and get back to me. Pineschi had a unique "in" with the city as the former personnel director.

August 21, 1987:

Chaney's application deadline came and passed.

August 24, 1987:

Our survey showed that seventy-two percent of the Dining Room's clients were housed or homeless residents of Roseville and twenty-eight percent regarded themselves as homeless nonresidents.

We knew that some folks who reported being "residents" were too ashamed to admit they previously had Roseville addresses but were currently homeless. Rather than question them further, we just lumped all housed and homeless residents into one category.

We now had proof that the Dining Room served more local people than transients. St. Vincent's was providing a needed community service.

August 26, 1987:

The day started off well enough when Pineschi called me back. He said that council members Byouk and Santucci would be meeting with a county environmental health official and Bob Hutchison to discuss the future of the public sector's treatment of St. Vincent's. Pineschi asked Byouk to work toward a compromise between St. Vincent's and the city. He said he would keep me posted as things developed.

Then everything changed. Chaney called at the rectory and left a message that she wanted to know how many people the Dining Room served on average.

Next, a City Hall source told me that eight of the business and commercial property owners around St. Vincent's met with city manager Bob Hutchison in a closed meeting and presented him with a letter asking the city to take action against St. Vincent's activities "that encourage transients into our area."

And finally, Wanda Patrick, a friend, St. Rose parishioner and a County Environmental Health Department sanitarian, called to let me know her colleague John Miners told her he had just met with Bob Hutchison and ten to fifteen people about St. Vincent's. She recounted to me what Miners had told her: He was surprised that the city folks were developing a strategy to "effectively proceed" against St. Vincent's.

City staff had asked Miners "Are they (St. Vincent's) in violation of the State health code?"

Miners replied that there were several things St. Vincent's needed to do to meet the current code. The environmental health department was working out a schedule to bring the Dining Room into compliance.

Patrick said that it was standard procedure for the department to help businesses address "out of code problems." It wasn't the county's policy to come down on people with a hammer. The environmental health department's protocol called for education and cooperation.

August 27, 1987:

I returned Chaney's call armed with our one-week survey data. I thought she should know how many local people used the Dining Room, and the information might soften her up. I told her that about seven hundred persons a week showed up for the midday hot meal, seventy-two percent of them from Roseville.

Chaney said it was nice that people could rely on the Dining Room for a meal, but the number of locals served was irrelevant. She just wanted to know how many seats we had.

Was she going to use seating as the criterion for the number of parking places? I told her we had nine booths providing seating for thirty-six people.

Then, I suggested the city examine Southern Pacific Railroad's lax trespassing policy and policing as the real reason the city was impacted by more homeless men than usual – a reason which probably was beyond the city's, let alone St. Vincent's, control.

I reminded Chaney that it was common knowledge that since the company's economic problems had gotten worse, Southern Pacific's police were not as effective as they had once been. Record numbers of transients were riding the rails, and everyone was hungry.

Jean Chaney seemed unmoved.

Around the same time, I tried to lobby Council member Crabb. Maybe he would help because in one of his earlier Council races, he had asked me to sign his nomination petition. Then he followed up by inviting me to drop over to his house for an election night party. We were neighbors, living just around the corner from one another.

I left a phone message with his wife, Jeanette, asking him to call me.

That night, he did. When I mentioned my concern about St. Vincent's, he invited me over to talk about it.

Assuming he knew something about the problem between St. Vincent's and the city, I started off asking for his help. He said " What problem?" After I gathered my wits, I gave him what I thought was the necessary background information.

Then I let him know St. Vincent's would like to work toward a positive solution—a deal outside of the hearing process.

Crabb said he would look into it and see what was going on.

The next morning I woke up with the sinking feeling I may have walked into a trap at Crabb's house: I'd told him something Father Mike and I hadn't told anyone else, that it was our intent to avoid the public hearing process.

A day or two later, on a visit to the County Environmental Health Department, I picked up three important pieces of information:

1. Copies of the department's notes on Chaney's July 6th telephoned inspection request, quoting her as saying she would like the inspection completed before the "city shuts St. Vincent's down";

2. Chaney's letter requesting a copy of the Dining Room's health code violations; and

3. Notes of John Miner's August 26th meeting at Roseville's City Hall.

The notes showed that the meeting was actually a forum for the city to pressure the environmental health department to act against St. Vincent's. Only one businessperson was at the meeting – Al Carruthers, who ran a tire shop on Riverside. Among the others were Council member Bill Santucci and department heads Chief Hall and planning director Steve Dillon.

The "eight people" that my City Hall friend erroneously thought attended the meeting were merely the signatures on a letter from businesspeople near St. Vincent's. The names I recognized were Wes Jones, Gordon Whitcomb, Mary Lou Flores, Al Carruthers, Steve Scott, Alberto Heredia and Dave Tognetti. Two others unfamiliar to me were Sylvia Slade and Sally Bragg.

August 30, 1987:
Council member Byouk and I had an opportunity to visit at a party at St. Rose Church. He was set to have a meeting with Hutchison and Santucci about St. Vincent's the following week. He was not sure about the details.

August 31, 1987:
Father Mike and I had recruited Jim Bush to join us for the scheduled meeting with the city brass in Hutchison's office. We were surprised that only the city manager, planning director Steve Dillon, and the mayor at the time, Phil Ozenick, were present.

The three men said they had a meeting the previous week with Bill Santucci and "some business people" who were "enraged" about transients being drawn into their area by St. Vincent's services. As I had discovered through John Miner's notes of the meeting a few days before, there were not "some business people" on hand. There was just one.

Hutchison said the main concern of "the business people" was the problem of transients "lying around." Dillon outlined what St. Vincent's needed to do to meet the city code specifications:

- File a request for a variance from the parking space requirement that the code laid out for the Dining Room, and
- Apply for a site review of the 111 Bonita building for use as a "non-residence."

He said that as far as he knew, the city had no other code concerns.

Dillon dominated the meeting and ran the show. He announced that Hutchison was no longer open to talking with us. The three of them, Hutchison, Dillon and Ozenick, delivered the message that from the department level up to the top on both the management and the political sides, the city was united in taking action against the Dining Room.

He mentioned an alternative to a public fight. Simply put, St. Vincent's should move the Dining Room out of downtown. That was what the city really wanted. It's what Chief Hall said to Ray Daniels and me at the Heritage. The city saw the Dining Room as a major impediment to redeveloping Riverside.

Dillon went on to suggest the following possibilities:

- The city might help St. Vincent's move the Dining Room to its new corporation yard on PFE Road or to somewhere in northwest Roseville, where the city could donate land;
- Different churches might take turns providing a meal at their locations; and
- Above all else, St. Vincent's should hire a security guard.

Ozenick floated the idea of moving the Dining Room to the fair grounds. I said the fair grounds' neighbors would love that.

Then he said he would support keeping the Dining Room open if we looked for another site where people from Rocklin and Lincoln could access the free meals. That was the extent of his involvement.

Hutchison's contribution to the meeting was minimal too. In passing, he mentioned that both Dave Tognetti, who owned the Baker Printing property across Riverside from St. Vincent's, and Steve Scott, who ran Roseville Upholstery, were the leaders against the Dining Room. All he offered after that was, "Get the transients off the street and out of sight!"

After our meeting, Bush and Father Mike surmised that Chaney and Hall were the just the messengers and the "bad cops," while Hutchison, Ozenick and Dillon, even though they were the instigators, wanted to be seen as the problem solvers and "good cops."

The two older and wiser men had figured out that the neighbors, business people and property owners were not the real threat. It was the city officials who planned to use public hearings to stir up citizen opinion against the Dining Room. The city still did not understand that we couldn't be coerced to give into its demands.

September 5, 1987:

At the St. Vincent's Board meeting, Father Mike, Jim Bush and I presented the results of our previous week's discussion with "the Big Three at City Hall." We listed the city's concerns with the Dining Room and shared Dillon's suggestions. The consensus of the Board members was that relocating was not viable.

I mentioned that Ministerial Association leaders, Pastors Tim Gentry and Virginia Pearson, advised St. Vincent's to adapt the existing facility to meet the city's requirements rather than attempt to move.

With that, the group opted to take another shot at solving the problem with minimum disruption to the meal program by offering a compromise. Moving the facility or having public hearings could not become part of the deal. Instead, we would:

- Cut the number of seats in the Dining Room from thirty-six to twenty-four to reduce the parking requirement we thought the planning department would insist on;
- Rent out the property at 111 Bonita to Project Home for family use;
- Fence the area where Dining Room clients waited for meals so they could relax while staying out of sight and off the street; and
- Hire a security guard from 11 a.m. to 2 p.m. to make sure that the clients behaved.

September 8, 1987:

I sent a letter to each of "The Big Three," informing them that there was no longer a need for a site review on the 111 Bonita house because we were going to convert it to a residence for a Project Home family. I added that we would hire a security guard, as Dillon suggested, and had asked Chief Hall for input on the job description.

Additionally, to refute any credence to the city's claim that the city's action was driven by business owners around St. Vincent's, I asked for a meeting with these merchants as soon as possible to ferret out their real concerns.

None of "the Big Three" replied to my letter.

I created a draft of a job description for the security guard position and asked for Hall's comments. Winnie Lavigne hand delivered the document to his office and mailed a copy to Hutchison.

Next, I called Chaney to ask her to come down to St. Vincent's to approve the location of the planned waiting area for the Dining Room clients.

We met later that afternoon on the sidewalk and walked around the location where the fence would be built. I told her there would be benches for the folks to sit on.

Chaney looked the area over and said that a visual check was not good enough. She needed a diagram. Then, she decided to go inside to check out the revamped Dining Room seating.

I showed her that three booths had been removed, cutting seating back to twenty-four and allowing the parking requirement to be cut back. She did not comment. We agreed to meet again the following week to discuss the parking matter further.

September 9, 1987:

It was the first meeting of the season for the Ministerial Association when Pastor Tim Brooks presented the letter I had written about the city's attack on the Dining Room. This was the first time some of the members had heard about the city's actions. After everyone was brought up to speed on the issue, it was decided that together they would develop a petition asking the city to back off its harassment of St. Vincent's.

The group created an "Open Letter" petition that they and their colleagues would sign. The plan was to deliver the signed document to Council members and city staff before the St. Vincent's site review matter could be brought to the planning commission.

After ministers from most of the major congregations in town had signed on, we kept the petition in our hip pocket, ready for use. The document pointed out that the city's off-street parking requirement was unnecessary for the following reasons:

- The Dining Room was open only two hours per day;
- Seating had been reduced from thirty-six seats to twenty-four; and
- Most clients were local residents who did not have cars.

Jim Bush and I would be the contacts for making sure the petition remained a hot topic among all the ministers in town.

Following the Ministerial Association meeting, I returned a call from Placer County Environmental Health's John Miners. We got some good news: Miners said that we did not have to submit any improvement plans until the problems with the city were cleared up. He was very definite about it. "Don't lift a hammer until (the) city problems are resolved." He also said his department would also consider easing up on other requirements in his report if we worked together on solutions.

By the end of the week, I was finally able to nail down Chief Hall about the security guard position. He was unusually negative and unfriendly. He let me know the draft was "wrong." The security guard should patrol just around St. Vincent's property, not the whole block. Hall said that he would stop by sometime the following week to go over the details. He went on to predict it would be hard to hire someone for the job because the position was only for three or four hours a day.

I responded that I already had more than ten applicants. Chief Hall never followed up on his promise.

September 15, 1987:

Chaney met me at St. Vincent's as planned and reminded me of the city's list of requirements for the Dining Room, including public hearings. I did not react, but rather handed her the diagram of the proposed new outside waiting area that included a screening fence (a fence that could not be seen through).

She wanted to check with the public works department to be sure the layout was okay, and said that Dillon was helping her draft a letter about the parking requirement. She assured me that the city would be lenient, given that most of the Dining Room patrons did not have cars.

She also let me know she was writing an ordinance to control what she called "future Dining Rooms and other undesirable services." St. Vincent's Dining Room and Food Locker would be "grandfathered in" when the ordinance was adopted.

September 29, 1987:

Fourteen days passed before I heard from Chaney again. When she finally called, I anticipated that the parking question would be answered. Instead, she said that a decision was still up in the air. Then she tried to make a joke by saying that, lucky for us, the city was not looking at the parking requirement for all of St. Vincent's activities, just the Dining Room.

I failed to see the humor. It felt more like a threat.

Chaney got serious and tried to reassure me she was only targeting 105 Bonita – the Dining Room. All the other uses and their parking areas were not in question.

In the next breath, she asked about the Dining Room's square footage and the same for the entire St. Vincent's facility so she could firm up the number of parking spaces needed.

Why did she need to know the square footage of the entire facility when she had just told me that the planning department was only concerned about the Dining Room?

Chaney reminded me that if we felt the planning department's recommendation for the number of required parking spaces was too high, we could appeal to the planning commission since there were not specific requirements for free dining rooms. She knew the public hearing process was the one thing we did not want, but was exactly what the city was hoping for.

Just to jab me a little more, she said she had checked again to be sure a public hearing would be required, pointing out that we would have to send notices to all neighbors within three hundred feet. Finally, she said it was okay to install the waiting area enclosure.

After Chaney hung up, I was so confused by her comments that I called her right back.

She again affirmed that the only issue open with the city was a public hearing requirement to determine the Dining Room parking question. She said the code called for restaurants to have one parking space for every three seats, but the planning department decided not to use that rule.

It was only then that she revealed that the city regarded the Dining Room as a "social service agency" because most of its users did not have cars. Therefore, the parking requirement would be less – only one space per two hundred square feet.

My internal reaction was one of relief. The Dining Room was very small, less than a thousand square feet. According to Chaney's new formula, the maximum number of parking spaces required would be five or less.

Abiding John Miner's admonition, I decided we would hold off on enclosing the waiting area. The whole process of trying to accommodate the city's wishes was getting so burdensome that the negotiations could collapse at any time.

I decided to have professionally prepared "to scale" drawings of the entire campus drawn up. Quality drawings that accurately showed the square footage of the whole facility might be enough to keep the city from changing tactics again.

October 5, 1987:
I delivered the "as built" plans of the St. Vincent's facilities prepared by Blue Streak Blue Printing to the city planning department.

Friday, October 9, 1987:
In a call to Chaney to see if things were progressing, I was told she wanted to check with Dillon about the number of spaces that would be required before doing anything else. She would get back to me the following Tuesday or Wednesday.

Wednesday, October 14, 1987:
Chaney's call never came.

October 16, 1987:

The Planning Department had skipped the courtesy call and instead issued its findings in a letter. The letter was a shock on two counts.

The first was that the Dining Room now needed eighteen parking spaces for thirty-six seats: one parking place for every two poor people using the twenty-four seat facility and six for three long-gone phantom booths.

The new mandate ran counter to what Chaney had told me in a conversation we had two weeks before, during the afternoon of September 29th when she had told me that the city would use the Dining Room square footage to determine the number of parking places, one for every two hundred square feet of floor space, meaning the Dining Room needed only five or six parking places. Chaney's assurances of leniency turned out to be bogus. After weeks of jousting with me about the seating requirement, the city had adopted the most punitive "solution" possible. The requirement that the planning department was trying to impose was more onerous than we ever anticipated.

The second punch to the gut was the imposition of an expanded public hearing process:

- Our application (which we had refused to file) would have to be first examined by the city's project review commission during a public hearing in which anyone could object to the whole idea of a free dining room, let alone express concern over parking spaces.

- Next, the application would be scrutinized by the planning commission during a second public hearing, giving opponents of the Dining Room the opportunity to take more potshots at the program. and

- Finally, if someone appealed the planning commission's findings, the matter would end up in a third public hearing before the elected members of the City Council.

The accumulating effect of three public hearings would certainly be disastrous for the Dining Room program. All the turmoil generated by the three public hearings would remain on the community's consciousness, serving as great material for not only the *Press Tribune* and the *Sacramento Bee*, but also for regional television. There would be no media focus on parking spaces, because the real story would be the hobophobic reaction of those in the community whose only desire was to destroy the free meal project.

Up to this point in time, even after both papers had called, asking about the problems with the neighbors, I was able to keep our press coverage positive for the most part. If the press got scent of a public fight, everything could spiral out of control, forcing us into "crash and burn" mode. The future of the Dining Room was at stake.

October 19, 1987:

The only way Father Mike and I could effectively respond to this assault was to confront it by fighting the planning department's findings, not in a public forum, but behind closed doors with the city planner. I called for an appointment with Dillon at 8:30 that Monday morning. He agreed that he and Chaney would meet us at 1 p.m. Father Mike and I wanted to go over the October 16th letter item by item.

As the afternoon meeting began, I told Dillon the letter was vindictive and unacceptable. Then I asked Chaney about the business of having to go through a project review commission hearing, as well as the planning commission, another layer of bureaucracy. She said that the project review hearing was necessary because the Dining Room was a new use that began in January 1984 after the 1983 original license for charitable services was issued.

Dillon seemed anxious. He kept looking down at the papers on his desk and told Chaney he didn't think that a project review was needed.

After a lengthy discussion, Dillon agreed to issue a new letter and destroy the original one so it wasn't part of the record. He appeared agitated by the uncertainty of what this would mean for his department. He was backing down – something city planners were not prone to do.

Dillon, now completely avoiding eye contact, seemed just to want the entire issue to go away. The whole thing had morphed into an undeserved political nightmare that landed squarely on his shoulders, a no-win situation for the ambitious young bureaucrat.

Finally, he could not take any more. He stood up from his desk, turned away, threw up his hands up in the air and said, "That's it. I'm going to let the Council decide this one!"

Were we driving Dillon nuts?

Chaney said she would come to the Dining Room to reevaluate the seating. She was back to "square one."

October 21, 1987:

As promised, Chaney showed up in the morning to measure the

square footage of the Dining Room, checking it against the plans. She said she would let us know when Steve Dillon would schedule the matter for the planning commission to determine the parking requirement. Yippee! The preliminary project review hearing had been eliminated; one down and two to go.

October 26, 1987:

Chaney called to confirm that the planning commission hearing was scheduled for December 10th. When I asked her for a copy of the staff report, she said it would be available the Friday before the hearing. I let her know that our attorney would represent us.

As soon as I ended the call, I sensed it was time to recruit a real live attorney. I knew where to start my search: I asked Steve Thomas. Thomas, a St. Rose parishioner, local developer and friend from my Sunrise Bank days gave me the names of six good lawyers he had worked with and what each one's strong suit was. The lawyer that stood out was Jack Willoughby, whom Jim Bush also knew. Bush called his office to see if he would help us. We got an appointment for the second week in November.

In the meantime, with all of this activity going on, Bush and I recognized that we would have to be resourceful to get some of the heat off of the Dining Room program. We launched a simple plan to show the merchants and the city that St. Vincent's was acting in good faith. We decided that Bush would talk with his church council, and then we both would meet with the St. Vincent's board to gain approval to move the Monday noon meal to the Methodist Church. Both groups unanimously agreed to the idea. The Dining Room was soon closed on Mondays.

Chapter 5:
A Meeting of the Minds
(Nov. 1987–Oct. 1989)

November 5, 1987:

Just two days after the city elections, top vote-getter Mayor-elect Santucci didn't wait to take the oath before swinging into action on the Dining Room matter. He had the city manager's secretary call Father Mike to invite all local ministers to meet with a group of business people at City Hall the following week. As mayor, he would finally be in control of the city's response to the homeless issue.

Father Mike and I were surprised at how anxious Santucci was to get a meeting going and how well he crafted his request. The meeting was to be on his turf – City Hall. As host, he would control the agenda and the conversation. When he had the city manager's secretary call, we took that to mean he did not want to talk to Father Mike about the issue before the get-together. And, by only giving five days' notice, he did not offer the ministers a chance to organize a plan for the meeting.

Father called some of the other churches and found that only one other pastor could make it. With that, he asked City Hall to put off the meeting until after the Ministerial Association had its monthly meeting

November 9, 1987:
Santucci took office.
Jim Bush and I met with Jack Willoughby at his office in the Sunrise Bank building. We both had great hopes for the meeting's outcome, and could tell right off the bat that Willoughby was very interested in our case. I handed him a background paper and copies of our correspondence with the city, along with other relevant documents.

He asked us what the specific problem was and what our goals were. We told him that it was our perception the city was trying to make it difficult for the Dining Room program to continue serving meals at all. By subjecting the operation to a public hearing process to determine how many parking places the Dining Room needed, the city could gin up public opposition to St. Vincent's presence on Riverside. Bush and I both told Willoughby our goal was to avoid the public hearing process by meeting with the "complainers" as soon as possible to defuse their anger.

When Willoughby probed us more about the city's motives, I suggested that he take a look at the correspondence and other documentation I had given him. That was enough for the savvy attorney to understand where the city wanted to go with this effort. After looking over the list of all the churches that supported St. Vincent's and a copy of the Dining Room floor plan, he suggested that Father Mike ask Santucci to set a firm date for the meeting of the ministers with the merchants. Bush and I were very surprised and grateful for the interest that Willoughby had taken in our case.

November 10, 1987:
Father Mike's letter requesting a meeting of the ministers with Santucci and the merchants was delivered to the City Clerk's office.

November 11, 1987:
At the Ministerial Association's monthly get-together, I gave an update on the Dining Room – city issue. I went on to suggest that the group ask to have a meeting with Santucci somewhere other than City Hall – maybe at the Dining Room.

Our first objective remained to negotiate a settlement with the city that would get the public hearings cancelled. We were not sure of what specific outcome Santucci wanted, but we were cautiously hopeful it would include a compromise we could live with, no public hearings.

Later that Wednesday morning, I contacted Steve Dillon to see if the planning commission hearing was still scheduled for December 10th. He said he'd call me back the next day.

Around noon Willoughby came to the St. Vincent's Dining Room for lunch with Bush and me. Afterward, the three of us took a tour of the entire property.

Before he left, we gave Willoughby a packet of information with copies of the Dining Room floor plan and the city approved client waiting area layout, as well as lists of churches that were providing meals, financial help and moral support to St. Vincent's on the issue.

After the meeting, Bush and I decided to expand the ministers' September 9 th "Open Letter" petition drive to as many churches in town as we could, asking the clergy and any members of their congregations who would like to support us to sign.

Before the day's end, I heard back from Dillon. He let me know he and planning commission chairman, Fred Lohse, had settled on the

December 10th date for the hearing (for which we still had not filed an application). Dillon went on to say that the hearing could be postponed and rescheduled for a later date, without indicating why. I did not ask any questions. The chance that the hearing might be put off was good enough for me. I felt like a stay of execution was in the cards.

In retrospect, I think that subsequent to the election, Dillon had asked Santucci to intervene in the matter. It was in the city's interest to bring the issue to a close as soon as possible. It could become an unnecessary distraction from the larger agenda that the city had: the establishment of the redevelopment agency, the new Auto Mall, a burgeoning electronics industry and mushrooming housing developments, among other projects.

November 13, 1987:
Willoughby sent a letter to Santucci requesting a meeting with the concerned business owners at the Dining Room around 5:30 p.m. or so "after work" on December 1st.

December 1, 1987:
The Dining Room meeting came off just as Willoughby planned.

Three key pastors in the community were there: Reverends Mike Cormack, Virginia Pearson and Tim Gentry. I represented St. Vincent's.

Mayor Santucci and Chief Hall represented the city.

Merchants and property owners Al Carruthers, Steve Scott, Dave Tognetti, Ken Wiener and the owner of the daycare center at the corner of Clinton and Bonita represented the business interests.

Willoughby, who Santucci trusted, facilitated the meeting, asking the property owners and merchants what they wanted out of the negotiations.

They summed it up by saying the transients had to be pushed out of the area. The business representatives were willing to help St. Vincent's serve local residents, but not the hard-core homeless.

When he asked Chief Hall and Mayor Santucci the same question, they replied they wanted the transients not only out of the area, but out of town. Hall said the Dining Room was like an open invitation for them. He claimed the Dining Room drew transients into Roseville from all over the country. He had no proof, but it felt like right reasoning to him.

By the time the meeting ended, we all agreed to consider one proposal: the Dining Room would be available to local people only, based on forms of identification that proved they were local. Families might not be required to have identification. Transients would be served a bag lunch to be distributed from a mobile unit at three locations along the railroad tracks – between Atlantic Street and Lower Vernon.

The business folks said they would help St. Vincent's find a mobile unit (they called it "a goodie wagon") and bring it up to code. Al Carruthers said he would maintain it and Steve Scott would reupholster it.

I was inclined to believe that what the property owners and merchants said they would do, and what they would actually do, were two different things. I would have liked to seen their offer in writing.

In any event, everyone seemed pleased that the "the goodie wagon" offer would definitely get city government support. The city, property owners and merchants admitted that the community had an obligation to feed hungry people. The only disagreement was where should they be fed?

At that point, Santucci excused himself, saying he had to leave for another meeting. As he stood at the doorway, he announced that if we could agree on a solution, the need for a hearing "would go away." Willoughby let him know he would keep things moving toward that goal.

I told the group that the Dining Room committee would have to sign off on any proposal, which I would present to them Friday afternoon. Father Mike, Virginia Pearson, Tim Gentry and Jack Willoughby agreed to be there, too.

Carruthers and Tognetti asked that the Dining Room committee brainstorm the idea of the goodie wagon. They were anxious for a follow-up meeting. We adjourned at about 7:30 p.m.

When I got home, I spent some time evaluating the situation. As far as I could see, the alternative to an agreement with the opposition appeared to be a long, drawn-out battle.

On the other hand, I had to discount the offer of the property owners and merchants because I figured there was a chance that St. Vincent's could end up being stuck with the all of the costs. They could back out of the deal at any time.

Either way, there would be a big increase in overhead and responsibility for St. Vincent's. Even if the property owners and merchants paid for the goodie wagon and its upkeep, St. Vincent's would still have to pay the ongoing costs:

- The salary of the person who had to be at the Dining Room door every day to manage and check the ID's of hard-core singles who wanted in. No volunteer would take on that job;

- The cost of keeping the goodie wagon up to the standards of the County Health Department;
- The cost of insurance and gasoline; and
- When volunteers weren't available, the employee costs of a two-person crew each day to operate, drive, supply and clean the goodie wagon, as well as pick up the litter around the stops.

In addition, the goodie wagon would have to be on the road every day that the Dining Room was open, and we would not be able to provide showers or clean clothes to transients.

December 3, 1987:

The first indication that we were on the right track toward a settlement with the opposition occurred when Dave Tognetti, the owner of the Baker Printing property across Riverside from St. Vincent's, telephoned to inform me that the merchants and property owners did not expect any changes until April. He went on to remind me that his group promised to help St. Vincent's buy the goodie wagon and keep it in good shape.

December 4, 1987:

Father Mike called me with more good news. Santucci just told him that "the parking issue had been pulled from the file." The item on the Planning Commission's agenda was cancelled – NO PUBLIC HEARING!

Later that afternoon, Father Mike, Pearson, Gentry, Willoughby and I met with the Dining Room committee to present the proposal of the city, merchants and property owners. In addition, I had developed seven alternative possibilities for discussion, giving the group a good selection of options. The choices ranged from doing nothing and waiting for a response from the city, to adopting the plan as proposed. All were reviewed and carefully considered.

Jim Bush was adamant that any solution had to include providing meals seven days a week somewhere in town, one way or another. Willoughby said that the bottom line was not turning away anyone who was hungry. All agreed to take a breath and meet later in the month to make a decision.

December 5, 1987:

That morning, at the monthly meeting of St. Vincent's Board, everyone was brought up to speed on the events of the last thirty days. There was lots of discussion about the proposed solution concocted during the negotiations with the city, merchants and property owners. It was felt that excluding the transients amounted to discrimination (no hobophobia here!).

The Board members agreed that because the Dining Room committee probably understood what was at stake better than they did, that group should work out a plan at its December 18th meeting and then bring it to the Board before presenting it to the other side.

December 8, 1987:

Father Mike received a letter from Ed Tiedemann, a long-time supporter of St. Vincent's. He and his wife Marian were members of Shepherd of the Sierras Presbyterian Church The letter was a copy of a blistering criticism that Tiedemann had written to the mayor and the other Council members, chiding the city for its attempt to impose parking restrictions on St. Vincent's as a "case where common sense and consistency has been forgotten. Some would characterize the city's actions as a case of harassment."

December 16, 1987:

Following Governor Deukmejian's executive order to make the state's National Guard armories available for temporary emergency shelters for the first time, sixteen armories around the state were used as shelters, while Roseville and Placer County limited their action to examining the consequences of opening the Roseville Armory. In other words, they were procrastinating.

The response to the governor's order by Placer County's director of emergency services Jim Armstrong was chilling. The *Press Tribune* quoted him as saying "I have not heard of any (homeless) problems in this area...People who don't have a home tend to gravitate to Sacramento." (translated: "We just dump 'em in Sacramento," which was true!).

Armstrong's negative comments spurred St. Vincent's and the Ministerial Association to agree to request that the County Board of Supervisors authorize the use of the Roseville Armory as an emergency shelter.

Pastor Tim Gentry of the West Roseville Baptist Church and president of the Ministerial Association would lead the effort.

December 17, 1987:

A new Dining Room problem popped up: our first negative press about the December 1st meeting showed up in the *Press Tribune*. Apparently one of the participants leaked the story. The paper reported that the merchants and property owners were upset that the Dining Room had impacted the neighborhood and businesses by serving meals to transients. The article claimed that most business and property owners wanted the Dining Room to limit meals to just Roseville residents and homeless families. Homeless single adults should get their meals from a mobile unit that St. Vincent's could operate, stopping at three locations along the railroad tracks.

The *Press Tribune* went on to detail that Southern Pacific opposed the idea, as did the transients, who were afraid that the railroad would get tough and not allow them to sleep in the yards anymore.

Mayor Santucci reportedly said that as an alternative to serving meals to transients along the railroad tracks, he would support the city providing a piece of land as long as:

- it was on the outskirts of town;
- the city was held harmless by St. Vincent's; and
- the merchants and residents were not bothered by the activity.

He had two parcels in mind. One was at the end of Berry Street (now part of Galleria Boulevard) and the other was at Hilltop, off of PFE Road (now the city's corporation yard), both far off the beaten path. Hobophobia was in control of city politics!

December 18, 1987:

When the Dining Room committee met, I offered a list of eight ideas as solutions to the problem. The committee narrowed it down to two, then after much discussion, to one. The selected proposal was very different than the one that came out of the meeting with the city, merchants and property owners on December 1.

The committee recommended that:

- St. Vincent's would serve hot meals only on Tuesdays, Thursdays, Saturdays and Sundays;
- St. Vincents would install a screened waiting area with seating on its property and require people waiting for a meal to sit there until called into the Dining Room.
- St. Vincent's would hire a security guard to be in place before, during and after meal times;

- The City Council would set up an advisory board of local citizens to formulate a comprehensive plan to care for the needy; and
- The city would coordinate an effort to develop a plan that included a shelter and meals component.

January 1, 1988:

Greg Cowart took over as police chief. He came to Roseville from Gilroy, California, where he had served as chief. His arrival brought a contemporary view of policing to our city as it continued to grow.

January 2, 1988:

The St. Vincent's Board approved the December 18th Dining Room committee recommendations. If the city, merchants and property owners accepted the recommendations, St. Vincent's would put them in place.

The Board also decided to implement other policies that would cut back on shower days, Food Locker hours and transportation vouchers – but again,

only if the Dining Room recommendations were accepted by the other side. The Dining Room continued to operate on its old six-day-a-week schedule until a formal agreement was reached.

Now that we knew what the St. Vincent's response would be to the other side, we were also set to reply to the leaked story about the December 1st meeting. We needed to get our momentum back and went public in a *Press Tribune* story detailing what St. Vincent's was actually ready to do.

We hoped that the article would report that a meeting had been scheduled with the business community, city and neighborhood members to discuss the two-part solution calling for a reduction in our services and an increased role for the city in caring for the needy. The article would let the other side know that we had rejected the December 1st proposal in favor of a solution that would move the city forward to meet its obligation toward homeless people, especially homeless single men and women.

February 1988:

Sherry Schiele, who oversaw the Project Home operation, and city representative John Sprague announced that the program would be receiving a thirty thousand dollar state and federal shelter grant for transitional housing through the city. But there was a problem: Project

Home needed to be a corporation to qualify for the funds. The program couldn't turn to Roseville's St. Vincent's for help either, because it, like Project Home, wasn't incorporated. The clock was ticking.

February 2, 1988:

Pastor Tim Gentry, the president of the Ministerial Association, with a group of his colleagues, asked the supervisors to consider the use of the Roseville Armory as a winter shelter as soon as possible.

County Supervisor Bob Mahan, who represented Roseville, did not warm to the idea at all, saying "We have plenty of programs around here to take care of the homeless." He went on to point out that he owned property across from St. Vincent's and that the transients who were attracted to the Dining Room bothered the nearby merchants and their customers.

Mahan's "no" to making the shelter request an agenda item meant we had failed. Without his endorsement, the Board of Supervisors wouldn't consider the request.

February 23, 1988:

The follow-up meeting with the city, the merchants and property owners at City Hall had all the players: Mayor Santucci, Council member Mel Hamel, Chief Greg Cowart, the assistant city manager, Chamber of Commerce executive director Leo Papas, several pastors (including Father Mike), a half-dozen merchants and property owners, Janette Sanders (Dining Room chair), Jack Willoughby (who facilitated the meeting) and yours truly.

Willoughby asked Chief Cowart to present an overview of the problems caused by homelessness. The chief set the tone, discussing the experiences of other jurisdictions and their progressive responses. The presentation put us at ease. Those of us from the caregiver and church community were pleasantly surprised by how Cowart's approach to the "homeless problem" differed from that of Jim Hall's. The chief emphasized that the problem should be managed, rather than confronted with force.

The merchants and property owners let us know right off the bat that they did not think the concessions we made in our proposal went far enough. They were sure that the transients drawn to the neighborhood on meal days would still be a problem because St. Vincent's would not maintain the security guard position after the heat was off. I tried to assure them that as long as I was overseeing the operation, a security guard would be on the job.

Leo Papas interjected that the local business community was obligated to help pay the cost of security because transients would be in the area whether St. Vincent's was there or not. He offered to send a letter to all the Riverside businesses, asking them to contribute to the cost of the guard's salary.

Even after my comments and Papas' offer, the meeting bogged down with complaints from the merchants and property owners, who continued to fuss about the folks waiting to eat. They were particularly concerned that the clients didn't have adequate access to toilets, especially when the only bathroom for Dining Room clients was occupied by someone taking a shower. We finally got the group to buy into our recommendations on a trial basis when we suggested installing a portable toilet.

The city representatives were much more receptive to the proposal, agreeing outright to our two recommendations. The results were immediate and long-term.

March 1988:

Implementation of our two recommendations for the city to take up came within weeks following the February 23rd meeting. Mayor Santucci
appointed an ad hoc "Blue Ribbon Committee" to study St. Vincent's free food activities, the homeless question in Roseville and the approaches of other communities to these issues. The seven-member group was made up of Lou Wilson as chairperson, Jim Bush, police chief Greg Cowart, another member of the police department and three representatives from the business community.

Cowart provided the Blue Ribbon group with some background information resulting from a survey of transients his officers had come in contact with during a one month period:

- 36% were California residents;
- 33% were from out of state;
- 31% did not have an address; and
- 13% of the California residents said they lived in Roseville.

The survey only listed people either looking like troublemakers or actually breaking the law, a total of one hundred forty-three males and four females.

The obvious flaw in the survey was that law-abiding homeless folks were omitted because, as Cowart put it, "The survey only spotlights those transients requiring police attention." Just the bad apples were counted. I was uneasy about how the committee might use the findings.

March 23, 1988:

Even though the property owners and businesspeople only accepted the settlement terms on a trial basis, we had already decided to put up the screened waiting area and hire the security guard as a sign of our good faith. Chief Cowart agreed to help us hire the right person for the security job.

The cost of the enclosure with seating was two thousand four hundred dollars for which St. Rose Parish picked up the tab. Neither the remodeling project nor operating day changes would start until we were certain the city would follow through on its end of the bargain.

That marked the end of the drama surrounding the city's attempt to leverage St. Vincent's into a public hearing process over the Dining Room.

Sherry Schiele announced that in her "spare time," she had discovered a pocket of county money that could be used to help qualify a large number of people for temporary shelter. These folks would have gone without housing if she had not learned the county would pay.

I never could figure out how Schiele uncovered those funds. For sure, the county did not advertise that they had the stash! She was a warrior for our cause, more than able to handle all the day-to-day operations of the Project Home program, plus write new grant applications, manage relations with city staff and give presentations to interested groups and individuals about the Project Home program. She was in good form despite her type 1 diabetes, feeling well and full of energy.

May 7, 1988:

Father Mike's comments to the St. Vincent's Board on the recent Blue Ribbon Committee meeting at the Food Locker assured everyone that we remained on course with the city. He said that with Jim Bush as member of the committee, we had the best person watching out for St. Vincent's interests. He went on to mention that Bush gave the committee a tour of the entire facility and answered questions about the Dining Room operation and what Schiele's job as social service coordinator entailed. Overall, the committee was surprised at how clean and large the operation was.

Following Father Mike's report, the group decided to move ahead with upholding its end of the deal. It was time to start the costly Dining Room remodeling and other changes required by the agreement with the city.

May 10, 1988:
Schedule changes, including closing the Dining Room on Wednesdays and Fridays, were in place. There were no free meals available two days a week. Something didn't feel right. People were going hungry! Something had to change!

May 13, 1988:
The Blue Ribbon Committee issued an interim report that unfortunately was critical of the Dining Room, saying, "...local merchants and residents have very legitimate concerns..."

The report had some positives, pointing out that Roseville should develop its own food program as a long-term solution. The committee also recommended the city conduct a thorough study to determine the actual number of transients, the specific needs of the homeless population, and the best ways to meet those needs. Another important suggestion was that the city should establish a detox center, something former police chief Hall had also called for.

Even though we did not like the committee's criticism of the Dining Room operation, overall, their effort looked like a "plus" for our side. The report, by stating that local government itself was part of the problem by not properly handling the homeless situation, put the onus on the city to come up with a permanent solution. This was a big shift.

July 1988:
The thirty thousand dollar grant that had been set aside by the state for Project Home had been hanging in limbo since February. Project Home, still unincorporated, remained unqualified to administer the funds. Without a legal entity to be accountable for the grant, the state would not release the funds.

Schiele and city representative John Sprague knew that time was running out. Our own local St. Vincent's, also unincorporated, could not act as proxy. The two had to get creative if they wanted Project Home to receive the money. Acting on a hunch, they were able to prevail on the Sacramento St. Vincent de Paul Society, which was incorporated, to agree to sign on to the deal on Project Home's behalf. Receiving the grant money was a breakthrough for both Roseville and Project Home.

The efforts of Schiele and Sprague finally paid off with all of the pieces finally coming together.

Ironically, shortly after, everyone was taken by surprise when Project Home's founders announced they were going to suspend operations for six months. They signaled that they were feeling overwhelmed. Schiele was moving too fast for them, expanding the program at a pace so rapid that it made them uncomfortable. Their floundering threatened to destroy all the groundwork Schiele had done with the city and put the option to purchase the Grape Street duplex in jeopardy.

July 26, 1988:

St. Vincent's Board formally notified Project Home that St. Vincent's would take over providing families with transitional housing and find a way to assume the pending grant. The program for homeless families would be operated under the new name Schiele chose, "St. Vincent's Home Start." She handled all the details of the transition just as smoothly as she had nailed down the grant in June.

There was one big problem that proved awkward to handle: St. Vincent's did not have the financial means to buy out Project Home's interest in the duplex. Thankfully, St. Vincent's members Ray and Kathy Daniels did.

The Daniels and I structured an agreement in which Project Home would assign its option on the duplex to them, enabling them to purchase the property and lease it back to St. Vincent's for the new transitional living program. The money the Daniels paid Project Home for the option was used to reimburse St. Vincent's for Schiele's wages that Project Home said it was still responsible for.

The Daniels agreed that they would pass title to the duplex to Project Home or its successor agency when it was able to purchase the property for the price specified in the option, seventy thousand dollars.

August 1988:

The remodel of the Dining Room was finally near completion. Father Mike arranged for St. Rose to pay for much of the cost by buying most of the new equipment – a ten thousand dollar donation. When the project was complete, Bishop Quinn led the rededication ceremony.

August 10, 1988:

Chief Greg Cowart, as a member of the Blue Ribbon Committee, made a presentation to the City Council on the transient problem. He recommended that the best way for the city to combat the situation was to offer increased social and mental health services, an overnight shelter and a detox program. The latter was a proposal in the May interim report of the Blue Ribbon Committee. Cowart suggested the shelter program be based on the model used in Santa Barbara.

He also asked the Council to adopt ordinances to increase penalties for public urination, drinking in public and carrying fixed-blade knives. His report evolved into a two-hour discussion with the Council members.

In the end, the idea of even considering a program like the Santa Barbara model was more than the hobophobic members of the Council could handle. They begged off following Cowart's progressive suggestions and just directed the city attorney to draft ordinances beefing up penalties for the infractions the chief had listed, making them misdemeanors. They also endorsed the Blue Ribbon Committee recommendation to expand the committee's investigation from just the Dining Room situation "to offer suggestions on the overall problem of homeless persons in Roseville." That request was about as close as city government ever came to resolving the homeless issue.

October 1988:

The Salvation Army expanded its presence in Roseville by adding the building next door to its offices on Lincoln Street, the former Presbyterian Church, to its operation. A few days following the dedication ceremony, the local commander Kit Wetter started to provide free sack lunches to all comers on the days the Dining Room was closed. The meal gap caused by the cut in St. Vincent's operating days had been filled.

November 1988:

The city quickly reacted to the Salvation Army's lunch program by shutting it down, stating that the Army needed a special permit to continue operations.

November 27, 1988:

When Governor Deukmejian authorized the use of the state's National Guard armories as emergency winter shelters for the second year, we began focusing our energies on getting a shelter established at the armory at the Roseville Fairgrounds.

We may have failed the previous year, but we recognized where things had gone wrong and were well-prepared. We had another chance to make the case and were not alone in our effort. The *Press Tribune*, in an editorial blasted the county for not having "any idea of the extent of the homeless problem...even though it spends millions in various social services to help the poor."

The Ministerial Association members lobbied the Placer County Board of Supervisors with a petition to open the Roseville Armory as soon as possible. Assistant County Executive Gloria Coutts gave us hope when she said we should wait until after the first of the year when three new supervisors would be sworn in to decide. She said the matter would probably be on the agenda the first or second week of January.

I also heard through the grapevine that Placer County Chief Executive Don Lunsford and Roseville City Manager Al Johnson planned to meet after Christmas to discuss issues surrounding opening the Armory. I knew the men were under a lot of pressure from folks on both sides and would be comparing notes on all the political ramifications involved. I put my two cents in a letter to them expressing the need for using the Armory as a shelter and offering the assistance of the Ministerial Association, St. Vincent's and St. Rose Church in any way that would help.

December 29, 1988:

After nearly ten months of meetings and traveling around the state observing how cities were addressing their homeless problems, the Blue Ribbon Committee issued a final report. In essence, the committee kicked the can down the road, recommending the Council appoint a broader-based committee to find solutions for a wide range of problems the city faced regarding homelessness.

January 3, 1989:

The Armory issue was finally put before the Board of Supervisors, with Roseville Mayor Santucci in the lead of our delegation. Supervisor Mahan, who represented the Roseville area, endorsed the move. The fact that both men supported the Armory shelter represented a transformational change in the political landscape in less than a year.

Mahan had always been calm, cool and collected, but, as I watched him that day in the Supervisors' Chambers, I saw a Bob Mahan who seemed touched to the core, yet conflicted by the change in his position. I think he sensed his true duty: It was up to him to do the right thing. The other supervisors were willing to accommodate any position he took on the issue, whether thumbs-up or thumbs-down.

In a gesture of generosity, Santucci committed Roseville to splitting the cost of operating the shelter with the county. He pointed out that even though he thought this financial commitment was more than Roseville's fair share because other Placer County cities would send homeless folks to the Armory, he wanted to get the deal done, sticking with his offer.

Mahan expressed how difficult the decision was for him, but also said it was what he had to do. After some anecdotal remarks, he took the lead and initiated the motion to open the Armory as soon as possible, accepting Roseville's offer of splitting the cost of operations. The motion was seconded and unanimously approved.

This was a watershed moment in Placer County history – one that was very emotional for me. I remember going up to the dais after the vote and thanking Bob Mahan as I shook his hand.

I'm sure that Santucci and Mahan, who were brothers-in-law and business partners, had many discussions about this issue during the previous eleven months. Both men were generally thoughtful and conscientious in their public service jobs and were inclined to do what was right as they saw it.

Placer County Welfare Director Ray Merz had always personally supported the idea of an Armory shelter. After the Board approved the proposal, Merz not only worked diligently behind the scenes with his staff, churches and service providers, but also recruited Volunteers of America to operate the program.

Yet, there were some in the community who were adamant that the shelter exacerbated "the problem" by drawing more homeless people to Roseville.

January 9, 1989:
Placer County and The Volunteers of America opened the Roseville Armory as an emergency shelter.

January 23, 1989:
An analysis of the facts illustrated that within weeks of the Armory opening, Roseville was safer and more peaceful than if the Armory had remained closed. The *Press Tribune* reported that Police Lieutenant John Barrow had noted arrests of transients were down by fifty percent. St. Vincent's records showed that there was no increase in the number

of people looking for a free meal, clothing or other services because of the shelter. In fact, "things seem to be much more orderly."

February 1989:
The good people at the Salvation Army were back in the meal business, serving a mid-day dinner on Fridays and adding a hot breakfast on Saturdays shortly after. About the same time that the Salvation Army started its hot dinner program, the First Baptist Church at Douglas Boulevard and Royer Street began serving noon meals on Wednesdays. Once again, there was at least one free hot meal in central Roseville seven days a week.

March 27, 1989:
The Armory shelter closed for the season after providing over three thousand shelter nights of housing (one person sheltered for one night equals one shelter night). About five hundred different people were served. There was always a good supply of fresh clean blankets donated by Sherry Schiele's "Blanket Brigade." Food for both an evening snack before lights out and a quick breakfast with hot coffee every morning was offered to all. The shelter had operated from 6:30 p.m. to 6:30 a.m.

Immediately after the Armory shelter shut down for the season, there was a jump in public safety incidents involving homeless men and women. It was easy to see that a year round shelter would be good for the community.

August 1989:
The second half of the year was a time when local government officials and St. Vincent's leaders worked hand-in-hand. Three key events seemed to bring them closer together.

The first occurred when Mayor Santucci commissioned his new Task Force on Homelessness in response to the Blue Ribbon Committee's recommendation. He went out on a limb with his commitment to find a solution to this long and vexing problem. The members of the committee were:

Pastor Roy Herndon of First Baptist Church, chairperson;
Lou Wilson, vice chair and community leader;
Jim Bush, St. Vincent's Advisory Board;
Max Dodge, Salvation Army Advisory Board;
Fred Lohse, community leader;
Diane Horton, businesswoman;

Al Carruthers, businessman;

Jim Wagner, businessman;

Chief Greg Cowart, Roseville Police Department;

Captain Chuck Knudsen, Roseville Police Department;

Ray Merz, Placer County Welfare Director;

Don Ferretti, Placer County Community Services Director;

John Tarson, Assistant City Manager; and

John Sprague, City Housing and Redevelopment Director.

This broader-based group had more authority than the earlier Blue Ribbon Committee. Task Force member Jim Bush, who had served with the first bunch, said this commission had been empowered to recommend policy changes to the Council and the Board of Supervisors, while the first one was limited to only creating a list of ideas. Bush, being his usual optimistic self, predicted, "I personally think a lot of good will come out of this."

Santucci indicated the committee could give insight into how to build a shelter program: "...this committee will ultimately focus on what a shelter will do and where it should be, how to get the property, that kind of thing."

The mayor also hoped that other cities and Placer County would take on more responsibility for the homeless problem.

Captain Knudsen became the Police Department's point man on homeless issues. Before he had focused on the matter, the department did not have anyone specializing in handling homeless problems.

The second key event would occur when the city and St. Vincent's partnered to ensure the future of Home Start by obtaining funding to guarantee its operation through 1990.

September 1989:

The third event of note occurred when Placer County proactively asked for proposals from service organizations to operate a "cold weather nighttime shelter...at the Roseville National Guard armory." The request for proposals was done both without any prompting from us and prior to Governor Deukmejian authorizing cities and counties to continue using National Guard armories for emergency winter housing.

Could the county's case of denial been cured?

October 1989:

Roseville City Council members put out feelers to other cities in south Placer County, hoping to receive help paying for shelter operations. The city got stuck with half the initial year's cost, twenty thousand five hundred dollars, which gave Council members political heartburn.

Assistant County Executive Gloria Coutts followed the Roseville request by lobbying the Auburn, Rocklin, Loomis and Lincoln city councils to help pay the shelter's operating costs. It was only right that they should kick in because the county was providing paid transportation from each city to the Armory site.

Chapter 6:
"...We're like a Rudderless Ship Bouncing Aimlessly on a Hostile Sea."*
(Nov. 1989–Jun. 15, 1992)

Press Tribune June 15, 1992

November 1989:

Placer County's Board of Supervisors voted to have Volunteers of America operate the shelter at the Roseville Armory as soon as Governor Deukmejian gave the formal statewide "go-ahead".

When the Armory opened, Placer's Consolidated Transport Services bused people to and from the shelter, and a Guardsman was on duty to oversee National Guard property.

I was hopeful Roseville and Placer County were maybe settling into a pattern of ensuring there were shelter services available every winter. It might even be a sign that the county was getting ready to take the next step: to provide shelter services regardless of the season.

When Bill Santucci's term as Roseville's mayor ended, Pauline Roccucci took over. The city's Homeless Task Force was in the midst of gathering information and investigating ways other communities around the state were handling the matter.

Santucci remained on the Council, working toward building agreement among all of the communities in south Placer County for a permanent solution to the homeless problem. His first order of business was to get financial commitments from them to help operate the current emergency shelter. A buy-in of Lincoln, Rocklin and Loomis would ensure the support of his fellow Council members for the Armory winter shelter and hopefully for a permanent facility. His position was that Roseville's commitment to help pay the cost of operating the Armory shelter was contingent on the other communities in south Placer doing their part.

Santucci's campaign was also an important introduction for other south Placer communities to his larger regional strategy. Their decision to make a financial commitment to the winter shelter was vital to paving the way to making a meaningful investment in the permanent shelter program. Each jurisdiction would be asked to support the effort based on the number of homeless people who said they were from that community.

December 4, 1989:
The Armory shelter began its second season of operation.

March 30, 1990:
When the shelter closed, records showed that six thousand one hundred sixty-five shelter nights of rest had been provided in nearly four months of operation. St. Rose hosted the shelter for one week in the parish hall while the Armory was being used for National Guard activities.

April 18, 1990:
After eight months of meetings, the Homeless Task Force submitted its final report to the City Council. Following its conceptual approval of the plan, the Council gave staff the go-ahead to apply for a one hundred sixty thousand dollar state grant to help fund future programs.

The report was absent any specifics for funding, building or operating a permanent emergency shelter. However, the document did urge the Council to retain someone to serve as Homeless Project Coordinator as soon as possible. The individual would develop a blueprint for creating a regional permanent emergency shelter and expanding transitional housing that included help for single adults. The report also proposed developing a center which would offer homeless services such as health care, mental health counseling, employment help, legal assistance and family counseling.

Mayor Pauline Roccucci affirmed that she liked the idea of a comprehensive service center being incorporated into the shelter plan. She observed that "Just feeding people doesn't solve the problem and just housing people temporarily doesn't solve the problem."

Councilman Crabb was flat out against any recommendations to provide additional services to homeless single adults, saying, "The only reason they're (homeless men and women) staying is because we accommodate them."

I testified before the Council that if we built a shelter to serve nonresidents, the St. Vincent's Dining Room would stay where it was to serve local residents and homeless families.

Even though the need for an emergency shelter outlined in the report was central to the Task Force's findings, it was downplayed by the city in official documents, publications and press. City government remained evasive and noncommittal about helping homeless people.

June 1990:

When Bob Mahan announced his retirement as the County Supervisor representing District 1, Santucci, Ozenick and Janice Palmer vied for the seat. Palmer was eliminated from the ballot in the primary, after which she endorsed Ozenick for the November runoff.

August 15, 1990:

Summer brought increased heat on the Council to move beyond its April "approval in concept" of the Task Force report to actually implementing its findings. Finally, after months of hemming and hawing, the Council agreed to consider the matter.

At the Council meeting, Pastor Herndon, the Homeless Task Force Chairman, emphasized that the report's top recommendation was the hiring of a Homeless Project Coordinator.

The report also called for:

- A year-round emergency shelter;
- More transitional housing units and beds;
- More motel and hotel emergency shelter vouchers for families;
- A network of coordinated emergency services; and
- A multiservice center for housing, meals, a clinic, showers, jobs and counseling.

The Council members' response was less than enthusiastic, as if they were not sure of their footing, expecting a possible political backlash. With a bit of courage and foresight, they could create a model program, one that could be emulated in cities across the country. During the entire public discussion, they even avoided acknowledging what kind of services might be available if a facility was authorized.

When Assistant City Manager John Tarson tried to draw them into a conversation to explore building a facility, they remained steadfastly and officially noncommittal about the whole concept. He went on to brief the group on the high probability that the city could qualify for five hundred thousand dollars in state and federal grant funds to finance the project, even suggesting a site, at the Hilltop property on PFE Road.

Tarson was also an enthusiastic backer of the Task Force recommendation to hire a Homeless Project Coordinator, someone who could focus on building funding streams for the facility. The Council members backed off and postponed taking a position on any part of the Task Force plan.

Instead, they rushed to formalize Santucci's long-term strategy to involve the other regional Placer jurisdictions, Rocklin, Lincoln, Auburn and even little Loomis. Crabb was the chief advocate for the plan, suggesting that all of them, including the county, should step up to the plate and contribute. He added that he would like to wrap up finding partners for the project in a year's time. The Council approved the motion.

October 10, 1990:

The Council didn't have to wait a year for an answer. The other cities fired back with a counter proposal in less than two months: Let's do a new, extensive study of the homeless issue in the entire area to see whose problem it really is.

The cost of the fifty thousand dollar study would be borne proportionately among the jurisdictions based on percentage of the area's total homeless population, meaning that the biggest share would be carried by Roseville. As Rocklin City Manager Carlos Urrita said, "It isn't fair (for Roseville) to ask the other cities in Placer County to pay to solve Roseville's problem."

When the reply from Roseville's neighboring jurisdictions about the item came up for Council discussion, Crabb's response captured the essence of the other members' sentiments. He brusquely responded, "We don't need to have any more studies. We already have too many studies."

With that, the majority unbelievably and immediately decided to hire a Homeless Project Coordinator as the first step in developing a comprehensive program to address the homeless problem. Four of the five members took the leap without the other jurisdictions.

Pauline Roccucci was in the minority. She kept her cool and said although she agreed with the concept, she remained concerned about funding the position. I interpreted her remarks to mean she did not think that hiring a special person "from the outside" to put the program together was a good use of resources.

I regarded the dollars spent to hire a coordinator as an investment in someone who would develop funding sources for the project. Plus, the cost of a coordinator was small change compared to the cost of the whole project. The salary could be paid from the grant funds that were successfully solicited.

October 18, 1990:
The *Sacramento Bee Neighbors* reported "The homeless program coordinator will acquire grants and develop programs to assist the homeless."

November 1990:
Santucci lost the contest for the Supervisor's seat to Ozenick by just eighty votes. Ozenick rewarded Palmer for her endorsement with an appointment to the County Planning Commission.

At the time of Palmer's appointment, the Placer County General Plan was up for review. The final document would govern Placer County's growth through 2004. Ozenick wanted his own novel concept incorporated into the plan. His "new town" model called for limiting Roseville's growth to one hundred thousand people and creating new, smaller communities abutting the city's growth line to absorb the increase in population over that mark. He expected Palmer to fall into line with his vision and push his plan.

December 1990:
The Armory opened as a shelter for the third season in a row. As basic as it was, I rested at home easier during those long winter nights, knowing that the homeless folks I looked in the eye in the daytime had a safe and warm place to sleep at night.

February 1991:
The city selected Pauline Tomlinson as the Homeless Project Coordinator. Tomlinson and city staff started to meet with the service providers and church leaders on a regular and consistent basis.

March 26, 1991:
The Armory shelter closed after more than three months of operation. During that time, families, service clubs and churches helped at the site with home-cooked meals and shoulders to lean on. The community as a whole seemed more at peace. No one had to spend the long nights of winter abandoned to the cold and rain.

The providers and churches continued meeting with Tomlinson several times a month, much more often than the business and residents stakeholders did. We helped her with design elements, policies and procedures.

"...We're like a Rudderless Ship Bouncing Aimlessly on a Hostile Sea."

Everything seemed to be running along smoothly, especially when we heard that the city had been tagged to receive state and federal grants totaling just under three hundred thousand dollars, enough to get the shelter project up and going.

April 1991:

The road to completing the shelter plan went from smooth to rough, turning into a difficult and emotional time for both Tomlinson and us. She started suggesting that services for transients be cut from the blueprint. We countered that unless the services for these folks remained in the proposal, there would be no reason for us to continue to work on it.

Tomlinson acknowledged our concern and backed off. We were assured our views would be incorporated into the final document for City Council approval. She was between a rock and a hard place, being pressured by city staff to make sure the final draft did not allow for any services to transients.

About that same time, we had a second hit: Our progressive police chief, Greg Cowart, had taken an appointment by Attorney General Dan Lungren as the Director of the California Department of Justice, Division of Law Enforcement. His replacement was Tom Simms.

Simms came from the City of Piedmont, where he was chief of a department of fewer than fifteen sworn officers. Piedmont, less than two square miles in size and with a population of no more than fifteen thousand, of which seventy percent were Caucasian, was surrounded by the City of Oakland. The tiny city had a median income and home prices twice the state average. It was a community of elites.

When Simms arrived in Roseville, it didn't take long for him to pick up where old-time police chief Jim Hall had left off with the campaign against homeless single men.

Early December 1991:

The Armory opened as the emergency shelter for its fourth winter of operation.

December 9, 1991:

Tomlinson took the bones of the shelter plan on the road for public scrutiny, making her first pitch to the Auburn City Council. The Auburn Council prudently deferred any action until the program could be studied further. They weren't going to be the first ducks into the water.

The Auburn folks were willing to consider the matter, but as Mayor Mary Bunnell said, their main concern was paying no more than their fair share. City manager Nick Willick remarked that one way of allocating the cost of the project would be to have each city pay based on its share of the total population of Placer County. That was as close as Tomlinson ever got to their wallets.

December 11, 1991:

Chief Simms revealed who he really was when he was the guest at a Ministerial Association lunch meeting at the West Roseville Baptist Church. It all began with his "grand entrance" as he came through the door. It was after we were all seated around a large table and had begun our meal.

He orchestrated it all like a pro, but it was over the top. The chief showed up in his uniform with pressed military creases and wearing his officer's peaked cap. His attire was complete with a gun belt and side arm.

After we ate, the members carried on a long discussion with him about the usual issues: neighborhood crime, drug abuse and school policing among them. There was one question that he had not been asked: What was his position on dealing with transients? So, I put it to him.

I remember he was standing up for some reason. When he took my question, he put his thumbs in his gun belt, postured and tersely replied he would run the tramps out of town!

I felt the anger in his voice.

February, 1992:

Our Homeless Shelter Committee submitted the proposal we had been working on for the previous twelve months to City Hall.

February 27, 1992:

The Armory shelter was suddenly shut down a month before it had been scheduled to close. The operators of the local facility, like those of other California armories, had planned to remain open every night until the end of March.

Unfortunately, the directive Governor Pete Wilson issued the previous fall only required that armories be used as shelters until the middle of February. After that, the state could close the shelters for the season the first day the weather reached forty-one degrees.

"...We're like a Rudderless Ship Bouncing Aimlessly on a Hostile Sea."

That was exactly what happened. When the temperature reached that mark in the coldest parts of California, all the armories were ordered closed.

According to Jennifer Harris, spokesperson for the State Department of Health and Welfare, all counties were told that their shelters could resume operations if the weather turned cold or wet again.

Of course, the weather did turn cold and wet again. It was still winter.

Even so, the Roseville Armory remained closed. There was no procedure in place to reopen the facilities with a minimum of fuss.

When the county tried to reopen the Roseville shelter for another four weeks, the National Guard commander refused. He was glad to have our guests out of there. Bill Hamilton, a former commander of the Armory, let it be known he was tired of homeless people "desecrating" the building, as if it was a sacred place.

Everyone, from state officials to the shelter occupants, was affected and subsequently upset to one degree or another by the closing. State representatives were ticked off at Placer County because bureaucrats had failed to relay the original closing directive to the contractor, Volunteers of America. The county was perturbed because the National Guard would not allow the Armory to reopen once it had closed. The service providers were in a tizzy because the homeless guests had nowhere to sleep. The guests were angry because once again, they were the victims of bumbling bureaucracies. They took to the streets, expressing their frustration by protesting in front of City Hall. City government was thoroughly embarrassed.

A local homeowner from the west side of the tracks decided to do something positive about the problem. Frances Barnum opened her backyard at 206 Grove Street for camping. City government found itself helpless about intervening. Its 1986 ordinance anti-camping ordinance only prohibited camping on public property. Barnum welcomed the homeless men, hosting seventeen to twenty guests at a time.

According to the *Press Tribune*, there were seven tents that stood "side-by-side in her back yard..." She and her friends cooked the meals while the men slept in shifts so they could take turns picketing City Hall for a permanent shelter. Chuck's Sanitation donated a portable toilet, and people contributed money to help out. A beautician, Julia Ortiz, gave free haircuts, and private citizens from all over the community supported the effort with donations of food, clothing and cash.

Within a week of Mrs. Barnum opening her backyard, the city proposed a new ordinance to control camping on private property without the owner's permission and prohibiting all campfires and bonfires for the first time.

March 2, 1992:

The *Press Tribune* editorialized in favor of City Council adopting the plan our group had submitted in February, which called for building a homeless shelter that served everyone, not just locals. The paper, which reported that our proposal was to come before the Council the following week, was hopeful that Roseville was on the verge of solving the homeless problem that had dogged the community since the late 1800s.

The editorial stated, "There will be room for the transient, typically a single male…simply condemning Roseville's entire homeless support system because of the railroad is akin to curing dandruff via decapitation." The point was made.

The same opinion piece commended the Salvation Army, the Methodists, the First Baptist Church and St. Vincent's for providing meals to homeless men, women and children. This was a big switch from the stand the *Press Tribune* had taken in the past.

March 3, 1992:

The city staff report on the shelter proposal was released for the following week's Council meeting, stunning everyone from the newspaper to the churches and service providers. City staff had removed any mention of food and shelter services for transients. The changes were not done publicly in a democratic way, but were crafted behind the scenes without public input.

We had enough political savvy to know that a staff report bound for City Council usually accommodated the anticipated preferences of the Council majority. The city manager, as a matter of routine, preemptively signed off on all documents, making sure that when they came before the Council, the majority looked good when they expressed their sentiments before, during and after the vote.

After reading the staff report, we knew there was a Council majority against our plan. Who were they? Pauline Roccucci and Fred Jackson seemed in favor of the plan. We assumed that Santucci, very much the pragmatist, would support it too. But Council member Crabb, who adamantly opposed any shelter plan, was sure to vote against it.

"...We're like a Rudderless Ship Bouncing Aimlessly on a Hostile Sea."

We wondered if Crabb had prevailed on Santucci, who was mayor at the time, as well as on Mayor Pro Tem Hamel, to side with him. If Santucci's about-face in his stand on the shelter was true, we had truly been hoodwinked. It was dramatically different from his track record which showed that he had been instrumental in:

- Settling the Dining Room problem;
- Initiating both the Blue Ribbon Committee on Homelessness and the Homeless Task Force;
- Starting the Armory program; and
- Hiring a Homeless Project Coordinator.

Was Santucci turning on us? An about-face would not have been something I could have seen coming. Had he become overly cautious because of Crabb's opposition to our proposal? I still believed in him.

I suspected that if he had turned on us, it was because of Crabb. Santucci had told me that if our original recommendations ever became city policy, Crabb would raise such a fuss that he would bring down Santucci's entire effort to solve the south Placer homeless problem. Plus, he would work against him in the 1994 Supervisor's race.

Santucci began acting like he might step on a political landmine any minute. His consternation became more evident when it came time for the Council to put its stamp of approval on the shelter package.

It turned out that he wanted time to put together a second city alternative to our plan, hoping to assuage Crabb's opposition and shore up public opinion before it got to a Council hearing.

In any event, the city apparatus was not going to let our recommendation for services to transients see the light of day. The remaining shell of our plan was molded into a transitional shelter program of fifty beds for families and thirty beds for single men, all of who were required to be residents of Placer County.

After learning of the changes, and despite probable Council rejection, several of us from the service provider stakeholder group publicly pointed out three major distortions in the staff report:

- The background information on the city's efforts to solve the homeless problem had been twisted;
- The proposed program goals and the eligibility requirements for participants had become more stringent; and
- The emergency shelter and drop-in food features had been entirely eliminated.

Our stakeholder group informed Pauline Tomlinson that the

changes to the proposal were deal killers. She assured us that a new staff report correcting the errors would be issued before the Council met on March 11th.

March 11, 1992:

City Hall remained in so much turmoil that the hearing for the scheduled shelter proposal was postponed. Besides our objections to the city's tactics, the homeless people displaced by the Armory closing were still picketing and adamant about their demands. Ms. Barnum's back yard remained their home base.

March 18, 1992:

The city's new "no camping" ordinance was enacted.

Because the weather was warming and the city wasn't budging, the crowd at Mrs. Barnum's dissipated. Even so, wounds from the battle were still raw.

March 24, 1992:

As promised, a new staff report for the Regional Homeless Facility was released to the Council for its rescheduled meeting. But the updated report was as much a rejection of our plan as the first. We had been led to believe it would include the corrections to the previous report we had asked for. But that assumption was false.

That evening, Santucci and staffer John Sprague arranged to hustle this new version of the plan on the city's TV channel. As a group of us watched the presentation at the St. Rose rectory as part of the St. Vincent's monthly meeting, we were dazed by how the city again had gutted our proposal.

Sprague started by outlining all the features we had fought against:

1. All existing meal programs and services would move from their downtown locations to the new shelter site;
2. No provision for any drop-in food or social services;
3. No services for transients; and
4. No emergency shelter services would be available.

Their proposal was for a transitional living facility only. To the average citizen, this appeared to be a good-faith effort and a generous gesture to help build a brand new facility. After the conclusion of the show, we reviewed our options:

- We could reject the proposal out of hand;
- We could cave in to the Santucci/Sprague version; or

"...We're like a Rudderless Ship Bouncing Aimlessly on a Hostile Sea."

- We could try for a compromise that would amend the city's proposal.

If we rejected their proposal, we might be accused of killing the deal; but giving in was not an option.

A compromise looked like our only chance. The Council members who were opposed to our original proposal might reject any plan on the pretext that we pushed them too hard, that we wanted the city to go beyond what they regarded as prudent. Rather than scrap with us any more, they could just walk away. We were upset about our prospects, to say the least.

March 27, 1992:

Roseville held a project briefing meeting to justify to all of the stakeholders why the changes were made in the February Homeless Shelter Committee's proposal. Anyone could see that the meeting was meant to grease the skids for the city proposal to slip through the political process with as little pushback as possible.

That didn't stop those of us representing the providers and churches from rejecting the changes. Still, the city wouldn't budge. The meeting was a waste of time.

March 29, 1992:

Tomlinson sent a letter to all stakeholders, City Council members, the city manager and Housing and Redevelopment Manager Sprague, attempting to calm the controversy caused by the staff's changes to the stakeholders' recommendations.

As I had expected, the coordinator's efforts were wasted on at least one Council member: Harry Crabb. He completely ignored any reference to our plan, and instead in a preemptive move to kill the Sprague-Santucci proposal, publicly labeled it as too radical. He went so far as to suggest putting the proposition on the June ballot as a referendum. It was my impression that if a referendum on the shelter proposal had been initiated, national media could have had a field day with it. The joke would have been on Crabb and spread like wildfire.

It appeared that Santucci and Sprague were caught between a rock and a hard place. To get out of the jam, Santucci immediately backed off any shelter plan, even the one he presented to the community. He told the *Tribune*, "I don't have an opinion on it yet."

I was astounded!

April 1, 1992:

At the Council hearing for the shelter proposal, we managed to diplomatically inform the members that the plan on the table was not the proposal that we had developed in our meetings. We also reminded the Council that nearly three hundred thousand dollars in federal and state grants might be lost if an acceptable plan was not approved.

I had the impression that the city was just going through the motions of a review before killing the whole deal. A year of meetings and subcommittee meetings, as well as tens of thousands of taxpayer dollars in staff and coordinator salaries would be going down the drain.

Maybe the Council members sensed our frustration. After some discussion, they postponed their vote for a couple of months to see if our differences could be reconciled. In spite of the setback, I remained optimistic, hoping that by the time the vote rolled around, we would have reached a compromise with the city. A "Santucci conversion experience" was what we needed.

April 8, 1992:

The City Council heard the first reading of an emergency ordinance to regulate expanding any free food sites or establishing any new ones. The ordinance was aimed at the free meal programs at St. Vincent's, the Methodist Church, the First Baptist Church and the Salvation Army.

No one from our side had been notified of the meeting.

April 13, 1992:

After reading a story about the April 8th Council meeting in the *Neighbors* section of the Sunday *Bee*, I met with Chris Robles at the planning department to learn the details of the ordinance. He said that a conditional use permit would be required either to open a free food site or to expand the size or the operating times of any of the four existing meal sites.

Two problematic features of this law were that the permits were valid for just one year; and to obtain or renew a permit, the applicant was required to go through the public hearing process.

That forced any organization subject to the new rules to endure the ordeal and expense of a public hearing every twelve months to continue its free meal program. It would be an annual trial by fire.

The ordinance also kept new free food sites away from residential neighborhoods and more than five hundred feet from schools and parks. Plus, any new free food site had to be a mile away from any other free food location. The effect would be to "zone out" any suitable new locations for free meal programs. All of the possible practical locations were within the core area of town and less than a mile from one another or from existing sites.

Robles told me that the ordinance had been in the works for a long time, but became an emergency situation when a rumor was floated that a new group in town was going to open a meal site. He was right to say that it had been a long time in the works. Actually, it was the one Cheney told me she was developing five years prior.

But the big problem I had with Robles' excuse was that it was not true. There was no new free meal program being planned to open either soon or in the foreseeable future. Everyone involved in the existing meal offerings would have heard about any new program in the works. In our minds, the ordinance was just another way to prohibit expanding our services.

It was doubtful that we would be able to block the Council's adoption of the emergency code amendment. But, what was more troublesome was that not one person in city government who was working with us bothered to give us a hint about what was going on.

That was in the days before agendas were posted online for everyone to see. The only ways for a person outside of city government to learn that something affecting them was going to be heard by the Council was ether by going to City Hall to see a copy of the document posted outside, or by being informed by the *Bee*, the *Press Tribune* or someone "in the know". We had been hoodwinked!

May 6, 1992:

Legal Services of Northern California attorney Vic Pappalardo had provided us with a position paper that outlined what we should say to the Council when we spoke against the ordinance. If the issue went to court, our comments would be part of the argument for overturning the ordinance. I was asked to be one of the spokespersons for the group.

During our dialogue with the Council, we were told that all four existing food sites were exempt from the law unless they wanted to expand hours, days of operation or the facility's footprint. Councilman Fred Jackson was brutally honest about the need for the ordinance, sharing his belief that the law was enacted to reduce the magnet (of free meals) that had been created for transients.

We failed to change any minds. The city was determined to move ahead. The objections and requests for a postponement by the

Ministerial Association, St. Vincent's and the Homeless Shelter Project Providers Committee didn't stop the Council from enacting the new law as written.

With the city's surprise homeless shelter proposal changes and this new law, we had been deftly outmaneuvered. In spite of our losses, we remained game for another round on the shelter proposal by offering a compromise.

May 14, 1992:

Our objective when we met with Santucci and the other city officials was to get his buy in on a "compromise" shelter plan ready for Council ratification. If Santucci could be persuaded that the compromise would be acceptable to the community at large, we would most likely have the three votes needed to pass the plan.

All of the homeless shelter project stakeholder groups were well represented at the City Hall workshop. Included were Council members Crabb and Santucci, city staffer John Sprague, shelter consultant Pauline Tomlinson, County Welfare Director Ray Merz, Pastors Roy Herndon, Tim Brooks and Jerry Angove, St. Vincent's representatives Elaine Willoughby and Fred Wight, Roseville residents Linda Burch and Jim Bush, Salvation Army commander Jim Durel, Sherry Schiele of Home Start, business owner and Chamber of Commerce President Ken Denio, Chamber of Commerce Director Leo Papas, a city stenographer to take notes and me.

Following our presentation of a compromise that would put a cap on services, including a noon meal limit of three days to non-residents (transients), Santucci and Sprague began arguing with us over details such as who was a resident and who was a nonresident. Santucci said, "We can't have any transients getting more than three free meals!"

Harry Crabb remained dead-set against any meals, saying, "Roseville is going to have more and more transients, then what? Where will the money be coming from? When the facility fills up, will we want to put up satellites?...The problem with the transients is not just downtown, but all over town...the service station at Keehner & Douglas." Crabb continued, "I'm interested in Roseville people. I only want to help them. I represent the community. I don't support a program that draws transients."

At the end of the meeting, Santucci was still noncommittal. We had failed to get his necessary buy-in. Crabb had kept Santucci in line.

May 23, 1992:

The members of the Ministerial Association persisted in their conversion attempts with Santucci. They still hoped that the Council would accept our compromise. To show Santucci that the shelter had broad community support, we organized a citywide petition drive among the churches, asking for a "yes" vote on the shelter project.

We began collecting signatures that weekend.

May 29, 1992:

Council member Pauline Roccucci agreed to meet me in the afternoon at City Hall. The first thing she said was that the shelter item would be on the first June agenda for sure.

Roccucci went on to say she was not concerned about start-up funds with the three hundred thousand dollars in grant money in the pipeline. She was apprehensive about ongoing funding for the project, "the big M."

I mentioned that the city would not have any contingent liability for funding or the ongoing operation of the facility. The nonprofit corporation that operated the facility would be totally responsible for fundraising. Even though the buildings would be on city property, the relationship of the city to the program would be that of a landlord, not as an operator or guarantor.

Another area of uncertainty for her was what would happen to the current meal sites if the shelter closed. My response was that the nonprofit corporation would be a separate entity from each of the current meal providers. I suggested that the city have an agreement with each provider, saying its program would close down when the shelter opened, and if the shelter closed, each provider would have the right to reopen, the new ordinance notwithstanding.

I felt that Roccucci was positive about the program, and I knew that she was a sure vote for the shelter proposal.

May 30–31, 1992:

Additional signatures were collected from churchgoers and then submitted to the city clerk for inclusion in the Council members' meeting packets.

June 2, 1992:

Roseville's shelter story gained statewide interest when the *Los Angeles Times* reported that Mayor Pro Tem Fred Jackson said "...(he) likes the proposal because it would not only stop transients' free meals but also relocate people who live in the downtown area who look like transients."

June 10, 1992:

Finally, the big day arrived; the Council would vote on the comprehensive shelter proposal. Those of us who had been working on this project for the previous eighteen months and on the emergency shelter issue for more than four years had done all we could to make it as easy as possible for the Council to adopt the plan:

- Each of us on the providers' shelter project committee had worked hundreds of hours with the city's chosen program director, Pauline Tomlinson, to develop a plan which would enable the community to settle the homeless problem;
- We had been responsive to Council members' reservations about the plan and had agreed to several compromises;
- We had developed broad community support for the plan from the *Press Tribune*, private citizens, the Chamber of Commerce, the Ministerial Association, and hundreds of individual members of church congregations; and
- We had met individually with each Council member to help allay any remaining concerns before they popped up as problems at the Council hearing.

The proposal had been shaped into a compromise offered in good faith, with federal and state grants still intact for its development.

After taking a good amount of time to consider the matter, two Council members, Roccucci and Jackson, were enthusiastically in favor of the plan and voted for it. Crabb, Hamel and Mayor Santucci cast their votes against it. Santucci had been the one Council member we had relied on to guarantee the building of a shelter.

Instead, he used his vote to detonate the charge that destroyed the four-year effort he had started. Thousands of hours of work by sincere and dedicated private citizens, as well as tens of thousands of dollars in city staff expenses, were thrown to the wind.

He rationalized "It (the compromise) goes too far." He seemed frustrated that the service providers had turned down the offer he and Sprague had presented to the community on the city TV channel.

I think Santucci was saving any remaining political capital he had for another day. His account was getting low, and with his plans for the future, he had to choose sides. Was it to be with the amicable Roccucci and the practical Jackson or with the obdurate Crabb and Hamel? Santucci caved in to power.

As for Crabb, this vote was the first time I could remember that when the subject of transients came up, he did not speak of his disdain for them as a class of people. Rather, he talked about his fiscal responsibilities, attempting to make a case that the project would be a bad investment for the community.

Hamel simply stated the Homeless Shelter Committee should not have asked the Council to buy into the plan. He said the project should have gone through the public planning process to obtain a use permit, just like any other proposal (so when it was appealed to the Council, he could vote "no").

The Council's decision confounded those of us who had worked for years to get a proposal to this level. This dream could have been built.

The residents and business owners against St. Vincent's who had been pushing to close down all services for transients were oddly absent from the meeting. I knew they opposed the plan. Maybe someone "in the know" had informed them that their presence was not necessary because the project was dead on arrival.

June 15, 1992:

The *Press Tribune* editorialized that the Council's action was hard to understand:

"Last week's decision by the Roseville City Council to reject plans for a homeless shelter leaves us bewildered...In the meantime, we're like a rudderless ship bouncing aimlessly on a hostile sea." In other words, "Where was our Captain (Santucci) when we needed him?"

A *Sacramento Bee* report implied that Santucci had washed his hands of the proposal, taking up Crabb's suggestion to "...support a ballot measure to resolve the issue."

The churches and the service providers remained determined. The Council's rejection of our plan was seen to symbolize the city's resistance to any genuine resolution of its "homeless problem." As city disdain for every attempt to aid transients persisted over the years to come, it became known in the legislative chambers of our state capitol as "the Roseville Syndrome."

Chapter 7:
Church Challenge Chafes City Chiefs
(Late Jun. 1992–Dec. 1992)

Late June 1992:

After Roseville had thrown our proposal under the bus, the city and county saw their chance to kill any further conversation about a permanent or seasonal shelter. They quickly made their moves during their June budget hearings, with the City Council being first, withdrawing support for the Armory winter shelter. Within days, the Placer County Board of Supervisors also voted against allotting money for the program. Supervisor Phil Ozenick, representing Roseville, had initiated the county move.

The death knell for our plan also brought the likelihood of the loss of nearly three hundred thousand dollars in government guaranteed grants for Roseville. During the previous year and a half, city staff had worked hard to secure the pot of state and federal money for the program, which was seen as an innovative response to homelessness that could serve as a model for other cities. It was an awkward situation. Staffer John Sprague put his take on the city administration's problem when he told the *Press Tribune*, "It's a credibility issue."

Yes, the city's credibility was in question. State officials had gone out on a limb for the project because they had been convinced by their city counterparts that developing this unique shelter project was a "done deal." Following the Council's June 10th vote against the plan, it was immediately evident that they were fed up with Roseville politics and were about to withdraw the funds. At that point, Sherry Schiele stepped forward with an idea that would "make lemonade out of this lemon," getting the city off the hook.

It was the opportunity she had been waiting for. Her St. Vincent's Home Start program had grown to housing nine families at one time in Phase One of the rehabilitation program. Clients lived in units scattered around town as they worked through the six-week residency program.

Phase Two involved up to two years of supervised independent living in the same housing. Each family was mentored by social workers and members of a sponsoring church who helped the family with day-to-day budgeting, parenting, employment searches and social skills.

Schiele was continually on the lookout for new units for her Phase One families. She knew she could accommodate more households more efficiently in Phase One if that part of the program was centralized. The grants, if the city cooperated, could allow her to achieve her vision. The three hundred thousand dollars was just what she needed to nail down an apartment complex for the program. She had two buildings in mind, one on Main Street at Berkeley and the other on B Street.

She had done such a great job selling the St. Vincent's Home Start program that it had become the darling of the community. Everyone from city government to local service clubs jumped on the bandwagon. Even white collar business suit types were getting involved. Organizations and groups like Roseville Rotary made special donations to champion the organization. Home Start was a hit because the organization helped homeless children with moms and dads who had run into problems. It was about saving the kids.

But Schiele's vision wasn't limited to helping families. She also wanted to build a program to accommodate homeless single adults. Completely separate from the Home Start expansion and behind the scenes, she continued to work on the emergency shelter front to help all homeless folks in the winter. While Schiele cooperated hand-in-glove with city staff on Home Start, she also planned this seasonal shelter project through the churches.

By the end of June, she had met with pastors of several churches about a shelter co-op idea.

July 1992:
Schiele continued beating the bushes and found a better location for her Home Start program, the old Flamingo Motel at 410 Riverside.

August 5, 1992:
Schiele received tentative City Council approval for St. Vincent's to pursue a lease for the Flamingo Motel property. If she was successful, the size of the Home Start program could be doubled in short order.

The Council held off giving final approval until the neighborhood had a chance to weigh in on the matter. Certain Council members didn't want to alienate any of their base. The fact that Roseville didn't have an ordinance on the books that controlled transitional or emergency shelters meant that a formal public hearing on the matter was out. The next best thing the city could do was to require Schiele to hold an open house at the old motel site so she could explain the program to the neighbors.

August 11, 1992:
The *Press Tribune* put its weight behind the Home Start move to the Flamingo with an editorial encouraging the city to save the grants and work with Schiele.

August 20, 1992:
Schiele held the open house.

September 2, 1992:
The *Press Tribune* wrote another editorial, putting the Council under increasing pressure to avoid further embarrassment if the grants were lost. The state expected the Flamingo to be ready to house families by October.

In an attempt to redeem itself, the Council went "over the top" supporting Schiele's new and larger version of Home Start. The members unanimously approved the project, with a stern reminder from Councilman Crabb, "At no point will singles be housed...No transients." Schiele, on behalf of St. Vincent's, agreed to the restriction for the duration of the grant.

To help finance the bigger operation at the Flamingo, St. Vincent's decided to cash in its interest in the Grape Street duplex. Still, one big hurdle remained: the motel landlord, Mr. Patel who lived back east, wouldn't sign the deal. While he had agreed to the monthly rental amount and to granting St. Vincent's a purchase option, he remained cagey about how much he wanted for the option. When St. Vincent's tried to pin him down with a number, he always jockeyed for more. Home Start ended up postponing the move-in.

The state warned that it would withdraw the grant money set aside for the program if the lease issue was not promptly resolved.

October 1992:
It looked like the deal was going to fall through until our friend, attorney Jack Willoughby, stepped in and convinced the landlord that he was going to lose a golden opportunity unless he got serious about making a deal. The message sank in and Willoughby prepared a revised contract and sent it to Patel, who quickly signed it.

November 1, 1992:

Schiele was disappointed that the city had failed to actually let loose of the two pending grants which had been allocated to Home Start. At the same time, she was busy planning for the grand opening of the church winter shelter group she had organized in June.

She called the coalition "the Interfaith Shelter Co-op." The participating churches agreed to take turns housing homeless persons nightly on a rotating basis over the winter. Schiele was determined to circumvent Roseville's blockade prohibiting anyone from operating a winter shelter. She pictured the emergency shelter program resurrecting itself, even as the city spent the summer and fall working to keep the idea in its grave.

Somehow, she managed to do all this without the city noticing. It was not that the city was not on guard. Rather, it was looking in the wrong direction — at Home Start. The Council majority's abiding fear that transients would be housed as part of the Home Start program had blindsided them. They thought they were on safe ground if they just sat tight on the grant money until they got a written agreement from St. Vincent's that transients would not be welcomed at the facility. The promise was to run concurrently with the terms of the grants, both expiring in twenty four months.

November 4, 1992:

Schiele continued to keep her shelter plan work completely separate from her Home Start activities. And the city was none the wiser. She told the City Council that signing the agreement would not be a problem.

As the opening time for the co-op emergency shelter drew near, she confirmed with Father Mike Cormack that he was ready to provide the St. Rose parish hall for use as the coalition shelter beginning in mid-November. Shortly after, he told the Catholic Herald, "I never realized this was going to happen, but I still think it was the right decision...It worked last year. It was the obvious thing to do."

St. Vincent's meeting minutes and St. Rose records from 1990 reported that the hall had been used as the county homeless shelter when the Armory was not available. And just like then, Schiele would run the 1992 program with volunteers. With that in mind, she just assumed that what had been proposed in theory for the current year should not have caused any waves.

We knew better. Our collective strategy was that if there was a strong rumor that church facilities would be used as the winter shelter, the subsequent public controversy would leverage local government into opening the Armory. We were willing to let the chips fall where they may.

November 10, 1992:
When the city caught wind that the parish hall would soon be used as an emergency shelter, Planning Director Patty Dunn jumped into action. She sent St. Rose a letter warning that it would be violating city ordinances. Of course, no specific ordinance was cited because the city did not have one governing emergency shelters.

Father Mike told me that he would never forget his meeting with Schiele after he received the letter. As the two of them discussed their options, she bluntly reminded him that he had to do the right thing – open the parish hall as an emergency shelter. With that, he reaffirmed his commitment to using the hall for as long as the Armory remained closed.

Schiele and the good pastors would not be kept from doing what was right. News that the parish hall was going to be used as a homeless shelter spread like wildfire.

November 11, 1992:
When St. Rose School parents heard about the shelter plan, they immediately brought the issue to the school board. The parents regarded the parish hall as part of the school or their gym, rather than as a parish asset for the benefit of the larger community. The thought of homeless people using the facility overnight was like sounding a fire alarm.

November 12, 1992:
The parents' anxiety escalated into organized unrest. Rumors became fact; pressure mounted. Schiele and Father Mike postponed the opening of the parish hall shelter to see how things played out.

November 13, 1992:
The hubbub reached the City Manager Al Johnson's office. The police department provided Johnson with a report analyzing police services pertaining to the Armory's use as a winter shelter. It was all music to our ears:

- Section 2, page 2, stated, "There did not appear to be an increase in transient-related calls for services during the period the shelter was open."; and
- In section 3, page 2, "There did not appear to be a significant increase in arrests for Drunk in Public while the shelter was in operation."

Police Chief Simms, not taking kindly to his own department's findings, tried to paper over them by attaching a cover memo to set a different tone – a very negative one. His letter was not as much an introduction to the report as it was an attempt to counter any thought that allowing a shelter was good city policy, irrespective of what his own department had found.

He cited the four-year-old, out-of-date results of the flawed March 1988 survey where only "transient looking" persons who had violated the law or were involved in "suspected activity" were counted. Simms also outlined every possible crime a homeless person could commit and every kind of medical and mental illness such transient might have that would require community resources. The list of offenses and infirmities was extensive.

The city manager's staff forwarded just the cover letter to Councilman Crabb.

It seemed that everybody in the parish had an opinion about opening the hall to homeless persons, polarizing those for and against.

November 14–15, 1992:

When Father Mike told the people gathered for Mass about the issue that Saturday and Sunday, he received ovations of approval and support. As the *Press Tribune* quoted him, "How can we as a church have a building for those who are comfortable in life when we have people out in the cold? I feel we are missing the whole point of being Christian."

Not everyone saw the situation as he did. Sunday morning marked the beginning of one of those life events that I cannot forget, so personal that it became a milepost on my spiritual journey.

It all began when Harry Crabb and his friends handed out fliers in the neighborhood, announcing that at 2 p.m., he and his wife would hold a meeting on their front lawn to:

"Discuss the issue of Saint Rose Church allowing homeless/transients all night lodging...Possible invasion by these people of our neighborhood should not happen! **HELP US PUT A STOP TO IT BY ATTENDING THE MEETING.**" Signed Harry & Jeanette Crabb, 612 Vine Ave.

The fliers were more like torches set to ignite a firestorm of hobophobia. This wasn't going to be a meeting to discuss anything. It would be more like a rally to scare the neighbors and to cement their fears about homeless folks.

The Crabb home made a great stage for the event. Crabb lived directly across the street from St. Rose Church. HIs house faced the church property with ample lawn and driveway space to accommodate a very large crowd. It was an ideal spot for him to mount his own pulpit to gin up public opposition to what he feared we wanted to establish, a precedent allowing churches to open their doors as shelters to homeless persons, even if the church buildings were in residential zones.

Crabb had prepared well for the meeting. TV stations were on hand to catch all the action. A crowd of over one hundred people had assembled.

When we arrived, the TV cameras were already going. The event started as a gathering of nervous neighbors and other interested citizens wanting to know what all the fuss was about. But, as Crabb laid out his case, the crowd got to talking among themselves, and the group's collective attitude morphed into one that seemed more that of an angry mob.

The rancor became palpable.

Council member, neighbor and parishioner Mel Hamel was there, standing with Crabb. His presence next to Crabb said it all. He was against us.

The crowd heard Crabb claim that he would seek an injunction through City Council action to keep St. Rose Church from housing homeless people. He stated as a fact that the church was violating an unspecified city ordinance and that he had four of the five Council votes to obtain a court order.

As Crabb spoke, people in the crowd started yelling at us. They got more fired up.

Just twenty minutes into the meeting, I saw a short, chubby Latino elbowing his way to the front of the mob. He angrily shook his fist in Father Mike's face as he accused him of having a mistress in Europe. A couple of minutes later, the same guy lunged at me, swinging his arms and screaming as he tried to connect with a punch. Luckily, some men pulled him back before he made contact.

Next, local Lutheran pastor Jim Patterson spoke. Pastor Jim had worked around homeless people in Sacramento. I had hoped he was there to bring some reason to the situation. But he had come at Crabb's invitation.

Patterson began his speech by vilifying homeless men, using all the standard clichés and stereotypes to demonstrate what he thought a hopeless bunch of human waste transients were.

The crowd got very intense and was in no mood to be reasonable or to even listen to us. Father Mike and I were shouted down when we tried to respond to the challenges and questions.

I had never experienced the real emotional taste of what human hatred is all about. These folks stopped being my smiling, polite neighbors and became a gang oozing...umm, I was not sure *what* to call it. I could not come up with the right word at that time to describe the unreasonable fear I felt emanating from Crabb and his vocal cadre.

Harry Crabb at St. Rose Church
Courtesy Sacramento Bee Neighbors

Crabb's attack didn't end with the afternoon meeting on his lawn. He had rallied a group of folks to picket the church before, during and after the Sunday evening Mass. They marched with signs on the front patio of the church building, outraged that the parish was even thinking about housing homeless people in the hall. The marchers looked so aggravated, that I remember leaning over to the reporter for the *Bee*

Neighbors edition, and saying, "I think they've been hit by hobophobia!"

November 16, 1992:

Monday turned out to be a busy, busy day. First, Father Mike, his staff and Jack Willoughby met with a delegation of school parents and neighbors in the parish house.

Kevin Valine headed the parent group. After everyone was seated comfortably in the living room, he handed Father a letter documenting their concerns.

Valine then carefully and diplomatically reiterated the position spelled out in his memo. The parents who Valine represented were uncompromisingly against housing homeless people in the "gym." Every possible reason the hall shouldn't be occupied for even one night by homeless adults was raised: homeless persons would leave germs that would infect the kids with airborne tuberculosis (TB) and hepatitis – and possibly AIDS; the neighborhood would be invaded by homeless criminals who would bring litter, broken bottles and mayhem.

We listened attentively. Nothing changed.

Some of the neighbors, parishioners and school parents understood what we were trying to do. As school parent John Olson told the *Press Tribune*, "The main drive (of sheltering the homeless at St. Rose) is to get the armory open again this year."

It was obvious enough; but some people, including Crabb and Valine, didn't have a clue.

Later in the afternoon, the City Council held a special session to deal with the St. Rose crisis. Father Mike was front and center delivering a challenge to the Council in these words: "...seriously consider whether it is in your interest to vote an injunction against our proposed accommodation of the homeless. Do you propose to tell us who to be, or what to do? Do you want to cross the boundary line of division between church and state? Do you want to put Roseville on the map as a city devoid of compassion?"

No decision was made.

Shortly after the meeting adjourned, we got our first break. Our legal counsel, Jack Willoughby, had a phone call from city attorney Mike Dean asking for a dialogue to determine how to proceed.

If there were any plans to obtain an injunction, they were abandoned as soon as we had left the Council chambers. As Dean told the *Press Tribune*, "(We) plan to sit down in a less emotional atmosphere and try to find some solutions acceptable to both sides...The issue of homelessness is something we as a society have to do something about."

The move to open the Armory had begun.

At this point, local officials were looking for a way out of the morass they had been dragged into. It seemed that their sentiment was that Crabb's response to the church's plan was perceived by the general public as inappropriate and unnecessary. Not that three of his fellow Council members might have cared about the homeless men and women we were trying to help. Rather, they probably saw the city in a losing political position.

Attempting to stop the church with an injunction, or worse yet, as mentioned in the hyperbolic press, arresting Father Mike, would have created a public relations nightmare that would have engulfed the city in a whole new level of criticism and ridicule. As Andrew Sorensen of the *Press Tribune* said more than once, "the city was backed into a corner." Sorensen thanked both Sherry Schiele and Father Mike for not letting the city slide on the issue.

It looked to him like opening the Armory would get the city off the "hot seat," presenting the least objectionable and most expeditious solution.

November 17, 1992:

A follow-up article in the *Press Tribune* noted that St. Rose legal counsel Jack Willoughby had made the case that the city was on thin ice for even considering Crabb's suggested injunction. Willoughby pointed out that just because churches existed in residential zones, it did not follow that they forfeited their duty and obligation to be sanctuaries for homeless folks.

Then, he made an apt reference to the fact that homeless persons have always been part of Roseville life, whether or not a shelter existed. He used the famous phrase from the movie *A Field of Dreams*, "if you build it, they will come" as an analogy. He concluded, "Well, we didn't build it, and they are coming anyway."

The same *Press Tribune* article reported that the city blamed the railroad for the transient problem. Officials claimed that Southern Pacific was not policing its trains as thoroughly as it should, allowing too many guys to hop a free ride.

On the other hand, railroad officials blamed the city, saying local government needed to control services to homeless people. The railroad spokesperson said there were too many "freebies" for the drifters in Roseville.

Placer County Welfare Director Ray Merz went on record that the county wouldn't "operate a shelter in a city that doesn't want it." I knew Ray and knew what he meant by that comment. It was code for when the city got around to asking that the Armory be used as a shelter that winter, he would take care of the rest. All Roseville had to do was to give the word, just like it had in years past.

The *Press Tribune* also reported that the city was not ready to say "uncle" to the move to open the Armory. "City officials do not want transients in town. Officials want the lunch programs shut down and they do not plan to open the armory this year."

November 18, 1992:

Negotiations continued. During the afternoon, Father Mike and Willoughby met with Santucci and Councilman Fred Jackson at City Hall. Santucci set the tone by asking for a constructive dialog. Jackson followed up by suggesting that the men should strive to find a "full solution" so the Armory problem wouldn't come up again. Willoughby added that the city should come up with more than just a solution, but also with an alternative site for housing the city's homeless men and women in the future.

Then, Santucci, pragmatic as always, broke the impasse. He suggested the Armory was the answer for this year. As the conversation evolved, Willoughby said St. Rose would put up ten thousand dollars plus additional funds as they were raised. Then the discussion shifted to how to get the Armory opened.

After some talk exploring ways for the city to save face, it was decided that the church, not the city, would take the lead by asking the county to ready the Armory as soon as possible. While St. Rose and the city would act together, Father Mike would be the principal spokesperson. He and Santucci would approach the Board of Supervisors the following Tuesday. Santucci and Jackson, hoping the shelter would be open by the last Friday in November, said the City Council would support the plan.

With that, everyone sighed in relief and agreed to take the rest of the day to cool off. Neither side would make a public statement that afternoon, even though the agreement of the four men was sure to stick. It was just what the churches and providers wanted.

November 19, 1992:

Father Mike and Willoughby met with Santucci and other officials to hammer out a one hundred five word joint statement in which the city and the church together would ask Placer County to once again use the National Guard Armory as a winter shelter. After the statement was finalized, Father Mike and Santucci presented it at a news conference at City Hall.

The two men announced the agreement, with Santucci adding that the Council had "reached a consensus in closed session Wednesday night...to pay up to fifteen thousand dollars toward the shelter's operation," and would hold an open meeting the first week in December to vote on the funding as required by law.

St. Rose contributed ten thousand dollars toward operations costs.

Just as Crabb had planned, the spectacle of an angry crowd on his front lawn railing against the church did bring the issue to a head. However, the result was not what he wanted. His attempt to restrict services to the homeless had backfired, with his fellow Council members embarrassed by the situation, wanting to put as much distance as possible between the public relations nightmare and themselves. The city had to back down.

Our ongoing strategy and strength came from the pastors of the three anchor churches: St. Rose's Father Mike, Roseville First United Methodist's Reverend Jerry Angove and Lutheran Church of the Resurrection Granite Bay pastor, Paul Carlson. These men made the difference. As Carlson said, "This is our mission. We seek to help people who can't help themselves."

Because the agreement with the city had yet to be presented to the county, we decided to hold off on our plan to use the St. Rose hall as a shelter until after the Supervisors' meeting.

November 20, 1992:

The *Press Tribune* listed two obstacles that needed to be overcome at the county level before the Armory shelter could open:

1. There was the usual county funding shortfall. The budget of every department had been cut or frozen because of a seven hundred thousand dollar deficit announced the previous week.

2. The deadline for requesting time on the Board of Supervisors' agenda for the upcoming Tuesday meeting had passed, forcing the city and the church to make an appeal during the public comment period. The paper said Father Mike and Santucci would

have to wait until next month to be on the agenda and have a vote. The shelter could not open until early December at best.

November 21 & 22, 1992:

St. Rose parishioners got their first chance to hear directly from the pastoral staff about what had happened. The whole week had been consumed by political jousting with lots of press coverage. After going through the wringer himself for the previous ten days, Father Mike asked me to bring everyone up to date at each Mass that weekend.

My remarks reflected on the events that had shaken up our parish life and were tied to the scripture readings as part of the homily. It was the Feast of Christ the King, with the Gospel reading from Luke 23: 35–43. Just as Jesus, the homeless vagabond, was rejected and crucified by some of the people of His time, the homeless stranger in our midst can be easily snubbed and persecuted, unless we are mindful that the life of every person is sacred.

It was widely known that among the four Council members who were St. Rose parishioners (Pauline Roccucci, Mel Hamel, Harry Crabb and Bill Santucci) that there was a wide range of opinions on the shelter matter. A *Sacramento Bee Neighbors* article delved deeper, asking whether, as Council members, they felt conflicted making a choice to uphold either their civic duty or their religious beliefs, as if the two were irreconcilable.

The three men found the situation spiritually troubling. Santucci said he was "braced for the worst – litigation." He went on to say "...it's like going against our mother or father." He went on to say that if the church was forced to open its hall to help the homeless because the county declined to open the Armory, he would uphold the law against the church.

Hamel said "It puts you between a rock and a hard place...You try to put aside your Christian principles, the emotional issues, to deal with the council issues."

Crabb, who was cited in the article as the Council member "most adamantly opposed to the church opening its doors to the homeless," said, "It's difficult" to be in opposition to his pastor.

As for Pauline Roccucci, the fourth Catholic Council member, she said she had "wrestled with the issue itself" more as a personal matter, not as a civic vs. religious matter. It was her opinion that the churches were looking for "...a permanent solution, not a Band Aid. I saw this (St. Rose's proposal to house homeless persons) as a cry for help." It was a way of keeping attention on the matter, drawing it to a head. She understood both sides of the issue, having worked with homeless persons through a Sacramento clinic. She was convinced much could be resolved "when you just sit down and talk about it." For her, litigation was not an option.

The three men seemed resigned to confrontation, while Roccucci recognized our overall goal and sought reconciliation.

Most feedback from the parishioners was amazingly positive. The issue was a contentious one that split the congregation – not 50-50, but more like 70% in favor, 20% vehemently opposed and about 10% who seemed indifferent.

November 24, 1992:

Mayor Santucci decided not to attend the Supervisors meeting, likely because Phil Ozenick was the Roseville area County Supervisor at the time. Santucci and Ozenick weren't the best of friends.

Instead, he had asked Council veteran Pauline Roccucci to take his place as the city's representative. Father Mike spoke for our group.

When Roccucci, Father Mike and Willoughby asked the Board to add the Armory issue to the agenda, Ozenick let it be known that he opposed the request. His opposition should have been enough to kill the Roseville delegation's request; but in this case, his fellow supervisors ignored protocol and adopted a motion to add the item to the agenda. Ozenick cast the lone vote against it. The fears expressed in the November 20th *Press Tribune* article suddenly became irrelevant.

After the item was added, the delegation made its presentation, asking the Board to authorize the use of the Armory as an emergency shelter. The *Press Tribune* reported that there was a plethora of "highly emotional testimony from a number of people opposing," as well as from those in favor of using the Armory as a shelter.

Old Town Restaurant owner Isabel Bravo, Ray Phipps of the Barker Hotel and resident Delores Manring were very verbal in opposing the Armory shelter.

Ozenick complained that he had become the victim in the issue, "taking the most heat." He insinuated that the matter was a Roseville problem; the city should deal with it and leave the county out of the picture. He went so far as to offer a motion to make Roseville, not Placer County, the lead agency. His motion failed to get a second.

With that, the Supervisors adopted a motion that Placer County would serve as the lead agency, directing staff to finalize arrangements with the state. The lead agency was the city or county which contracted with the State Military Department by signing the operating license.

After all of his fussing and apparently lacking the power of his own convictions, Ozenick joined the majority, making the vote for Placer County to be the lead agency unanimous. The Roseville delegation was asked to come back within a week to firm up the deal.

With the Armory shelter approved by the Board of Supervisors, Roseville Ministerial Association president Pastor Jerry Angove and Father Mike co-authored a letter to the twenty-seven members of the association to update them on preparations to get the Armory up and running as an emergency shelter. They asked the members to hold a special offering to help support the effort and the costs of operation.

December 1, 1992:

The Supervisors decided to have the facility ready by the middle of the month. They seemed to be keeping their fingers crossed that the Armory would not be forced to close before the usual end of March.

Pauline Roccucci and Father Cormack provided the Supervisors with details on how Roseville and St. Rose would help fund the shelter project. St. Rose increased its pledge to fifteen thousand dollars, and other contributors included Placer County with eleven thousand dollars, Placer County Transportation Commission with fifteen thousand dollars, other cities with ten thousand dollars and other churches with five thousand dollars. County Welfare Director Ray Merz estimated that the total cost would be seventy-four thousand dollars. Roseville would decide the following Wednesday night on its contribution.

Roccucci pointed out to the Supervisors that local governments coming together to find a solution was critical. If they failed, the state might intervene with its own solution. Ozenick took a page from Harry Crabb's political playbook and suggested that if Roseville continued to use the Armory as winter shelter, there might be a move to put the issue on the ballot for local voters to decide.

December 2, 1992:

The City Council finally voted to allocate fifteen thousand dollars toward operating costs of the winter shelter at the Armory. The vote was four to one to support the Armory opening, with "guess who" dissenting.

Willoughby presented the St. Rose check for fifteen thousand dollars at the meeting. St. Rose parishioner and Chevron franchisee Kurt Gould also handed over a check, one for two thousand five hundred dollars from Chevron USA.

Police Chief Simms said that his department would diligently enforce the law and cooperate with property owners to minimize problems caused by the Armory shelter. Even with these assurances, he was quick to point out there would be "transient problems" anyway.

December 14, 1992:

The *Press Tribune* ran an editorial resurrecting the memory of the colossal blunder by city officials, who in June had rejected the proposal to build a regional shelter, even after they had adequate state grants in hand. The paper made a point of rubbing their noses in it.

The editorial chastised especially the Council members who voted against it. Among other things, it said "The council's decision (to vote down the regional shelter proposal) has forced some Placer County residents who are suffering from the area's weak economy to live on the streets...Those residents could have gotten back on their feet quickly (if the shelter had been built)." It went on to say opening the Armory was a good thing, but the community really needed a year-round shelter.

December 15, 1992:

As planned, the Armory began operating as an emergency shelter for the fifth straight winter.

December 17, 1992:

The *Bee* reported Bill Santucci saying, "Belief that a shelter serves as a magnet to railroad-riding transients has given way to reality."

Santucci shared another insight; any shelter would have to belong to the region, or at least be located outside city limits, even though the problem was eighty percent Roseville's. His new strategy was to obtain regional buy-in for the project by picking players from all jurisdictions for hands-on participation in its design and implementation. These would be representatives from all of the local governments, churches and homeless provider organizations.

The *Bee* also announced that Santucci was going to hold a meeting with the region's mayors the following week to launch his new effort.

That same morning, Chamber of Commerce Executive Director Leo Papas called to ask me to participate in the design group. Papas confirmed that Santucci was pushing the effort from behind the scenes with a sense of urgency, seeing the state's decision not to make armories available for shelter after the 1993–94 season as a potential problem. He did not want another face-off between the city and the churches. The focus of the design would be to set up a regional shelter and to relocate the free meal sites and other services to it.

This was the first time the Roseville Chamber of Commerce would have a direct and active hand in helping develop a homeless shelter proposal for the Council – a big plus!

During the conversation, Papas nervously confided that he had a pragmatic reason for jumping into the thick of the planning process. Apparently, he had been swamped by member complaints during the holiday shopping season when St. Rose Church confronted the city for being against the winter shelter.

While the press had a field day portraying Roseville as hard-hearted and bereft of compassion, retailers were innocent bystanders splattered by the mud. As the guardian of the business community's reputation, Papas said he felt compelled to neutralize the problem.

Given those conditions, it was no surprise that Papas was nervous. As I revisited my notes from the call, I imagined the scene of a frantic Papas grabbing Bill Santucci by the lapels and begging him to get the shelter problem resolved.

As novel and funny as that was, getting the job done remained serious stuff. Like Santucci, for years, I had known that the biggest obstacle to any solution was Council member Crabb. I figured he had to be dealt with, but I did not know how.

Santucci saw the solution to the Crabb problem differently. His pragmatism was what made him an effective politician. Santucci knew that the best way to deal with Crabb was not to deal with him at all.

Instead, he would work around him, achieving consensus from surrounding cities to build a shelter, and then bringing the plan to Roseville's Council. By putting the shelter outside city limits and funding it with financial commitments from all the jurisdictions in the region, our City Council, with or without Harry Crabb, would likely buy into the solution.

Papas tried to persuade me that the providers would not get jilted in this go-round. His big selling point was that the final agreement would have staying power because the Chamber would back it as one of the agreement's creators, as well as a sponsor. He calculated that the weight of the Chamber's heavy involvement would keep the city from flaking out on us, as it did earlier in the year. Plus, he said, as we drafted the agreement, we would be sure to interface with the city to keep everyone on board.

Papas also suggested we could have a speakers' bureau, making certain everyone in the community was up to speed on all the facts as we went along. He said the first committee meeting would be in January, and his co-chair Pastor Jerry Angove would contact the churches. Like any good pitchman, when he felt he had me hooked, he drew me in by asking what I thought.

I hesitated, but I was so committed to getting some kind of winter shelter facility for Roseville that I let my heart get the best of me. Foolishly, I jumped on board. I felt we had already been snookered twice by the city, first on the matter of the homeless shelter proposal developed with the Homeless Coordinator and then by the city's adoption of the emergency anti-free food ordinance. Still, I felt compelled to give it another shot. The spectacle of those hungry people I had met in the past who did not have a safe place to bed down was an image I couldn't get out of my head.

I told Papas I would go along with the plan as long as the proposal would not deny services and food to anyone – transient or not. He said he could "accept that understanding."

I can say that neither Papas nor Santucci were looking for a solution for the sake of homeless people. Rather, they were searching for an answer that would quell criticism of Roseville and allow them to start rebuilding its reputation. The two men's interests were economic and political, not humanitarian or spiritual.

Santucci believed that pushing a regional shelter was good for growing his political career. He planned to run for Placer County Supervisor in 1994, so the time he spent organizing and leading the mayors' group would be an excellent investment.

His choice of Papas to be his envoy was great because Papas was the consummate insider. Papas, in turn, chose Pastor Jerry as co-chair because he was, by all appearances, the leader of the local religious community as president of the Ministerial Association.

Santucci had laid groundwork for deploying his strategy for the shelter project, with Papas and Angove co-chairing the design team.

December 21, 1992:

Santucci made his presentation to other area mayors at Roseville City Hall. Mayors Kathy Lund of Rocklin, Carl Malotte of Lincoln, Walt

Scherer of Loomis and Auburn vice-mayor Bud Pisarek showed up.

The meeting did not produce any movement toward an agreement on how to proceed, but merely affirmed what Santucci already knew: It was going to be a long, hard slog. Santucci summed up his challenge this way: "We have another year to go (using the Armory), then what do we do?" The new coalition was his last chance to build a facility that would be in place by the winter of 1994–95.

He firmly believed that if the public sector did not come up with a shelter by that deadline, the churches and providers would go ahead and open their own facility. Plus, the longer the shelter issue remained unresolved, the stronger the Crabb camp's clamor for a city ban on shelters would be. The next mayors' meeting was scheduled for the first week in February.

The turmoil and political bickering over the homeless issue in 1992 provided the *Press Tribune* with so much copy that the paper proclaimed it the top local story of the year.

Chapter 8:
"Let's get down to business!"*
(Jan. 1993–Sep. 15, 1993)

*Leo Papas, Executive Director, Roseville Chamber of Commerce

January 1993:

The city shifted the nearly three hundred thousand dollars in grant funds to St. Vincent's Home Start. The Flamingo Motel site had been cleaned, painted and repaired by volunteers. Fourteen families were in the six-week Phase One portion of the program.

Home Start Executive Director Sherry Schiele said twenty of the thirty motel rooms would be used to house families, four rooms would be dedicated as a children's' center and the balance of the space was for administration.

Schiele noted that she was looking at the budget for 1994 to develop ways to cover the overhead, especially utilities. She planned to double her grant writing efforts and fundraising as soon as things settled down.

January 8, 1993:

At 7:30 a.m., the first meeting of Leo Papa's committee was held at the Roseville Chamber of Commerce office. Co-chair Pastor Jerry Angove and members Del Stephenson, Elaine Willoughby, Ken Denio, Jim Bush, Mr. and Mrs. Scott, Jim Durel, Father Mike Cormack and I made up the gang. The folks who Papas had invited from Rocklin, Lincoln and Auburn, including providers, business people, residents and politicians, failed to show up.

It was our job to design a comprehensive proposal that would keep as many of the south Placer area politicians on board as possible. We had our work cut out for us. Our homework for our second meeting was to explore the issues that kept last year's proposal from being implemented. In other words, we had to find a scapegoat for the failure. We had to wipe the slate clean of blame before we could proceed.

Our group knew we couldn't fault Santucci for not resisting the political pressure from Crabb and Hamel. That would not be politically acceptable. And the blame could not be thrown at the feet of the caregiver group. That would have flown in the face of the facts. The simple and surest solution was to blame both sides, guaranteeing that neither could point the finger at the other.

January 15, 1993:

We came up with a couple of good excuses for 1992's failure, labeling them euphemistically as "missed opportunities for compromise."

The first was the failure to agree on the kind of services that should be offered, such as: How many meals? How many days of shelter? How much free clothing should a homeless person receive?

The second, related to the first, was articulated by St. Vincent's president Elaine Willoughby. It was a failure to agree that different homeless persons have different needs that require different responses.

We all should have acknowledged the simple fact that our response to a person who wanted a chance to improve his life should have been different than our response to a person who just wanted free food, clothes and shelter.

We should not have presumed that just because some persons were transients that they all should be treated the same way.

After we had developed a rationale for 1992's failure, we thought we were ready to start fresh. But we had forgotten about the two big unresolved problems lingering that stared us in the face.

The first was whether we should recommend that the hot meal programs stay put or be moved to a less central location. Families and local homeless single adults were not seen as the problem. Transients were. I floated the idea of moving only meals for transient men and women to a separate site. Families and local homeless single adults would still be served meals at the four existing meal sites.

A program for transients could be located in the industrial areas of town or even outside of city limits. Having their meal center away from the center of town would meet the concerns of residents, business and government. If the facility included a shelter, it would also meet the concerns of the providers.

The second job we faced was to reach common ground on what kinds of services each category of homeless single persons should receive.

January 26, 1993:

It was about halfway through the shelter season when the Board of Supervisors was given a report on the Armory's operations. Ray Merz told the Board that fewer, not more, transients were using the shelter, indicating "the magnet theory is pretty much down the tubes." Merz outlined instances of the broad community support that was coming from the entire region in the form of donations and pledges.

After all the good news, Supervisor Ozenick complained that the new system of busing people to the Armory from downtown Roseville locations, as well as from outlying areas, was too expensive. He also claimed there was general opposition to using the Armory as a shelter. His fellow Board members let his comments roll off their backs.

By this time, we had cobbled together a package for the February mayors' meeting. The proposal provided a service matrix that Elaine Willoughby had designed. The document had four separate groupings of homeless persons, with different levels of service for each group. It was a great tool to visualize the needs of different segments of the homeless population:

- Group 1: Homeless single residents from Roseville and outlying areas and homeless singles who could not prove local residency, but who were on SSI or General Assistance. These folks would receive long-term help through existing programs.
- Group 2: Nonresident families and homeless resident families, who would be directed to Home Start.
- Group 3: Nonresident singles and other homeless singles regarded as transients. The individuals would be eligible for food, shelter, clothing and referrals to medical and other services for a maximum of three days. All aid to this group would be provided at a campground with toilets and showers, security and minimal structures to protect the campers from the environment. Meals would be brought in from one of the existing meal sites by a canteen wagon.
- Group 4: Singles who qualified to be in a church-sponsored transitional living program that lasted up to twelve weeks maximum.

The four existing meal programs would remain open to all persons except those in Group 3. The Group 3 folks would be taken by van to the campground for meals.

February 1, 1993:
At the regional mayors' meeting, Papas and Angove made the presentation our committee had put together. Elaine Willoughby accompanied them.

February 4, 1993:

The *Sacramento Bee Neighbors* reported that at the mayors' meeting, Pastor Angove had mistakenly conceded that our group was prepared to limit services to "hard-core" transients to one 24-hour period before asking them to move on.

February 5, 1993:

Our group received a recap of the mayors' meeting from Papas, Angove and Elaine Willoughby. All three commented that Santucci seemed fidgety and anxious to cut to the chase throughout the presentation and explanation of the service matrix. In fact, as soon as they finished their spiel, Santucci asked "Why aren't the other religious leaders here?"

- Angove, the Ministerial Association president, told us he responded, "Our group (the church group) is willing to submit to significant compromises." Angove's actual words, according to the *Sacramento Bee Neighbors*, were, "We would be willing to have a compromised proposal in order to see a greater good happen."
- Santucci followed Angove's remark by saying that "any shelter would be least offensive if it was five feet beyond our (Roseville's) border!" referring to the campground shelter that would be provided for Group 3.
- When Elaine chimed in that it would be up to the city and the county governments to pick the site, Santucci asked Merz to have the County inventory its surplus property that might be suitable for a shelter for a presentation at the next mayor's meeting.

We were told that by the close of the meeting, Santucci looked relieved and a little more at ease, suggesting an update in six weeks. The next regional meeting was scheduled for April.

February 24, 1993:

Like most successful chamber of commerce executive directors, Papas had lots of political savvy and was well-connected to City Hall. Often, he would share his insights with city officials about issues affecting the Chamber's members, making him feel he had an inside track when it came to local policy and political matters. He routinely received "a heads-up" briefing about important topics that would be heard at future meetings of the various commissions and the Council.

Not this time!

When the usually on-top-of-things Papas read the February 25th Planning Commission Meeting agenda, he was stunned. He discovered that the city had initiated an anti-shelter ordinance. He was furious, seeing the proposed ordinance as the city's attempt to gain leverage over his shelter committee.

In a call to the planning department, Papas learned the official line was that St. Rose Church and St. Vincent's planned to open a shelter program in the near future. The city had to head the plan off with the ordinance.

Papas did not buy it. This was the same excuse the city had used to enact the emergency anti-free food ordinance the previous year. He telephoned the Shelter Committee members to ask for a special meeting.

February 25, 1993:

The Shelter Committee members met that morning to sign a joint letter Papas had drafted to the Council objecting to the ordinance.

He gave us a thorough briefing at the beginning of the meeting, including the details of his consultation with Jack Willoughby, who was the Chamber's legal counsel as well as for the church and St. Vincent's. The two agreed that Willoughby would contact the city attorney to ask that the item be pulled from the agenda. As the attorney for all three organizations, Willoughby could assure the city that no emergency shelter was planned for the foreseeable future.

The letter of protest that Papas drafted was approved and signed by the committee members:

"We cannot help but believe that the timing of this proposal (the ordinance) is nothing short of a slap in the face of those of us who have been working diligently, with your knowledge and tacit consent to devise a long term solution to the homeless problem in the Roseville area."

By late afternoon, the city had agreed to withdraw the ordinance from the Planning Commission agenda in exchange for Willoughby's promise that neither St. Rose Church nor St. Vincent de Paul would open a new shelter within the following ninety days. He followed up with a formal letter outlining the understanding.

February 26, 1993:

The very next morning, during our regular Shelter Committee meeting, Harry Crabb and Mel Hamel walked in, totally unannounced.

They tried to characterize their visit as a goodwill gesture.

The two supposedly stopped by to inform us that they would go along with delaying the anti-shelter ordinance until the June planning commission meeting. June was when our proposed plan was due for submission to the Council.

I guessed that they also had at least two additional reasons for dropping in. First, they were compelled to let us know they were in charge of the ordinance's destiny, not the city attorney or anyone else in the city administration, not even the mayor and certainly not our committee. And second, they wanted to know what this semi-official advisory board was doing.

We realized that we were not just another ad-hoc committee put together by Council member Santucci; we had some kind of a quasi-formal standing with city government.

March 4, 1993:

Jack Willoughby was appointed to the bench by Governor Pete Wilson, meaning that he was required to discontinue all attorney-client relationships. John Haluck of Dieppenbrock, Wulff, Plant & Hannigan, took over as St. Rose Church's pro bono attorney.

March 22, 1993:

Bishop Quinn led the dedication of the new Home Start facility.

March 26, 1993:

Our committee turned in our shelter proposal for the Council's review. We informed the city in the cover letter that "we feel we have gone as far as we can (in developing a plan that would help the community address the problems of the homeless population) without your leadership." We asked the Council to appoint two of its members to work with us. "These members would ensure that the plan...would conform to the long range needs of our community."

The report was immediately set for the Council's review during the first week in April. We were surprised the hearing was scheduled less than two weeks after the document's arrival at City Hall. The usual time spread between arrival and a scheduled hearing of any outside report was several weeks because of staff review and recommendations to the Council. Not for us!

Why were we getting "special treatment?" It was all very strange.

Contrary to Santucci's timeline, now the Council would see the report before the regional mayors reviewed it at their mid-April meeting. We could not understand what was going on.

We knew that Santucci's strategy had been for the region's mayors to approve the plan before it got to the Roseville Council. Was someone trying to throw a wrench into the works?

Coincidentally, on the same day, a source at City Hall let me know that Crabb had convinced Hamel to change his mind about putting off the homeless anti-shelter ordinance until June. The two had agreed to have it heard at the April Planning Commission meeting.

I passed along this new development to the other committee members. We wanted to get to the bottom of this.

March 30, 1993:

John Haluck, Father Mike and I went to City Hall with other committee members at 4:30 p.m. to confront Crabb and Hamel about their change in position. With the city attorney at their side, the two men stated they were concerned that putting off the ordinance until June would make it impossible for the city to have it in place before winter. That would make the city powerless to stop any group from opening a shelter if it wanted to.

The committee members took the Council members at their word. During the next hour or so, they tried to address the concerns the two had raised, making what they thought were necessary concessions that would lead to the ordinance being put off again.

Before granting any concessions, the committee members told Crabb and Hamel that it was their hope to obtain agreements with city and county governments by June for a shelter site and by mid-August for a shelter program based on the March proposal. Then we gave our word, which would be followed by a letter from John Haluck, that no one on the church and provider side would even attempt to open a new shelter in Roseville until one of the following conditions occurred:

1. Ninety days after we gave written notice of our intention to open a shelter, or
2. When the anti-shelter ordinance was put on the Planning Commission's calendar, or
3. Ninety days after August 15th of the year.

And, to show that our group was serious about playing ball, we went along with what Pastor Angove had conceded at the mayors' meeting: We agreed to limit services to "hard-core" transients to one twenty-four hour period before asking them to move on.

This was done hastily to make a deal, a bad one at that. In the proposal the committee members had recently submitted, they had provided for three days services for transients. Here we were, already compromising by making this huge concession.

In exchange, all Crabb and Hamel had to do was allow the Council to pass a resolution to remove the anti-shelter ordinance from the April Planning Commission agenda.

Once Crabb and Hamel had extracted a grand bargain from us, they let us know what they thought of our committee, complaining that they were not being kept in the loop about our work (code for Santucci was doing a good job of keeping them in the dark).

Furthermore, after we conceded, they were no longer interested in talking about transients. Instead, they focused on how the temporary and transitional shelter programs for residents and homeless families would be configured.

I understood that Crabb and Hamel did not trust our committee even if the leadership of Leo Papas and Pastor Angove had given us some credence. Father Mike and I were still rebels and lawbreakers in their eyes – and maybe even worse, we might be Santucci's operatives.

After the meeting, Father Mike shared his reservations with Haluck and me about what our committee had just given up. In a follow-up letter to Haluck, on which I was copied, he reminded us of what even he had forgotten in the rush to make a deal:

- "(If we regard the anti-shelter ordinance as either) a violation of the human rights of a certain group of people (or)...an infringement on the mission of the Church, likewise we should not be involved."; and
- "...the caregivers in giving up the right to feed transients may be dangerously near compromising their values."

In other words, we all should have considered the ramifications of our actions, taking time to think twice before getting involved in any possible entanglements that compromised the rights of others.

We were overly anxious to prove we were acting in good faith and ended up making a deal with the devil.

April 7, 1993:

The Council combined our shelter report with the compromise and the motion to remove the anti-shelter ordinance from planning commission consideration into one agenda item.

I was astonished that when it came up for discussion, Crabb and

Hamel moved quickly to emphasize our committee's new concessions, overshadowing its report.

Hamel set the tone, saying the Council would not commit to any part of what we had submitted in the report. At the same time, he clung on to our agreement to narrow the stay for homeless single men and women from three days to one. The deal was now etched in stone.

It was understood that the only reason the planning commission hearing on the anti-shelter ordinance was delayed again was because the providers promised not to open a shelter program unless certain events occurred.

Our request that the Council appoint two of its members to consult with the committee was completely ignored.

As the discussion rolled on, it was evident that Crabb and Hamel saw themselves as being in the driver's seat. I thought to myself that they had outgunned Santucci, making sure our work on his committee was slowly becoming irrelevant.

After the meeting, it dawned on me that the two men possibly had a bigger scheme in mind than just dealing with us. It appeared that they wanted to derail Santucci's entire strategy. Scheduling both the Committee report hearing and the ordinance proposal before the regional mayors' conclave certainly worked to their benefit. Hamel and Crabb had officially reshaped the report before the other mayors had a chance to see it. We had paid a high price for the anti-shelter ordinance delay.

April 12, 1993:
The regional mayors' meeting produced more upsets. They pushed the plan into an even more pronounced downward trajectory – a change that we didn't anticipate. Papas and Angove were there, but didn't try to influence any decisions. The two sounded almost fatalistic when they recounted the events to our committee later:

- The mayors' group agreed to Roseville's tighter regulations without batting an eye. I was really shocked when Papas and Angove told us that the mayors pushed for even stricter limits on services to homeless single adult males and females than we had ever thought of. They eliminated any chance for an emergency shelter. This would mean that transients just passing through would get only one day of meals and nothing else, not even a shower or a place to sleep.
- The mayors then molded the size of the facility into what they

wanted, nothing like what we had in mind. There would be only ten intake beds and twenty transitional living beds, all at the same location.

- Their next move was to saddle our committee with the job of preparing a comprehensive proposal, including a financing strategy and a site, for their May meeting. The only good thing about their directive was its time frame. It fit with the arrangement we wanted to make with city and the county for a shelter site by June.

- We were also informed that Auburn vice-mayor Bud Pisarek said that he'd help us put the package together. I didn't hold my breath on that one.

- Then we were told that in response to Santucci's February request that the county look for shelter sites on its surplus property list, fourteen locations had been identified. The fourteen would be presented to the Board of Supervisors the first week of May, with the sites in the Roseville area being prescreened by Roseville city staffers John Ford and John Sprague. That meant that the Supervisors would put their stamp of approval on the Roseville locations before we had a chance to recommend any of them to the May mayors' meeting.

After the briefing, I had to sit back for a minute to try to take in what I heard. I had thought up to that time that Santucci wanted to get the mayors to build a plan that we as providers could accept and the Roseville City Council wouldn't veto. Now, it looked like they were developing a plan the Council would accept and we couldn't live with!

While I was still in a daze, the other committee members started talking about how much we had to get done if we were going to have a proposal ready for the politicos' May meeting. Our workload was split among the various committee members, each focusing on a different portion of the final proposal, and bringing the work accomplished to the larger group for approval. Finding the appropriate site and developing a financing mechanism were the two details that the politicians and bureaucrats had kissed off because those were the toughest parts of the plan.

Papas and Angove volunteered to design and assemble the final report. I decided to develop a list of potential sites in addition to the fourteen properties the county had. I figured that all of the fourteen locations would be shot down by the time they got to the Supervisors.

Others on the committee teamed up taking on tasks such as

designing the program and determining facility specifications, as well as obtaining cost and permit fee estimates.

The financing piece – raising the dough for the project – was the orphan. We felt that, for the time being, we would kick the money part back to the politicians and bureaucrats. They were the ones who held the purse strings.

But what if local government was too slow to act on a good deal for a site? In a pinch, I was set to front the money, just as I had when buying the St. Vincent's facilities on Riverside. And what if the public sector failed to produce enough financial support for ongoing operations? I felt we could always fall back on having a fundraising campaign. It had been done before; like old proverb says, "Where there is a will, there is a way."

Our group was determined not to allow the politicians and bureaucrats to use a lack of funding as an excuse to wiggle out of their commitment to the project.

April 15, 1993:

The next sign of political trouble I saw for our shelter proposal occurred by chance while I was at the Chamber of Commerce office. While I stood at the public counter waiting to pick up some papers, I heard a distinctive baritone voice resonating from the open door to Papas' office. It was that of Planning Commissioner Earl Rush. His comments were loud and clear. I couldn't help hearing what he said.

Rush was trashing the homeless shelter project that Papas and the team had been working on. He was urging Papas to give it up, that it was a waste of his time to develop a shelter plan. Rush's tone of voice made it seem that he was almost making fun of the Executive Director's efforts.

He went on to say that he and his friends on the planning commission were prepared to do all they could to destroy any shelter proposal that came their way. They would load it down with as many conditions of approval as they could to make it impractical to build and operate. Items like operating hours, staffing requirements, number of beds, location and who could be served under what conditions were all features which could be inserted into the plan as city mandates. This was in addition to the probable hobophobic opposition from a certain segment of the public that would try to organize a crusade against a shelter being built in "their town" with taxpayer money.

With that, I walked behind the counter, passed the front desks and went to the door of Papas' office. Rush was seated in a chair with his back to me. Papas was at his desk, so he could look past Earl and see me standing in the doorway.

When I gave Papas a big, knowing smile, he sheepishly grinned back. When Rush turned and saw me, he was not at a loss for words. In his usual smooth, calm manner, he told me in a condescending way that he hoped I knew I was wasting my time, too.

It was an ugly experience.

April 28, 1993:

When shelter committee co-chairs Papas and Angove handed out their semi-final draft of our committee report for the next mayor's meeting, I felt they were trying to move too fast. The meeting was more than four weeks away. As we read the report, we understood why they were pushing us. We were being asked to make another compromise – a big one.

They wanted us to water down our proposal further by asking the providers to move all free meals to the shelter site when it was developed, completely closing down the neighborhood meal programs. Apparently, someone at City Hall had promised to make a stink unless we made this concession.

Papas and Angove led with remarks that the First Baptist Church would go along with such a move. However, they failed to identify anyone we knew as their contact at the church, nor did they say why the Baptist Church was asked to take a position and the rest of the meal providers were not.

After some questioning, it was obvious that they never talked with the church's pastor, Roy Herndon, at all about the change. They did not have the nerve. I doubt if Pastor Roy would have said "Hell no!" But that was what he would have meant. I smelled a rat.

It looked like their tactic was to raise the issue with the full committee and hope that the majority, who were merchants, property owners and residents, would back the change and then force the providers to give in. But their plan failed to work.

I remember looking over at my fellow committee member and friend Jim Bush, a leader in the Methodist community. I could see that when he heard the proposal, he moved into his scrapping mode. He crossed his arms, rocked back in his chair and glowered at Jerry Angove. It looked like he might be preparing to say "Maybe it's time we find a new pastor!"

Elaine Willoughby didn't look pleased either. For my part, I felt manipulated. In the end, the committee rejected the change.

May 1, 1993:

Father Mike Cormack retired as pastor of St. Rose. The new pastor, Father Dan Casey, picked up where his predecessor had left off. From the beginning of his tenure, Casey and I worked well together.

May 18, 1993:

The Board of Supervisors was ready to look at shelter sites. When County Deputy Chief Executive Gloria Coutts reported on the fourteen surplus properties which might have been appropriate for a shelter, she said that not one of them passed muster with either Roseville or Placer County staffs.

Coutts explained that initially one hundred thirty-eight county-owned properties were considered. One hundred twenty-four were weeded out, leaving just the fourteen. It did not surprise me that the county and the city did not find any of the properties suited for a homeless facility. Both were looking for a way to get out of the site-finding business.

Then, a battle unfolded in front of our eyes. Supervisor and Board Chair Phil Ozenick started the fracas. He said he had taken the liberty of asking the state about using the Auburn Armory for a shelter, instead of Roseville's. He had a written reply from the state right in front of him.

He announced with "gotcha glee" that the state said either site would be suitable for a shelter.

He told the other supervisors that while the shelter was the subject of discussion, the Board should consider moving the upcoming winter shelter from Roseville to the Auburn Armory. It looked like Ozenick had cornered his colleagues. He said, "It's not fair for Roseville to bear the brunt of it where there is an alternative that could work."

The Auburn politicians emphatically argued that they did not want the shelter in their backyard. During the discussion that followed, both Board member Ron Lichau from Auburn and Auburn vice-mayor Bud Pisarek pointed out that the majority of the folks who would use the shelter would be from Roseville. Since the cost of transporting them to Auburn was a waste of resources, it didn't make sense to change the shelter location.

After the majority of the Board refused to consider his idea, Ozenick bitterly noted, "I'm going to tell the people of Roseville that their Board of Supervisors doesn't even have the guts to look into something that will get it off the hook for one year."

With all the heat the Board was under from cities, churches and businesses to acquire a permanent site, the Supervisors, to the obvious surprise of county staff, moved to have them look into buying private property for a regional shelter.

The staff was less than thrilled, but knew the drill. All they had to do was just to sit on the request until further notice.

May 24, 1993:

The south Placer mayors agreed to have their jurisdictions budget for the Armory emergency shelter for the next winter.

May 26, 1993:

Papas followed up with a letter to Mayor Santucci, notifying him that there was no way our program would be ready for the coming winter, and that the city should set money aside for the Armory shelter.

June 1, 1993:

The City Council had sold the hospital on Sunrise to Sutter Health and enacted an ordinance requiring that proceeds from the fourteen million eight hundred thousand dollar sale be placed into a special trust called "the Citizens Benefit Fund."

Ordinance No. 2788 also established the guidelines for managing the new pot of money, as well as providing for a Grants Advisory Commission. The Commission would evaluate proposals from city departments, as well as from nonprofits (including the homeless services providers) for projects that would ultimately be approved for funding by the City Council each year.

June, 1993:

During Roseville's budget hearings, the Council allocated fifteen thousand dollars as the city's contribution toward the winter shelter. This wasn't a signal that the Council had voted for Roseville to participate in the winter shelter program. It just meant that the money was there if the majority did vote to participate.

To ensure that the city would follow through with funding to support the shelter, I wrote a letter to City Finance Director Phil Ezell. He suggested we meet with Mayor Santucci and Mayor Pro Tem Jackson in July to confirm the city's intent to use the Armory as the shelter.

It was very important to keep Roseville as a partner in funding the winter shelter. If the city backed out of the plan, all of the other jurisdictions, including the county, would jump ship, too. Roseville was the lynchpin, holding the whole process together.

I still hadn't found the right spot for a shelter. My son Paul and I continued our search for a location. Waiting for the city and county bureaucrats would get us nowhere. The first property we came across was an industrial building at 217 West Ivy at a great price of one hundred thirty five thousand dollars. Unfortunately, it was too close to a residential area.

We investigated more locations in and around Roseville. I made offers on two. One that looked promising was for lease at 2131 March Road, but the partners couldn't agree among themselves to lease it for a shelter. Another industrial property with a large and modern building was for sale at 2010 March Road. But, it was grabbed up before we could put our offer together.

July 1, 1993:

While Home Start celebrated getting its sixteenth unit at the old Flamingo Hotel up and running, our committee was prepared to present the shelter design and program to the city councils in the area. The mayors were already on board after they had tinkered with our proposal. Our strategy still remained to build agreement among the members of the governing authorities of all the separate jurisdictions in the region, going to the Roseville City Council last. I was asked to make the case to the Rocklin Council.

July 8, 1993:

The meeting scheduled by Roseville's Finance Director Ezell with Santucci and Jackson went well. The two councilmen agreed that the city would request the county open the Armory as a shelter during the upcoming winter.

July 27, 1993:

The committee members took the shelter program on the road to get the buy-in from the jurisdictions around south Placer before trying to extract approval from Roseville.

In my pitch to the Rocklin City Council members, I didn't ask them to just approve the concept of a regional shelter project, but also to make a down payment on its share of the cost, which our committee had calculated to be seven thousand dollars.

Kathy Lund, a member of Santucci's mayors' committee, jumped right out in front and took ownership of the project. The other Council members, especially Pete Hill, were less enthusiastic. They asked the staff to bring back a more comprehensive report on how the shelter would benefit Rocklin.

By this time in the process, the plan had become so watered down by the Roseville powers that I had to admit to the Rocklin folks that most shelter services would be restricted to Placer County residents only. In effect, transients had been segregated out.

The single exception for transients was they would be given meals for one day before being asked to leave town. The meals were touted by Roseville as a carrot to get them out of the downtown area before being "deported."

As I explained the plan to the Council, I was overcome with shame. Our effort to help homeless single men and women had turned into an attempt to lure them with food and then round 'em up and ship 'em out.

After the Rocklin Council meeting, I came close to resigning from the Committee. But I realized if I did, others might do the same. If we fell apart and disbanded, there might not be any shelter project. That would be just what the Roseville City Council majority probably wanted. The Council members could then wash their hands of the issue and point to us as unwilling and inept partners.

It was best for everyone on the Committee to hang in there. Even if we failed to build a shelter, we would be able to keep the Roseville political elites in the game and maintain our credibility with the community.

July 28, 1993:

Roseville Mayor Pro Tem Fred Jackson resigned from the Council unexpectedly. Even though nature abhors a vacuum, especially when it comes to politics, the four remaining Council members resisted the urge to fill Jackson's spot by appointing someone to serve out the remainder of his term, which was all of three short months and few days.

However, they did determine that in the interest of the city, one of them should be chosen as mayor pro tem. They drew lots to select who among them would get the title. Harry Crabb was the lucky guy.

August 7, 1993:
Rocklin approved the concept of the regional shelter project and appropriated its initial seven thousand dollars toward the cost. Council members George Magnuson and Clarke Dominguez followed Mayor Kathy Lund's lead and endorsed the program. Member Pete Hill still expressed reservations about the program even after the Rocklin city staff provided answers that should have assuaged his concerns.

August 12, 1993:
To ensure Roseville city government was in firm control of any shelter proposal outcome, city staff urged the planning commission to recommend that the Council adopt the anti-shelter ordinance. Putting it in the pipeline provided a legal point of reference – a critical move allowing the city to crack down on emergency shelters during the upcoming winter.

The law nominally called for regulating homeless shelter operations. In reality, it was so restrictive that its intent was to stop any homeless shelter from opening, including shelters like the one St. Rose was ready to open the year before.

The ordinance defined "Transient" and "Homeless" as being a "person lacking a dwelling unit in which that person regularly resides," former Roseville resident or not. The description was so vague that it could have applied to anyone, even to someone, whether it be man, woman, child, invalid or mentally disabled person, who took a few days to move from one residence to another. John Haluck expressed our opposition to the proposed ordinance in a letter to the planning commission, as did the Catholic bishop's attorneys, Desmond, Miller & Desmond.

When the planning commission recommended that the Council okay the ordinance, surprisingly, there were two dissenting planning commissioners, hard-liners Jay Kinder and Earl Rush. I was certain that these two guys couldn't have cared less whether or not homeless people were hurt by the new law. These two wouldn't support a shelter under circumstances.

As Kinder said to the *Press Tribune*, "It is a waste of the taxpayers' money to house people who choose to be irresponsible. This ordinance talks about emergency situations, but I don't see one iota of emergency about somebody riding around in a rail car all day and hopping out to find a place to stay at night."

August 13, 1993:

The planning commission action was followed by city staff's revised but official version of our shelter plan. That was folded into the Council members' briefing packets for their next meeting, replete with changes that denied all services and meals to transient men and women.

Because we had no idea what was in the staff report before it was released, we didn't have a chance to submit a timely letter countering the staff recommendations.

Over the span of the previous eight months, I had watched as our recommendation of three days of meals and services for homeless men and women was changed so that none were allowed at all – not only in Roseville, but throughout the south Placer region. The developments were disgusting.

August 17, 1993:

The Board of Supervisors approved the concept of the regional shelter.

August 18, 1993:

Roseville's City Council went along with Placer County and Rocklin to okay the shelter project, which brought it one step closer to becoming The Placer Community Care Center (PCCC).

Then, the city delivered a knock-out punch. In a rare move from his chair on the dais, City Manager Al Johnson, using the provisions of the new ordinance in progress, sternly reminded those of us in the provider and church community that any motion for approval of a shelter "needed to include the requirement for completing the city planning process" (i.e. going through the ordeal of a public hearing).

Johnson's comment meant three things to me:

1. City officials were going to make it clear that the shelter proposal was no longer theirs, but owned solely by the shelter committee;
2. The city was affirming that the burden of finding a site had fallen to us, the committee members. Johnson saw it as our job to alone come up with the site and then plod through the hearing process; and
3. The city had made sure the shelter would be subject to the new anti-shelter ordinance that the planning commission had recommended just the previous week.

The public hearings on our plan, at both the planning commission and the City Council levels, would provide our adversaries with the opportunity to gin up opposition to the shelter proposal before, during and after the public vetting process.

Once more, deferring to our better judgment, we chickened out and decided this Council meeting was not the right place to question all the changes being thrown at us, even though they were major. We allowed the city to steamroll right over us.

The city staff report bristled with bravado as it suggested the alteration of our program "...meets the goal to eliminate services to homeless adults i.e.: transients."

Our recommendation had been sanitized and neutralized. The report proposed busing transients out of the downtown area to a location that remained undetermined. It went on to say that homeless single men and women who took the van ride would not be entitled to any meals.

Question: Why would any person take a van ride away from the downtown meal sites to go to the shelter unless he was going to get some services – like a meal?

A *Press Tribune* editorial countered the Council's position on the shelter plan. The newspaper proposed a slightly more humane version of the concept.

While both the city's version and the *Press Tribune* version called for existing downtown food programs to serve only local residents, the paper stated that transients who did not want to participate in a transitional living rehabilitation program would be served one meal at an alternate location before being asked to leave town. Very generous.

Our only victory was that we were able to make it evident during the Council meeting that in our opinion the ordinance was legally flawed, meaning it would be challenged in court if the city used it to try to stop us from operating a shelter.

August 24, 1993:
While I was scratching around for a way to stop the Roseville Council from adopting the ordinance, I got together with Hamel, then with Santucci, in separate morning sessions at Kava's Coffee House on Vernon Street.

I was surprised when each man told me in one-on-one conversations he hoped the ordinance would be delayed for at least a year. Their reasoning was that in a year's time, the new shelter project, such as it was, would be up and running, making the new regulation irrelevant.

I had learned something new. I realized that the ordinance probably wouldn't be enacted. With Jackson's seat empty, there were only four votes in play. Hamel and Santucci had told me that they were not for it. But I was positive they wanted a promise of cooperation from the providers and churches if they were going to ensure that there would be no majority on the Council to vote for adoption of the ordinance.

Both men had seen Jack Willoughby's letter of February 25th to the city attorney guaranteeing that neither St. Vincent's nor St. Rose parish would open a shelter within the following ninety days. Santucci said that if I was able to get the providers and the members of the Ministerial Association to sign a pledge similar to either the St. Vincent's-St. Rose letter or the one the Homeless Shelter Committee members had agreed to on March 30th, he would have the ordinance pulled from the Council's agenda. He assured me he had talked with Steve Bruckman, the Assistant City Attorney, who had given him the green light to plan to pull the ordinance.

I drafted a letter to the Council as a pledge that would be signed by the providers and ministers stating that they would not open a shelter or endorse the opening of a shelter without giving the city ninety days' notice. The document also noted that the providers and ministers were making this promise on the condition that either the city or the Placer Community Care Center (PCCC) would have a winter shelter plan in place by September 1st of each year.

That afternoon, I dropped off the draft of the pledge for Santucci at his home. His wife, Norma, said that when he got back that evening, she would have him call me. When he telephoned late that night, he let me know that he liked the letter, but wanted "to check out a few things at City Hall" before I should start gathering signatures.

August 25, 1993:

Following Assistant City Attorney Steve Bruckman's review of the letter, Santucci gave me the go-ahead to collect signatures. I spent the day tracking down the providers and the members of the Ministerial Association to sign it. I thought that a dozen signatures would be enough to show the city that the provider and religious community would abide by the pledge.

Midday, I had lunch with Jack Willoughby. Although he was on the bench, he was still keenly interested in the homeless issue and remained a loyal and constant friend with good practical advice.

"Let's get down to business!"

Throughout August, I had continued my search for a shelter site. I looked at several properties and made many calls. There was commercial property for lease at 129 Linda, but it was too close to the Salvation Army and several residences. I could not get a response from the owner of a commercial building at 207 Kenroy for lease. Two others on Kenroy, 211 and 215, had parking problems. One on Penryn Road would have worked, except that it was too remote from Roseville.

Finally, I found a perfect property with a big house and a barn on acreage at 1555 Bedell Lane, just outside the city limits. The plan was for me to buy it and eventually turn it over to the committee when the funds had been raised.

Santucci and I walked the site and the surrounding properties together, agreeing it held lots of promise. He told me that the city would hook up the property to the city sewer system if the owner agreed to have the city annex the property at some future date. Plus, he said City Manager Al Johnson assured him the city would provide road access from Foothills Boulevard to the site if we purchased it, providing a direct and quick connection from a major street to the property. This would alleviate any potential traffic problems that could come up on the narrow county roads that then served the property.

As Santucci's excitement about the Bedell Lane site increased, the sellers' interest in moving the property decreased. When they discovered what the intended use of the property would be and that my purchase was just a front for the committee, they withdrew the property from the market. Their action was legal because the site was zoned for industrial use.

September 2, 1993:
Santucci called to tell me that "the (anti-shelter) ordinance that Harry (Crabb) wanted" since last year would be shelved at the next Council meeting. He said the pledges from the pastors provided adequate proof that the ordinance was not needed for the time being.

He remained hopeful about the Bedell Lane site.

September 12, 1993:
In an emotional statement to the *Bee Neighbors* a few days prior to the Council meeting, when it looked like a majority vote against his position was certain, Crabb said, "...we need to have a new ordinance for transients. I can't emphasize the word 'transients' enough."

September 15, 1993:

The members of the Council signed off on the ministers' letter of agreement meeting and directed staff to put the proposed ordinance restricting overnight shelters on the shelf. Finally, we had an agreement to have a winter shelter plan in place every year.

Crabb was the lone holdout and let it be known he wanted the ordinance immediately. The three other Council members felt they had come a long way in the last year. All of them, except for Crabb, remained comfortable with their decisions to fund the Armory for another season and to approve the PCCC project.

That was followed by Pauline Roccucci motioning and Hamel seconding that the Council approve the staff recommendation that Roseville ask Placer County to use the Roseville Armory as our shelter for the coming winter. With the exception of Crabb, the Council adopted the motion, making this the Armory's sixth season as the shelter.

Hamel stated he would not be party to any motion that called for Roseville to be the lead agency in operating a shelter. He went on to say the city could wait on the anti-shelter ordinance because "they've (the providers and the churches) agreed they won't open a shelter..." He also remarked, "For the first time, the (shelter) proposal is the most promising I've seen in my six years up here. In that spirit, I'm willing to make a compromise."

He then motioned to accept Item 30 (the letter of agreement from the providers and ministers) and to drop Item 31 from the agenda (the zoning ordinance amendment relating to overnight shelters). Pauline Roccucci seconded the motion.

The city attorney noted for the record that that the current ordinance on the books was adequate to require a church in a residential zone to have a use permit for a homeless shelter. Santucci reiterated the point by saying, "It (the existing ordinance) would suffice."

When I looked through the city zoning code after the meeting, I couldn't find any provision similar to the one which the city attorney and Santucci were talking about.

Chapter 9:
City Council Does the Chicken Dance
(Sep. 21, 1993–Jul. 1994)

September 21, 1993:

Local politics were fraught with intrigue, not only among the Roseville City Council members, but also on the County Board of Supervisors. While the homeless issue drove city shenanigans, it was the revision to Placer's General Plan that caused the County fracas. At the center of the storm was Supervisor Phil Ozenick, who represented the Roseville area.

During the ongoing process of updating the plan to 1994 standards, Ozenick saw his chance to put his stamp on the future growth of Roseville by advocating for his "New Town" model, which called for limiting Roseville's growth to one hundred thousand people. New and smaller communities, which would abut the city's growth line, would absorb the increased population over that mark. The 1994 document was planned to govern Placer County's growth through 2004.

When Ozenick learned that the County Planning Commission members, including his appointee from 1990, Janice Palmer, disagreed with his "New Town" concept, he was furious. The planning commission members wanted the plan to "direct most new urban growth to the existing cities," e.g., Roseville.

Ozenick regarded his appointee's difference of opinion with him as a betrayal. He went on a mission to have her "fired," which required the votes of a majority of the County Board of Supervisors. He rounded up the other two votes from allies Ron Lichau of Auburn and Kirk Uhler of Granite Bay, the three tossing Palmer out on September 21, 1993. After the vote was taken, Chairman Alex Ferreira remarked in disgust with words to the effect "Is there any level lower we can sink to?"

Ozenick appointed an old Roseville ally, Al Saracini, to take Palmer's spot.

Needless to say, Ozenick's vision and ideas not only created a fracture in relations between Roseville and County government, but also a controversial City-County lawsuit.

November 2, 1993:
Four of the five Roseville City Council seats were open on Election

Day, with only Bill Santucci, whose term was up in 1995, not running for office.

When all the dust had settled, Hamel received the highest number of votes and was seated as mayor. Pauline Roccucci came in second, becoming mayor pro tem. I thought we were safe. These two, along with Santucci, gave us the votes we needed for advancing the shelter program. We considered them friends to our cause. Third place went to newcomer Claudia Gamar. Crabb managed to hold onto a seat by placing fourth.

I thought that with Hamel as mayor, our chances of getting the shelter project up and running were significantly enhanced. A few weeks before the election, I had assured him that I would do all I could to help his candidacy. He was very appreciative and in return shared his intentions to support the program.

Former Mayor Pro Tem Jackson had backed Gamar from the sidelines. Their joint involvement in promoting the agenda of the Chamber of Commerce, where he had served as president, gave Gamar the boost she needed to pass up Crabb.

Gamar also had a strong constituency of voters in the Cherry Glen and Thieles neighborhoods that surrounded St. Vincent's. The two groups had recently organized with a primary goal of eradicating St. Vincent's and any services to transients in Roseville.

November 7, 1993:

On the Sunday after Hamel's victory, I met with him to discuss the unfinished business of the Placer Community Care Center (PCCC) project. After congratulating him, I segued into a discussion of St. Rose's support for him during the election. Then, I mentioned that the homeless shelter committee wanted to focus its energies on creating a project that would meet the terms of our agreement with the city – one that would help not only those who could help themselves, but also those who could if they had a little needed encouragement and mentoring.

He accepted the idea without any complications. I thought we were on the same page.

Then, we reviewed some recent developments. I told him that Leo McFarland of Volunteers of America was now on the shelter committee and was possibly interested in having VOA run the PCCC program. Hamel commented he thought VOA would be a good fit.

I also mentioned that Santucci had called a couple of days after the election to give me a heads-up that the county was interested in buying the excess property at the new city corporation yard on PFE Road, a great spot for the PCCC shelter.

What I didn't mention to Hamel was that Santucci had also strongly advised that the committee meet with City Manager Al Johnson as soon as possible to get his backing. Up to that point, the committee had worked primarily with Santucci when he was mayor, letting him be the one to pass the info onto others in city government. A meeting with both the city manager and the new mayor was in the works for December 5th.

In my conversation with Santucci, he emphasized the importance of Johnson's position in influencing city policy, especially when a new mayor takes over. He said the city manager's opinion was as important as a new mayor's in a matter like this. I had the feeling that Santucci was letting me know I should not assume anything about Hamel's political leadership abilities.

As Hamel and I talked about the county's involvement, he reiterated what he said in September, that he would never support a move to have the city operate, own, or sponsor a shelter facility for single adults. That was the county's job.

But, he added, he would back a transitional living facility at the new corporation yard all the way through the planning commission process if the county owned the land. He would be happy with either the PCCC (shelter) committee or VOA operating it.

I thought to myself that all this would be welcome news to the shelter committee. Half a loaf was better than none.

We also covered the importance of the south Placer mayors' group. Hamel said he appreciated everything that Santucci had done to get the group functioning, and he wanted to assure the members that they should remain active and be a vital part of the process. He said that given the City-County tension that had been created by Ozenick's anti-Roseville growth antics, the mayors' group could become an important opportunity to rebuild political relationships.

Then Hamel shared that at the regional mayors' October meeting, it was unfortunately decided to not convene again until a site for the PCCC facility was found.

Our discussion ended on a second downbeat note when he told me that he was troubled by the prospect of a confrontation with Crabb over the shelter project. Hamel went on to predict that if a shelter was approved anywhere in Roseville, "Harry will take it to the streets!"

December 5, 1993:

We had our meeting with City Manager Al Johnson and John Sprague about the shelter proposal. I was relieved to see Santucci sitting with Mayor Hamel at the table.

Going into the meeting, I felt both Santucci and Hamel had our backs. They both had assured me of their positions before and after the election. But, I had a gnawing feeling that Johnson and Sprague were looking for any possible weakness in the Council's commitment to the project so they could drop it.

When we wrapped things up, Papas summarized the day's events by saying he had no doubts that the Chamber of Commerce would continue to work with providers and churches in building out the Homeless Shelter Project.

I was certain that that Johnson and Sprague understood that the course remained steady ahead toward completion of the project, with Hamel and Santucci unambiguously enthusiastic about it, and Pauline Roccucci firmly in our camp.

Later, Santucci confided in me that he was at the meeting to be sure there wasn't any mistake or misunderstanding about the shelter project's importance to the city.

December 15, 1993:

The Armory opened for its sixth winter of operation as support for the program continued to broaden. Churches and civic groups, including the Placer County Bar Association, provided hot meals, hygiene kits and friendship.

Late December:

Leo Papas announced his plan to retire at the end of the year. His replacement, Wendy Gerig, former Executive Director of the Benicia, California Chamber of Commerce, was already hired and prepped to step in. Papas seemed certain that Gerig would be supportive of our cause.

I first met Gerig when she started attending St. Rose Church shortly after the announcement that she would be the new Chamber's Executive Director. She began attending Homeless Shelter Project committee meetings on a regular basis asking lots of questions, but always hanging out at the fringes.

By year's end with Hamel and Gerig in Roseville leadership positions as uncertain quantities in their new roles, the committee members moved quickly to firm up our position with Johnson. We knew that he understood where his bread was buttered. If he felt the Council's power and the chamber's leadership were changing course, he would jump into the lead, just like he had at the August 18th Council meeting. With that in mind, I felt we were smart to make sure the city administration would not attempt to duck out on us again.

January 1994:

The rumor was that Bill Santucci was campaigning to replace Phil Ozenick on the Board of Supervisors. I thought that just based on Ozenick's record, the spot was Santucci's for the asking. If Ozenick had any political skills to protect Roseville's long-term interests, he had failed to use them.

It was not an exaggeration to say that as his fourth year in office began, he had done such a poor job that Roseville and Placer County were at each other's throats. It seemed as if almost every organization with a political bone in its body was looking to oust him.

Ozenick called me and asked to sit down with him for a chat. When we met, he was his usual self – very blunt, but very nervous. He wanted my support in his bid for reelection. He seemed disturbed that Santucci was going to run, even though he had not formally announced.

I said I wanted to stay neutral in the race and wouldn't take sides unless someone tried to make political hay out of the homeless issue. I tried to signal to him that I thought there were plenty of bigger issues to talk about without dragging homelessness into the political discussion.

He pushed me to reconsider. I put him off, saying that it would be best for all of us if I stayed out of it. I didn't want to jeopardize our committee's progress on the PCCC project.

A couple of weeks after Ozenick's visit, Santucci formally announced that he was running to unseat Ozenick from the Placer County Board of Supervisors.

February 1994:

About halfway through the 1993–94 shelter season, the County held an "update meeting" on the shelter. After Health and Human Services Director Ray Merz and VOA Executive Director Leo McFarland reported that the operation was going smoothly, it was decided there would be enough money in the pot to keep the program going through mid-March. The average number of folks being sheltered to date was forty-nine per night, ten percent of them women.

In city politics, it looked like new Council member Gamar had teamed up with Crabb to advocate for the Cherry Glen and Thieles neighborhood associations in an effort to dislodge homeless single men and women from the community. The first account of Gamar and Crabb supporting the two groups occurred when special city resources were funneled to the associations to enable them to more effectively combat what they labeled "the transient problem," The goal of the aid appeared to be the dismantling of St. Vincent's.

This city assistance was above and beyond the normal Neighborhood Watch Program and police patrols. It included:

- City development of association organizational skills and liaison links with city Housing and Redevelopment staff, as well as with Council members who supported them;
- City development of strategies that the neighbors could use to document the activities of homeless people in the neighborhood, especially those close to St. Vincent's.
- City education and coaching of the association members on how to target and record these events so they could be used as evidence in litigation.

March 14, 1994:

When the county failed to make a move to buy the shelter site at the new city corporation yard, it looked like we had come up empty-handed again. Then a glimmer of hope appeared on the horizon: There was the chance of a donation of some barracks-type buildings which could be moved to a site if we found one. St. Vincent's volunteer Dave Sorensen came up with the idea.

Sorensen's day job was managing transportation for the western region of Southern Pacific Railroad. He knew that the railroad had a group of modular buildings behind the Barker Hotel off of Lincoln Street that once had been used to house train crews during their layovers. The buildings had been vacant for some time, and Southern Pacific was looking for someone to move them off the site.

A few members of our committee, along with city representatives, took a close-up look. Joe Ivanusich, who was in charge of railroad facilities, provided a guided tour. There were eight buildings, each one made up of two sixty-by-twelve-foot sections joined together. The buildings were in pretty good shape. In fact, they were ideal! Lack of a site didn't stop us from asking Southern Pacific to hold them for us until we found a location.

Sorensen let us know that his boss said our request for the hold was all he needed as a first move. That would allow the railroad to put the best political spin on the buildings' removal. The company would like to say something such as the buildings were removed at no cost to the railroad, as opposed to saying they were given to a homeless program.

If we could finagle the modular buildings from Southern Pacific, we could easily have them moved to the site at the new city corporation yard.

March 21, 1994:

I called County Supervisor Ozenick early in the morning to ask for his help in having the county acquire the excess land at the new city corporation yard. He said he had heard about the land deal, but was not sure where it stood. He acted like the site might be the answer to finding a location for the shelter facility. We talked about the PCCC leasing a portion of the land for a nominal price, say one hundred dollars per year.

Ozenick said he would look into the status of the transaction. Then he mentioned that Placer County Health and Human Services Director Ray Merz was the person to coordinate with. He went on to say that he would ask Merz to give me a call.

May, 1994:

The Cherry Glen and Thieles neighborhood associations' members had completed their training on how to document what they regarded as "neighborhood problems." The video camera became their favorite tool.

I personally witnessed how the more earnest association members rushed out of their homes and businesses to video any transient looking person who hesitated long enough to remain in the their line of sight, even if he was not coming from or going to St. Vincent's.

Pressure was mounting.

As the Ozenick and Santucci campaigns for County Supervisor ramped up, both candidates stayed in close contact with the Homeless Shelter Committee. They made repeated pitches to us, bidding up the help they would offer if elected, all the time reminding us of the influence a county supervisor had, especially as it related to getting a shelter up and running. When one man showed up at our meetings, it was just a matter of time – maybe a week – before the other would pop in on us.

May 3, 1994:

A group of city and county staff members headed up by John Sprague had been previously asked to represent the committee's interest in acquiring a site for the shelter from Southern Pacific Railroad. We needed an alternative to the new corporation yard location, which we understood looked like a dead deal.

That morning, Sprague reported his findings at our weekly meeting. It had taken him some time to contact the right people who all worked out of the bay area. The railroad had several parcels for sale near the Roseville yards that would be sold only as a group totaling fifty acres. The people in control made it clear that, in any event, none of the land would ever be for lease as a location for a transitional housing program. Another dead end.

Coincidentally, Ozenick then showed up and threw us a bone to make us feel better. He stated for the record that since an alternative plan for housing homeless single men would not be in place by winter, he would vote, as he had in the past, to use the Armory as an emergency winter shelter.

May 10, 1994:

As we had expected, county supervisor candidate Santucci made an appearance right on queue at the beginning of our 7:30 a.m. shelter committee meeting, one week after Ozenick's visit. He parroted just what his opponent had promised us, that he too would definitely back the Armory's use for the coming winter. Then, he sweetened the pot by committing to support locating the new facility at the Berry Street landfill (now the Galleria Boulevard area). He went on to say that even though the chance to obtain a site at the corporation yard on PFE Road had probably fallen through, he would try to breathe new life into it.

Besides hosting local politicians, we worked to finish our proposal, which we hoped might include some sites for the Council's consideration and completed drawings for the facility.

May 18, 1994:

Our work was nearing completion. Our committee was ready to hand off the final draft of our proposal to the City Council.

May 31, 1994:

The last formal committee meeting to wrap up the project focused on reviewing the project timeline after local governments had received our report. Our final proposal recommended that the city and the county together be responsible for acquiring a site.

There were four potential shelter locations listed, none of them strong possibilities. The only location that might have been viable was the one that Santucci mentioned a few weeks before – the Berry Street landfill. But that was inside the city limits, a feature not acceptable to Crabb.

When Greg Cowart had been our police chief, he had suggested an ideal location would be somewhere in the county equally accessible from Roseville, Lincoln and Rocklin, as did Ozenick in 1987 and Santucci, in 1993.

But after investigating those possible locations, we found that the parcels were too remote, too big or lacked the necessary infrastructure of sidewalks and lighting and municipal water, sewer and transportation services.

Another unresolved issue was what to do with the Southern Pacific modular buildings. The railroad still wanted to give the buildings a new home. Sorensen checked with me to see if we were ready to accept them. But without a site, our hands were tied. We stalled for time.

June 3, 1994:

In his report to the Board of Supervisors, Placer County Health and Human Services Director Ray Merz said that during the previous winter there were five hundred eighty-five different people housed at the Armory over a period of ninety days. The guests were bused in at night and out in the morning, dropping the folks off at the same stops where they were picked up. The busing program had begun in response to resident complaints coming from the neighborhood around the Armory. Homeowners did not want the area to become a dumping ground for homeless persons.

Merz was positive in his remarks about the importance of volunteer support and the donated meals that helped make the program a community success. He ended his report saying, "I am hopeful that this spirit of cooperation will continue until a more permanent solution to the problem of homelessness can be found."

Later that day, I learned that city operatives had a new solution to the homeless problem: Just don't fund Roseville's share of the upcoming winter shelter Armory cost. That was exactly what had happened. During the city's budget hearings, the city's share of the Armory shelter costs for the upcoming winter had been omitted.

Previously, Santucci had committed to supporting the winter shelter and Hamel had led me to believe that he also did. I thought the funding was a foregone conclusion. Additionally, everyone familiar with the PCCC project realized that the new shelter would not be up and running by November. All of these factors made it certain that the oversight was intentional.

When I discovered this "budgeting mistake," I got on the phone to Santucci. He was out of town.

Next, I tried to reach Hamel and left a message asking him to return my call.

I contacted the City Finance Department and spoke with Nadine. She implied that the winter shelter funding decision might have been shoved over to the newly created Grants Advisory Commission, which would recommend to the Council whether some of the interest proceeds from the previous year's hospital sale could be allocated to support the Armory shelter.

And finally, I tried to get in touch with City Manager Al Johnson. He, too, was out of town. Instead, I spoke with John Tarson, the Assistant City Manager. He said the city's budget was pretty well firmed up, but he would be sure to let Johnson and the Finance Director know they needed to make provision for the fifteen thousand dollars in shelter money. It would not be forgotten.

June 4, 1994:

First thing in the morning, City Housing and Redevelopment Manager John Sprague called for me at the rectory and asked that I contact him ASAP. When I returned his call that afternoon, he told me that he heard I was concerned about the shelter funding. He said the money would be made available, but there had been some changes in the funding process.

He went on to say that after he had talked to the new Chamber of Commerce Executive Director Wendy Gerig, the city staff decided to recommend to the Council that the city's traditional share of the winter shelter funds be budgeted when the staff asked the Council to request the county open the Armory.

Then he told me that the old Community Promotions Fund that had been the source of the city's share of Armory operating money no longer existed. He wrapped it up by saying if the churches preferred to see the fifteen thousand dollars allocated up front, they could go to the Roseville Grants Advisory Commission to request the money.

After thinking about the consequences of the new procedure, I realized the city could use it as a tool to avoid asking the county to open the Armory shelter altogether. If the staff or the churches and providers waited to ask the Council for funding in the fall, Council members who were opposed could say arrangements should have been made at budget time. No funding, no shelter.

Hobophobia could get people to do cruel things.

It looked like Sprague and Gerig thought they had devised an effective roadblock to funding the winter Armory, one that Assistant City Manager John Tarson was not aware of. Gerig had effectively moved the Chamber from our camp into that of our opponents.

I telephoned Mayor Hamel to bring him up to speed on the shelter funding issue. He thanked me for the heads-up, saying that he wanted to keep it out of the upcoming Santucci- Ozenick County Supervisor race.

June 30, 1994:

At the city's budget hearing, Hamel had the funding for the Armory shelter program restored to the budget.

July 3, 1994:

The *Press Tribune* reported that the Council included fifteen thousand dollars in the budget for the Armory shelter for the coming winter. What now concerned me most was that Sprague had been attending our committee meetings on a regular basis as the city's liaison during the same time period that he was attending the meetings of the Cherry Glen and Thieles groups. After going through this little budgeting ordeal, I had a pretty good idea of where his loyalties lie: They were not with us.

From his position, he could keep track of what was going on in both camps. I wondered how he used what he learned from his enviable perch. Who on the other side benefited from the information he gained? I was certain it wasn't the mayor. Hamel had just made a decision to help the homeless folks in our community the coming winter. Or was it the mayor?

July 28, 1994:

After nineteen months of committee work, we submitted our final report with a list of four possible shelter sites for Council action. The cover letter pointed out that the Placer County Board of Supervisors and the city councils of Auburn, Rocklin and Roseville had approved the project in concept. Now, we needed a location. We asked the Roseville City Council to schedule hearings in the next four to six weeks to select a site.

July 29, 1994:

The very next day, we got a startling surprise: the *Press Tribune* announced, "At the behest of Mayor Mel Hamel, the city has hired area negotiator Steve Barber to moderate the (homeless) forum..." The *Press Tribune* went on to say "Four potential sites for (the) shelter are expected to be revealed at the upcoming forum."

The committee members felt betrayed. I personally came to label the city's deceit as Roseville's version of "The Chicken Dance." Using some fancy footwork, the bureaucrats and politicians had managed to sluff off our shelter report onto the Homeless Forum participants. The mayor and his compatriots never intended to take the heat that would come with evaluating the sites.

The forum was billed by Housing and Redevelopment Manager Sprague as "an opportunity" to bring a variety of government and civic groups, as well as other interested persons, together to discuss solutions to the homeless problem in Roseville. He announced that the city was looking to the Homeless Forum process for "productive recommendations and goals."

Hamel, who once was able to pass himself off as the great conciliator, found that his political capital was eroding quickly. His Council was split on how to deal with our proposal. Crabb and Gamar were strongly against any shelter while Santucci and Roccucci were seen as on our side.

That meant Hamel could be left standing alone – right out in the open, caught in a political crossfire between not only his fellow Council members, but also between our committee and the Thieles and Cherry Glen Neighborhood groups – unless he did something proactive and politically furtive.

As the neighborhood groups' influence grew, they were no longer content with either having a say in the homeless shelter proposal or eliminating the presence of any homeless person who might amble by on their sidewalks. They became emboldened to dream that they had the power to eradicate any program in Roseville that provided services for homeless single adults. Hobophobia!

Chapter 10:
"Baby, It's Cold Outside!"*
(Aug. 1994–Dec. 10, 1994)
*music composer Frank Loesser, 1944

August 1994:

The Cherry Glen and Thieles neighborhood associations dominated the Homeless Forum process. Sally Bragg and Sylvia Slade, both of whom told the *Tribune* they had arrived in town in 1990, emerged as the leaders, saying their personal interests were "beautification and renewal" of their neighborhoods, which were merely euphemisms for getting rid of transients and St. Vincent's.

Their goal made good business sense. Property values in Cherry Glen and Thieles had begun to escalate rapidly, catching up with those in the newer parts of town. The potential upside in the value of their real estate investments was fantastic.

Bragg and her husband, Mike, had purchased older residential properties in Cherry Glen with an eye to build new homes on the lots or upgrade the older ones, possibly flipping them for a comfortable profit.

Slade and her husband, Mike Papier, bought a commercial property that had been shuttered for years. It was a run-down shell of a building across the street from St. Vincent's that had been a neighborhood liquor store. Besides the storefront, the lot had a separate apartment and garage building in the back. They were able to acquire the site at a discounted price, transforming it into a stylish hair salon.

Both couples were employing a time-tested method of making money by purchasing distressed properties and improving them. Their next move called for an "area cleansing." Their main target was St. Vincent's.

The area cleansing strategy can work in a variety of situations and often allows opportunities to maximize profits. A theoretical example is the real estate developer who buys a farm property next to a dairy and then has his property rezoned for residential use. Soon after, he claims that the effluence and smell from the dairy cows is a health hazard, drawing flies and vermin. The cows' presence is running off potential homebuyers – a nuisance, even though the dairy had operated for years before the real estate developer even thought of buying next door.

A court rules in the developer's favor, forcing the dairy owner to close his operation and find a new site.

In the case of Bragg and Slade, St. Vincent's was like the dairy. Their argument was that the charity was creating a nuisance by providing meals and services not only for poor residents, but also for homeless men and women. Even though the program had been at the location for several years before they had arrived, they claimed the charitable activities infringed on their property rights, that St. Vincent's was keeping them from remaking the neighborhood in their own image. St. Vincent's and its clientele had to go.

Both women were politically savvy and took time to develop strong ties to Council members Crabb and Gamar to help them with their plan.

When the Homeless Forum process evolved into a series of meetings and started to take on a life of its own, Slade and Bragg were able to make their entrance onto the larger Roseville public stage.

August 2, 1994:

In her newspaper debut in the article entitled "Roseville residents bristle at transient population," Slade told the *Tribune*, "I think this could be a wonderful little street. As long as the feeding (at St. Vincent's) is going on, this street doesn't have a chance."

August 6, 1994:

The Forum group held its first meeting far away from City Hall, at Maidu Center on the east side of town. Both the neighborhood activists and providers from central Roseville were rounded up and asked to meet in a large conference room to go at it. Pauline Roccucci said meeting was more "like the Hatfields and the McCoys!"

To set the tone he wanted, City Housing and Redevelopment Manager Sprague distributed copies of a handpicked package of thirty-five newspaper articles favorable to the City of Roseville in its handling of the homeless problem. Each forum participant had a set in hand for reference at that first meeting. At that time, my own collection of articles on the subject numbered over two hundred reports from the *Sacramento Bee* and the *Press Tribune*.

At the end of the first meeting of the Homeless Forum, I felt that we had been had. After failing to get city buy-in on some form of homeless shelter project proposal over the previous six or so years, I didn't believe we stood a chance in this new venue. It seemed that Slade and Bragg were just the obstacles that the Council majority had been looking for to fend off our efforts, and maybe this time permanently.

There was no good option for us other than to go along with the Forum process. We just hoped that somehow the tide would change.

August 11, 1994:

Council members Crabb and Gamar, along with city staffer John Sprague, made an appearance at a Cherry Glen and Thieles neighborhood rally held at the Chamber of Commerce offices. The meeting room they occupied was the same space that Leo Papas had held meetings just months before to develop the homeless shelter project plan. The Chamber and its new executive director, Wendy Gerig were giving the Cherry Glen and Thieles neighborhood associations as much support as possible without formally endorsing their conduct.

The city's political elites used the rally to let the folks know that they were on their side when it came to cleansing their neighborhoods of unwanted people. As Crabb said to loud applause, "We do want to get the transients out of town." That was followed by Sprague's statement, "We can only go as far as you are willing to go with us."

August 12, 1994:

The *Press Tribune* optimistically encouraged community participation in the Homeless Forum and its "Interest Based Negotiations," implying that with more community involvement, a broad consensus on a solution could be developed.

The problem, as always, was that the homeless issue was the narrow focus of two very different special interest groups with opposing views of the world – one dedicated to expanding humanitarian aid and the other determined to constraining it.

Outside of these two groups, most of the remaining folks who attended the Forum meeting were curious but uncommitted resident bystanders who liked to learn about recent events in the media, but were unwilling to venture more than an opinion on the matter.

The *Tribune* also reported on the future goals and objectives of the Cherry Glen and Thieles neighborhood associations. The article detailed how the associations' members had fully implemented their plan to gather evidence to use in litigation. The paper noted that they were set to take their next concrete step toward court action that held "landlords financially responsible for the loss of area property values...crime, vacant properties, nuisance problems, transients living in and around vacant properties and other problems..." That next step, according to the article, was to install "drug-free zone" signs that would put offenders on notice.

But, as Sally Bragg, in her best attempt to sound innocent, pointed out to the *Tribune*, "We're not a vigilante group..."

The paper went on to say that the associations were "documenting transient problems and meeting with lunch providers (St. Vincent's) about those problems." The meeting part of their claim was a bit of a stretch.

The reality was that the Homeless Forum process talks were the only contact we as "lunch providers" had with them. The fact was that that neither neighborhood organization had attempted a direct dialog with us about any of their gripes with homeless single adults.

With coaching from city officials, association leaders Slade and Bragg had probably studied the Berkeley, California model of neighborhood activism or a similar one used in Arizona. The Berkeley strategy used small claims lawsuits to target landlords who wouldn't remove tenants involved in drug activity on or around their properties.

The two women likely came to the conclusion that there was no reason the Berkeley plan wouldn't work in Roseville. They must have fantasized that with the support of both the City Council majority and the police chief, they could easily fire up their troops to steamroller over St. Vincent's.

August 17, 1994:

At that evening's Council meeting, our May shelter proposal turned up on the agenda "for show" as Item 42. There were actually two items on tap concerning the homeless issue – Items 41 and 42.

The staff had arranged the agenda so that the Council would first adopt a schedule of four more Homeless Forum meetings in Item 41, and then discuss evaluating Item 42.

Item 41 began with a briefing on the Homeless Forum by Sprague, who staged a great presentation. He tried to show what he termed "the progress" that had been made by bringing various factions together. He recommended the city sponsor up to four more Homeless Forum sessions, suggesting everyone might be able to reach an agreement.

An agreement? In his dreams!

The Council approved his request and scheduled the dates of August 29th, 30th and 31st, with a final meeting to be held sometime in September. The stage was set for Item 42.

Item 42 was the suggestion that the Council, "looking through the lens" provided in Item 41, evaluate our shelter project recommendations as part of "the overall review of the Homeless Forum results" and then consider "arriving at one solution during the upcoming forums." Translated, this meant that Sprague had got the political heat off of Hamel, just what the mayor had hoped for. It looked like he had avoided a scrap with Crabb.

August 19, 1994:

The *Press Tribune* must have observed the Council meeting that night through rose-colored glasses. It reported that city officials acted to "focus on budding negotiations that involve the entire community."

September 1994:

By summer's end, we had lost any political advantage we may have had.

With the balance of power on the Council shifted against us, the annual rite of political handwringing by the city and county over whether to open the Armory shelter had also changed. Both the city and the county rubrics deviated from the norm in a number of ways.

For example, The Roseville City Council requested that the Auburn Armory be used instead of the one in Roseville. The county met the suggestion with disbelief. Claudia Skaggs, Chief Deputy Health and Human Services Director, said in unusually frank terms, "It just doesn't make any sense."

September 21, 1994:

After the laughter had died down at the county's offices at the DeWitt Center, the Council reluctantly accepted reality and motioned to ask the county to operate the usual Armory winter shelter in Roseville.

Testimony against the proposal was more hostile than in any previous year. Homeless Forum participants and activists Charles Curtis, David Battles and Matt Hodges from the neighborhood groups mocked the providers and church leaders with comments like "Let's trade places," and "Take (the transients) into your neighborhood and see what it's like."

The Homeless Forum participants who opposed using the Armory shelter were not in any mood to back off their position. In fact, they had been charged up by the Forum meetings.

Then we witnessed the first overt Council move away from the providers and toward our opponents. Members Santucci and Hamel indicated they were fully aware that they both were in the doghouse with the shelter opponents. To make amends and ingratiate themselves with them, they added two new elements to the annual request to use the Armory as a shelter:

- Representatives of groups opposing the Armory shelter, such as leaders from the Cherry Glen and Thieles neighborhoods, would be included in the planning process for opening the facility; and
- Homeless persons using the shelter would be required to participate in a work program.

I felt that while Hamel seemed to want to keep his word to us, he remained under high pressure from powerful sources on the other side – the politically active neighborhood groups and Council members Crabb and Gamar. He let us know in no uncertain terms that 1994 was the final year that he would support the Armory's use as a shelter. All future bets were off.

Santucci found himself with his political neck on the chopping block. With the County Supervisor election just around the corner, he tried to justify his vote: "We have to be in control. Once we allow the churches to open shelters, we've opened Pandora's box."

He was alluding to the real possibility that if the city defaulted on its 1993 agreement with the ministers to either provide a winter shelter plan by September 1st or allow another entity such as a church to do so, the churches would be free to open their doors when winter arrived, forcing the Council to resort to litigation to stop them. Given the City's weak laws on the matter and its binding promise to the ministers, Santucci feared that the ministers would prevail in a legal battle.

To boot, the merchants and residents disagreed with Santucci's analysis. Sylvia Slade, representing the Cherry Glen and Thieles neighborhood associations, astutely observed, "If the churches opened shelters, that would help the (Homeless Forum) process. Then we'd have other people recognize the issues we're dealing with here." She added the Armory neighbors and many of her members would be up in arms and join the chorus to stop all services for the homeless.

Retired National Guard Colonel Bill Hamilton added to the offensive. Hamilton said he had not complained in past years about the Armory shelter because he was on active duty. But, since he had retired, he could say what he wanted. He said a lot!

Hamilton claimed guardsmen were being demoralized by the presence of the homeless men. Even if there was zero evidence to support his claim, his comments made for great rhetoric.

As the time for the Council vote drew near, everyone on our side knew how allies Gamar and Crabb would vote. Their positions on denying help to the homeless had been well staked out. Gamar, with a big balance of political capital on the books, had invested it well with the neighborhood associations. Her political future looked bright. At that point, I felt that the civic establishment had its guns trained on us, using whatever methods and means were available to stop our work with the homeless population.

Surprisingly, when all was said and done and the vote was taken, the motion to ask the county to open the Armory as a winter shelter passed three to two. Council member Pauline Roccucci led by voting for the item, as did who I felt were a reluctant Hamel and a skittish Santucci. As sure as the sun rises, members Crabb and Gamar voted against honoring the city's 1993 covenant with the ministers.

Accounts in both the *Tribune* and the *Bee* caught the tone of the meeting perfectly. Hamel and Santucci had tried to straddle the fence, but instead ended up trapped between a rock and a hard place. The *Bee* reported that "Councilman Crabb sided with the speakers against the motion, saying that the feeding of the homeless by organizations such as St. Vincent de Paul attracts transients."

September 23, 1994:

Father Dan and I filed the paperwork with the California Secretary of State to incorporate the nonprofit *Placer Community Care Center*, which would operate the shelter that was being planned by the Homeless Forum Process.

October 1994:

As the day for the County Supervisors' vote on the Armory winter shelter drew near, I received a call from Ray Merz. He said the Supervisors' meeting had been cancelled because of a lack of a quorum. Merz indicated that the Armory winter shelter vote would be put off until sometime in November.

I was not surprised by the news, given that the Santucci/Ozenick contest for the District One Supervisor's seat was less than five weeks away.

Coincidentally, Ozenick called me shortly after I got off the phone with Merz. My notes show that he told me he "...did not want to see homelessness become a public campaign issue and hoped the vote (for the shelter) by the Board of Supervisors could be delayed into November."

October 20, 1994:
Santucci called. He was upset and asked if we could sit down to go over some campaign literature.

When we got together at St. Rose, he pulled out an Ozenick political hit piece that had been mailed to targeted Roseville households. The flier lambasted Santucci (as well as Roccucci and Hamel) for the vote to ask the county to operate the Armory shelter.

The mailer was an obvious breach of the gentlemen's agreement I had with Ozenick and Santucci that neither of them would make homelessness a campaign issue. Now, because of Ozenick's ad, it had become not only an issue, but a significant one.

That was when Santucci and I decided that he would do a targeted mailing, too. His would be a letter from me explaining the opportunism of the piece against him and the agreement that Ozenick had broken. The mailer went out on St. Rose letterhead to two thousand five hundred homes, creating a stir, most of it positive for Santucci.

October 28, 1994:
Placer County Health and Human Services Director Ray Merz telephoned Father Dan to tell him that the Board would hear Roseville's request to use the Armory shelter at the end of November.

November 8, 1994:
The election results for county supervisor were solidly against Ozenick. He had been so divisive during his term that he lost the seat to Santucci by a fifteen percent margin. Although the main issue in the race was land use, Ozenick's position and actions on the homeless question cost him votes as well. Voters dispatched him to the political junk heap. Comparing his loss by nearly two thousand votes to his razor-thin victory in 1990 of eighty votes was enough to demonstrate the poor impression his four years of service had left on the public.

November, 1994:
After Santucci won his seat on the Board of Supervisors, The *Press Tribune* confirmed rumors that a civil lawsuit or lawsuits by property owners, businesses and residents around St. Vincent's was in the works. The litigation would claim that the Dining Room was a public nuisance.

It looked like the opponents of St. Vincent's were out to finish the job, once and for all.

As a follow-up for the record, I wrote to St. Vincent's president Elaine Willoughby, asking her if she had heard anything about a lawsuit. While I waited for her reply, I did a little more detective work on my own.

First, I spoke with John Kintz, Roseville's chief building inspector. I asked him if he had heard about possible legal action to shut down St. Vincent's activities and if he had anything in his files about our buildings being a public nuisance.

He assured me that he had no valid complaints about St. Vincent's in his files and would call me directly if anything came in. He added that the nuisance abatement and code violation provisions did not apply to our buildings because they were in good shape. He did say there were two dilapidated buildings in our area that he was after – the Mahan building across the street from St. Vincent's on Bonita and the big multifamily building on the southwest corner of Bonita and Clinton.

Kintz asked who was behind all this. When I told him it was likely Sally Bragg and Sylvia Slade, he admitted that he knew about their activities and of the Cherry Glen and the Thieles groups' hostility toward St. Vincent's. He went on to say he had stated in public meetings that they ought to try to work with St. Vincent's rather than fight us.

Next, I called Placer County Health Department Supervisor Thom Carmichael at home to see if there were any complaints against St. Vincent's. He said there weren't any and everything was okay. He would let me know if there were any changes.

I continued to keep my ear to the ground and began preparing for an attack ahead.

November 29, 1994:

On the day the County Supervisors were set to vote on the shelter at the Roseville Armory, there were only four supervisors present. Supervisor Ron Lichau from Auburn was missing, in the hospital recovering from a cellulitis attack. When the *Auburn Journal* interviewed him about using the Armory shelter, he told the reporter from his bed "I feel fairly confident in saying we'll do it one more year and that's it...The way I see it right now, the city is depending on the county continuing the shelter for another year. For us to bail out at this time would be irresponsible."

Meanwhile, back on the Supervisors' dais, Ozenick seemed

dejected, probably ruminating over his trouncing at the polls. But, when it came time for him to voice his opinion against our request, he came to life.

During the shelter hearing, he was joined by Roseville old-timers Phillip Tafoya and Melba McClain, who showed up to testify, as did Ozenick backer Thanti Powers. The three let the Board know they were tired of what they perceived as problems the patrons of the Armory caused in their neighborhoods every year.

When the vote was taken, as we expected, Ozenick went against us, as did Supervisor Kirk Uhler from Granite Bay. Uhler said, "I find it ironic that Roseville wants to play lead agency on all the positive impacts of growth, but not on the negative consequences of growth."

Normally, two negative votes out of five on the Board would not stall a motion. But, there wasn't anything normal about this year's attempt to use the Armory. The vote was a tie, and Chairman Ferreira said he would call for a new tally when Lichau returned.

Both Ozenick and Uhler gave assurances that their minds were made up. The *Sacramento Bee Neighbors* quoted Ozenick as saying, "We've stood it in Roseville 'one more year' too long."

Kirk Uhler told the *Auburn Journal*, "I will not vote for the county to be the lead agency, even if it means the shelter doesn't open."

The truth was that Lichau, Ozenick and Uhler often voted as a block. The three frequently threw up obstacles attempting to curb Roseville's increasing political dominance in the county by actively trying to block the city's growth boom, using the planning process. Lichau was protecting Auburn's clout as the political center of the county, and Uhler was trying to erect a barrier against Roseville's growth and political influence to the east.

November 30, 1994:
I spoke with Supervisor Lichau and asked for his support on the Armory matter. Unlike what he said to the *Auburn Journal*, he told me that he was not sure how he would vote. When our phone conversation was completed, I was so alarmed that I contacted Santucci, who said he would talk to Lichau and call Board Chairman Alex Ferreira to try to keep Lichau's vote in the "yes" column.

December, 1994:
More warnings about possible legal problems! Friends told me that property owners, business people and residents around St. Vincent's

were planning legal action. The Berkeley model kept popping into my head. I knew their claim would be that the Dining Room was creating a public nuisance.

I sent another letter to Elaine Willoughby to bring her up to date about the threatened legal action. I suggested she take appropriate steps to protect our shared interests.

That was followed by another development, this one at a Forum bargaining meeting, coming from our side. For the first time, St. Vincent's offered to discuss moving its meal program to another location, on the condition that the other side would voice support for opening the Armory. The opposition wouldn't even take the proposition under advisement.

December 2, 1994:

The *Tribune's* editorial "Playing Politics Too Much" slammed our city officials' playbook of negativity and questioned their sincerity when it said it was time "...for our politicians to get off their soapboxes and seriously address the problems facing us as a community." The paper called out the city's leaders by saying they were satisfied having homeless people sleeping on the streets even during the winter.

The *Press Tribune* did not stop there, going on to say, "The script is becoming familiar...The program is thrown into a tizzy...a crisis develops, all sides finally agree...and a last minute scramble is made to open the temporary shelter..."

December 6, 1994:

Supervisor Lichau was back on the dais for the meeting and the second hearing on the Armory request. When the item came up for consideration, Roseville anti-homeless activists Sylvia Slade and David Battles voiced strong opposition.

After public testimony ended, Lichau surprised us all by introducing a motion to return the matter to Roseville because it was a Roseville problem, not a Placer County one, effectively washing his hands of the whole issue.

I could see from my seat in the audience that Ozenick and Uhler comfortably rocked back and forth in their swivel chairs, glancing at one another with self-congratulatory smiles as they voted with Lichau.

The three of them had carefully crafted the outcome long before the meeting started. Supervisors Ferreira and Bloomfield voted against the motion.

Ozenick's reasons for his vote remained unclear for a man on his way out. Who was he trying to hurt? Was he on an ego trip; was he swinging wildly at the Roseville City Council and administration; or was he simply angry over his circumstances as a loser?

The Board's 3–2 vote meant the county was out of the shelter business for the first time since January 1989. Sylvia Slade and Sally Bragg were as tickled with the vote as a couple of Kings cheerleaders on a winning night. They knew that they had a majority of the Roseville City Council eating out of their hands. Now it was apparent that the Board of Supervisors was also on their side.

Slade told the *Bee*, "The transients are people who have chosen that lifestyle. Part of that lifestyle is that it's pretty darn cold out there." I understood her to imply that choosing to be a transient was a rational decision made by someone who was as mentally competent as she was.

She also postulated to the *Press Tribune*, "I think we now have the beginnings of being able to rehabilitate our downtown streets." Her statement sounded like she was pleased that one big obstacle was out of her way, even though other people would suffer.

Those of us supporting the Armory's use felt unsure where to turn. We were reluctant to ask Roseville to be the lead agency. Many members of our coalition remained optimistic that the Homeless Forum process held out some hope for our cause. The majority of the group didn't want to confront the Council with a request to ask the state for the Armory to open. They saw the move as a risk, jeopardizing a possible compromise on a permanent shelter proposal – a dream!

December 9, 1994:

After a few days of bitterly cold nighttime temperatures, the ministerial leadership of the Methodist Church, the Salvation Army and St. Rose agreed that the situation was intolerable.

People were needlessly suffering because of a bad political decision by three county supervisors – a decision that seemed to be based on self-interest, ego and spitefulness. The three churches sent a joint letter to City Manager Al Johnson, asking for time on an upcoming Council agenda to address the matter of opening the Armory shelter. Under the plan, St. Rose would take full responsibility for operating the shelter.

The state guidelines for operating an armory shelter only required a county or the city where the armory was located to request its opening. The regulations allowed a private nonprofit or church to operate the program.

It was certain that Crabb and Gamar would oppose our move, Crabb on the grounds of his unrelenting dislike of homeless single men, and Gamar because she wanted to keep the Cherry Glen and Thieles Neighborhood associations in her pocket. Hamel's support was doubtful due to his previous statements in opposition to making Roseville the lead agency in operating the Armory shelter.

Additionally, he had gone on record telling the *Bee*, "We've had the armory open for several years. Let's see what happens if we don't have it for a year."

In my optimism, I was silly enough to regard Hamel's comment as just political posturing. The *Bee* interpreted it in a similar light – as a "more neutral view" than that of either Crabb or Gamar.

Ray Mertz read something else into it. He told me he failed to understand why Hamel was so against the city signing the license for St. Rose to run the Armory. Mertz postulated that Hamel had said it to provide him with good cover for his real objective – to kill the shelter option once and for all.

The leader of the Cherry Glen Neighborhood Association, Sally Bragg would have loved that. She was right out in front with her opposition to our request: "The issue is still the transients. This is certainly no way to expedite a solution (to her conflict with St. Vincent's). It's only going to alienate the stakeholders – the residents, businesses and property owners."

We had to at least take a shot at getting the motion approved. Johnson said the request would be on the Council agenda for the 21st.

December 10, 1994:

Sacramento station *KXTV,* Channel 10 interviewed Hamel to follow up on his comments to the *Bee*. He declared that he was no longer aligned with Santucci and Roccucci, but was firmly in the Crabb/Gamar camp and would vote against opening the Armory winter shelter to keep the homeless out of Roseville: "The first thing (people opposing transients) told (the city) their biggest problem was the transients who hang around, live around, walk around, defecate on their property and scare their families. We'll take care of Roseville residents, but we're not going to take care of everybody on the road."

Somehow I missed that interview. My ignorance provided only temporary bliss.

Chapter 11:
"I'm happy when the Armory is open…"*
(Dec. 11, 1994–Dec. 23, 1994)
*homeless man Juan Lara to *KCRA, Channel 3 TV*

December 11, 1994:

On this crisp and clear Sunday morning, I was greeting folks leaving church after Mass. I had preached the homily and was still vested in my deacon outfit.

A man walked up and introduced himself. I thought he was a new parishioner. He had a great smile and a friendly way about him, appearing to be every bit the Roseville professional. I soon learned his name was Archie Mull, a name I recognized. He was a well-known attorney in Sacramento and a good friend to Father Dan Madigan, founder of the Sacramento Food Bank. I had known Madigan for years.

Mull was on a mission. He said that he had read the *Bee* account about the problem we were having convincing the city and county to offer shelter. He thought it was shameful.

He wanted to help us find a solution. He handed me a personal check for twenty-five thousand dollars and said we could use it any way we wanted, providing it helped people have winter shelter and we kept his identity confidential. He hoped that his donation when added to the rest of the pot would be enough to get the Council to change its collective mind.

WOW!

I invited him into the parish house to meet Father Dan. After introducing the men, I handed the check to Father. He was overwhelmed. The three of us talked for some time.

Father and I were suddenly more hopeful than we had been in a long time, all because of Archie Mull. His encouragement and belief in our cause energized us, providing a turbo blast to get the Armory opened.

I wanted to share the news with Mayor Hamel, who I thought was still on the fence concerning how he would vote on the Armory shelter. At that point, I remained unaware of his Channel 10 interview which had aired the night before. Maybe our good news of that morning would be enough to sway him. The donation could be the final touch in our appeal – one that Hamel couldn't resist pragmatically or in good conscience.

December 12, 1994:

Coincidentally, Hamel had called the St. Rose rectory from his office at Spanger Elementary School and left a message that he wanted to talk with me.

When I returned the call, I tried to set up a meeting. He said he didn't have the time and wanted to speak to me by phone.

I was still under the impression that he was of two minds about the Armory issue. I thought he was calling to see how much he could leverage his upcoming December 21st vote to get a better deal for the city. I then proceeded to tell him about Mull's twenty-five thousand dollars gift, which would enable St. Rose to take on the shelter program without any liability to the city; and the parish was ready to indemnify the city and guarantee the funding for the project.

Hamel stopped me and said that our group should go back to the County Supervisors with the twenty-five thousand dollars to see if it would change their minds.

At that point, I should have listened more and talked less. I would have heard what he was really saying: if there was going to be a shelter, the county would have to be the agency responsible for getting it operational, not the city.

Instead, I continued to tell the mayor about the two great options for the city – options that would be politically sound, enabling providers to manage the project with no obligation on the city's part. He patiently told me to go ahead with my thoughts. I said that under either scenario, we would throw in our usual parish support for the project, plus Archie's twenty-five thousand dollars.

I went on to explain the first possibility in detail: the City Council would ask to have the Armory opened and then turn the operation over to the 501c3 "Placer Community Care Center" corporation that Father Dan had in place for the shelter project. The 501c3 would handle all the interactions between Volunteers of America and the governmental agencies, including paying the bills, collecting contributions, supplying a licensed security guard to supplement police patrols and, most of all, providing appropriate insurance.

I also mentioned that I had been getting price quotes for the insurance with the help of Leo McFarland from VOA. All the city had to do was be the lead agency on paper and contribute the fifteen thousand dollars that had been budgeted the previous summer. We would do the rest.

The second option depended on whether or not St. Rose could be the lead agency under California law. The city manager was having city staff determine that as we spoke. If St. Rose could be the lead agency, the only part the city had to play was to contribute its fifteen thousand dollars for the operation. Hamel seemed more reserved than usual.

Then I threw out what I thought would be a carrot, something that would really entice him, and the neighborhood groups had been harping about for over four months. I told him I would make a major concession by supporting moving the meal site from St. Vincent's to a new permanent location as soon as one was available. Up to that point, I had insisted that the meals remain available at the Riverside location for local folks.

I thought that as Hamel cast his vote for opening the Armory, he could also announce that he had secured a deal that all of the St. Vincent's meals would be moved when a new location was found. He would be a hero. And that might be enough to make Slade, Bragg and their crew back off from their litigation plans.

Hamel was not a man given to chance. He remained noncommittal.

After I finished my spiel, I told him I would be meeting with Santucci at 1 p.m. to brief him on the same information. Hamel said he would take my comments under advisement.

I later came to understand that the intention of his call was to confirm that he had switched sides, hoping I had seen his Channel 10 interview. When he understood that I didn't know about his new position, it was probably more than he could do to admit that he had caved in to Crabb and Gamar.

There had been several cold nights during the first part of December, with temperatures hovering around freezing. I was determined to give the folks who were forced into the winter weather some protective shelter, a place where they could rest and get a good night's sleep.

When I mentioned the Hamel news clip to Sherry Schiele, she said she hadn't seen it and immediately suggested that we should make contingency plans. Schiele, Father Dan, Dave Sorensen and I developed a strategy for moving forward.

The four of us did a lot of soul-searching and made some calculations, both political and monetary. We had to prepare for the worst and determine when and how we would make our move after the

Council vote, if needed. Fueled by Archie Mull's twenty-five thousand dollars, we decided we could accomplish our goal.

Throughout northern California, the public's interest in the Roseville shelter issue continued to run high. The buzz from the Channel 10 story was still in the air when the *Press Tribune* and the *Bee* ran several articles, and Channel 3 did a lengthy human interest piece. The *Bee* pointed out that St. Rose Church was ready to take full responsibility for the Armory's operation if the city or the county would just get permission to open the facility. The paper got it right when it said that we were ready to sign any contracts, provide any staff and collect the funding for operation of the shelter.

Both papers urged the city to make the Armory available as a homeless shelter.

December 13, 1994:

The *Press Tribune* had a triple header – three items on the shelter issue.

In a front-page piece, the paper detailed the state's procedure for opening an armory as shelter. According to the state's military department, only cities and counties were allowed to apply for an operating license. That did not preclude the licensee from contracting with an operator like St. Rose to operate and indemnify the licensee from any liability or harm.

In an opinion piece entitled "'Good will toward men at stake" the *Press Tribune* editorialized in favor of having the Armory opened on humanitarian grounds. "Many of these people, (who are homeless) due to an assortment of problems such as alcoholism or mental illness, are incapable of taking good care of themselves. Although it is easy to disregard those who have no home, it will not be easy for our public officials to ignore constituents who feel inaction in this matter borders on irresponsibility and a lack of humanity."

In an accompanying news article, Councilman Crabb reaffirmed his strong opposition to providing shelter in Roseville. "'People in Sacramento are even saying that they can handle it. So why are we even bothering...'" Merry Christmas!

December 19, 1994:

In the spirit of the season, the providers and church stakeholders were prepared to reach an agreement with the Cherry Glen and Thieles groups that would entice them to back the Armory shelter.

Unfortunately and unbeknown to us, the Homeless Forum meeting for that night was canceled at the last minute.

December 20, 1994:

A *KCRA* Channel 3 news crew showed up at St. Vincent's to ask several of the folks waiting for the noon meal how they felt about the Armory being opened. A guest, Juan Lara, volunteered in broken English, "I'm happy when the Armory is open. It is cold! The Armory is warm. The food is good…"

December 21, 1994:

The Council meeting was an eye-opener for me. Mel Hamel was not any more interested in the carrot I offered than the neighborhood and merchant groups were. In my blind optimism, I had underestimated their new power. With the support of Crabb, Gamar and the police chief, their strategy was to close the St. Vincent's Riverside-Bonita location without providing an alternate site. The Homeless Forum meetings had become their platform from which they employed inflammatory rhetoric to ratchet up their political clout. They had the momentum.

The environment was hostile. Our hopes for a new comprehensive shelter program in Roseville were doomed. The opposing coalition would make it impossible for us.

Hamel justified his vote against the Armory shelter on the grounds that it was inappropriate for the city to be the lead agency (to contract with the State Military Department by signing the operating license). He said that liability for the operation was something the city should not expose itself to. He told the *Press Tribune*, "If the city has to be the lead agency, then whatever happens at the armory, we're responsible." Hamel, just like County Supervisor Ron Lichau, had found a way to wash his hands of the whole issue.

Ray Mertz was right on the money with his assessment of Hamel's position.

When Hamel had done the political calculus, he found that with Santucci leaving the Council for the Board of Supervisors, he would be at a severe disadvantage for the remainder of his term – unless he aligned himself with Crabb and Gamar. He did not want to be caught between those two on one side and Pauline Roccucci, our now Lone Ranger, on the other.

Plus, the Council members would be selecting someone to take

Santucci's seat after the first of the year. Hamel needed to be on the side that ultimately chose that person. He had to be part of the new majority.

The Council vote was three to two not to consider our request to be the lead agency. Hamel, Crabb and Gamar were in the majority with Roccucci and Santucci in the minority. The Council destroyed the delicate bridge of trust that had been built between the religious community and the city.

December 22, 1994:

The Council's "no" vote broke the city's agreement with the ministers and churches. We announced a three-pronged emergency shelter project to help homeless persons wherever they came from:

1. St. Rose funded a motel voucher program and gave out free pup tents through the St. Vincent's Office on Riverside. Each tent was stenciled with a large label reading "Roseville Homeless Project" and was numbered sequentially;
2. St. Rose leased a van to provide free rides daily to Sacramento's Loaves & Fishes, where homeless folks could get a lift to the shelter at Cal Expo; and
3. Home Start would begin a shelter program on January 5th, offering overnight accommodations for families and singles for the rest of the winter.

Funding for the winter the program came from two sources. The first was from the Community Services Planning Council that had set aside twenty-four thousand dollars in FEMA money for Volunteers of America of Sacramento for operating the Placer County Armory shelter.

When VOA discovered that the Armory project had been nixed, VOA's CEO, Leo McFarland, worked with Schiele to redirect the funds to Home Start.

The second source was the St. Rose winter shelter fund, which had nearly forty thousand dollars, including the twenty-five thousand dollars donated by Archie Mull. These funds were distributed mainly through Home Start and St. Vincent's. St. Rose provided some aid to the Salvation Army when the city balked at reimbursing the Army for vouchers issued to help Roseville homeless individuals.

Once the scope of the city's nasty plan to end any aid to homeless single adults became apparent, Schiele and I began collecting evidence for a federal civil rights complaint against Roseville for violations of the Fair Housing Act.

"I'm happy when the Armory Is open…"

The Act, since its inception in 1968, has prohibited denying housing and shelter to any person by most private entities and by government agencies when the denial is based on the person's race, color, religion, gender (homeless single men, for example), or national origin. The law

ROSEVILLE EMERGENCY SHELTER PROJECT

1. Overnight Housing
Shelter at Home Start, 410 Riverside
Apply 10:00 am - 4:00 pm Daily
I.D. Required

2. Free Pup Tents at
St. Vincent de Paul, 139 Riverside
Report for 3 days to St. Vincent de Paul
And on 3rd Day Get a Free Tent
Photo Required on 1st Day
I.D. Required
Closed Sunday

Warning: In Roseville City Limits, it is illegal to camp on private property without owner's permission and on any public property.

Emergency Shelter Project Flyer, January to March 1995
Boudier Collection

has its foundation in the Fourteenth Amendment, which guarantees everyone equal protection under the law and freedom from discrimination.

December 23, 1994:

The first tragedy that could be attributable to the Armory closure occurred. The *Auburn Journal* – not its sister paper, the *Roseville Press Tribune* – reported that the nude body of a Hispanic man was found on the bank of Dry Creek in Roseville. The corpse was later identified as being that of the homeless man, Juan Lara, who had been interviewed about the Armory by KCRA TV at St. Vincent's.

His death might have been avoided if the Armory shelter had been operational. There was no doubt in my mind that some of the responsibility for the homicide rested with Roseville's City Council and the Placer County Board of Supervisors. The failure of Roseville to even lift a finger to open the Armory was seen in Sacramento as heartless, crass and mean:

- The *Sacramento Bee* reported that Sacramento officials understood the implications of the Roseville City Council vote: a calculated return by the Placer County establishment to its old ways, dumping its homeless population on Sacramento for shelter.
- Sacramento City Manager Bill Edgar said that Roseville's decision was unfortunate and would worsen the strained relationship over the homeless issue between the two communities;
- Loaves and Fishes Executive Director LeRoy Chatfield called Roseville's nixing of the Armory shelter program horrible, especially given the season of the year and the story of the homeless Christ Child; and
- Sacramento Mayor Joe Serna put a whimsical twist on the whole issue, noting "let's just say that in the end, Santa knows who's naughty and who's nice." What goes around comes around.

I had recorded the Roseville Council meeting on video at home, giving me a chance on a bad night for TV to review the antics. I was impressed at how comfortable Pauline Roccucci seemed just being a conscientious voice on the Council – no political games. Conversely, I found it fascinating to observe Crabb and Gamar seated next to one another as the group discussed the Armory issue.

The two took very different approaches to obtain the same end – obstructing any move to provide aid to homeless single men and women. Each had a different political style.

Crabb was direct and visibly upset, blurting out opposition to the idea. He glowered as he repeatedly said he would only vote for a program that took in Roseville residents. All others should be turned away.

He told the audience his position had not changed from the very beginning. "I've been opposed to it before, and I continue to be opposed to it," he said. "Roseville should not be a haven for transients…I'm not going to support transients in Roseville."

Gamar came across as emotionally tormented by the prospect of having to vote against the motion to be the lead agency. She gripped a hankie tightly in one hand and explained to both the TV audience and the audience in the chamber that "This is the hardest thing I've ever had to do." She said it over and over again and was sure to add that Roseville was a place that cared about others, stating, "We are a compassionate community."

It looked like she was ready to shed a tear. But none flowed. There was no need for the hankie.

After the vote to dump the Armory, Gamar made an effort to demonstrate that at some level she really did care about people being out in the freezing night without shelter. She suggested a voucher system. The city could offer vouchers to some of the folks by using the money that was set aside for the winter shelter.

The video showed that Harry Crabb, who was sitting right beside Gamar on the dais, reacted to her suggestion by immediately turning toward her. Like an old uncle, he scowled at her and, with almost a conditioned reaction of alarm, exclaimed that nonresidents might get vouchers by mistake!

Crabb quizzed her. "Is this voucher program to support everybody, transients and the homeless?" The implication was, how would the city keep undeserving outsiders from getting something for nothing? Gamar stared back at Crabb with a befuddled look on her face like a startled rabbit caught in the glare of headlights, not knowing which way to go.

After she uttered a confused reply, Crabb pronounced he would vote against anything that allowed unwanted outsiders to get help. "I guess I need to know then what kind of people we are going to give the vouchers to. I can support a voucher program, but not for particularly transients…It seems like we are defeating the purpose if we all of a sudden give them a voucher to stay in a hotel…I think our goal was to move the transients out of the community."

Gamar took another stab at clarifying her position. And when she realized she still failed to meet Crabb's expectations, she withdrew her motion.

At that point, Council member Pauline Roccucci jumped in, hoping to develop a positive consensus for a voucher program. She offered a motion that the hotel voucher program be considered as a means of offering aid to the homeless and that staff bring back recommendations to the next meeting.

Santucci seconded the motion.

When it came time to vote, Crabb uttered a simple but definite "No – because you included transients." He was the only dissenting member.

In the end, that meeting of the Council members did nothing of substance to remedy the shelter problem. They certainly did not succeed at getting the heat off the city.

After the meeting, everybody was so confused about what the Council decided that City Manager Al Johnson had to unravel it for the newspapers. He told the *Press Tribune,* "You have to look at what the council actually did. They ensured families would not go without shelter and they supported our residents. The action was against the transients."

When I saw that in print, I understood why the residents and business owners had canceled the last forum meeting. They were "in the know," that the vote was going to go their way. They had no reason to compromise.

Chapter 12:
"Scrooge found in Placer County!"*
(Dec. 29, 1994–Apr. 6, 1995)
*paraphrasing *The Sacramento Bee*

December 29, 1994:

A *Sacramento Bee* editorial chided both the Placer County Board of Supervisors and the Roseville City Council for being more like Scrooge than the Magi during the Christmas season. The paper urged City Council to think about the implications of its decision and suggested that a new vote be taken to open the Armory.

Then the Sacramento Housing Alliance bestowed an unexpected honor of dubious distinction on the Roseville City Council – its "Scrooge Award."

Roseville Councilman Harry Crabb responded, "I think, as usual, people who come up with those brainstorms don't understand the local situation. They just kind of shoot off their mouths."

Bishop William Weigand of the Sacramento Catholic Diocese shared his sentiments in a letter to Mayor Hamel, asking the Council to reconsider its decision. The Salvation Army, St. Rose Church and the First United Methodist Church joined in, petitioning the city to rehear the item. The Armory matter was again placed on the Council agenda.

The shelter issue was not going away. In fact, it just heated up. City operatives were caught off-guard when they discovered we were giving homeless men and women free pup tents. They quickly claimed that we were encouraging them break Roseville's anti-camping ordinance. City Manager Al Johnson's frustration was evident in his comment to the *Press Tribune* when he emphatically proclaimed, "Tents cannot go up in public property in order to help control camps being set up. That includes the creek beds and parks."

January 1995:

According to a City Hall insider, the US Department of Housing and Urban Affairs (HUD) would soon be on the city's back, probing into what was happening in Roseville. My source told me a representative from the agency had visited John Sprague and Al Johnson with concerns about the housing issue (i.e. "the shelter hubbub").

Locals remained split on whether shelter should be given to homeless single adults. Vernon Street business owner Doreen Giles seemed to speak for those in town who were delighted by the city's hard line against anyone who looked like a transient. The *Bee* quoted her as saying, "I've seen a very significant decrease in the number of transients since the Armory has not opened. There is no panhandling or harassing."

Folks like Giles thought "With no Armory shelter, there are fewer transients." They all seemed to have trouble connecting the dots. What they missed was the effectiveness of our three-prong emergency initiative launched December 22nd. We had moved the homeless men and women off of the streets and into our own shelter program, many of them into facilities at Home Start, just a few blocks away.

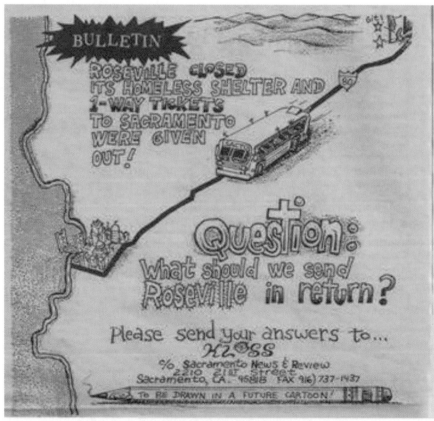

Sacramento News & Review, January 5, 1995
Courtesy of John Kloss

"Scrooge found in Placer County!"

January 3, 1995:

Bill Santucci was sworn in as a member of the Board of Supervisors. One of his first behind-the-scenes moves was to try to persuade the Board to vote again on the Armory opening.

For the matter to be taken up again, one of the three supervisors who voted to dodge the Armory issue would have to introduce a motion to reconsider the question. Ozenick had been put out to pasture, and neither Uhler nor Lichau was interested. The shelter question was dead at the county level.

January 4, 1995:

We finally had the opportunity to ask the Roseville City Council to reverse its vote. Our last hope to get the Armory shelter going had arrived.

During the hearing, Bill Hamilton, the retired commander of the Roseville Armory spoke again against opening the Armory to homeless people. When he took the podium, he went on a tear, claiming that having "those people" in the Armory created a "myriad of problems concerning health, sanitation, safety, security, morale and welfare" for the National Guard troops.

I felt sorry for him. His claims were accusations from out of the blue, made by an emotionally shaken man to a sympathetic Council.

For the Council to legally reconsider its vote, the same parliamentary procedure as at the county level applied: One of the three members who voted not to open the Armory would have to introduce a motion to reconsider, either Gamar, Crabb or Hamel.

There were just three Council members at the meeting: Roccucci, Crabb and Hamel. Santucci's seat had been vacated when he stepped up to the Board of Supervisors, and Gamar was absent. Pauline Roccucci's hands were tied by parliamentary procedure. That left only Crabb and Hamel who could reintroduce the matter. Those two had made up their minds long before the meeting and were certain not to budge. Reconsideration was a dead issue.

Before the Council members could proceed on to the next agenda item, Crabb and Hamel wanted to make statements for the record. Crabb capped his refusal to reconsider the Armory question with this observation: "I'm once again taken by some comments that are continually being made...that we have our own agenda at the City Council. We don't have our own agenda...I will not help transients coming through the city..."

Mayor Hamel then related a story that he must have thought justified his position: ("I had)...a personal experience again a couple of years ago, a family enrolled at (Spanger) school was living at the Home Start program, and when I walked them out the door, they were driving a car with a New York license plate. I asked in my mind, wondered, if there is such a demand for problems (sic) in Roseville, why are we taking in people from New York? I don't know how that happens."

This was followed with another statement from Crabb reinforcing the Council's decision about the Armory: "I checked with the police again today...there are fewer problems and fewer transients in our community now, than we had prior to the December meeting and the decision not to open the Armory."

Betty Melligan of Willow Avenue backed up Crabb: "I can count on one hand the amounts (sic) of transients I've seen come into the neighborhood. It's nice to know I can empty my trash without being frightened."

Hamel then announced that the Council would move on to the next item on the Council agenda. But before the Council did so, a voice from the far end of the dais that couldn't be ignored said, "Mel!" Hamel noticed that Pauline Roccucci had something to add. Roccucci made sure that those watching the action in the Council chambers and on TV knew that this was not the end of the homeless discussion.

Roccucci said she had talked with city staff leadership before the meeting to assure that the city would continue to work on "a greater solution with the churches" to the homeless problem, one "that we can all live with...This isn't something that is going to go away...We need to deal with it squarely. We will continue to work with the nonprofit groups in that respect."

Then, she referenced her December motion, calling for a humane and inclusive emergency shelter voucher program, trying to ensure that no city official had closed the door to helping all who needed shelter during the winter: "My motion at that meeting was that we would make sure that no one has to go cold – has to freeze during the winter."

Compassion and courage are wonderful qualities.

January 5, 1995:
Even though we had no idea when the neighbors would spring their law suit offensive, St. Vincent's president Elaine Willoughby told me she had asked attorney John Haluck for advice as to how we should proceed in response to the threat of legal action. I wondered who at

City Hall was in charge of guiding the neighbors' ship.

After several sessions of the Homeless Forum over a five month period, the meeting chatter came to a screeching halt. The tenor of the relationship of the Council and the neighborhood group leaders with us became so strained that communications had abruptly snapped – broken off. The stated goal of reaching a community consensus on how to address homelessness seemed all the more elusive.

As sobering as the times were, Father Dan reassured me that our efforts to nail down a site for the shelter would continue. We didn't have to wait for the Homeless Forum to complete a plan and endorse a site. Bottom line, we didn't believe that the city and neighborhood groups had any intention of letting the job get done. We kept our noses to the ground, hoping to find the right location for the shelter.

My son Paul, who was now a realtor with Coker Ewing Real Estate, put together a portfolio of industrial locations that might be possible candidates for a shelter. Father Dan and I examined the fifty-page list. Those in the Sunset Industrial Park were too far away from the core area of town, and one on Washington and another on Church Street were adjacent to residential neighborhoods.

A third location on Derek Place was right on top of the busy Southern Pacific's north-south mainline. When we checked it out, we found that the rumbling of the passing freights suffocated the sounds of every living thing and shook the ground. It was not a good spot for a shelter.

We did find one parcel that might work. It was located on the northwest corner of Viking Place and PFE Road, just to the west of the city corporation yard and outside of the city limits.

While the shelter issue remained unresolved, solid progress was being made on another front. Sherry Schiele, with St. Vincent's blessing, incorporated "Roseville Home Start, Inc." on January 5, 1995.

Her new Board of Directors consisted of Wayne Terrell as President, Wanda Bourgeouis-Phillips as Vice President, Rev. Paul Carlson as Treasurer and Rexine Brewer as Secretary, with Steve Hargadon and Rev. Freddie Simpkins as additional Board members. St. Vincent's president, Elaine Willoughby, volunteered as a consultant to the new Board.

Schiele began making the organization ready to provide emergency shelter for homeless singles and families immediately following the Council's negative December vote. It was part of her larger plan developed to make Home Start an independent entity, separate from St.

Vincent's.

During the previous couple of years, there had been a growing acrimony on the St. Vincent's Board of Directors between Schiele and the volunteer chairpersons of the Food Locker and the Dining Room, who claimed that Home Start was taking more than its fair share of financial resources. In fact, they expressed fear that Home Start might bring the entire organization to financial ruin. The other members of St. Vincent's Board had put up with all the flack that they could handle, while Schiele chomped at the bit to go independent.

Even though Schiele seemed to accomplish the split quickly, she had also carefully timed it to make Home Start independent not only of St. Vincent's, but also of the 1992 city agreement which contained a restriction that kept Home Start from housing homeless single adults. The city had forced St. Vincent's to sign the two-year agreement before it would shift nearly three hundred thousand dollars in state and federal grants to the organization for Home Start's use. The transfer took effect on January 3, 1993.

That twenty-four month restriction didn't apply to the new incorporated Home Start:

- It was St. Vincent's Home Start, not Roseville Home Start, Inc., that the agreement applied to;
- The grant money had been totally expended; and
- The two year agreement had taken effect when the city transferred the money to St. Vincent's two years and two days prior to Schiele incorporating Roseville Home Start, Inc. on January 5, 1995.

An independent Home Start had been freed of the restrictions that had been heaped on the back of St. Vincent's by the City Council.

January 6, 1995:

Those of us managing the emergency shelter program realized that offering free van rides to Sacramento was a flop. During the first fifteen days of operation, there were only nine riders. On that note, Father Dan, Sherry Schiele, Dave Sorensen of St. Vincent's and yours truly decided to drop the service.

In an informal poll of homeless men in Roseville about why the shuttle was not successful, they cited two factors:

1. They came into town on the rails and wanted to go out on the rails. The trains out of Roseville were easy to hop, and there were more departures from Roseville than from Sacramento.

2.More importantly, the men found that Sacramento was too violent. If they had to make a choice between sleeping outside in Roseville or going to a big city shelter in Sacramento, they would choose Roseville.

The next project on the providers' list was to get the City Council's emergency shelter voucher system going. John Sprague, Pastor Jerry Angove, Jim Durel, Dave Sorensen and I met to develop a plan and policy the Council would accept. We worked out a deal that Sprague said might fly. The agreement called for the fifteen thousand dollars that had been allocated in the city budget for the Armory to fund the voucher program. The city's money would be used on a matching basis, meaning every dollar expended by local charities would be matched by a dollar from the city.

The proposal would help homeless families, irrespective of residency, but Roseville residents would have priority. Homeless singles and couples who could prove they had lived in Roseville immediately before becoming homeless would also qualify for the plan. Nonresident singles or couples would not be accepted for the voucher plan under any circumstances. We all agreed that Sprague would present our idea to the Council.

January 18, 1995:

From the time Santucci left the Council to become a member of the Placer County Board of Supervisors, the *Press Tribune* had reported on the considerable controversy about his successor.

The debate centered on whether a Council majority should force the selection of someone with similar political stripes to their own, or act more democratically, seating the person who received the next highest number of votes after Gamar and Crabb in the 1993 election, Joe Tadlock, who just missed the cut.

Community members who pushed for the former idea were the supporters of Crabb and Gamar from the Cherry Glen and Thieles neighborhood associations. Those who supported Tadlock were from the churches and service provider community.

As to how the balance of Roseville's population felt about the issue, no one seemed to care one way or the other. They just soaked up the drama.

The way it all played out, as documented by the *Press Tribune*, reinforced my hunch that a new power center had developed on the Council, and that the Council's selection process was just for show – a lot of ballyhoo. The Council members had their positions staked out long before the public discussion began that evening.

When it came down to the decision on who to select, all four members concurred that the slot should not be given to Tadlock. They then proceeded to nominate their own candidates. Roccucci and Hamel backed Jim Gray, a veteran of local government and a seasoned observer of Roseville politics. Crabb and Gamar favored Planning Commissioner Randolph Graham.

When the vote was taken, there was a 2–2 Council impasse on the appointment, with the members disagreeing on which of their friends should get the seat. The outcome seemed to set Mayor Hamel back on his heels, even though he realized he had Roccucci's continued backing for Gray.

Hamel must have known that neither Crabb, once he made up his mind, nor Gamar, once she stated her position, would change.

The mayor was supposedly in charge, but when it came time for the second vote, it looked like he waffled, leaving Roccucci to fend for herself. His stated rationale was the Council needed to move on and not rehash the same issue two weeks later for a third vote. It was my impression that he had given in too easily, allowing his integrity to be hijacked. When Roccucci realized she would be the lone holdout against Graham, she joined the other three to make Graham's selection unanimous.

At that point, there was no doubt who would control the Council until the next election. With Graham at their side, Gamar and Crabb were clearly in charge. They didn't need Hamel; but Hamel needed them. Our Cherry Glen and Thieles adversaries were as pleased as punch. They were assured of a warm embrace by four of the five Council members and by those on the city staff anxious to advance their civil service careers.

Following their triumph, Gamar and Crabb, with Hamel on the line, dove into the other controversial item on the agenda: the homeless voucher proposal that we had designed with city staffer John Sprague. The three proceeded to dismantle the program and then to layer its remains with a hideous list of restrictions that any homeless person would be challenged to overcome. They had twisted the voucher plan into a hobophobic tool to effectively deny shelter to almost everyone. At the same time, they managed to create just enough cover for their failure to open the Armory and to give the appearance that the city had taken a decent shot at providing emergency shelter.

"Scrooge found in Placer County!"

I was ashamed to have had anything to do with the mean-spirited revisions. Despite months of bad publicity that Roseville had been hammered with, the Council majority remained intransigent in its opposition to any kind of winter shelter for outsiders.

Pauline Roccucci responded to their tactics by coming out strongly in favor of helping everyone: "I want to make it clear that when I made the motion in December to look into a voucher program, it was with the intent to keep all the homeless out of the cold."

Crabb immediately countered Roccucci: "We need to shelter our homeless, but I continue to have a problem with nonresidents." Roccucci caved in when it came down to vote, resulting in four to zero in favor of a program that excluded almost all aid to nonresident homeless families, as well as to all singles.

The program's guidelines were so restrictive and mean-spirited that based on principle, St. Rose Church, St. Vincent's and Home Start opted out of participating. Only the Salvation Army agreed to administer the voucher system on the city's terms. The guidelines made the city look cheap and stingy.

I sensed that from that time forward, a hostile reaction from the Council was a certainty whenever a new homeless service initiative was proposed. Irrespective of the spadework that would go into designing it, the governing majority would forthwith scrap the proposal, even if it had been created by consensus.

I found that over the previous few months, the Council had flipped one hundred and eighty degrees, prohibiting spending any city shelter funds on anyone, child or adult, who could not prove Roseville residency to the Council majority's satisfaction. The swiftness with which Crabb, Gamar and Hamel had dispatched our voucher recommendation to the junk heap seemed almost spiteful, in our face, and definitely intended to show us who was boss.

January 30, 1995:
St. Vincent's volunteer Dave Sorensen let me know he had received the green light from the operations folks at Southern Pacific to offer us the eight trainmen's housing modular units for a total cost of eight hundred dollars. The next step was to get the deal approved by Southern Pacific's legal department.

February 1, 1995:
Archie Mull and Father Dan Madigan asked Father Mike Cormack,

Father Dan Casey and me to meet them for lunch at Fat City in Old Sacramento. I had met with Mull shortly after New Year's to share my son Paul's list of possible sites, showing how slim the pickings were.

When Mull told Madigan about our situation, it appears that they decided it was time to intervene with their own plan. After we sat down around our table, Madigan led off saying that he had a building he would like to donate and would have Norm Montgomery's house moving company bring it up to us from Del Paso Heights. Then, Mull said he was prepared to front up to seventy-five thousand dollars to secure the land as soon as we found the spot for the building.

What a change! One day, we had nothing to work with. Two days later, we had financial backing to purchase a location and two different options for buildings.

February 2, 1995:

I met with County Supervisor Bill Santucci to discuss how to go about acquiring a sixty-nine thousand one hundred twenty square foot portion of the Viking Place property for a shelter.

I had first talked with the owner, Mike Besoyan, in early January when I was going over our list of sites. He had used the property for his construction business, but was experiencing tough times during the building slump in 1994–95. In fact, his property was under Chapter 11 bankruptcy protection. Besoyan was desperately trying to market his entire site, including an office, a warehouse and a parcel of raw land fronting PFE Road. We were only interested in the land.

Santucci and I discussed the obstacles we would have to overcome to close this deal: the bankruptcy court issue and how to work with the lender, Sacramento Mercantile Bank, who had a Small Business Association (SBA) guarantee on the loan.

What this meant was that even if Besoyan accepted our offer, we would still have to convince the court and the bank to release the portion of the property we wanted.

I suggested that it was time to get Father Dan in the room with us so we could decide on how to proceed.

February 3, 1995:

Santucci volunteered to contact Fred Yeager, Placer County Planning Director to determine how to split the lot and to ask if we needed an administrative permit to operate a shelter. He told Father Dan and me that he also wanted to get City Manager Al Johnson on board to determine what was needed to extend city sewer and water to the property.

February 26, 1995:

The harsh terms of the city's homeless voucher plan didn't escape the notice of the *Press Tribune*. The paper led with a front-page piece and banner headline "Voucher plan fizzles over proof of residency." The article provided examples of actual Salvation Army cases demonstrating how the Roseville City Council micromanaged the program, monitoring each application for aid and ultimately denying help to otherwise qualified Roseville residents. For example, the Council would not accept a driver's license, letters of testimony from an applicant's relatives or pastor, or even documentation from the Salvation Army's files as reasonable proof of residency.

February 28, 1995:

The paper editorialized that the Council might want to reconsider the program's tough rules: "The council wanted to show its compassionate side, but it may have established too many hoops for some area residents to jump through."

Sherry Schiele was more direct in her criticism of the program. She told the *Sacramento Bee Neighbors,* "It was a joke. Even the priests at St. Rose (Catholic Church) couldn't qualify; they didn't have rent receipts."

The program was just like the old Police Department Benevolent Fund from the '80s. The money was only to help homeless families. The only catch was it was impossible to pry it out of the city's hands.

Even Cherry Glen transient activities watchdog, Doug Selby, told the Council, "I just wanted to encourage the council to get the bugs out of the voucher system."

Unfortunately, but not unexpectedly, the Council majority dug their heels in with no changes forthcoming, leaving city staff with the job of papering over the mean-spirited policies in the voucher plan.

Part of the repair job was a staff-prepared editorial to be run in the *Press Tribune* extolling what the city called "the voucher plan's fairness." Before asking the paper to print it, city bureaucrats had the nerve to ask the president of Roseville Ministerial Association for permission to use the Association's name as an endorsement of the editorial. I immediately let the Association know it was being misled by the city in an attempt to justify its ruthless tactics. The ministers' group declined to endorse the editorial. Instead, John Sprague had to strong-arm a self-serving endorsement out of the Salvation Army for the newspaper piece.

The homeless voucher program administered by the Salvation Army that winter managed to help only twenty-two local households with rent and utilities.

City government ironically became the program's biggest beneficiary because of its ownership of the municipal electric, water, sewer and garbage utilities. It was a tidy mechanism to collect past-due amounts on a few of the city's most delinquent accounts, meaning that a good portion of funds released by the city to the Salvation Army to pay for past-due utilities came back to the city when these bills were paid. In effect, the city not only recouped its money, but also indirectly took funds from the Salvation Army, because the charity was required to use its donors' contributions to match the city's portion, dollar for dollar.

March 1995:
Kevin Daley and Ken Jaros joined the Home Start Board of Directors.

March 7, 1995:
Father Dan Casey and I committed to taking the Southern Pacific modular buildings in a letter to D.J. Seil, Southern Pacific's Roseville Division Superintendent.

March 8, 1995:
Several supporters of the city's tough anti-shelter policy went before the Council to attest to its positive effects. Doug Selby of Clinton Avenue told the Council that the transient situation had improved: "Every year when the Armory is in effect, the transient population in the downtown and the parks is up – noticeably up. This year without the Armory being open, the transient population in town has been down."

Selby went on to say "(Homeless) children are innocent victims of adults' discretions (sic) whether it being monetarily or drugs, and the Armory was patronized by all types of people of unknown repute."

Sally Bragg, chairperson of the Cherry Glen Beautification Committee, was effusive in her praise of the Council members for attending her meetings and for their support of the association's effort to rid their neighborhood of transients. She reserved special praise for the police department's good work.

The locals remained convinced that their quality of life had been enhanced with enforcement of the new anti-homeless policy. It was hard to believe none of them realized that a new shelter had operated since early January (and without any major incident) at Home Start, right in the heart of the Thieles/Cherry Glen area. In fact, on many early mornings, I saw Betty Melligan taking her stroll with her walking partner on Riverside Avenue, passing immediately across the street from where these homeless men and women were being housed at that very moment.

How could the Council, Chief Simms and our other adversaries have been so clueless? What Home Start had been doing was no secret. There was lots of evidence floating around town about the project:

1. We had printed and distributed fliers announcing the new Home Start Overnight Housing initiative for anyone needing it. The only requirement was an I.D; and

2. Simms' own officers utilized Home Start when they came across homeless individuals who needed a place to stay. Officers delivered them to Home Start's front door on a regular basis.

March 10, 1995:

Archie Mull formally offered to purchase Besoyan's property on our behalf for seventy-five thousand dollars cash.

Mull's contribution would be the down payment on the total cost of relocating and rehabbing the modular buildings, as well as paying for site improvements, utility installation and other start-up costs.

It was all a long shot, but it was the only shot we had. Besoyan was open to the offer. Now all we had to do was get the court and the bank to release the property.

March 12, 1995:

After Sunday Mass, Phil Kister, a member of the Roseville Grants Advisory Commission and a reliable source of information, told me that the word was out that the city was going to call a halt to the Homeless Forum process. He said the matter had been discussed when the Commission members recently met.

I had hoped that the authorities would at least continue to encourage the Forum discussions. But it looked like city officials felt that the Homeless Forum had served its intended purpose, and it was time to cut their ties to the entire process, walking away with three major victories in their pocket:

1. The implicit agreement our committee had with the Council that it would select a site for a shelter facility had been trashed;
2. The heat over the closure of the annual Armory shelter program had been safely dissipated; and
3. Our homeless shelter committee report, which had proposed the construction of a facility, was dead, and the Placer Community Care Center, the non profit corporation which Father Dan had set up in 1994 to run the operation, was put back on the shelf.

When the rumor that the Forum had died became fact, Forum process facilitator Steve Barber quickly offered to revive it by continuing to provide his services. He said he had a plan to help residents and businesspeople resolve their differences with the providers. His offer was music to my ears. Whether intended or not, Barber's move blocked the city's attempt to sneak out the back door. The providers quickly agreed to continue talks.

March 15, 1995:

The Roseville Grants Commission's nondiscrimination policy was officially outlined: "The Roseville Grants Commission does not contribute to organizations that discriminate on the basis of race, religion, national origin, ancestry, physical or mental disability, Veteran status, medical condition, marital status, age, sex, or sexual orientation."

The Roseville Emergency Shelter Project operated by the St. Rose, St. Vincent's and Home Start coalition closed as planned. Our report to the community documented that:

• Just seven hundred one person shelter days of emergency housing were provided to three hundred twenty single males and one hundred twenty-eight single females through Home Start;
• Two hundred eighty-five shelter days of rent assistance and motel vouchers had been provided by St. Vincent's;
• One hundred forty-three men and women received pup tents and sleeping bags; and
• Fifty-three individuals were helped with transportation.

March 22, 1995:

The City Council appointed Doug Selby to the planning commission, taking Graham's old spot.

March 30, 1995:

The deadline for submitting offers on a piece of surplus Caltrans property that I thought was a good candidate for a shelter site had arrived. The two plus acre parcel was located on Taylor Road just beyond the Highway 65 overpass at the north edge of the city limits, complete with easy access to public sewer and water. It was an out of the way location and probably could be had at a reasonable price. The minimum bid was one hundred seventy thousand dollars, with credit terms at ten and one half percent. But, as *Bee* reporter Art Campos said, "The (Roseville) City Council indicated...it isn't interested in the idea..." No bids were received.

April 6, 1995:

Homeless Forum facilitator Steve Barber sat down with representatives from all the stakeholder groups to work out the ground rules for resuming the Forum process, including who the representatives of each group would be:

- City: John Sprague and Robyn Graham (the wife of Council Appointee Randy Graham)
- Residents: Sally Bragg and Planning Commissioner Selby
- Merchants: Sylvia Slade and Dave Kelly
- Providers: Rev. Jerry Angove and Herb Whitaker from Legal Services of Northern California.

From the get-go, the deck was stacked against us. Our provider representatives were outgunned by a margin of six to two. At the same time, I believe that the Council majority remained determined to put as much distance as possible between them and anything resembling a compromise on its hobophobic stand against homeless single men.

The meeting resulted in these format changes:

- Only the eight delegates would meet with Barber in a step-by-step series of meetings to resolve the shelter issue.
- In turn, the delegates would take the decisions back to their respective groups for an okay on that portion of the plan.
- The providers were charged with preparing a "straw design" document that would bring together agreed-to concepts from general discussions and meetings. The straw design would include recommendations for a facility location and layout. It would also incorporate policies covering what services should be

available, where transient meal programs should be located, how they should be administered and funded, and what the standards of accountability to the community would be.

- The process involving all stakeholders would be restarted by introducing the straw design to the individual stakeholder groups, supposedly giving all common ground to further refine a solution.

- Following each stakeholder group's input, a general meeting would be held where the design could be modified. At the general meeting, the various stakeholders could come to a final consensus on the blueprint for a facility.

Though Roseville's homeless issue had been front-page news for the *Press Tribune* and had interested patrons of the *Sacramento Bee* and Sacramento television stations for years, it was only of real concern to a small base of locals. Neighbors and merchants around St. Vincent's, the providers, ministers, political insiders and a group of bureaucrats all stayed laser-focused on it. But, too bad for an embarrassed Roseville business community: The unresolved problem stuck to the city's reputation like fresh pine sap to a white shirt.

As for neighborhood and merchant representatives Sally Bragg and Sylvia Slade, it looked like they had placed themselves as the only contacts between their members and the larger Forum group. They were the lone voice and ears of their constituents. All communication was channeled through them. For those they represented, their word must have seemed like the gospel truth.

Chapter 13:
The City's Rush to Crush Home Start
(Apr. 11, 1995–May 19, 1996)

April 11, 1995:

Alarm bells went off at City Hall when City Manager Al Johnson reported that Home Start was housing homeless single adults overnight. Newly appointed Council member Randy Graham had relayed the news to Johnson after being alerted by Thieles neighborhood resident Kristi Kinzel.

It was true. Following the March 15th closure of the Roseville Emergency Shelter Project, Home Start continued to house single adults in both an overnight shelter operation and a new transitional living program that Schiele had developed over the winter. Those in the transitional program were being kept on until they were ready to enter independent living.

Whether or not homeless singles were being sheltered in April, it was hard to believe that it rated as news or would shock anyone. Home Start had very publicly provided shelter for singles for the previous three months. But when Crabb, Gamar and Hamel were informed, they felt they had been tricked and immediately retaliated. This was despite the fact that the grant agreement signed in 1992 by St. Vincent's had expired, and Home Start had become an independent agency.

The resulting city guerilla tactics were orchestrated through Johnson's office by the City Council itself. In one of the first moves against Home Start, Council members directed the planning, building, fire and housing departments to bring the full force of their resources against Home Start. Inspectors showed up at the facility with ever-increasing frequency to cite building and other code violations that had been overlooked in the past.

City Housing and Redevelopment Manager John Sprague was instructed to contact state and county agencies, Home Start business supporters and local churches in an effort to cut the agency off at the pockets. The city refused to sponsor any new grant applications for the charity and withdrew support for applications that were in the pipeline.

Planning Director Patty Dunn suggested a quick overhaul of the old overnight shelter ordinance that had been sitting on the shelf since the fall of 1993.

The city also tried to stop Federal Emergency Management Agency (FEMA) money from "passing through" to Home Start. Those funds had been earmarked to help Volunteers of America (VOA) operate the Armory shelter. Since VOA was not operating the shelter and Home Start was, VOA handed the funds over to Home Start. When city staff members discovered that Home Start had inherited the twenty-four thousand dollar grant, they appealed to the Sacramento Community Services Planning Council to recall any remaining funds and to bill Home Start for what the agency had spent, claiming that Home Start had no right to the money.

But the Sacramento Planning Council found Roseville's claim groundless. Home Start's facilities met the standards for an emergency shelter, and the agency was in compliance with FEMA regulations.

Sprague seemed determined to vilify Home Start. He stoked the political fires, exaggerating that the agency "began providing eight rooms for as many as 50 single adult men and women per night in January."

His incendiary remarks were off the charts. Our report showed that over the sixty or so calendar days of the shelter operation, Home Start provided only seven hundred one nights of shelter for homeless singles, fewer than twelve per night. How he felt he was justified to inflate that number to fifty is beyond comprehension.

Hamel, Crabb and Gamar remained in a tizzy over the news for weeks. They acted like victims, rather than the instigators that they were. It had been the City Council majority who had broken faith with the religious community by ignoring their September 15, 1993, agreement with the providers and churches.

April 20, 1995:

A new front in the battle between the city and Home Start opened up. The members of the Cherry Glen and Thieles Neighborhood Associations met and circled their wagons. They responded to the Home Start singles program with shrills of outrage that Home Start had fooled them.

Here they were thinking they saw fewer transients in the neighborhood only to find out that Home Start was sheltering them. Was the situation during the past winter really better, or were they just delusional?

In any event, they sent a complaint letter to the Council claiming

Home Start was "in violation of their stated purpose and use of the facility as presented to the neighbors on August 20, 1992 (at the open house)."

April 25, 1995:

In a General Information Memo, city staff claimed that Home Start had violated the 1993 agreement by failing to give the city ninety days' notice prior to opening a shelter.

The memo conveniently omitted the fact that the 90-day notice was only required if the city proactively "implements by September 1st of each year a proposal to shelter the homeless..."

It was a matter of fact that only when the city defaulted on its responsibility on December 21, 1994, did Home Start moved ahead with plans for a shelter program of its own. The timeline was irrefutable.

April 27, 1995:

Home Start Executive Director Sherry Schiele promptly responded to the accusations in a *Sacramento Bee* article. She let *Bee* correspondent Art Campos know not only that the information presented by the city was inaccurate, but that the restrictions imposed on St. Vincent's in January 1993 no longer applied because Home Start had become an independent entity.

May 1995:

Phil Kister confided in me that when he had learned from "the powers that be" at City Hall that Home Start had been housing homeless single males during the entire winter right under the city's nose, he became extremely agitated.

Kister's understanding of the city/provider relationship was skewed by his loyalty to the establishment and the anti-transient policy of the Council majority. He told me that he would no longer support any Home Start applications that came to the Grants Advisory Commission for review.

Kister's timing in complaining to me about Home Start was amusingly perfect. Unbeknownst to him, I had just become a Home Start Board member.

As the rhetoric surrounding the Home Start crisis heated up, the Council found itself more deeply mired in "the homeless morass."

May 17, 1995:

Crabb summarized the Council's sentiments that night about what he characterized as Home Start's end run around city rules. He said, "In effect, they're telling us to stick it in our left ear."

Earlier in the month, the Council had not only tightened its grip on Home Start, but also attacked its former parent, St. Vincent's, declaring grant requests from either agency wouldn't be approved by the city because they were in cahoots to provide aid to homeless single males. Instead, the Council redirected the grant money to nonprofit groups such as the Placer Women's Center (PWC). Part of the deal the city made with the PWC was that the organization would discontinue its working relationship with Home Start and remove its offices from the Home Start campus.

In a private conversation with Sherry Schiele, PWC Executive Director Arla Gibson Buckwalter indicated there was substantial pressure from the city to terminate the connection. Her agency had received major funding through the city's Grants Commission program.

There was another factor that may have influenced Buckwalter's decision to follow the city's directive: in September, P.E.A.C.E. For Families, a shelter dedicated to helping women and children escape domestic violence, opened a facility at 120 Main Street. The new shelter allowed Buckwalter to turn to P.E.A.C.E. For Families as a sister agency. Her need for an alliance with Schiele and Home Start had evaporated.

In its crack-down on St. Vincent's, the city sent Associate Planner Mike Wixon on a reconnaissance mission to the charity's Riverside location. He dropped in unannounced to inspect the facility at a time while St. Vincent's president Elaine Willoughby was absent.

When volunteer Terry Anderson asked him to return later, Wixon stood fast and insisted that the inspection was immediately necessary so that he could document for the record the various buildings in the complex, determine their uses and diagram the spaces that each use occupied. This documentation meant "Any future expansion or modification of the facilities or services...are subject to city approval. These approvals could include but are not limited to a building permit and conditional use permit" (City of Roseville).

Ms. Anderson's written report reflected that the element of surprise appeared to be a key part of Wixon's visit.

Bill Santucci's gift for diplomacy would have come in handy at this point. If Santucci had been on the scene, he would have kept the Council on a middle course and not allowed Harry Crabb to take control.

The tactlessness of the strategies being employed pointed to Crabb calling the shots at City Hall even though he was not mayor. It looked like Crabb just wanted to lash out against the charities. There was no reasoning with him.

Another means of resolving the situation was to have Home Start and the city enter into a new Memorandum of Understanding. The agency would be required to limit services to transitional living programs for families in exchange for the city's endorsement of state and federal grant applications. But, the time was not right for that solution in the eyes of either Home Start or City Hall.

The Home Start Board had determined that the agency would continue to provide shelter to homeless singles as long as possible – or until an alternative shelter solution for them was provided.

The powers controlling the city had other plans, too. They had no intention of entering a new MOU until after proper retribution had been doled out. Actions against Home Start remained merciless.

May 20, 1995:

I informed City Manager Al Johnson that the St. Vincent's Board had voted to terminate the hot meal program at the Riverside location if and when the Homeless Forum had set up an alternate site with easy access for anyone in need.

May 23, 1995:

The US Department of Housing and Urban Development (HUD) investigation of the City of Roseville was initiated by my telephone call to the HUD office in Sacramento. Schiele and I decided to keep her name off of the complaint because of her position as Home Start's executive director. While the Board members could come down hard on her, they would have a more difficult time pushing back against me as their peer.

May 24, 1995:

David Philipson, HUD's monitor for Roseville, telephoned, asking for a meeting with our group after his next visit to the city at the end of the month. Philipson suggested that we get as many provider and church representatives as possible to the meeting. Our discussion would focus on the mechanics of a gender-based discrimination complaint, documenting the city's campaign against Home Start and the men it housed.

Specifically, Philipson intended to show us how to file a Section 109 Title 1 complaint based on the Housing and Community Development Act of 1974. The 1974 law covers discrimination in government programs and activities receiving financial assistance from HUD's Community Development and Block Grant Program. There was also a possibility that the complaint could address violations under Title II of the Americans with Disabilities Act of 1990, which prohibits government disabilities-based discrimination.

June 1, 1995:

Sherry Schiele, Elaine Willoughby, Rexine Brewer, Salvation Army Captain Jim Durel and I met with Philipson at the St. Rose Rectory to lay the groundwork for lodging a gender discrimination complaint against the City of Roseville. This was our first step in filing a formal civil rights complaint on behalf of the transients. I gave Philipson a packet of information on the issue.

As embarrassed as I was that there were only five of us who took the time to meet with him, the low turnout did not seem to faze him. He listened and then gave us pointers on how we should proceed. He suggested that the first thing we should do was to file the complaint as soon as possible with the HUD office in San Francisco. It should be gender- and disability-focused. Philipson reminded us that because there was a short statute of limitations on complaints, we shouldn't waste any time putting the documentation together.

He asked us to send him a summary of Home Start's records on the gender and race of the singles sheltered with a letter attesting to the truth of the statistics. He suggested we also send a copy to the City Council. That was no problem for our side. We had kept comprehensive records.

Later in the day, Father Dan and I heard back from the bank attorneys managing the Viking property bankruptcy. They were against helping us buy the site for use as a homeless shelter and were just waiting for the opportunity to foreclose, putting the bank in the position of exercising its SBA loan guarantee and recovering its money. When we contacted Besoyan, he reluctantly told us that he felt that would be the best out for him, too. One more shelter possibility bit the dust.

June 7, 1995:

While the city kept the neighbors steamed up and the pressure on Home Start, the Home Start Board tried to calm everyone down by using diplomacy. After all, the fuss was really only about a dozen or so homeless people needing a safe place to sleep each night. The city and the few neighbors who had it in for transients acted like it was hundreds.

At the Council meeting that night, Home Start President Steve Hargadon and Sherry Schiele answered questions from the Council members and Home Start's opponents in the audience. Hargadon announced that Home Start would hold a public forum at its next board meeting and invited interested parties to attend. But even mild-mannered Hamel would have none of it. He said, "If they want to mend some fences, they need to realize it's no longer winter. It's not wet and it's not cold, so put an end to housing the single transients."

Several people spoke out against Home Start:

- Sylvia Slade, representing Riverside Avenue merchants
- Sally Bragg, leader of the Cherry Glen Neighborhood Association
- Charles Curtis, Cherry Glen Neighborhood Association member
- Linda Williams, Cherry Glen Neighborhood Association member
- Fred Lohse, Oak Street resident, former planning commission chairman and later a member of the project review commission
- Terry Lesh, C Street resident
- Kristi Kinzel, representing the Thieles Revitalization Committee
- Don Koenes, representing the Roseville Chamber of Commerce.

Schiele responded, "We're doing what we feel we have to do because no one else is doing it." She blamed the city and the county for creating the problem by not asking the state to open the Armory the past winter.

"We couldn't leave the homeless outside," she said.

Sally Bragg threatened legal action, citing a successful suit in Arizona where the courts ruled a program like Home Start was a nuisance. Schiele fired back, "Let them file. We have a couple of lawyers willing to go to bat for us."

Council members Crabb and Gamar got their licks in, too. Both questioned the Home Start Board members' credentials citing, that all but two came from outside Roseville. Crabb received a round of applause from those opposed to Home Start's shelter program when he proclaimed, "It's not fair for you to come from Granite Bay and set up a homeless shelter in Roseville."

Council member Roccucci was composed, suggesting that the program be modified to offer emergency housing to singles for no more than three days so they could be evaluated to determine if they could handle a commitment to the transitional program.

In the end, a staff report put the city's problem in a nutshell, declaring, "The city has no contractual agreement which it could enforce to persuade Home Start to discontinue its service to homeless single adults."

The report also laid out what seemed to be the city's fallback position and a thinly veiled attempt to save face by sermonizing how Home Start should not disregard the good-faith intent of any past agreements it had with the community.

When Sherry Schiele heard that suggestion, she retorted, "Obviously, we're supposed to have more sense of responsibility to the City Council than to the homeless people of Roseville."

After a raucous hearing, the consensus on the Council was that city staff would investigate if it was possible to place restrictive occupancy limits on the Home Start facility.

Later in the evening, the Council directed staff to move ahead with the Congregate Residence Ordinance that had been sitting on the shelf since 1993. The jury-rigged draft was dusted off and spruced up by City Planner Patty Dunn and City Attorney Mark Doane. The ordinance would impose controls that would make developing a shelter program with services for homeless adult single males nearly impossible.

Associate Planner Mike Wixon reminded the Council that any new ordinance would not obligate Home Start to modify its program. The Council majority was not pleased.

With no conventional tools to counter the Home Start program, the anti-homeless Council majority became defensive. They interpreted what started as our efforts to rescue homeless singles from the winter's long, cold nights as more an act of cunning than of kindness.

They realized that having no lawful control over Home Start's new transitional living program for singles, over the winter shelter project or over St. Vincent's established services for homeless single males put them at a significant disadvantage, possibly enabling us to leverage the city into building a shelter. As Mayor Hamel said, "To use this issue as a bargaining chip (for obtaining a transitional center through the Homeless Forum process) and as a way to hold the community hostage will never bring any resolution."

Neither the Council nor the six Forum committee members representing the city, neighborhood and business interests would be coerced into giving a thumbs up to any shelter project. They would not be stampeded into a quid pro quo in which Home Start or St. Vincent's would give up serving transients in exchange for agreeing to endorse a permanent transitional shelter and meal site.

The truth was that neither St. Vincent's nor Home Start had any such strategy in mind. Both organizations' goals remained simply to welcome homeless men and women to a home-style meal and a safe place to sleep.

June 13, 1995:

As promised, Home Start held its board meeting and public forum. The crowd was so large that the meeting had to be moved outdoors. Pauline Roccucci was the sole Council representative, and only three members from the neighborhood and businesses spoke up: Kristi Kinzel, Sally Bragg and Sylvia Slade. Many of the people were there out of curiosity.

The three women opposed to Home Start housing singles were quick to voice concerns that Home Start had broken a promise that it would house only families with minor children. They cited the open-house invitation that they had received in August of 1992.

The reality was, as Steve Hargadon and Rev. Paul Carlson pointed out, the flier said that Home Start only housed families with minor children at the time. It was not a promise about future developments, such as what Home Start might do if the city refused to honor its commitment.

We tried to keep the meeting positive, asking for ideas to make the program better. Some suggestions were:

- Performing background checks before allowing singles to stay at the facility;
- Following through on the idea of using one of Home Start's rooms as a neighborhood police substation;
- Limiting single adults' stay to three days if they were unwilling to participate in a transitional program;
- Appointing a community member to the Home Start Board to add transparency to our operations and to build trust;
- Visiting other cities to investigate how they handled similar issues; and
- Introducing the possibility of a new shelter site.

Later that afternoon, I returned to my office at St. Rose, fixated on the spectacle of the board meeting public forum, and all the events that prompted it. It seemed there was something odd about the residents' and business owners' pattern of comments to both the Council and the media regarding the transient situation: At any moment, their statements reflected what they wanted to believe was going on regarding the number of transients in town, rather than what was actually happening.

Then, when our opponents found out that Home Start was providing emergency shelter for singles, they complained that the transient problem had immediately gotten worse, even though the shelter situation had been the same for months. The dialog at Council meetings between the Council members and the neighborhood leaders went from self-congratulatory pats on the back to fist-pounding demands that Home Start pay for its sins.

Just for fun, we could plot the attitude fluctuations on a graph and call it "The Roseville Hobophobia Index." The ups and downs would show the residents' and business peoples' beliefs about transient activity at any point in time, regardless of the facts. The Index could run from a low of one, when the concerned residents and businesses perceived the hobo situation was well under control, to a high of ten, when they saw it as being completely out of hand.

Based on public comment, and using the Index, we could assign a score of a cool two from February to the beginning of April. But as soon as it was announced that Home Start had been sheltering homeless single men and women during the same period, the rating would jump to a red-hot nine!

As much as the city remained obsessed with stopping Home Start from housing single adults, those of us affiliated with the charity worked to carry on both the emergency shelter and transitional living programs for singles. We were holding out against what amounted to a siege, remaining hopeful that the larger Roseville community would somehow come to the rescue. We still believed there was a possibility that these services could become an integral part of a comprehensive system of care for homeless persons, such as the one developing through the Homeless Forum.

Unfortunately, the establishment seemed to be holding all the good cards.

Late June 1995:

Kristi Kinzel accepted our invitation to join the Home Start Board as the community member.

July 1995:

We formally folded the Viking site deal, empty-handed again. Archie Mull assured me that even though this offer fell through, he would remain on the scene.

August 1995:

HUD had begun requiring consolidated plans from local and state governments in 1995 as management tools to help them create blueprints for shelter and housing in their jurisdictions. Roseville's Consolidated Plan proved to be less of a tool and more of a misrepresentation, with the city trying to sidestep the issue of its hostility towards homeless single men. Here are two examples:

- The Plan's entire focus was on women and families, who already had a substantial number of beds set aside for them. At the same time, it omitted any proposal for sheltering those in the community who were at the greatest risk of being homeless: single men. This was despite the fact that Roseville did not have even one bed dedicated for their use.

- The Plan didn't accurately describe Roseville's relationship with the church and provider community. Instead, it was chocked full of euphemistic statements masking over city enmity toward them for championing the cause of homeless single men. An example of such deception is the following quotation portraying the city's relationship with Home Start as almost "harmonious": "(Home Start) was consulted by mail and by telephone to assess the Roseville homeless' needs as well as the number of persons in need. In addition, the City of Roseville has had ongoing, formal and informal meetings with this organization."

It was well-known that the city's policies and practices with the agency at that time were downright hostile and overtly aggressive with intent to destroy.

In addition to a Consolidated Plan, Roseville, like other jurisdictions lining up for federal funds, was required to submit an Analysis of Impediments to Fair Housing document. Both documents were submitted to HUD, with the city knowing full well that the dollar amount riding on providing the proper paperwork for the following fiscal year could be as much as four hundred forty- nine thousand dollars. The funds would be delivered in the form of a Community Block Grant for local housing and shelter projects to help meet "the most urgent low income housing needs of the city..."

Schiele and I had accumulated a mountain of material from the city's Consolidated Plan, Analysis of Impediments to Fair Housing document and other sources to support HUD's probe of Roseville's violations of the rights of homeless single males. Our information was divided into four categories:

1. The city's failure to include in its ninety page HUD Consolidated Plan:

    - Its acrimonious and often public disagreements with the service providers and churches as they struggled to provide assistance to homeless single males;

    - Its overt support of the small but vocal Cherry Glen and Thieles neighborhood groups, their negative characterization of the transient problem and their agenda to defeat any proposal for a shelter; and

    - Its opposition to any program which would encourage the development of outreach, shelter or housing for homeless single males;

2. The city's sugarcoating of its 1995 Analysis of Impediments to Fair Housing document to HUD, which omitted any reference to Roseville's regionally known discriminatory policies and actions toward homeless single men;

3. The city's attack on Home Start for housing homeless single men; and

4. The city's refusal to abide by its September 15, 1993 agreement with service providers and churches to facilitate the establishment of an emergency winter shelter. We had plenty of evidence to back up our claims:

    - A three-page list of recent quotes by City Council members showing they were adamantly opposed to providing shelter or allowing housing aid of any type for homeless single males;

    - A description of the city's token winter shelter voucher program, which explicitly excluded transients and discouraged other homeless people who could not meet the restrictive provisions for proving residency as a condition of receiving shelter; and

    - Documentation of the punitive actions by city officials against Home Start when they became aware that the agency was operating overnight and transitional shelter programs for homeless single males.

As a result of our input, HUD returned Roseville's Consolidated Plan for corrections. With some scrubbing and polishing, the city was able to overcome HUD's concerns.

Roseville still had to work on its Analysis of Impediments to Fair Housing submission to HUD. The Introduction and Executive Summary of HUD's instruction booklet for preparing the document stated "Impediments to fair housing choice are any actions, omissions, or decisions taken because of race, color, religion, sex, disability, familial status or national origin which restrict housing choices or the availability of housing choices."

When city staff commenced preparing its Analysis of Impediments to Fair Housing document and asked for public input, Herb Whitaker of Legal Services of Northern California and I both submitted information. The list of impediments which Schiele and I had prepared included four pages of testimony with sixteen supporting exhibits.

August 29, 1995:

Susan Sears from Caltrans informed me that Roseville city staff did ask if the California Transportation Commission would transfer the two plus acres of surplus Caltrans land fronting Taylor Road to the city as surplus property for the shelter project. Sears said Caltrans declined.

Instead Caltrans re-advertised the property for sale, this time with a minimum bid one hundred twenty thousand dollars and ten-year credit terms at 9%. The property was scooped up by an investor and developed as a mini-storage project. Looking back, I realize that this was an opportunity that I should have helped facilitate.

September 1995:

Home Start was hit with a comprehensive two-page list from the city building division detailing code violations that needed correcting if Home Start intended to continue its operations at 410 Riverside.

September 25, 1995:

Forum stakeholders were notified that their individual groups would meet to review and fine-tune the proposed shelter development document. The individual group meetings would be followed by a general meeting the first week in December to iron out any remaining wrinkles.

While it all sounded too easy, those of us in the provider group were hopeful.

October 1995:
Arla Gibson Buckwalter, Placer Women's Center's Executive Director reported that the city mandated move of her agency's office from the Home Start campus was finally completed.

Fall 1995:
The city decided to discontinue providing Home Start with its annual fifteen thousand dollars supplement for a social worker position. It also successfully pressured United Way to deny Home Start's request for grant funds for computers, all because of the singles issue.

That didn't stop the H.B. Fuller Company and State Farm Insurance from underwriting the cost of needed repairs at the facility. In addition, H.B. Fuller employees, led by Sharon Archuleta, a buyer for the firm, gave the buildings a fresh coat of paint and created a fenced play yard, complete with swings, slide and sandbox, as well as a redecorated kids' playroom complete with a Disney mural.

November 1995:
It came as no surprise that after Harry Crabb took over as mayor and Claudia Gamar became vice mayor, the strained relationship between Home Start and the city worsened. The city's punitive policies had become as inflexible as seasoned concrete. The question was, "How long would it be before Home Start was brought to its knees?"

With Home Start on the run, the city decided not to offer its emergency shelter voucher program. Given that it had been an ineffective flop the previous winter, its absence wasn't going to be missed by anyone. And the plan's principal architect, Mayor Crabb probably didn't want it around anyway. Any program to help the homeless folks of Roseville that winter, irrespective of how lame it was, would take away the thrill he must have been getting watching Home Start go down.

The Home Start Board, for its part, focused more and more on the agency's diminishing cash flow, forcing it to count its pennies to make it through the winter in the face of the city's siege.

November 29, 1995:
Sherry Schiele told me that city housing and redevelopment staffer

Jan Shonkwiler had made an unusual request: She had attempted to extract a statement for the record from Schiele that the city had not been retaliating against Home Start over the previous seven months. Shonkwiler had told Schiele that the city was concerned about the extensive list of items I had submitted in August for inclusion in the city's Analysis of Impediments to Fair Housing document – the material we had compiled documenting how the city bullied the providers.

That was the first indication we had that the city was concerned about our opposition. We both understood that it was more important than ever that our material remain included in the official report that would eventually be given to HUD. After further assessing Shonkwiler's request, the two of us wondered if the city, even with Crabb and Gamar in the saddle, could ever be pushed far enough to tone down its policies and practices towards homeless single men in exchange for our withdrawal of our comments.

About a week later, I contacted Shonkwiler in an attempt to begin a dialog to see if a compromise was in the cards. What would the administration be willing to do to avoid the possibility of HUD intervention? There was only one way to find out. This might be the opportunity we were waiting for.

December 1995:

State Farm came through again with another grant award. Home Start celebrated when they received seventeen thousand two hundred dollars from the company. The grant, along with generous support from area churches and individuals, enabled Home Start to continue operations for the time being.

But the money failed to overcome the city's throttlehold on Home Start. Schiele gave the Board the following bleak report on expected income:

- St. Rose Shelter Fund: amount unknown, but could be up to nine thousand five hundred dollars.
- Holy Family Shelter Fund: amount unknown.
- Miscellaneous donations from various other churches: amount unknown.
- FEMA: up to fifty thousand dollars. Home Start received twenty four thousand dollars the previous winter over Roseville City Council's objection.
- Schiele also had a magical wish list of improbable funding

sources.

Considering that Home Start was four months behind in its four thousand dollars per month rent, Schiele's unfailing optimism was admirable and infectious. It kept us going.

December 7, 1995:

As that evening's general session of the Forum began, the providers' representatives tried to break the ice. They shared their report that included a recommendation to move the meal programs and Home Start to a new location.

The majority of the four constituencies' members saw the plan as a step in the right direction. But, as the conversation continued to develop, two major problems stopped us in our tracks.

The first was that Schiele and Hargadon felt it was safer for Home Start to remain where it was. Both expressed fear that the city would use a new ordinance that they had heard was in the works to continue its punishment of Home Start rather than enable the group to move.

The second problem was that several Forum participants were exhibiting signs of frustration. Sally Bragg was for sure, as was "observing" Council member Harry Crabb, along with a few other folks. I was jolted when they simultaneously blurted out that the process was headed in the wrong direction. They felt that it was supposed to lead to the conclusion that no services would be provided to transients or transient looking individuals. As Crabb said at the time, "If we offer services to transients, then they're going to come."

Crabb and his gang still hung onto the *Field of Dreams* myth years after Jack Willoughby had debunked it with actual data. Some people never learn.

I realized that I had somehow been led to believe that the issue of "services to homeless single males" had been settled as a condition of restarting the Forum process the previous spring. I had assumed it was understood that these services would be moved to a neutral location and that they would be provided on a limited basis as a compromise, a point of reconciliation between the two sides.

Apparently I had it all wrong. At that point, I was totally disillusioned. I was frustrated, too. I had enough.

After talking to Father Dan and Schiele, I wrote to Steve Barber, informing him of the decision to withdraw St. Rose from the Forum process. Schiele handed in her notice, too.

With the St. Rose and Home Start withdrawals, the Forum process was effectively pushed back to August 1994 when the basic St. Rose and Home Start positions were:

1. All existing meal programs would remain at their existing locations and offer services to all comers without restrictions; and

2. Transients and "transient looking" individuals wouldn't be segregated as a separate class of people and denied services.

If the neighbors and merchants wanted to gain control over the meal programs and services, they would have to agree that transients and transient looking individuals would be eligible for basic humanitarian services.

December 28, 1995:

A *Sacramento Bee Neighbors* article reported that Sally Bragg proposed that the residents and businesspeople should look at other means "to eradicate" Roseville's transient problem, such as filing a lawsuit against Home Start as a public nuisance.

January 2, 1996:

Efforts to resuscitate the Homeless Forum process were once again in the making. The involvement of Home Start and St. Rose proved to be essential for the Forum meetings to continue.

January 5, 1996:

The follow-up meeting to my early December telephone call to Jan Shonkwiler began at 8:30 a.m. at City Hall. My fellow deacon, Pete Silott, accompanied me as my witness as I attempted to introduce the possibility of a compromise with Shonkwiler and her boss, Housing and Redevelopment Manager Sprague. My part of the bargain would be the withdrawal of the material Schiele and I had submitted for inclusion in the city's Analysis of Impediments to Fair Housing document. In exchange, the city would soften its policies and practices against services for homeless single males.

As the conversation began, Sprague seemed unusually tense. He opened the discussion right away with a challenge: He questioned whether I had the authority to withdraw St. Rose from the Homeless Forum process in December and to submit the list of Impediments to Fair Housing on St. Rose letterhead. He seemed rattled by the candor of my remarks in the letter.

I informed him I absolutely did have the authority and assured him that it was a matter of policy that I would not send out any parish communication, especially to the city, without the pastor's concurrence.

In what seemed to me to be a fallback position, he suggested that the language in the St. Rose letter about Impediments to Fair Housing should be toned down. He objected to the use of phrases such as "retaliatory action" by the city and "token voucher program" in particular.

Sprague went on to remark that the first occasion he had to really digest my comments was that morning. He said (and Shonkwiler confirmed) that his first question to her after reviewing my submission was, "Has the city attorney seen this?" He followed up with the comment that what I had documented looked like it was preparatory to a lawsuit. They both became very defensive.

Sprague was also concerned that St. Rose and Home Start would continue to use their withdrawal from the Forum process as a tool "to get our way." I told him it was unlikely, and it remained my hope that the initial withdrawal was adequate get everyone to refocus on the central issue: creating an alternative site for comprehensive services for all of the homeless members of the community, whether they were transients or homeless families.

I also questioned whether Bragg and Slade as the neighborhood representatives were merely voicing their personal preferences to the other participants or truly representing the views and interests of their constituents.

Sprague wound things up by letting us know that I had until January 11th to revise the list of Impediments to Fair Housing if I decided to. There was no talk of a compromise.

January 10, 1996:

Representatives of the various groups met again to work out details of restarting the Forum process. Dave Sorensen, St. Vincent's newly elected president, had taken Jerry Angove's spot for that night. I stayed home.

Both Herb Whitaker and Sorensen contacted me and provided their individual recaps of the meeting. They both said the final shelter design would include limited services to transients and transient looking individuals.

That was all I needed to hear!

I telephoned Schiele to give her the news. We agreed that St. Rose and Home Start would return to the Forum. Now maybe the shelter design could be completed. The next general meeting was planned for Saturday, March 9th.

January 11, 1996:

Sprague called in the afternoon to ask if I was going to make any modifications to my HUD Analysis of Impediments list.

I told him I was going to keep the package as it was submitted. The conversation was over. There was not even a hint of a compromise coming from the city. I should have known better than to try, considering who was in charge downtown.

At that juncture, I thought I should give HUD "a head's-up" about this new point of tension. After I spoke with David Philipson, the HUD monitor for Roseville, not only about my list of impediments to fair housing, but also about the list that Legal Services had submitted to the city, I sent copies of the documents to both him and to Andrew Quint at the HUD Fair Housing and Enforcement Center.

January 23, 1996:

City Hall lashed out at Home Start for the first time under Crabb's leadership. I thought it was in an odd and transparent way, something I had seen used a couple of times before by the city to justify its crackdown on services to homeless single males:

- the city's 1992 passage of its anti- free food ordinance after it created the myth that another charity was planning to open a new meal facility in town; and
- its February 1993 attempt to pass an anti-shelter ordinance when the city created another rumor, this one that St. Rose Church and St. Vincent's planned to open a shelter before the city had a chance to put adequate restrictions on the books.

Both actions were based on falsehoods, as this new one seemed to be. In a letter to Home Start, Roseville City Attorney Mark Doane so much as said that the planning department, the building division and his office had heard rumors that Home Start was planning an expansion project. Doane was reminding the organization that any expansion would require a Conditional Use Permit in compliance with the city's Congregate Residence Ordinance.

He followed with another statement that we found strange: "according to the records of the Roseville Building Division, the Home Start facility had a maximum occupancy load of seventy persons as of the September 1, 1995, the effective date of the Congregate Residence Ordinance...If Home Start plans to increase the number of individual persons served...that will constitute an expansion...and require Home Start to obtain a Conditional Use Permit..."

Based on our calculations and recent written correspondence from the same Building Division, we knew that the correct occupancy number was more like one hundred thirty-eight. We were initially puzzled about Doane's intent.

After we let it all soak in, the list of whom Doane copied revealed more about the intent of the notice than the notice itself. It read like a Who's Who at City Hall, the mayor, members of City Council, Al Johnson (City Manager), John Sprague (Housing and Redevelopment Manager) and Patty Dunn (Planning Director).

The letter was composed in the midst of a Roseville expansion boom, with the city apparatus dedicated to working at top speed to accommodate the totality of that activity. Yet, the City Hall power elites felt compelled to set all that aside in order to focus on little old Home Start.

I saw the letter as nothing more than a manifestation of City Hall's frustrations under the Crabb-Gamar administration. The city must have received tremendous pressure from the Cherry Glen and Thieles neighborhood associations that caused its attorney to fabricate a letter that was so easily refuted by facts. We had the building division's September 28th, 1995, letter to Sherry Schiele, which endorsed the higher occupancy number. The city's left hand didn't know what its right hand was doing.

Mark Doane's missive was only a temporary distraction and just another instance in which the city wanted to apply pressure, to continue nipping at our heels, never letting go. Our real problem was the ongoing struggle to keep Home Start on its financial feet.

In the face of all the financial difficulties and city harassment, the Home Start Board voted to formally back the HUD civil rights complaint that had been initiated on May 23rd. Home Start partnered with the Placer Community Care Center to move the HUD complaint forward.

St. Rose pastor, Father Dan Casey, had created the corporation for the shelter project in 1993. When the Council killed the project in 1995, St. Rose parish kept the shell corporation alive for use when a viable shelter program was developed. In the meantime, as a nonprofit corporation, it could still lodge the HUD complaint. As its agent for service of process and custodian, I had the sole responsibility for filing the HUD complaint in its name.

February, 1996:

Home Start's financial crisis deepened. Even with the cash infusion of more than twenty two thousand dollars from the winter preaching campaign I had conducted at St. Rose, Holy Family and Saints Peter & Paul Parishes and with the a FEMA grant of fifteen thousand six hundred forty dollars, there still was not enough cash to pay five months of back rent and keep the operation afloat. My cash flow projections showed that we could be as much as fifty-five thousand dollars in the hole by year's end. The problem boiled down to either resolving the standoff with the city or closing shop. As the guy recently saddled with the job of Treasurer, I called for a special board meeting to review our options.

To prepare, I met with Leo McFarland, the Sacramento Volunteers of America CEO, for lunch. I had asked him several times before to consider joining the Home Start Board. He had always declined. That wasn't going to keep me from asking him again. I also needed a chance to explain the dire situation Home Start was in and to ask for his advice on how to convey the seriousness of the circumstances to the other Board members.

In addition to operating several homeless programs in Sacramento including the county's annual shelter program, his agency had run the Roseville Armory shelter from 1989 to 1994. More importantly, he was a friend, was respected in Roseville and understood our political situation.

Unlike past occasions, when he had put me off about serving on the Board, this time McFarland said yes. What a relief!

March 9, 1996:

The Homeless Forum general meeting resulted in an agreement by all stakeholder groups to take the "straw design" to a "working design" phase. New committees formed and began developing the various elements of the final product, including scope of service, transportation, location, estimated development costs, operating policies, an annual operating budget, governance structure and accountability. It looked like the consensus of the Forum participants was finally to recognize that everyone, regardless of residency, would receive aid.

March 12, 1996:

After setting up a special meeting of the Home Start Board at 3:30 p.m. to discuss the financial crisis, I was disappointed that we didn't have enough board members to take any action. Only members Kevin Daley, Rev. Carlson, Kristi Kinzel and yours truly showed up, along with Sherry Schiele and guest Leo McFarland. We waited fifteen minutes for other members who might wander in; but we had a hunch that wouldn't happen.

McFarland and I stuck to our plan of breaking the bad news to the others present. They needed to know the depths of Home Start's financial problems, including the possibility of a forced shut-down because of the desperate funding shortfall. Kevin Daley took the minutes.

I could see that Schiele was heartbroken. I had told her before the meeting what McFarland and I would be revealing. But, knowing Schiele, I could have banked that she believed the Almighty would not let her down – that He would intervene with a miracle, sending manna from heaven to save the singles program just in time.

As far as the attending Board members were concerned, they understood what we were saying, but were hesitant to suggest what we should do to avoid disaster. McFarland and I were forced to wait for the regular meeting later in the month for a decision.

In the interim, I did some politicking with the remaining members, briefing them on the financial crisis that was looming.

March 26, 1996:

We finally had a quorum at the regular monthly Home Start Board meeting. Leo McFarland was elected to the Board – one of the few positives that came out of the session. Even after presenting the financial data, McFarland and I were the only ones willing to discuss the financial problem, and more importantly, the reason for the problem – the ongoing beef with the city over housing singles.

To help the Board members evaluate how to respond to the financial crisis when juxtaposed with the discrimination matter, I reminded them that the Home Start-Placer Community Care Center joint HUD complaint about the city's discriminatory actions against homeless single adult males would not be going away, irrespective of how the Board moved ahead. Whether the Board voted to settle with the city or keep on fighting, the complaint would live on.

HUD was formulating at least two formal civil rights actions against the city for its treatment toward these men. Although the complaint had been filed with the Board's consent, authorizing the formal civil rights actions would require another vote.

I pointed out that there was only one positive way the Board could respond to the complaint situation: fold the singles program, and encourage HUD to move ahead with an investigation. With that approach, we would be complying with the city's demands, while at the same time retaining our integrity.

I soon understood that I was moving too fast with too many ideas. The other members were not ready to decide how to deal with either folding the singles program or continuing to support the complaint matter. They were so shocked by the funding issue that all they wanted to do was to try to process what they had heard and talk.

At that point, McFarland and I realized that we would need another special board meeting to refocus the members on the issues of discrimination juxtaposed with finances. We wanted one scheduled as soon as possible.

April 3, 1996:

After many phone calls and one-on-one conversations with other Board members, McFarland and I had received an adequate number of commitments to schedule a vote at a special board meeting that afternoon. We had decided to have Schiele invite her staff, Machel Stokes, Phil Regalado and Pam Moyer, as well as volunteer Lynda Frost, to the meeting. The three of us agreed that the best way to stop rumors was to give everyone a chance to hear the discussions firsthand. Machel Stokes recorded the minutes for Rexine Brewer, who left early.

Once the members had reviewed the new financial information and began weighing their options, McFarland started the discussion by stating what he thought Home Start's mission was: to provide transitional housing and guidance to homeless families with children. Following a considerable amount of chatter, the members settled on that definition. But, they also said they felt unsettled and conflicted. After all, they had invested a lot of time and energy into helping the singles with shelter, too. The thought was that if Home Start abandoned these men and women just because times were tough, their rights would be steamrolled by the city.

Then, the reality of the financial crisis began to sink in and the discussion shifted to what was needed to salvage the program for families with children. The fact that the city's deadline for grant applications to the Roseville Grants Commission was fast approaching was also discussed. These two elements forced the members to concede that the singles programs had to be phased out.

I moved that the Board agree to do what the city required: that Home Start enter into a Memorandum of Understanding which provided that after April 8th, the only singles who would be housed were parents who entered the rehabilitation program with children. Kristi Kinzel seconded the motion. It passed with five "yeas" and one abstention.

Immediately following that vote, I introduced a second motion that the Board would do what was necessary to enable HUD to complete its investigation of the city's actions against homeless singles. Ken Jaros seconded the motion. The vote was again five for and one abstaining.

Next, Kevin Daley moved that we request that the city provide emergency shelter for its homeless population and set up a year round sheltering program for the homeless singles in town. All voted for the motion. Schiele was asked to draw up the concession letter to the city for Paul Carlson's signature as soon as possible, getting it delivered to City Hall and to the Roseville Grants Commission by the end of the week.

April 16, 1996:

I had received two formal documents from HUD to begin the investigations of the complaints against the city. They arrived just in time for the board meeting. There was one for Home Start to act on, outlining the city's harassment of the agency for housing single men, and a second for the Placer Community Care Center detailing the city's attempt to use its new Congregate Residence ordinance as a means to deny housing and shelter to homeless single men.

All that was needed to get HUD into the fray on a legal level was for Home Start Board Chair Carlson to sign its complaint and for me to sign the other. But, Carlson was focused on the MOU.

The city was so anxious to wrap up the problem, it had quickly prepared the MOU, signed and dated it and forwarded it to Home Start in time for our board meeting that day. The city even sent an uninvited guest to that meeting to witness our vote, Jan Shonkwiler.

McFarland moved that the Board adopt the MOU. I seconded his motion and the eight members approved it.

Then, I brought up the unfinished business of the HUD investigation. I solicited suggestions as to how Home Start should proceed, being careful to refrain from motioning for approval. I was very leery of moving ahead too quickly, as I did on March 26th.

What had been an animated meeting became extremely quiet. Several members sat with arms folded across their chests. Their uneasiness was palpable. Any discussion had to be drawn out of them. A few Board members backpedaled, making a consensus impossible. Some argued that continuing to help HUD investigate the city for civil rights violations would be seen as inconsistent with capitulating to the city on the singles shelter issue. Such an action could be characterized as being unfair.

I sensed that the problem was Shonkwiler. Her presence threw a wet blanket on the proceedings. Most of the Board members felt their backs were against the wall. I discovered that there was a big difference between firing the Home Start Board up to initiate a HUD civil rights action and getting them to follow through by signing on the dotted line. There was no action on the HUD matter.

April 19, 1996:

I sent a letter to HUD stating the Board had postponed its vote until the next scheduled meeting. That would be the first opportunity I would have to make another pitch. Maybe the Board members would agree to postpone the HUD resolution until the Homeless Forum process wound up. If the process collapsed or if the city declined to accept and promote a shelter proposal that included services for homeless single males, then we would sign on with HUD for the investigation.

While the group's majority must have seen the decision not to move ahead on the HUD issue as wise, Schiele, Rexine Brewer and I were taken aback by what we regarded as their cowering in front of the city's representative. After the meeting, the three of us discussed what Shonkwiler must have thought of our Board. With the rationalizing that went on that afternoon, we were sure her report to City Hall would be welcomed with a chuckle of relief.

Surprisingly, HUD was OK with the decision to wait for another month for a vote.

May 14, 1996:

The day arrived when a majority of my fellow Home Start Board members reneged on their decision to press the HUD complaint. When they voted to let the city off the hook, I felt betrayed.

I could only guess that they were acting out of fear. While they were making excuses about being two-faced, it looked to me that they were just fretting that the city folks would cut us off at the pockets again once HUD showed up on City Hall's doorstep. If that was the case, they were wrong. HUD's presence at the doors of City Hall would be enough to keep the bureaucrats and politicians honest.

Home Start's capitulation to the city's demands had devastated Sherry Schiele. During the tumult of the final few months of confrontation, she had not been monitoring her type 1 diabetes as closely as she should have. As a result, she developed sores on her feet. Following a trip to the emergency room, she was restricted by her doctor to bed rest at home. She also had to modify her diet and keep her legs elevated.

May 19, 1996:

Home Start President Paul Carlson dealt the deathblow to the HUD complaint. He wrote a letter to Andrew Quint of HUD stating it was the Board's decision "to forego implementation of the Housing Discrimination Complaint filed...on 1/23/96... (it is our belief that) the City of Roseville continues to support the Homeless Forum process and it is our expectation that they will stay true to their commitment to assist in actualizing the final plan."

I was sure, after seeing how the Home Start program was nearly decimated by their attacks, that city officials envisioned a future free of any further uprisings from the provider community. After all, Home Start had been forced back in line, city homeless policy was firmly controlled by the four-person Council majority of Crabb, Gamar, Graham and Hamel, HUD eventually gave Roseville a pass on its Consolidated Plan and Analysis of Impediments to Fair Housing and the Homeless Forum process was scheduled to wind up in an orderly fashion in a few months.

Even at that, all was not well with Roseville. The city had been put on notice by the feds that it would risk new sanctions if it renewed its acts of impunity towards its homeless population. And as equally important, a new HUD intervention would reveal that Roseville had suffered another embarrassing outbreak of hobophobia!

Chapter 14:
The Straw Design Goes up in Flames!
(May 28, 1996–Aug. 13, 1996)

May 28, 1996:

The providers and churches optimistically planned for the Homeless Forum process to conclude, with the shelter straw design becoming a completed blueprint by the end of summer.

But all was not peaceful. Four months after Deacon Pete Silott and I met with John Sprague and Jan Shonkwiler about the Analysis of Impediments to Fair Housing document, and a week after Home Start had caved in to the City, Shonkwiler "coincidentally" called to see if I had decided to withdraw my written comments for the Impediments package. She left a message saying the final documents were being gathered for Council approval and suggested that I might want to leave mine out.

She claimed that back in January I said my submission was just for information. My notes of that January discussion indicated her recollection was faulty.

Shonkwiler telephoned again at 4:20 p.m., again while I was away from the office. Her message stated that she was going to take it upon herself to remove my comments from the Council package. She explained that she thought it would be what I would want, given the bluntness of the Council members' quotes against homeless single men I had included.

May 29, 1996:
I returned her call next morning and left a message telling her to keep what I had submitted in the official Council package.

June 1996:
Even though Home Start's HUD complaint had been killed, my PCCC filing remained alive, but on life support. As the agent for that organization and as a Home Start Board member, I wondered if pursuing the PCCC complaint might impair Home Start's attempt to rebuild a healthy relationship with the city. The PCCC was still a shell corporation, and unlike Home Start, hadn't suffered any economic

harm.

And then there was the prospect that the Homeless Forum might produce a blueprint plan for building a shelter. Any proposal would have to be sanctioned by the City Council before any part of it could be funded.

With my involvement in the Homeless Forum and my hostile relationship with the city, I felt that it would be better all around if I held off signing the PCCI HUD complaint. I wrote to HUD, saying "The (Homeless Forum) proposal is due to go before the (Roseville) City Council in August or September. If the Council does not act affirmatively on the proposal, then we will look to file a new complaint."

June 6, 1996:

A Homeless Forum general meeting was held with participants focusing on nitty-gritty topics like construction costs and the annual operating budget, projected at around two hundred ninety one thousand dollars. We figured a little more than one hundred thousand dollars of that should come from local governments. In Roseville's case, most of its share could come from its annual allotment of the federal CDBG grant funds or the Roseville Grants Advisory Commission.

I was worried about the reaction when folks saw those numbers. But, if anyone had sticker shock, it wasn't evident. Instead, people seemed to agree that the process could be completed by August. Steve Barber suggested that all stakeholder groups complete their assignments by the beginning of July to make the final document ready in time for an August conclusion.

June 7, 1996:

A *Press Tribune* article featured a comprehensive summary of the meeting and an interview with John Sprague. He tipped his mitt when it came to discussing financing the venture, specifically the city's position on putting money into any part of the project. Apparently, his comments reflected the view of some of the other participants. As Sprague said, "Is it realistic to expect one hundred thousand dollars from the city? The citizens will have to decide if the city can afford and is willing to support a (homeless) facility."

After reading the article, I realized we were dreaming if we thought this Council would support the project with any financing, let alone one hundred thousand dollars a year. The Crabb majority would oppose any CDBG or other grant money going toward a homeless shelter, when the dollars could be spent on improvement projects that directly benefited their constituents in Thieles and Cherry Glen.

Based on my past experiences and what I had read in the paper, I was skeptical we would make it over the finish line by summer's end. But by all outward appearances, it looked like there was still hope. We were too close to a consensus on the final product to ditch the effort.

Mid-June 1996:

Regional homebuilder John Mourier expressed interest in helping Home Start with funding.

Since Schiele was on disability leave and I was going to be away on a long-planned six-week vacation, Rexine Brewer said she would meet Mourier's point person, Karen Wertenberger, and invite her to the next board meeting in July.

I would also miss the hearings for Council approval on the Analysis of Impediments to Fair Housing document that were set for July 10th and 24th. Father Dan was going to be out of town on those dates, too. He suggested we make a presentation to the City Council before he left in mid-June, stating for the record our objections to the city's representations in the document.

I thought it would be more effective to present our case at the last meeting in June, closer to the hearing dates. That meant I would be the spokesperson for our side. He joked that his absence would be best, in any event. It would keep him from losing his "cool" with the Council members. He was notorious for having a short fuse.

June 26, 1996:

The only option I had to speak at the Council session was during the Public Comment portion of the meeting, when my presentation was limited to five minutes in accordance with Council policy. But our written documentation would be part of the Council's record and could be as long as needed to make our case. What Father Dan and I had prepared noted each half-truth we saw in the report and cited all of the city's acts of discrimination against Roseville's homeless single male population that I could dig up.

To assure that the oral and written comments for the meeting became part of the official Council record, I gave complete copies to the city clerk at the meeting.

As I delivered my remarks to the Council, I was so anxious to get the presentation process behind me and to move into vacation mode that the hard, but vacuous stares from Crabb, Gamar and Hamel just bounced off of me. It didn't matter whether their glares were fueled by anger shrouded by feigned indifference or if they were genuinely composed. I remained unaffected and on point.

I could see that they were at their controlled best, completely ignoring anything I said. Instead, they steamrolled ahead with plans to make it more difficult for homeless men and women to receive free meals in town by holding the first reading of an amendment to "the Free Food Distribution Center Ordinance."

The old ordinance prohibited any of the existing free dining rooms from making "any alteration or expansion involving ten percent or more of its floor space, (which would make it subject) to the specific requirements of (that part of the code)."

But, the new language that would be written into the law included a provision that if any of these older facilities closed for more than thirty days

- A conditional use permit would be required to reopen;
- It would be forced to remodel to meet all the provisions of the Roseville code; and
- The use permit would have to be renewed every year.

After I left the Council chambers that night, the memory of what I had just been through hit me with a deep-in-the-gut realization that what I had said to the Council about our well-documented record of discrimination didn't matter to Crabb, Gamar or Hamel one bit. They were determined to forge ahead with their agenda.

The only way to get them and the city administration to change their policies and practices was with a swift kick. And I figured that the best entity to deliver that kick was HUD. As I had discovered the previous year, HUD was programmed to respond quickly to citizen complaints of discrimination. With that, I decided to file new paperwork.

I had to be quick. Annette and I were planning to leave for our extended trip to Canada at the end of the week.

I called several of the Home Start Board members and spoke with Sherry Schiele, St. Vincent's President David Sorensen and St. Rose Pastor Emeritus Father Mike Cormack about filing a new complaint.

The consensus was there was no problem with me initiating a new HUD grievance as long as neither Home Start nor St. Vincent's were asked to be signatories. Also, as long as it was my neck that was on the chopping block, there was broad support for the prospect that the city would finally be held accountable for its discriminatory policies and actions directed at homeless single males.

After I wrote a quick letter to the HUD Intake Branch of the Office of Fair Housing and Equal Opportunity in San Francisco, I asked the St. Rose office staff to watch for a reply. I would call them on a weekly basis for messages. It was important to stay in the loop not only about word from HUD, but also about the preparations for the August Homeless Forum meeting when the comprehensive design for the new shelter would be presented for approval.

July, 1996:

While the city's formal acceptance of the Memorandum of Understanding with Home Start marked the end of that battle, Bragg and Slade remained so charged up that their frustration boiled over onto the out-of-state owners of Home Start's property.

The anti-homeless leaders and their allies on the Council had once dreamed of putting an end to both St. Vincent's and Schiele's Home Start in one fell swoop. But, with the MOU, the city lacked justification for going after the family program.

The new strategy was that the neighborhood groups would peck away at the out-of-state property owners in hopes that the lease would be cancelled and that St. Vincent's would be taken out by litigation. If Home Start was still around after all that, it would be their final target.

July 10, 1996:

At that evening's Council meeting, Home Start Board Secretary Rexine Brewer echoed the concerns I had outlined the month before with ten minutes of detailed remarks concerning the shortcomings of the City's Impediments to Fair Housing report. Her comments made the point: The city document had been turned from its intended purpose of being an instrument of self-examination regarding discrimination into a whitewash of city bias against the homeless single males in our community.

That didn't stop the Council from adopting the staff's version of the Impediments to Fair Housing report. The final vote was uneventful and predictable – unanimous and void of discussion.

July 15, 1996:

I telephoned the St. Rose office. An envelope from HUD's Fair Housing and Equal Opportunity section had arrived. I asked St. Rose staffer Bertha Chavez to open and read it to me. It was from the Acting Chief of the Intake Branch, Paul Smith, asking me to complete a comprehensive Pre-Complaint Questionnaire for his office within ten days. If more time was needed, we had to notify a Ms. Irene Green in his office.

Chavez was quick to call Ms. Green to ask for an extension – until the latter part of August, a couple of weeks after I returned to Roseville.

July 16, 1996:

Ms. Green returned the call and left a message saying she would advise us if she encountered any problem with the change.

August 2, 1996:

The Roseville Council adopted the anti-shelter ordinance proposed by Planning Director Patty Dunne and City Attorney Mark Doane. It was dubbed the Congregate Residence Ordinance; its restrictive provisions became part of the Roseville Municipal Code as Ordinance 2908.

Enacting the ordinance was followed by a two-day citywide campaign by Roseville police, park rangers and Southern Pacific police to round up homeless men and women. The cops combed public parks, staked out the downtown library, plied the streets and alleys, and raided hangouts on the railroad's right-of-way.

The homeless singles caught up in the sweep who had outstanding issues with the law were cuffed. The others were escorted out of town often by the seat of their pants by the firm hand of railroad officers like Lieutenant Larry Colvin.

August 11, 1996:

As soon as I got back in town, the first thing on my to-do list was to go through the stack of mail on my desk. At the top of the pile was a delivery notice from the Post Office dated August 2nd reminding me to pick up a certified letter. The letter was from Sally Bragg. I set the delivery notice in a special pile. There was not much time left before it would be returned to the sender.

In my stack of phone messages, I found a note from the St. Rose office staff saying that someone from Cochrane's Funeral Home had tried to contact me on August 2nd, saying that a representative of the merchants' association had asked the management to sign a petition for a class action suit against me personally. The funeral home called to let me know they had declined to participate, but thought I should know what was going on.

With these two messages in hand, I could see that our opposition was getting ready to pounce.

August 12, 1996:

I met with Father Dan about shelter project developments. He let me know that he supported the shelter concept and said St. Rose would do its part.

August 13, 1996:

At that morning's providers' meeting, the news was good for the most part. Pastor Angove, Leo McFarland and Herb Whitaker reported that County Supervisor Santucci and County Health and Human Services Director Merz supported the shelter design that would be presented at that evening's meeting, a positive sign.

With the political heat that the neighbors had created and the negative disposition of the Council majority, I doubted that any shelter that served homeless single males would ever be built within Roseville's city limits unless HUD intervened. The county would have to provide a site.

Leo McFarland had completed estimates for building and start-up costs for the facility at eight hundred forty-six thousand dollars, with annual operating expenses of two hundred ninety-one thousand dollars.

St. Vincent's President Dave Sorensen said his organization would definitely move to a new location when the new site was up and running; but there was no site on the horizon. Sorensen also pointed out that planning a move would mean two things:

1. Dining Room guests would need transportation; and
2. If the city or county failed to approve the new location, then the old location would remain open.

Angove said his church would work toward the same resolution. Whitaker noted that Captain Simpson, the new Salvation Army commander, would do likewise.

The providers voted for Sorensen to announce at that evening's Homeless Forum meeting that St. Vincent's would close the Dining Room if an alternate temporary site was operational and if construction of the new permanent shelter facility was near completion. Even though closing the Dining Room had been on the table several times before, most Forum members were probably not aware of it.

Sorensen also said he would look into hiring a security guard for the St. Vincent's meal program as soon as possible.

Then we hit a sour note. Some members began sharing their take on the Homeless Forum stakeholder representative meetings that had occurred while I was out of town. The consensus was that our nemeses Bragg and Slade seemed laser focused on getting the meal providers to move if a temporary site was found, even if the larger project was not even near completion. And the two women appeared disinterested in the new permanent shelter cost estimates that McFarland was working on – a very strange reaction by the pennywise women.

Those two observations together meant something besides a shelter plan was brewing for that night's Homeless Forum meeting .

The meeting had been billed as the granddaddy of all them all – the summit, the conference at which all parties would be called upon to adopt the eight-page straw design as a blueprint for constructing a shelter facility.

The provider committee had "excused" me from attending the meeting because I had become a lightning rod, an unnecessary point of controversy. I was asked to find something else to do.

After that night's meeting, I got a call from Sorensen. He said that all of the regulars were there, and the complete working design was presented. Discussion moved along well until the last half-hour.

Sorensen characterized Slade and Bragg as being shocked and agitated when the projected cost of the facility was discussed. He was not sure if they were genuinely upset because the price tag was higher than they anticipated or were just using money as an excuse to break off negotiations. Budget figures similar to these had been floated at the Forum stakeholder representative meetings for several months.

Then, Sorensen described how the Forum process collapsed once and for all. First, the two women adamantly insisted that services to transients in Roseville be terminated. Next, when they failed to get their way, they simply walked out.

It was all over.

It looked like Slade and Bragg had used the Forum as a tool to build their court case and boost their credibility – to make it seem that they had gone through all the motions in good faith, seeking a solution to the transient problem. They could tell a court that they tried to solve the matter without bringing legal action, and then blame the Forum for not yielding the results they wanted. That was what "made them do it."

Chapter 15:
Let's Get Litigious!
(Aug. 14, 1996–Aug. 31, 1996)

August 14, 1996:

I woke up still puzzled by Sorensen's summary of the events of last night. What was this latest kerfuffle all about? The morning *Bee* quickly shed some light on it.

Bragg was quoted as saying, "The residents want their tax dollars being spent to revitalize the community."

So now I knew it was not about money in general, but rather about the cost of any project that helped homeless people using tax dollars.

I needed time to think, and it was a beautiful morning. So I went outside to clean out the motor home after our long trip.

At 7:30 a.m., less than twelve hours after the Forum collapsed, Bragg and Slade showed up at my house. I was astonished to see them. They had never been there before, and I was certain they were not there to tell me they missed me while I was on vacation.

As they approached me in my driveway with a letter in hand, I continued to attend to my chores. After I declined to take the letter, Slade assured me it had nothing to do with a lawsuit.

With that, I accepted the letter and invited them to sit down with me on the porch while I looked it over. I quickly discovered that, once again, I shouldn't have trusted Slade.

No, it was not about one lawsuit; the document was about four-dozen lawsuits and an ultimatum that either I evict St. Vincent's from the Dining Room facility within seven days or face the fact that "48 neighbors are prepared to sue you in Small Claims Court for maintaining a public nuisance. As you may be aware, numerous claims have been upheld by the courts and neighbors have been awarded up to five thousand dollars each." The total award could be two hundred forty thousand dollars.

So much for the women's honesty.

I felt their appearance at my home was their version of "Pearl Harbor"! Homeless Forum Coordinator Steve Barber later called it "The surprise." I preferred to label it for what it was, "The surprise attack."

Slade and Bragg had opted for a new strategy They had decided to go for the jugular and close the meal program down without regard for a new location. I was sure they had also factored in that if they succeeded in shutting the program down for thirty days by court order or by my decision to evict St. Vincent's, it would mean the end of the Dining Room. The facility could not reopen until it met the new city ordinance requirements, which would be never.

Now, I was convinced that the two women were responsible for engineering my absence from the previous night's meeting. After all, it could have proved awkward for them to negotiate in good faith with me at the meeting and then show up the following morning at my house threatening to sue me.

And, I didn't have to conjecture long as to whether they had worked a good part of the night composing the neatly typed letter threatening to sue me. The letter was too well-thought out for that.

It seems probable that the document had been resting on the seat of the car as they drove to the Forum meeting the previous night. I would have bet it was all set for delivery the following morning, topping off the act they had staged to end the Homeless Forum meeting – their spontaneous walkout in a huff!

I wondered if they had laughed over a nightcap and cigarettes the night before as they reveled at their own cunning.

This was the move I had been warned about for some time. Slade and Bragg finally had sprung their trap. That was all right. I did not waste any time initiating a response to their assault:

- By 9:45 a.m., I had faxed a copy of the letter to Legal Services of Northern California's Herb Whitaker and asked him to call me.
- By 10:00 a.m., copies of the letter were on Father Dan's and Father Mike's desks. Both men suggested I fax a copy to the bishop.
- Shortly after, I consulted with Archie Mull by phone. He asked me to fax a copy of the letter to him.
- Between 11 and 11:30 a.m., during a phone call from Herb Whitaker, we came up with a list of eight items that could become part of our strategy:
  1. Confirm with everyone possible on both sides who had attended the Forum meetings that St. Vincent's had been on the record as ready to relocate services if an appropriate alternate site was found;
  2. Meet with the forty-eight potential Small Claims plaintiffs and compile a list of their complaints;

3. Remember that Bragg and Slade were not authorized to represent the plaintiffs because they were not attorneys;
4. Examine the Small Claims actions to determine if they represented an incidence of an "abuse of process." For example, if we determined that that the plaintiffs were threatening court action to coerce us to close down the Dining Room, without intending to follow through with a court action, they could be liable for abuse of process;
5. Compile a list of local supporters – residents and merchants;
6. Develop a dossier about the two neighborhood groups, their leadership and their interactions with the city staff and politicians;
7. Work hand-in-glove with St. Vincent's to ensure our strategy of cooperation was seamless; and
8. Gather evidence showing that transient problems were primarily due to the railroad, the businesses that sell alcohol and the city for not properly policing public areas along Dry Creek illegally used for camping, bathing and partying.

At noon, St. Vincent's President Dave Sorensen and I had a chance to discuss the situation. We decided that he would develop a report listing the number of people St. Vincent's had helped over the previous twelve months with meals, shelter, food locker services, office services, showers, transportation, clothing, furniture and other aid.

He would also put together a binder of policies that the organization had developed for managing services to clients, especially single males who frequented the Dining Room.

And finally, I spoke with him about what I felt were three important points:

- I had made a promise when I was St. Vincent's president in December 1987, to employ a security guard to monitor the Dining Room clients;
- I had written numerous letters to the presidents who succeeded me about the importance of keeping that promise; and
- The fact that the guard position had been vacant for over seven years helped lead to this critical problem with the neighbors.

Sorensen wasn't aware of the roots of the commitment and again assured me that he would get the security guard job filled as soon as possible. After that conversation, I faxed a copy of the Bragg-Slade letter to Catholic Bishop Weigand and to Leo McFarland.

By mid-afternoon, I finally got some good news: Archie Mull

telephoned to say he would donate one of his attorney's services from his office – at least through the initial stages of litigation. He had handed the Bragg-Slade letter to his staff to do some research.

Mull urged me to write a letter to Bragg and Slade telling them that I did not take kindly to their threats, and if the forty-eight small claims suits were filed, we would initiate a suit in Superior Court naming each Small Claims plaintiff as a defendant. He asked me to think about it and to call him the next day.

I got busy drafting my response to the two women.

That evening, the *Press Tribune* confirmed what I already knew when it quoted Bragg after she left the forum meeting; "I was asked to compromise and I felt we compromised to the point where we were giving in and giving up." She continued, "We don't want any tax dollars spent on this."

The actions of Bragg and Slade affirmed that the whole Homeless Forum process was a sham – a Council tool to stonewall any shelter recommendations.

August 15, 1996:

Whitaker called early in the morning for a lengthy chat. After his initial comments on the situation, he expanded on the ideas he had posited the day before. He pointed out:

1. As Mull mentioned, we could have all the Small Claims cases moved to Superior Court and ask the court for relief from the interference the suits posed to our property rights.
2. If the plaintiffs wanted to prove that St. Vincent's was a nuisance to them, they had to establish that the Dining Room:
   - Somehow conspired with local liquor stores and bars to sell liquor to homeless people;
   - Forced the railroad to bring homeless people to Roseville; and
   - Kept the city from adequately policing transient camping and drinking on the creeks.

On the other hand, if they wanted to prove that the Dining Room was a public nuisance, they had to demonstrate that it was a nuisance to the whole community and not just to their little area of town.

Their plan was flawed from the beginning.

Whitaker was very thorough and helpful. Before we ended our conversation, he let me know we needed to determine if the incidents with transients and others increased when St. Vincent's operated the meal program.

By early afternoon, I had finished the Bragg-Slade draft and faxed it to Mull and Whitaker for their feedback. Basically, the letter asked the women to list the facts or instances in which they felt St. Vincent's acted illegally or caused a serious or public nuisance. I also wanted to meet with each of the forty-eight neighbors that they said they represented to find out what their individual concerns were.

Both Mull and Whitaker said that the response would do the job.

August 16, 1996:

Irrespective of what we thought of Bragg or Slade, it remained important to keep the communication going. I delivered our reply letter to Sally Bragg's mailbox shortly after 5:00 p.m.

August 17, 1996:

I wrote a letter to the St. Vincent's Board members, recommending that if they wanted the Dining Room program to survive, they should do the following as soon as possible:

- Pass a corporate resolution hiring legal counsel and indemnifying and defending Annette and me against any legal actions the plaintiffs may take, as provided for in the lease;
- Collect any letters of complaint, police communication and/or any other information for the attorneys that could be used to either prove or negate the merchants' and residents' claims; and
- Hire a uniformed professional security guard to show the merchants and residents that St. Vincent's was making a sincere effort to monitor and respond to any actions by Dining Room clients that might aggravate the situation.

August 18, 1996:

Archie Mull had a solid legal strategy mapped out and was ready for the small claims suits when the time came. His plan covered seven points:

1. Request all of the small claims suits be moved to Superior Court and heard as one action;
2. Ask the court to determine if the Dining Room was a nuisance and what the respective rights and responsibilities of the plaintiffs and St. Vincent's were, without awarding any damages (i.e. an action for Declaratory Relief);
3. Round up individual letters of support from Ministerial

Association members testifying to the court about the beneficial community service that the Dining Room provided;

4. Circulate three different petitions for review by the court showing the broad community support the Dining Room enjoyed among its more friendly residents, church members and businesses;

5. Hold a press conference when the lawsuits were filed to ask for public support and point out that St. Vincent's has been on the record since May 1994 as willing to move the Dining Room program;

6. Provide the public, in follow-up news articles, with evidence that the city had aided and abetted the residents and merchants to sue by having personnel, including the police chief and other staff, along with Council members, attend their meetings and encourage the action; and

7. Whitaker would represent one or two Dining Room clients who had relied on the Dining Room as a basic source of healthy meals while Mull and his staff of attorneys, including Allen Haley, Jeffery Jones, Marsha Leach and John Bilheimer, would represent St. Vincent's, Annette and me.

August 20, 1996:

Bragg and Slade hand-delivered a reply to my August 16th letter. Their response claimed that the meal program attracted homeless single males who engaged in illegal activities which threatened "the peace and harmony" of the neighborhoods.

They levied multiple complaints, from irrational to unrealistic and finally to what I saw as absurd. Their list of crimes by the Dining Room guests included panhandling, making threats, camping and loitering on the sidewalks, in the gutters and in the alleyways before and after meals were served, urinating and defecating in neighbors' yards and around business buildings, littering, throwing broken beer bottles and stealing clothes from laundry lines.

It also decried the presence of the outdoor portable toilet at St. Vincent's. I thought that this was a legitimate complaint and one we could remedy. It was time for the Dining Room to have better toilet facilities.

The letter went on to claim that the area's old folks and children were living under the constant threat of transients, being denied the security they deserved. It argued that the only way "Mayberry" could be restored was by closing down the Dining Room. This assertion was totally unrealistic. The only way to get what they wanted would be to reroute the railroad.

And finally, the ladies let their rhetoric overcome reason when they declared that the alleged activities caused so much mayhem that it made "the people in this area fearful for their life." Hyperbole trumped reason!

They said that members of their group had declined our suggestion to meet with us one-on-one. Instead, they invited us to a group meeting on the evening of the 26th in the conference room at the Chamber of Commerce building.

I knew the room well. It was where several city-sanctioned shelter development committee meetings had been held.

St. Vincent's President Dave Sorensen, Annette and I accepted the invitation. We asked Herb Whitaker to attend as an observer to represent the interests of the Dining Room clients.

August 22, 1996:
A uniformed security guard was on the job at St. Vincent's from 9 a.m. to 5 p.m. Sundays, and 8:30 a.m. to 2 p.m. the other four days the Dining Room was open.

August 26, 1996:
Mull had a draft of our Superior Court suit asking for declaratory relief. The suit would include not only the St. Vincent de Paul Society, Annette and me, but also Roy Worley and Kathy Benitez, long-time Dining Room patrons and local residents as plaintiffs. They would be stand-ins for hundreds of individuals who for years had relied on the Dining Room for food.

The defendants were Bragg and Slade, as well as Does 1 through 100.

Before the meeting with the residents and the merchants, Whitaker joined Annette and me for dinner at our house. I was full of questions for him – hypotheticals like "How far should we bend to calm down the neighbors?", "Should we be as agreeable as necessary to avoid the filing of the suits?" and "What were the odds that we would win?"

In short order and to her credit, Annette made it clear that we had to stand our ground to keep the Dining Room open at all costs.

With that, the direction of our strategy was set. I was charged with telling the residents and merchants that the Dining Room was staying put with the same schedule until an alternate site was found. Whitaker also said that I should lay out why we were meeting with them: to listen to their complaints about misconduct at the Dining Room, share our understanding of our responsibility, and let them know we would correct the issues the best we could.

When we arrived, I let Bragg and Slade know that we were going to record the meeting and that a tape would be available to anyone who wanted one. The fact that the two women were going to be held to what they said verbatim did not sit well with them. From then on, the evening went downhill.

As we entered the room, I estimated that there were about thirty people on hand, including those standing along the walls. When I looked up and down the long conference table, I was disappointed to see the faces of folks I thought I knew pretty well, like Rudy Martinez. Annette and I had been acquainted with him since the early seventies when he was dating one of our Fosters Freeze employees, Paula Rinker. The pair married and raised their family in the Cherry Glen neighborhood, where they lived happily for years.

Jim and Barbara Avilla were there, too. I had been more than acquainted with them since the early sixties when Jim's dad leased my ranch property as a dairy. Then, Annette and I had bought furniture from Barbara in the sixties and seventies when she worked at Miller's Maple Shop on Riverside. Later, in the nineties, I had officiated at Jim's mother's funeral.

Two others I knew were Ken and Vera Lonergan, looking on as observers. They were gathering more information as stand-ins for Vera's elderly aunt and uncle, Paul and Lou Lunardi. The Lunardis lived down the street from the Braggs.

In addition to the ringleaders Bragg and Slade, other militants on hand were Joe Ciraulo, Jr., Dave Tognetti, Doug Selby and David Battles. Some of the remaining folks I had seen, but had not met personally. A few of them attended St. Rose Church.

Soon after the meeting started, I understood that our adversaries simply hoped that we would be so afraid and intimidated by their numbers that we would cave in to their demand to close the Dining Room. They were half-right. I was afraid, but not intimidated. Instead of giving in, I tried to create a dialog to find out what their specific complaints were.

Within minutes, the meeting took on the flavor of a pep rally. Bragg blasted, "Cherry Glen has five times more police calls than any other neighborhood. Why?"

The unified crowd's response was a loud "St. Vincent de Paul!", followed by applause.

Another woman in the room yelled, "Isn't our goal and desire to have the place shut down?!"

The pack shouted, "Yes!" to more hooting and clapping.

The cheerleading and responses sounded like they had been rehearsed. Maybe it was a ritual they went through at every meeting to get pumped up.

Then a woman hollered at me, "Will you do it?"

I gave a straight-out "No! Because of the harm it would cause most of its users."

With that, there were groans, hoots and laughter, followed by nasty comments about the Dining Room and the people who ate there.

A man asked me, "Bill, then will you stop serving homeless single males?" It sounded like he thought he was offering a compromise.

I said "No" without reservation.

More boos.

Slade then made a campaign-style appeal that riled up the crowd, emotionally pleading, "Bill, could you first for a second understand that each and every one of these people each single day are confronted by an issue that you bring specifically to our neighborhood? We are sick of it! We will do everything in our power to have this nuisance and safety issue taken out of our neighborhood."

The crowd erupted with a loud ovation.

After the whoops of approval died down, the evening disintegrated into an exercise in frustration and eventually degenerated into a near-mob scene.

The meeting only lasted a little more than thirty minutes before it exploded.

Then, out of the blue, two police officers walked in and suggested that the four of us leave. Their arrival at the Chamber of Commerce building was bizarre. Officers dropping in by coincidence?

Maybe someone made a cell phone call. Of course, I could have been so distracted by everyone yelling at us that I just didn't see it.

August 27, 1996:

The next day, I talked with Rudy Martinez, telling him I was surprised that he was part of the Bragg-Slade gang. He said he joined after he had a run-in with a transient on a Friday (which happened to be a day the Dining Room was closed). After the altercation, he followed the guy who landed at the "St. Vincent de Paul corner." That was the last straw for Martinez.

He told me how Bragg and Slade "managed" the Small Claims group. He said he went to three meetings over the last few weeks, and the women had the papers for people to sign. They brought his to his house to sign, and told him this would take care of "the problem."

Martinez went on to say that he didn't want any money damages and didn't have a copy of what he signed. He just did what Bragg and Slade told him to do. He said he only wanted the transients out of the neighborhood. Then, he repeated that he wasn't looking for any money and that Bragg and Slade were handling everything. He paid his fifteen dollar filing fee and was told that it was all he could possibly lose.

August 28, 1996:

I delivered our final letter to the two women. As Archie Mull and Marsha Leach had suggested, I offered the possibility that the two sides work toward a genuine compromise over the issues that could be addressed, rather than maintaining polar opposite positions.

I followed up with Mull's August 18th suggestion that the merchants, residents, St. Vincent's and Annette and me jointly ask the Superior Court to determine if the Dining Room was a public or private nuisance and then abide by the judge's decision.

If the Superior Court determined some of the activities or features of the Dining Room program constituted a nuisance, we could either modify or completely eliminate them to the judge's satisfaction without having to terminate the whole program.

For instance, if the judge found the outdoor porta-potty to be a nuisance, it would be eliminated. The same would hold true if he ruled that clients' loitering around the neighborhood before or after meals was a nuisance; we would institute a policy of keeping the area clear during those times by enforcing a "no meal and no services policy" for clients who refused to cooperate.

I also mentioned that St. Vincent's had hired a security guard.

I wrapped the letter up with three points:

1. "...If small claims actions are filed against us, we would immediately cross-claim in Superior Court against each and every plaintiff, seeking declaratory relief...Each small claims plaintiff would have to respond to our suit in Superior Court in a timely

manner."

2. "We, along with St. Vincent de Paul, are ready to sit down to discuss realistic compromises at any time. A neutral third party facilitator would ensure that each person has the opportunity to be heard and listen to alternatives."

3. "Please pass a copy of this letter on to...the interested parties."

Slade and Bragg responded with a letter saying their members declined joining us in an "Agreed Suit," and they intended to move ahead with the small claims actions. They confidently added they were ready to respond to the possibility of a Superior Court action if they had to. I felt they were bluffing on the last count. They had already stated in the letter that a reason they were not joining us in an "Agreed Suit" was the cost of a Superior Court action.

This concluded the pre-litigation communication. Each side professed to having done everything possible to avoid a confrontation in court. All of the jousting, sending letters back and forth, and meetings were relegated to the past.

August 29, 1996:

I was finally able to refocus on HUD's Pre-complaint Questionnaire that had arrived while I was on vacation. I outlined three instances of housing discrimination by the city toward homeless single males:

1. The retaliation against Home Start for housing homeless single males;

2. The coercion of Home Start into an agreement to discontinue serving the men; and

3. The misrepresentations of facts to HUD in the city's Analysis of Impediments to Fair Housing report.

August 31, 1996:

The St. Vincent's Board adopted a comprehensive corporate resolution committing the organization to retaining legal counsel, indemnifying Annette and me, and defending its right in court to operate the Dining Room program.

Chapter 16:
"This is a nuisance?"*
(Sep. 1996–Nov. 1, 1996)

*Judge Joe O'Flaherty, October 30, 1996

September 4, 1996:

The City Council became desperate to overcome the years of negative press about the never-ending homeless fracas it had brought on itself. The members were so distressed that they voted to resurrect the emergency shelter voucher program that they had abandoned the previous winter. Vice Mayor Gamar proclaimed "We were previously accused of being hard-hearted. This program shows that we do care and we want to care for those who need help,"

Only one charity signed up to hand out the vouchers: the Salvation Army. The other charities avoided it like the plague because of its Scrooge-like stipulations:

• The unrealistic residency rules; and

• The mandated charity-match. The Salvation Army had to match dollar-for-dollar each expenditure the city made from its pot of fifteen thousand dollars.

The city had no shame, again extracting money from the charity on an ongoing basis to make its delinquent utility accounts receivables look slightly better – all under the guise of helping homeless folks.

September 8, 1996:

We had no idea who most of the small claims plaintiffs were until the merchants and residents group held a press conference in front of Slade's salon, directly across from St. Vincent's. Todd Patterson, our security person, went over to hear what the gaggle was telling the press. One of faces interviewed by a TV crew was Don Fisher, who owned the La Rosa Club a block south of the Dining Room.

After the media left, chatter among the gang members continued, rehashing what they had told the reporters. Patterson overheard Fisher telling Doug Selby, "Some of the news people asked me what I thought the solution to the problem was. I said to take some gasoline and a match to the place." He went on to conclude, "...the news people will probably cut that part out."

Later, when Mull's office asked me who I thought the plaintiffs were, I included Fisher's name along with the names of the folks I knew: Bragg, Slade, Barbara and Jim Avilla, Bud Miller, David Battles, Joe Ciraulo Jr., Doug Selby, Donald Wilson and Dave Tognetti. I wasn't certain who the others might be. Bragg and Slade had refused to give out any names.

September 11, 1996:

By the time the small claims suits were filed, the actual number of cases against us had grown to fifty-two. The small claims trial date was set for November 7th at 8 a.m. in Judge Joe O'Flaherty's Municipal Courtroom in Roseville at Taylor and Royer Streets.

September 12, 1996:

We quickly realized how lucky we were that the liability insurance carried by St. Vincent's was SAFECO. The company proactively began to evaluate the strength of the allegations of the residents and merchants. SAFECO's representative, Sally Carmody, asked for a copy of every document I had on the matter.

SAFECO Insurance also notified us that the firm would be defending us in the small claims actions to the extent possible under the rules, which was limited to providing advice and counsel behind the scenes.

Feeling more confident, we agreed with Mull's office that it was time to file the Superior Court suit his staff had prepared and ask the court to determine if the Dining Room was a public or private nuisance. Each of the fifty-two small claims plaintiffs would be become defendants in the Superior Court action and would be served with a summons. Mull paid all of the costs.

The final document contained two important additions to the draft: the first was that bar owner, Don Fisher, became a named defendant along with Sylvia Slade and Sally Bragg, in addition to Does 1 through 500. The second was a request that the court determine if business establishments selling alcohol in and around the Cherry Glen and Thieles neighborhoods were the actual public or private nuisances claimed by the defendants. This action was called "a request for a determination of comparative fault."

If the court determined that these businesses were a root cause of the transient problem, it would also establish to what extent they were responsible and obligate them to repay us if we had to compensate the residents and merchants for damages.

We finally learned who each of the small claims people were when one of us was served with the papers. When Mull and Whitaker both told us that it was important to determine where these fifty-two plaintiffs lived or owned property in relation to both the creek and the Dining Room, we plotted their addresses on a map. Surprisingly, Don Fisher had not filed a small claims suit and only five plaintiffs lived or had property within shotgun range of the Dining Room.

The map was an eye-opener, a great tool to demonstrate to the court that the root causes which brought transients to the Thieles and Cherry Glen neighborhoods were the railroad, the sellers of alcohol and the poorly patrolled brushy creeks. After the court saw the map, it would then be able to settle on who was responsible for what.

We discovered that fourteen of the plaintiffs lived one-third of a mile away or farther from the Dining Room and most of those fourteen lived within a block of the creek, the notorious refuge for transient camps and parties long before the Dining Room was on anyone's radar.

The four plaintiffs who lived on Willow Avenue had the creek at their doorsteps, but were more than a quarter mile from the Dining Room. They were adamant that the Dining Room, not the creek, was the source of their problem.

The sixteen folks with homes on the 100 block of Irene Avenue and on the 200 block of Earl who filed actions against us were located equidistant between the creek and St. Vincent's. Like their neighbors, they also swore that St. Vincent's, and not the creek, was to blame for their transient troubles.

SMALL CLAIMS COURT PLAINTIFFS – ALL 95678 Zip Code
September 11, 1996

First Name	Last Name	Residence or Property Address	Estimated Distance from Dining Room
Joe Jr.	Ciraulo	225 Riverside Ave.	100 Ft.
Michael	Papier	210 Riverside Ave.	100 Ft.
Silvia	Slade	210 Riverside Ave.	100 Ft.
David	Tognetti	220 Riverside Ave.	200 Ft
Merle	Bailey	138 Clinton Ave.	100 Ft.
John	Wingate	207 1/2 Clinton Ave.	400 Ft.
Victoria	Wingate	207 1/2 Clinton Ave.	400 Ft.
Doug	Selby	127 Clinton Ave.	500 Ft.

Linda	Selby	127 Clinton Ave.	500 Ft.
Robert(Bud)	Miller	416 Riverside Ave.	1,200 Ft.
Eric	Fuerstenberger	421 Clinton Ave.	1/3 Mile
KC	Fuerstenberger	421 Clinton Ave.	1/3 Mile
Andrew D.	Rhoads	227 Earl Ave.	1/4 + Mile
Linda	Williams	228 Earl Ave.	1/4 + Mile
Robert E.	Williams	228 Earl Ave.	1/4 + Mile
Gordon	Healy	239 Earl Ave.	1/4 + Mile
Virginia	Healy	239 Earl Ave.	1/4 + Mile
Irene E.	Weber	240 Earl Ave.	1/4 + Mile
William J.	Weber	240 Earl Ave.	1/4 + Mile
Michael D.	Bragg	334 Earl Ave.	1/4 + Mile
Sally	Bragg	334 Earl Ave.	1/4 + Mile
Robert C.	Bowman	405 Earl Ave.	1/4 + Mile
Amarylliss	Bender	119 Willow Ave.	1/4 + Mile
Michelle	Gregson	132 Willow Ave.	1/4 Mile
Wayne A.	Gregson	132 Willow Ave.	1/4 Mile
Betty Ann	Melligan	201 Willow Ave.	1/4 Mile
Barbara	Avilla	210 Fern	1/4 + Mile
James	Avilla	210 Fern	1/4 + Mile
Christopher	Brown	112 Irene Ave.	1/4 Mile
JoAnne	Wells	112 Irene Ave.	1/4 Mile
Hans	Moeller	124 Irene Ave.	1/4 Mile
Colleen H.	Koebbe	125 Irene Ave.	1/4 Mile
Kenneth	Koebbe	125 Irene Ave.	1/4 Mile
Donald S.	Wilson	127 Irene Ave.	1/4 Mile
Juanita D.	Wilson	127 Irene Ave.	1/4 Mile
John	Bauchmann	136 Irene Ave.	1/4 Mile
Sandra L.	Bauchmann	136 Irene Ave.	1/4 Mile
Dee Ann	Phillips	243 Irene Ave.	1/3 Mile
Leigh R.	Bacco	301 Irene Ave.	1/3 + Mile
Peter J.	Bacco	301 Irene Ave.	1/3 + Mile
Wallace F.	Stewart	312 Irene Ave.	1/3 + Mile
Eunice P.	Johnsrud	317 Irene Ave.	1/3 + Mile
Norman K.	Watkins	318 Irene Ave.	1/3 + Mile
Robert	Johnson	320 Irene Ave.	1/3 + Mile
Michael	Rodrian	338 Irene Ave.	1/3 + Mile
Joe Sr.	Ciraulo	214 Cherry St.	1/4 Mile
Rudy E., Jr.	Martinez	322 Cherry St.	1/4 + Mile
Toni Marie	Gish	419 Cherry St.	1/3 Mile

Julie	Lawrence	625 Vernon St.	1/4 Mile
Doreen	Giles	100 Block Vernon	1/3 + Mile
David	Battles	305 Fifth St.	1/3 + Mile
Kathleen	Battles	305 Fifth St.	1/3 + Mile

Why did the small claims plaintiffs try to pin the transient problem on a charity when we could so easily show that the railroad, the purveyors of alcohol and the city were to blame?

I believed the answer was that St. Vincent's was easier pickings.

The plaintiffs would only face that truth if they had to respond honestly to three simple questions:

1. Who gave the transients a free ride to Roseville?
2. Who sold the cheap alcohol? , and
3. Who failed to do their job of patrolling the creeks to arrest violators of open container laws and of illegal camping and fire ordinances?

These were questions only a court could get answered. For example, a court could show that one result of the recently announced Southern Pacific sale to Union Pacific Railroad was that the city would finally have a willing partner to keep the trains free of transients. For years, because of Southern Pacific's economic woes, its rail police had been cut back, giving free riders easy access to the freights.

The word among the homeless men was that U.P. had a heavy-handed police force, with a track record of enforcement on its existing network. Free rides on the U.P. were an exception, rather than the rule.

Here is a handy illustration of how city policy influenced the handling of the transient problem on the local level: Roseville's new fifteen hundred foot-long fence along Vernon Street to keep transients from using a trail between the rail yards where the men hopped freights and the "Cheaper Food & Liquor" store.

September 19, 1996:

Before Union Pacific Railroad officially took over Southern Pacific Railroad operations, the new owner's executives met with local officials and concerned citizens. A new agreement was negotiated with Union Pacific that specified beefed up security and law enforcement in the rail yards.

As we continued to prepare for court, both our side and the plaintiffs had access to police statistics on incidents involving selling alcohol to transients, intoxicated or not, showing a pattern involving purchases at three neighborhood stores: "Chief's" at the corner of Clinton and Darling Way, "Deluxe Liquors" on Riverside and "Cheaper Food & Liquor" at the junction of Douglas, Riverside and Vernon.

The pattern showed that men and women would buy a bottle or a twelve-pack and head for the creek or the rail yard to party. While the plaintiffs saw the data as evidence for their case, we realized we could turn the facts against them. We could prove that it was poor police patrolling of Dry Creek, not the Dining Room, that caused a big part of their problems:

- The Cherry Glen streets with the majority of police calls for alcohol-related incidents were Earl and Irene, two of the three closest streets to the creek.
- A vast majority of the plaintiffs lived in closer proximity to the creek (where the guys drank, camped and partied) than to the Dining Room.

Only a handful of the residents of the Thieles neighborhood, which was on the side of Riverside closer to the rail yard and further from Dry Creek than any of the Cherry Glen plaintiffs, filed small claims actions. In fact, dozens of Thieles residents and merchants signed declarations of support stating the Dining Room was a community asset. Another twenty-six Cherry Glen residents, most of whom lived closer to the Dining Room than the plaintiffs, also signed declarations of support.

As we gathered momentum, I felt sure that we would prevail. Failure would have been devastating, not only to the Dining Room, but also to any meal program in any community which faced community hostility like we did. There was no telling how far beyond Roseville the ripple effect of a defeat would extend. These plaintiffs had followed the Berkeley model used to shut down drug houses. If they succeeded in this case, it could become a precedent, providing angry people in other cities with "the Roseville model" as a template to close down free meal programs they disliked. We couldn't allow that to happen.

We set up volunteer patrols to drive through the plaintiffs' neighborhoods during the period from one hour before the Dining Room meal was served until one hour after. The volunteers wrote up reports stating how many homeless single men were walking, loitering or drinking in the neighborhoods.

Bill Spencer and Vivian Prince coordinated the effort for six weeks with Bob Carvo, Alma Zehrung, Machel Stokes, Sherry Schiele, Maggie Racco and Father Mike Cormack helping out. The only transient activity the crew reported was of men and women walking through the residential area directly to or from either the vicinity of Royer Park or downtown. There were no instances of loitering or bad behavior.

One Sunday after Mass, Rodney Phillips, a videographer, talked with me about a unique way that he could help our side in the dispute: He volunteered to develop a video to use in the courtroom. The footage would be a documentary that would help a judge visualize the circumstances of the case better.

Phillips and I wrote the script, he produced and edited it and I narrated. The finished product was an eighteen minute presentation that included a summary of all St. Vincent's services, a detailed description of the Dining Room program, interviews with long-time patrons and a thorough overview of the business district, the neighborhood and of what we saw as the real problem – camping and drinking along the creek.

On the legal front, Mull's office moved ahead with an amended Superior Court complaint listing by name each small claims plaintiff as a defendant. The plan was to serve papers to each of them by the first week of October on both the Superior Court action and a request that the Small Claims judge transfer the neighbors' complaints to Superior Court.

We combined the two because:

- Twenty-eight of the small claims plaintiffs who alleged that the Dining Room was a nuisance specifically asked that the nuisance be abated, giving us the option to have those cases transferred to Superior Court; Section 116.220 of the California Code of Civil Procedure stated that the authority to order the abatement of a nuisance was beyond that of small claims; and
- If the remaining twenty-four cases stayed in Small Claims Court, they would have to be decided simultaneously with the Superior Court cases. That didn't make sense: It would have been inefficient to tie up both courts over the same issue.

October 3, 1996:

Municipal Court clerk Lorraine Bickel told me that Small Claims Judge Robert McElhany was quick to grant our request which would send the entire bunch of small claims to Superior Court to be consolidated with the higher court case.

October 4, 1996:

Judge O'Flaherty signed the order and Ms. Bickel saw to it that all the Small Claims cases were transferred.

When the Cherry Glen members were each served with the Superior Court action and the transfer request, their collective reaction seemed to verge on panic. Several plaintiffs' commitment to the cause evaporated. The first person I encountered who broke ranks with Bragg and Slade was Rudy Martinez. He called me to see how he could get out of the Superior Court suit.

Others talked openly about jumping ship. Bragg and Slade were furious. Their coalition was showing signs of crumbling.

Police Chief Simms tried to come to their rescue by putting his political weight behind an effort to move the cases back to Small Claims Court. He tried pressuring the judge. A friend of mine who worked in the municipal court building told me that Simms and O'Flaherty were overheard talking about the St. Vincent's lawsuits in the judge's office.

The comment that stood out to my friend was Simms' admonition to O'Flaherty: The chief said the plaintiffs wouldn't forget if he failed to get the suits moved back to Small Claims. Simms warned that such a failure would be regarded as a betrayal – something the judge would have to face the next time he was up for election.

So much for "blind justice!"

The pressure on O'Flaherty must have been more than he could handle. He had the cases returned to his desk.

October 17, 1996:

We received a notice that a Small Claims hearing to reconsider the earlier move to transfer the cases to Superior Court was set for October 25th. I played for time, writing a letter to the judge asking for a postponement.

October 18, 1996:

Bud Miller withdrew his Small Claims action with prejudice, meaning he could not sue us over the same issue again. Shortly after, Betty Melligan did the same.

SAFECO Insurance retained the Law Offices of James Biernat in Sacramento to handle our case. The Biernat firm specialized in liability issues such as the predicament we were facing. Attorney Jeffrey Steele was assigned "to head off" any attempt to place responsibility and extract money judgments from us. The fact that attorneys can't represent clients in Small Claims Court did not stop Steele from coaching me on how to present our side of the story to O'Flaherty.

Steele spent at least an hour with me and said that the most important thing we could do was to take advantage of the opportunity to inform the judge about all of St. Vincent's activities and community support. He suggested I do it in a simple, concrete and direct way, as soon as possible – in a letter to O'Flaherty. That would give the judge time and space to not only read it, but also to digest and integrate the contents before evaluating the neighbors' claims.

October 25, 1996:

On the day of the hearing, O'Flaherty's courtroom was packed. Attorney Jeff Steele was on hand to observe the proceedings. There were so many people in the gallery that a few, including Father Dan, sat in the jury box. When the judge entered the room, he was shocked to see the spectators jammed in like sardines. In his opening remarks, he said that the crowd that day was the biggest he had ever seen in his courtroom.

Most of those on hand were St. Vincent's members and supporters who had been helping build our case. There were also a number of ministers and clients who were regulars at the Dining Room. The rest of the folks were curious onlookers. There were only a few plaintiffs. Most were absent because it was a work day.

The hearing lasted ninety minutes, but it seemed like eight hours. Bragg and Slade spoke for all the plaintiffs, even though the plaintiffs were supposed to represent themselves. The two women seemed to go on-and-on. Dave Sorensen was on hand to join me as the St. Vincent's representative; but the judge seemed to like having the two women duke it out with just me. O'Flaherty' jumped in once in a while for a punch or two himself.

The appearance that O'Flaherty favored the other side didn't bother me. I believed the hearing was merely to determine if the actions would be given over to Superior Court.

In any event, the judge put on a good show for the press and the Cherry Glen voters. When I mentioned that we were asking to have the cases heard in Superior Court so that there would be finality to the question of whether or not the Dining Room was a nuisance in the eyes of the law, he shot back, "Clearly I have the power to stop individual filings. If that's what you are claiming on, (sic) that narrow issue, I'm inclined to reject that."

"This is a nuisance?"

He must have realized that was not the point I was trying to make. I hoped he would admit that it was best to have all of the cases sent to Superior Court to resolve the issue once and for all.

Irrespective of what O' Flaherty said about these cases, we were going to follow through with our Superior Court suit.

The judge continued to be sympathetic to the neighbors. As Art Campos reported in the *Bee*, "a somewhat testy O'Flaherty" glared down (at me) from the bench, saying, "You've got (the residents) riled up, so there's something going on. I hope you appreciate the magnitude of the problem."

As the hearing wound down, O'Flaherty stated that he would rule in two to three weeks. Obviously, he would postpone the trial set for November 7th, although he didn't indicate what the new date would be.

He vowed to investigate the situation thoroughly by touring the neighborhood, interviewing witnesses, conferring with police and dropping in at the Dining Room. As he said, "I'm entitled to go see these things myself. I won't just get one side and not the other. I'll get both sides."

October 27, 1996:

The next two defectors from the Bragg-Slade camp were Jim and Barbara Avilla. They approached me late in the afternoon as Father Mike and I were walking west on Lincoln Street near Vernon. As they came around the corner from Vernon Street toward us, they spotted us and rushed up and began talking to me in a hushed tone.

Jim told me he had heard a rumor that the cases had been moved to Superior Court. In the next breath, he said that the two of them did not want any trouble.

I was pleasantly surprised. They asked me how they could get out of the litigation. What could they do to show that they did not mean any harm to St. Vincent's or us? They admitted their mistake of letting their anger get the best of them.

I told them I thought it would be pretty straightforward for them to get out of the Superior Court case. As far as I was concerned, all they had to do was to ask the Small Claims Court Clerk that their complaint be dismissed with prejudice and then take a copy of the dismissal to Mull's office.

They looked relieved and thanked me over and over again. They assured me they would visit the Small Claims Court clerk to put the whole matter behind them.

October 30, 1996:
Judge O'Flaherty stopped by the St. Vincent's Dining Room at about 11:45 a.m. – fifteen minutes before mealtime.

He walked in and introduced himself to the cooking crew. Our all-around handyman, Bill Mosher, overheard the discussion and dropped what he was doing to rush into the office to tell me, "Here comes the judge!"

By the time I arrived, the crewmembers were having a friendly talk with O'Flaherty, explaining what went into preparing a hot dinner for an average of one hundred twenty people. He seemed very interested and receptive to everything the ladies were saying. So, I just stood to the side, sure to shut up and listen.

About five minutes before the door was scheduled to open to the folks queued up for the meal, I glanced out the big window overlooking the sidewalk. What I saw was stunning! The sight caught the attention of everyone in the room. The place went silent and all of us, including Judge Joe, gawked at the spectacle.

What we witnessed was not homeless men and women standing in line for a meal, but an orderly parade of about fifteen neatly dressed children with six or seven women, probably moms, walking toward the entrance gate of the waiting area.

Why were these kids here and not in class? On school days, the number of children who came to the Dining Room was minimal.

Mosher ran to open the door. He got there just in time to greet them, "Women and children first!" Soon, they filled the line at the serving counter as they patiently waited their turns.

Judge Joe stood back and watched in amazement as the kids and moms got their food and sat down to eat. Finally, with a rhetorical question articulated with what I thought was surprising clarity, he revealed the sentiments of his heart. With an astonished look, he asked, "This is a nuisance?"

Those four words, I think, represented his expression of a profound sense of awareness. He recognized that the Dining Room was an important asset to the community. I believe with that, O'Flaherty had made up his mind. He would rule against the neighbors' request.

I never saw the children or the moms again.

Back at City Hall, apparently the staff and the Council majority had been preparing to land the knock-out punch to the Dining Room in the event the small claims plaintiffs were successful in having it declared a nuisance. I received evidence of the plan from a City Hall source, who handed me an internal city memo.

The memo suggested that the city had options it could pull from its bag of tricks to close the Dining Room permanently. If the plaintiffs were victorious in having the Dining Room closed because it was a nuisance, and if the facility remained closed for more than thirty days, the draconian requirements in June's revised Free Food Distribution Center ordinance would automatically kick in, allowing the city to resurrect the unsettled 1987 Dining Room parking question, claiming the Dining Room had never been sanctioned to operate.

That meant that St. Vincent's would have to survive at least two public hearings prior to qualifying for a permit to reopen. The public hearings would provide the Dining Room's opponents with a fresh platform to raise the nuisance issue, allowing them to demagogue it to death. Even if by some miracle St. Vincent's made it through the hearing process, the organization would still face having to upgrade the facility to meet the outlandish standards of the June ordinance at a prohibitive cost.

if the plaintiffs weren't successful against the Dining Room, the city still had options. For example, it could employ a dirty trick that had been used against Home Start to force that organization into line: harassment with city inspections and threats of citations for code violations.

October 31, 1996:

The gradual withdrawal of the neighbors' suits was a solid setback for City Hall and for Bragg and Slade. Even with the desertion of their troops, the two women seemed unfazed and determined to carry on their fight. It looked like they were on their own, with no support from other residents and businesses. That wouldn't stop them. They retained Roseville attorney Renee Nash to represent them in Superior Court to answer our request for declaratory relief.

Later that afternoon, we discovered that Don Fisher, owner of the La Rosa Club and a defendant in our Superior Court case, had filed a petition to have our action against him dismissed. He claimed that he was included in our suit in retaliation for his remarks at the press conference. His attorney, Geoffrey Wong, argued that our action against him was a "Strategic Lawsuit Against Public Participation" suit, or SLAPP suit, attempting to punish him for expressing his views on the Dining

Room situation, which were protected by the First Amendment.

Fisher, like Bragg and Slade, misunderstood our intentions. He didn't know that by the time we saw his complaint, we were planning to dismiss the whole action because the controversy had been resolved by the withdrawal of the small claims suits.

November 1, 1996:

The *Press Tribune* interviewed some of the Cherry Glen residents to get their reaction to the hullabaloo surrounding the lawsuits. An old-timer told the paper that the lawsuits had changed the whole ambiance of Cherry Glen for the better. Valeta Wall said, "It is quiet for the first time since (the Dining Room) was opened up. But, before it was terrible...I didn't know what a good night's sleep was." Doug Selby confirmed her take on the situation, but he went on to say, "They've cleaned up their act before. I know it will go back to the way it was."

Amazing! The residents contended that by just filing lawsuits against St. Vincent's, they had improved conditions in the neighborhood. What they said was merely another manifestation of what they believed as being true, not what was really true. My Roseville Hobophobia Index, which had been stuck at a red-hot nine for the past eighteen months, had just chilled to a one. Bragg told the *Bee* it wasn't up to Roseville to offer homeless single adults shelter from the winter cold. "If they choose to be transients and choose not to work, the choice is theirs to solve their own problem. (A shelter) would be damaging the people who live here and pay taxes here and try to act as appropriate citizens."

Chapter 17:
If You Wanna Play, You Gotta Pay!
(Nov. 3, 1996–Jul. 1, 1997)

November 3, 1996:

A long-time St. Vincent's client, Palla Andrade, called me at home, very upset. After she calmed down, she told me about Sally Bragg's latest attack on Roseville's homeless folks. Andrade said she had witnessed Bragg and her neighbor, KC Fuerstenberger, that afternoon trying to use their vehicles to intimidate and block Abundant Life Church members from serving their weekly Sunday meal to hungry people in Royer Park. She said the two women drove their cars off of the street and onto the park grounds, aiming for the assembly. Some of those waiting for the meal were families with children.

It seemed that Bragg was literally out of control.

Andrade said the police were called. The officers defused the situation, dispersed the crowd and told the church group to pack up their food, saying that if they wanted to provide a meal in the park to local homeless people, they needed a license. The police allowed Bragg and Fuerstenberger to drive off.

Following that incident, Bragg told a couple of key people in the neighborhood group that she and Slade had new plans that would take St. Vincent's back into court with a big lawsuit. Their attorney, Renée Nash, was getting set to file a Superior Court action in which each neighbor who participated would sue for fifty thousand dollars in damages, rather than the five thousand dollars they were limited to in Small Claims Court.

The ladies must have fanaticized that most of the fifty-two small claims plaintiffs could be convinced to underwrite the open-ended financing required to sponsor what could become a major piece of litigation. Their assumption was that splitting the legal fees among fifty or so plaintiffs would make the cost palatable.

My neighborhood sources also indicated that no date had been set to file the new action.

On our side, a suit of that scope meant that the potential liability for damages that SAFECO would have to pay out could be as much as two million five hundred thousand dollars. In any event, Bragg and Slade would have to bear the costs of initiating a new Superior Court case as plaintiffs if they wanted to prolong the battle.

With all the preparations Mull's firm had made and with SAFECO on board, we were ready for anything. I felt that we would just have to endure going through the legal system one final time to vindicate our position and affirm the legitimacy of the Dining Room.

I had a chance to catch my breath and address the underlying cause of the recent fuss – St. Vincent's substandard operation of the Dining Room. For the previous seven years, the operation had been run with minimum oversight by St. Vincent's presidents and boards of directors. Their management continued to be slipshod and unprofessional, even after I had called them on it time after time.

Prior to Dave Sorensen becoming President, I had disagreement after disagreement with St. Vincent's leadership about matters such as hiring security, conforming to the Health Code and keeping the site clean. At the same time, I became the target of the city, the residents and the businesses, taking the heat for the sloppy Dining Room operation. They blamed me for the state of affairs that led to the fight that became a community-wide feud.

I was through being the patsy. It always seemed too easy for St. Vincent's administrative leadership to lean on me when the organization got into a scrape.

November 7, 1996:

Word of O'Flaherty's reaction to his Dining Room visit must have spread like wildfire. Within eight days of his visit, all the remaining small claims plaintiffs had withdrawn their cases before he had a chance to act. Five of the cases were withdrawn with prejudice and forty-seven without prejudice, meaning that the forty-seven could sue us again. We weren't out of the woods.

November 16, 1996:

In a letter, I let the St. Vincent's organization know that it would have to take full responsibility for the Dining Room program, including relocating it if that was what the larger community decided.

I also affirmed my interest in seeing the Dining Room program move to new location. I took the opportunity to step back from my responsibilities at Home Start, as well.

November 19, 1996:
I gave Schiele my Home Start resignation letter and asked her to deliver it to the Board.

At that point, the city maintained a throttling grip on the organization; I wanted to pursue expanding services to homeless single adults. I knew that my activities in that regard, especially considering the pending HUD complaint, made the other Board members nervous. They did not want to be linked to it, either personally or as a group.

Late November 1996:
As it worked out, Don Fisher signed a settlement agreement drafted by Marsha Leach in which each side dismissed with prejudice any action against the other. He paid his own attorney's fees, and Mull absorbed ours.

On the heels of Fisher's settlement of the anti-SLAPP complaint, Bragg and Slade spread the word that they were not finished with us. Bragg let *Press Tribune* reporters Carol Crenshaw and Robyn Eifertsen know that the members of their group "have not backed down on their demands..." In fact, she told the paper that "...many more people are asking to become involved."

December 5, 1996:
Nash tried to put the best spin possible on her clients' decision to curtail the recent small claims litigation. In a letter to St. Vincent's attorney Marsha Leach, Nash reshaped the facts making it appear that her clients had agreed to return to the bargaining table in exchange for our dismissing the Superior Court lawsuit. There was a quid pro quo.

We had dismissed our claim, but were certainly not bound by any agreement to do so. The point of the small claims suits became moot when they all had been withdrawn. We had won that battle!

Nash's letter expanded on the deception by setting conditions for renewing negotiations, the most significant ones being:
1. Bragg and Slade, as well as any others who might join them, would be represented at the bargaining table under the umbrella of a new organization identified only by the acronym CORR;
2. The negotiations would commence at the beginning of January and be held for two hours, one day per week over four consecutive weeks; and
3. Each side "will agree to refrain from making any statements to the media..."

When Leach told me she thought Nash's letter was odd, I set it aside.

December 6, 1996:

A news story about the stance of the residents and merchants broke on the front page of the *Press Tribune*. Bragg and Slade instigated the story, but arranged for one of their minions, Doug Selby, to serve as the front man.

The *Tribune* quoted Selby as making a veiled threat that our side was under the gun: "If the Boudiers and St. Vincent de Paul work with business owners and residents to resolve the problem, then we won't file a suit. But if they don't, there is a strong possibility we will file suit in Superior Court. We have no plans of going to court now, but the option is out there."

We knew that Selby's comment that his group did not have plans to go to court was absolutely false. We knew Nash had a Superior Court complaint on her desk, signed, dated and ready to be filed.

December 12, 1996:

Leach sent a response to Nash emphasizing that the sole reason we dismissed our complaint was that there was nothing to sue about after the withdrawal of the small claims actions. She made it plain that we did not dismiss our complaint with the intention of getting anything in return from the neighbors. There was no quid pro quo. Why did Nash insist on what was absolutely false?

I pointed out to Leach that Nash's proposed meeting schedule seemed designed to undermine a renewed attempt to resuscitate the Homeless Forum process by facilitator Steve Barber. He had proactively tried to restart the Forum negotiations as soon as he learned that the lawsuits had been dropped. He wrote to all of the forum participants in the spirit of cooperation, inviting them to a meeting on January 21st to restart the Homeless Forum deliberations.

December 13, 1996:

My suspicion that Nash's meeting schedule was timed to undercut the Forum process was confirmed in a phone conversation with Doug Selby following a *Press Tribune* story. I asked him about his take on Steve Barber's proposal. Selby's aversion to the idea came across loud and clear. He saw it as an obstacle to achieving the neighbors' goals.

January 6, 1997:

Despite their talk about negotiating, Nash, Bragg and Slade launched a New Year's attack, a barrage that landed us in Superior Court for the second time. They asked the court for:

- Preliminary and permanent injunctions, ordering the closing the Dining Room;
- fifty thousand dollars in general damages for each member of CORR;
- Compensation to offset the decreased value of each of the member's real property "according to proof";
- Five million dollars in punitive damages;
- Costs of the suit; and
- Any "other relief as the court may deem appropriate."

These people were out for blood. Their suit bore no resemblance to our earlier Superior Court filing which simply asked for declaratory relief – merely to determine if the Dining Room was a nuisance. Their complaint asked the court to throw the book at us.

Events moved swiftly. The filing of the suit was followed by a press conference orchestrated by Bragg and Slade on the sidewalk in front of Slade's salon. John Englander of the *Sacramento Bee* called me afterward, asking for a comment.

I told him his call was the first time I had heard that the litigation had been filed. He gave me the details, including news that a uniformed Roseville Police Department representative, Lieutenant Bill Hughes, was standing with Nash, Bragg and Slade as they announced the lawsuit.

When I asked Englander who the named plaintiffs were, he responded that there was only one, an organization called Citizens Organized to Revitalize Roseville, referred to as CORR. I assumed that because Hughes was present, CORR must have been part of the new Roseville Coalition of Neighborhood Associations (RCONA), which was unincorporated and controlled and promoted by city government at the time. He and Pam Harlan, also of the police department, had been trying to set up RCONA neighborhood groups throughout Roseville, two of the first being the Cherry Glen and Thieles Neighborhood Associations in 1993. RCONA wasn't an independent corporation until February 28, 1997.

My first thought was that if Hughes was allowing CORR to use his status as a peace officer to leverage support for the organization in this private property dispute, he had strayed way over the line, abusing his position. His presence was just one more sign that Chief Simms was once again stepping up his campaign against homeless single men.

In fact, the city was off base if it had allowed CORR to become part of RCONA. The blatant use of public resources to interfere in a private, civil property rights lawsuit seemed a reckless and irresponsible act by a local hobophobic government out of control.

Right after the conversation with Englander, I returned a call from Carol Crenshaw of the *Press Tribune*, who had also been at the news conference. She wanted to know my reaction to the new court filing. I first let her know that I thought the suit would undermine any chance of reviving the Homeless Forum process. I also told her I felt that CORR would find it difficult to prove the allegations in the lawsuit.

The reporter calculated that the total amount of potential money damages involved could be more than seven million two hundred thousand dollars, figuring the five million dollars in punitive damages and fifty thousand dollars in damages for each of the forty-five members CORR was thought to have. My first reaction was that this kind of money would ensure that the insurance company would put up a damn good fight. I gave her Jeff Steele's contact information.

Crenshaw mentioned that Nash said that her clients would probably drop the demand for money if we agreed to move the meal program. I thought that was an unlikely proposition, coming from the attorney representing Bragg and Slade. After all, these two women had spurned each of our many attempts to negotiate a move of the meal program. I got the distinct impression that Nash had no idea of the depths of hostility that Bragg and Slade had for St. Vincent's and me.

That evening, I had a long talk with Father Dan about the day's events. He had a good head for business. In a matter-of-fact way, he observed that the police department stood with the plaintiffs at the news conference because the city had already sided with CORR. He recounted that the police had shown up at the August Homeless Forum meeting almost like they arrived on cue. He also reminded me that we had thought the police had coached the neighbors on how to file the small claims lawsuits. Everything he mentioned fit together like a puzzle.

But then, he surprised me. He offered, "Bill, how can I help? Do you need any money?"

What a generous offer! As kind as it was, I think he had forgotten about St. Vincent's SAFECO's insurance coverage. I expected it to kick in any day. Father Dan's gesture of generosity was one that I will always remember.

January 7, 1997:

Jeff Steele from SAFECO Insurance brought me up to date on things from his end, even though he had not been officially assigned to the case. He said he was sure he would be handling the matter and was waiting for word from Richard Williams, SAFECO's adjuster.

I also heard from Marsha Leach. Much to my surprise, she expressed an interest that led me to feel I could rely on her help if SAFECO fell short in some way. That was welcome news! I regarded her judgment and understanding of our problem as being right on the money.

A couple of key observations Leach made were that CORR was not formed to improve the community as much as it was to harm St. Vincent's and me, and that there was no legal precedent which stated that needy persons were a nuisance.

January 10, 1997:

Early in the afternoon, I received a letter from Williams, letting our side know that SAFECO would manage our defense once it was certain that we were covered by the policy. I immediately called to thank him for the letter and ask that Jeff Steele be assigned to the case.

Mid-day, I found out the Homeless Forum process was formally finished. Steve Barber had thrown in the towel. His office called and said the meeting on the 21st had been canceled.

Yes indeed. Nash and her associates had changed from a course of "negotiation" to one of litigation in a few short weeks. They had launched a major lawsuit, successfully killing the Homeless Forum process and at the same time had implicated the city, especially its police department, as a partner in their endeavor.

January 12, 1997:

Jim Bush said the word on the street was that both the Union Pacific police and Roseville police were cracking down on rail riders, driving them out of the yards and beyond city limits. The *Press Tribune* corroborated the rumor.

Using an obscure 1872 law, city police officers warned owners of liquor stores and bars to stop selling to a handful of hard-core repeat offenders or face being cited. Lieutenant Joel Neves had his men distribute handbills with pictures and names of some of the men to about twenty businesses selling liquor in central Roseville.

January 16, 1997:

Activity opened up again on the HUD complaint. I received a letter from Gloria Flemister, Director of HUD's Enforcement Division for the Office of Fair Housing and Equal Opportunity. The letter was the first indication we had of HUD action against the city. Flemister asked if HUD could disclose my identity and other personal information to the city in the course of investigating the complaint. I presumed that it was in response to a Freedom of Information Act (FOIA) request to HUD by the city.

I had serious misgivings about allowing the move:

1. It was no secret that I had filed the complaint. I had signed and mailed it only after I had told Home Start's Board I intended on doing so. Certainly the new community representative on the Board, Kristi Kinzel, who was tight with city officials, had given them a heads-up;

2. Whether my name was used or not did not alter the fact that the city was violating the law with its housing policies and ordinances. Confirmation from HUD of my initiation of the complaint would allow the bureaucrats to shift the discussion away from their transgressions and onto me as the messenger; and

3. I felt that it would be more difficult to pursue the HUD complaint if it was formally connected to me at that time. The neighborhood plaintiffs might insist that I drop the complaint as part of settling the Superior Court case.

I asked Marsha Leach for advice on how to respond to HUD. She said I should talk with Archie Mull, who did have some great insights. He told me that I should assure HUD that I would help in any way possible to show that the city discriminated against homeless single men. Fighting that discrimination was the basis for my complaint and was at the heart of our defense against the neighbors' new lawsuit.

January 20, 1997:

SAFECO confirmed that the company had taken the case, though it would take a few weeks before we saw the actual lawsuit. I was tired of waiting.

January 23, 1997:

St. Vincent's yard manager Kevin Stone made a special trip to the courthouse in Auburn to pick up a set of the documents CORR had filed.

"If you wanna play, you gotta pay!"

We distributed copies to Marsha Leach, SAFECO's Jeff Steele, Herb Whitaker and insurance agent Fred Festersen. Our side was savvy and solid.

I got word that Mull's advice regarding HUD was on target. Within a week of my reply, HUD let me know they had all the tools needed to conduct a focused monitoring review of Roseville's housing programs, policies, ordinances and procedures. HUD's purpose was to determine if the city had discriminated against anyone on the basis of race, color, age, disability, national origin, religion, sex or familial status.

When I asked David Philipson why HUD did not call the investigation what it really was – an investigation – he would not give me a straight answer. Instead, he said for all practical purposes an inquiry like this one was an investigation irrespective of what anyone wanted to call it.

Philipson also did not tell me that HUD regarded the withholding of my identity as the equivalent of never formalizing the complaint. Looking back, I would have probably still withheld my identity had I known that fact at the time, given the lawsuit situation and the excellent results that Philipson had already obtained.

February 5, 1997:

The leaders of St. Vincent's naïvely started their own public relations effort to save the Dining Room by inviting neighbors and businesses in Cherry Glen and Thieles to an open house as part of a strategy to dissuade them from joining the CORR lawsuit. It was a wrongheaded idea, one that I believed would flop.

February 6, 1997:

The next day, St. Vincent's President Dave Sorensen followed up with me and said that the open house, in his own words, "went well." He declined to say how many people had showed up, but mentioned that Bragg, Slade and Nash, as well as Father Dan, Fred Festersen, Doctor Bill Keenan and the St. Vincent's Board members were there.

Keenan was a local pathologist and entrepreneur. He was very confident that his presence on the scene would facilitate moving the problem along to a successful resolution. He learned otherwise in the days ahead when he tried lobbying members of the Council whom he mistakenly thought he knew well.

Nash, Bragg and Slade suggested a new committee be formed to search for an acceptable Dining Room site. They said significant differences could separate this endeavor from past attempts. For example, a Council member or even the mayor could sponsor the location, and only members of CORR and St. Vincent's would serve on the committee.

Sorensen told me that Nash, Slade and Bragg also suggested that they might like to buy the St. Vincent's property from Annette and me. I was sure they thought they could get a deal at a bargain price.

I immediately pointed out to an unsuspecting Sorensen that if we even expressed an interest in selling the property to the other side, St. Vincent's ability to find a new location would be completely undercut. In fact, the very idea of relocating the Dining Room project would get a good laugh from the folks at City Hall. It did not take long for the ideas of the three women to crash and burn.

February 14, 1997:

The process server working for Nash had a problem: he was unable to locate Annette and me to deliver the documents. Apparently, he didn't know where we lived or that we didn't hang out all day at the St. Vincent's office. The guy waited around the office for days, finally giving up and attempting to serve the papers to office manager Charlotte Magennis as she walked to her car.

Magennis refused to accept them. After she got to her car and began driving off, he ran alongside and tossed the papers through an open window. So much for doing the service of process the legal way!

About the same time, the city began a public relations campaign to garner support for revitalizing the Riverside Avenue corridor. The street looked drab and dated. The new Auto Mall on the other side of town had pulled most of the new car dealers away from the area, leaving empty old buildings and lots as monuments to Riverside's better days.

It was my impression that city insiders believed this new Superior Court lawsuit would deal the Dining Room a deadly blow. All that had to be done to finish off St. Vincent's was to wait for us to give up or to be run over in court. In their book, with the cleansing of the street by removing St. Vincent's, the stage to revitalize Riverside would be set.

February 15, 1997:

City resistance to a Dining Room relocation effort was confirmed by an insider who told me that Harry Crabb had asked the Council to meet in closed session to review the status of the CORR lawsuit, and to consider whether or not to recommend that the city get involved by joining CORR's cause.

According to my source, this was the second time Crabb would bring up the matter in closed session. His first try was in January – ostensibly to help the cause for Riverside Revitalization. Crabb was copying a move by the City of Sacramento, which the LA Times said "had aired its gripes against Loaves & Fishes in an extraordinary way. Astonishing advocates for the homeless across the country...Sacramento sued the religious charity...declaring parts of its operation a public nuisance and demanding that it stop serving food on Sundays."

It looked like Crabb was willing to go down the same path and actually expose Roseville to ridicule by having the city join CORR as a plaintiff. I thought he must have deluded himself into thinking he was a hero, leading the cause for Riverside's revitalization. He was oblivious to what he was really doing – again making Roseville look foolish, mean-spirited and narrow-minded. It appeared he thought he could freely work his will with fellow Council members Gamar, Hamel and Randy Graham.

March 5, 1997:

Crabb's closed meeting attempts to involve the city in the lawsuit flopped when the legal action that the City of Sacramento had taken against Loaves and Fishes turned into a public relations nightmare. Sacramento was forced into mediation to resolve its complaint.

March 10, 1997:

Bragg wrote to the City Council as the chairperson for CORR and "...on behalf of St. Vincent de Paul Board of Directors," the very organization she was suing. She stated that both organizations have agreed "to work together in the areas of concern with the operation of the Dining Room and hope that the city would be a willing partner." She also requested to make a presentation to the Council.

The names of individuals who Bragg claimed were behind the lawsuit and represented to be CORR's members were revealed. These were, by and large, the same names that had shown up in the small claims litigation. Some were folks who had dismissed their small claims with prejudice, which meant they couldn't sue us again about the Dining Room issue.

March 11, 1997:

Steele was ready to file his response to the CORR suit. His strategy was to demur to the complaint, rather than respond to the allegations. He would argue the complaint was defective on its face because it failed on several points:

- Because CORR failed to list any members in the official court documents, the court had no way to determine if the organization represented the considerable number of persons required to label the Dining Room a public nuisance, as required by California law.

- Because CORR failed to identify a considerable number of persons who were subjected to the alleged nuisance, it failed to show that a public nuisance even existed.

- Because CORR did not demonstrate that it suffered a special injury different than might have been endured by the community as a whole, it failed to prove that it suffered a public nuisance.

- Courts had determined that a private nuisance is "a civil wrong based on disturbance of rights in land." But CORR did not hold any private property interest and apparently was not representing any other parties, based on the documents filed with the court. and

- Steele noted that the portion of the complaint alleging that the Dining Room was a private nuisance was so poorly drafted that there was no way the court could determine whether the claimed private nuisance injury was suffered by CORR or by its members. He pointed out that the ambiguity alone was reason enough to sustain the demurrer on the additional grounds of uncertainty.

After the demurrer to the complaint was reported in the press, CORR began a downhill slide. Nash went on the defensive, telling Steele in a phone call that she was withdrawing from the CORR case because "she had suffered a severe personal illness."

Steele immediately informed me of Nash's call.

Bragg withdrew her offer to "work together." City Clerk Carolyn Parkinson told me Bragg said, "It was no longer an option...Things have changed."

March 20, 1997:

Slade launched a disinformation campaign. While she was chairing a Riverside Revitalization meeting, she got right to it by challenging some of the points in Steele's court filing. A reporter from the

Sacramento Bee Neighbors, Nick Budnick, was on hand. Slade apparently thought the meeting was the perfect opportunity for her to lay out her take on the lawsuit. Her CORR infomercial zeroed in on four points:

- The organization was founded as a neighborhood group to work with city government;
- CORR had closely collaborated with the Police Department;
- Vicki Wingate, a Cherry Glen resident and neighborhood leader, had filed papers for CORR to become a full-fledged nonprofit; and
- CORR was flourishing and had grown from just five people into a large citywide organization to get rid of St. Vincent de Paul.

John Sprague, Roseville's Housing and Redevelopment Manager, was on hand. He immediately distanced the city from Slade's claims. He flat-out said that city government was not involved with CORR. Two other city employees, Rick Fowler from Engineering and Robin Graham, Councilman Graham's wife and Sprague's assistant, just sat and listened. Seven Riverside area property owners and merchants also were present to hear Sylvia's litany: Sonny Eskridge, Bill Lesh, "Bud" Miller, Tom Romeo, David Schmidt and me.

The Riverside Revitalization project effort began to fizzle when Bragg and Slade canceled all Revitalization Subcommittee meetings and shifted their focus to the lawsuit and building up CORR.

March 24, 1997:

Bragg and Slade were scheduled for a meeting at the police department.

March 26, 1997:

Because Nash had not severed her representation of Bragg and Slade after she had told Steele that she was opting out of the case, Steele felt he needed to remind Nash that it appeared that a basic tenet of legal ethics had been broken by her and her clients more than once. The first occurrence was when she, Bragg and Slade (plaintiffs) interacted with Dave Sorensen and his board at the open house hosted by St. Vincent's (a defendant). A second came when Bragg wrote to the City Council that she represented St. Vincent's.

Steele wrote to Nash, putting her on notice that as long as she was CORR's attorney of record, she and her clients were not to communicate with or claim to represent either St. Vincent's or any other named defendants, and that any correspondence and all negotiations were to be channeled through his office.

March 27, 1997:
Unfortunately for Slade and CORR, the article written by Budnick about the meeting the week before focused on Riverside revitalization and ignored Slade's representations about CORR.

March 31, 1997:
The CORR group met at the Chamber of Commerce offices.

April 2, 1997:
After a long day, as Annette and I settled in for the evening, the telephone rang. When I picked up the receiver, I heard a familiar voice. It was Lou Desmond, the bishop's attorney.

I was surprised that he had called me after 6 p.m. An after-hours phone call was out of character for any attorney. Following an exchange of pleasantries, Desmond asked me how our prospects were shaping up with the new Superior Court lawsuit.

I told him that SAFECO had retained some very good attorneys to develop a solid strategy to defeat the plaintiffs' claim. The company certainly had the motivation to put some heavy hitters into the game based on how much was at stake.

At that point, I was feeling relieved to finally get some feedback from the bishop's office about our ordeal. I presumed that Desmond was building up to an announcement that we were going to receive some form of moral support from the bishop, just as we had received support from both Father Dan Casey, the pastor of St. Rose Church and from Pastor Emeritus Father Mike Cormack, as well as from several of my Protestant minister friends in town.

Desmond did not waste words getting to the purpose of his call. He bluntly said that Annette and I, as well as St. Vincent's, would not get any support, moral or otherwise, from the diocese. His exact words were, "You are on your own."

When I heard those words, I was crushed not only by the message, but also by the fact that Weigand himself did not deliver it. Why had he preemptively opted out of providing any support, public or otherwise, for our cause? I am still not sure.

The Church's negative response to our legal challenge was something I had not expected. I had put myself and my family at risk by trusting the institution and its leader. I had mistakenly presumed that Bishop Weigand was as much a social justice advocate as Bishop Quinn had been during his tenure. Quinn lived by what Jesus said. It seemed that Weigand just mouthed the words.

I remembered that in the months immediately following his installation as Bishop of Sacramento, Weigand spoke to the deacons and their wives gathered for a spiritual retreat. He told us he would appreciate our reporting any action or situation to him directly that might adversely affect his office or the Church and its ministry. He reminded us of an early Church saying which describes the foundational bond between bishop and deacon: "The deacon is the eyes, ears, mouth and heart of the bishop."

With that ideal in mind, and as had been my routine in dealing with the small claims actions, whenever I had received important new information on this new Superior Court case, I made sure Bishop Weigand's office was appropriately informed. Every week or so, I personally traveled to Sacramento to deliver news articles, as well as the latest legal documents, correspondence and meeting notes to the Pastoral Center.

I took our new bishop at his word. Why shouldn't I? The only bishop I knew well was Bishop Quinn. His word was as good as gold.

Weigand retreated when faced with potential risk to the Church, failing to grasp a golden opportunity to promote the gospel values of justice, charity and compassion for one another.

I no longer saw Weigand as my leader, and certainly not as a man of courage.

April 17, 1997:
Nash notified Bragg that she was dropping the case – a month after we got the word.

April 25, 1997:
According to Bragg's letter to the Superior Court, Nash alleged that she had an "...illness which makes her unsuited to represent CORR..."

I decided to do some checking about Nash on my own. Her legal office telephone number had been recently disconnected. Was Nash shutting down her practice? I called the antique co-op where I knew she had an office the previous December.

When I asked the person who answered the phone about Nash cutting off her law office phone line, she told me that Nash had just changed the phone number.

I mentioned that I had heard Nash had been ill. The lady said that to the contrary, she seemed quite well. In fact, Nash had just left the store to return to her new Oak Street office. Nash was still in business.

But, Bragg and Slade were without an attorney and found themselves in deep trouble. The case management hearing was just a couple of weeks away. To Bragg's credit, she tried to fill the void left by Nash's exodus and appealed to the court for an extension of time for CORR to obtain legal counsel. The extension wasn't granted.

May 1997:

The police department received three twenty-five thousand dollars U.S. Department of Justice "COPS" (Community Oriented Police Services) grants to study the damage homeless persons caused the business community in Old Roseville – the area on both sides of the rail tracks along old highways 40 and 99E.

The premise underlying the study was that homeless people in the Old Roseville area were running off potential business customers who opted to shop in upscale malls. Its stated goal was to find ways to curb transient-related problems.

I thought it evident to anyone with any business sense that the real cause for Old Roseville's economic decline was not a sprinkling of homeless people in the area. It was a group of outdated and irrelevant retail stores occupied by undercapitalized mom-and-pop shops one step away from folding.

Bill Lesh, a friend from the Thieles neighborhood who worked with me on Riverside Avenue's revitalization, told me he was skeptical of the city's intentions regarding the grants. He felt it was a political boondoggle the city took on to keep the litigious neighbors happy and to squeeze a few dollars out of the award for the police department computer system, rather than as a search for real solutions, such as stepping up patrols.

I had the same feeling as Lesh. We decided to contact the police department to validate our hunches.

May 5, 1997:

Bragg was upset that Jack Willoughby, who was the presiding judge of the trial courts, was personally handling the CORR case management hearing.

Jeff Steele later recounted the blow-by-blow banter that went on among Bragg, Willoughby and himself during the hearing. After opening remarks, Willoughby let Bragg know she couldn't represent CORR because she was neither an attorney nor a named plaintiff. She didn't have standing in court.

That was followed by Bragg's request that Willoughby recuse himself from the case because she felt he would be biased in our favor. Willoughby bristled at the implication, saying that the case management meeting was procedural and another judge would be assigned to handle any issues of substance.

Willoughby set November 16th for the court trial. Steele responded that he needed more time to prepare because of the complications of discovery. He had no idea how many CORR plaintiffs there were, which meant that the number of depositions and possible interrogatories was open-ended. Willoughby replied that it remained to be seen as to whether or not the November date was too soon.

May 6, 1997:
Another judge whom none of us had met, Larry Gaddis, sustained Steele's demurrer. That put an immediate burden on CORR to file an amended complaint that would trump our objections. Gaddis gave Bragg until June 16th to reply.

May 20, 1997:
When a formal order sustaining Gaddis' decision was signed by Judge Roeder, Steele saw that the whole CORR case was on the verge of collapse. If he could get the reply date moved up, he could wind up the matter in short order in our favor with a Bragg default.

May 28, 1997:
Council member Mel Hamel surprised the community when he announced his decision to retire from his job as Principal at Spanger Elementary School and resign from City Council effective mid-June. His term did not end for another sixteen months, but he was walking away.

There were plenty of people who wanted Hamel's spot on the Council. Following the Council's decision to appoint a replacement rather than call a special election, twelve locals filed applications.

June 8, 1997:
A regional meeting co-hosted by Placer County Social Services was held at Shepherd of the Sierra Presbyterian Church of Loomis.

Volunteers from area churches and charities were invited to examine and discuss the impact on families and singles of the new nationwide welfare reform law enacted the previous August.

The conference turned out to be a great opportunity to network. I made several new contacts who would help overcome south Placer County's homeless problems down the road: Jim Williams (a County Supervisor at the time), Bev Anderson and Deb Koss.

June 13, 1997:

For my birthday, I got a little present from an unexpected source: Bragg threw in the towel. She filed a dismissal with the court clerk, withdrawing her suit without prejudice, which would allow CORR, or any other party, to sue us again. It was better than nothing.

July 1, 1997:

Bragg's dismissal was thrown out by the court because Nash was still the attorney of record for CORR, and Bragg was neither an attorney nor a named plaintiff in the action.

Judge James Roeder, whom none of us on the defense knew, vacated Bragg's dismissal without prejudice.

In its place, he dismissed CORR'S complaint with prejudice, entered a judgment in our favor, and awarded us recovery of all costs. For all practical purposes, the issue of whether or not the Dining Room was any kind of nuisance had been permanently resolved in our favor.

Luckily for Bragg and Slade, the costs were minimal. Archie Mull had donated all of his fees and SAFECO Insurance picked up Steele's tab. But Bragg did have to reimburse Steele's office seven hundred forty-two dollars in filing and motion fees plus bear any expenses of the case she incurred, including funds spent for court and attorney fees. Hopefully, Sylvia Slade helped absorb the costs.

For the record, there was never a corporation or formalized association named "Citizens Organized to Revitalize Roseville (CORR)." Apparently the phantom organization was an invention of the imaginations of Nash, Bragg and Slade – a convenient vehicle to spin a yarn they wished was true.

As their story played out, reality took over, and both Bragg and Slade learned a not-so-subtle life lesson: If you wanna play, you gotta pay!

Chapter 18:
City Cited for Short Shrift of Shelterless Singles
(Jul. 9, 1997–Dec. 1997)

July 9, 1997:

The dispute Ozenick started in 1994 between Roseville and Placer County over community growth issues, specifically the city's development rights over lands west of Fiddyment Road, was settled.. The Roseville City Council approved a Memorandum of Understanding with Placer County that effectively made Roseville the major economic hub of both south Placer County and northern Sacramento County.

In essence, Roseville had become Placer County's nine hundred pound gorilla which Placer County officials had no desire to tangle with.

The agreement's conciliatory tone was facilitated by County Supervisor Bill Santucci. For Santucci, the MOU was his legacy, polishing his reputation as a peacemaker.

The second big item on the night's Council agenda was settling on who would replace former Council member Hamel. Two names were placed in nomination, Jim Gray and Earl Rush. Both had appropriate credentials and substantial records as local political insiders.

Gray was the former chair of the city's grant commission, a former member of the parks and recreation commission and had served on the planning commission for eleven years. He was also the current personnel director for Placer County.

Earl Rush was also a member of the planning commission, a post he had held for nine years, and was the former Crime Stoppers president.

When the vote was taken, Council members Roccucci and Graham were for Gray, while Gamar and Crabb wanted Rush. When the dust settled and a second round of balloting got underway, Gamar surprisingly broke with Crabb, giving Gray three votes to Crabb's one for Rush. Gamar justified changing her vote by announcing, "I couldn't in good conscience cost this city and the general fund one hundred thirty thousand dollars for a special election."

July 16, 1997:
Jim Gray was sworn in as a Council member at high noon. I was glad that he was selected. Rush's opposition to helping the less

fortunate was well-known.

July 22, 1997:
An editorial in the *Sacramento Bee* was sharp in tone and went to the heart of our homeless issue. The title was perfect. "Roseville's Homeless – Boomtown can't continue to shirk its responsibilities." The editorial pointed out the moral obligation of the community to provide for the needs of the "Social misfits, the mentally ill, drug addicts and alcoholics (who) hide in boxcars that rumble into the largest switching yard west of the Rockies.... (A homeless shelter) would give Roseville a place to fulfill its responsibility to serve the legitimate needs of the down-and-out, as well as a way to manage and contain a difficult population, one that's not going to disappear."

As the *Bee* reported, between the beginning of the year and mid-July, two hundred eighty-three people had been cited or arrested by Union Pacific Railroad police. The company was enforcing a rule its predecessor, Southern Pacific, had on the books for years but failed to fully implement because of cost: UP's zero-tolerance policy. Trespassers were subject to arrest or citation instead of being just run off.

The result was a noticeable drop in the number of transients showing up in Roseville, which meant fewer meals at St. Vincent's. As Union Pacific police officer Blair Geddes said, "Word had gotten out that Roseville is a hot yard, meaning unfriendly."

Union Pacific, which was not hobbled by HUD regulations that kept city police in line, had promised Roseville to that they would use every tactic permitted by law to reduce the rail rider problem over its entire network. They meant business.

July 25, 1997:
John Sprague sent out an invitation to those in the service provider group to attend a meeting to view a document he and Shonkwiler had cooked up over the past three months called "The Continuum of Care" or "CoC ."

The CoC process was a new yearly requirement by HUD. It called for each community seeking federal funds to get public input to determine what the community's housing and shelter needs were. The needs and request for funds were to be ranked by priority in the CoC document.

The meeting was to rubber stamp the document, which had never seen the light of day. Sprague and Shonkwiler, alone in the privacy of their offices, had fabricated Roseville's CoC proposal. There were no public hearings or collaborative meetings with the service providers. The process was totally absent any transparency.

August 1997:

Sherry Schiele and I traditionally met once or twice a week after morning Mass to discuss business, usually in the St. Rose parking lot.

We often commiserated over the probability that the City of Roseville and Placer County would again escape responsibility for housing homeless persons during the upcoming winter.

As it was, there would be a few people who would qualify for housing help, exceptions who would manage to muddle through the maze of rules for the city's penny-pinching homeless voucher program or meet the exacting requirements of a random program the county might offer to families.

The two of us always made sure the programs we were associated with were ready to come to the rescue. St. Vincent's would try to help by offering free pup tents to singles and motel vouchers to families on the waiting list for the Home Start program. Home Start would take in as many families as possible at its Riverside location. Additionally, St. Rose would continue to provide monthly stipends of over one thousand dollars to each agency on a year-round basis. Other churches and donors helped out, as well.

Sometimes I tried to joke with Schiele about what I had labeled "the County Express," the occasional trip by a Placer County Health and Human Services employee to Sacramento to dump some poor soul at the door of Loaves and Fishes. Usually the victim would have some physical or mental issue and was stranded in Placer County or maybe had just been released from jail or the hospital.

A few of Police Chief Tom Simms' men were known to use similar tactics. It appeared that they thought solving the homeless single male problem in Roseville was easy: either drive the men to the Sacramento county line or, more brutally, break up their camps, confiscate their personal items, including their I.D.s, throw the works into the creek and tell them to get out of town.

The plight of homeless men and women in Roseville was never something Schiele took lightly. She worried about them day in and day out, and her concern grew as the winter drew near. She knew it would take a miracle to meet the needs we would be faced with this winter.

During one of our confabs after Mass, Schiele told me she wished there was an organization in Roseville that would broadcast across the city that caring for homeless folks was what Jesus wanted us to do. She wished for an organization "...that would be in their face about it!"

Schiele continued her thought and then questioned out loud, why shouldn't there be an organization in Roseville named "What Would Jesus Do?" With that, her eyes lit up, and she suddenly said, "I need to go to Sacramento!"

When I asked what for, she said she wanted to check with the Secretary of State's office to see if the name was available.

I asked, "What name?"

She said "What Would Jesus Do?"

Schiele was back in Roseville before noon, thoroughly delighted that she was able to put the name on hold.

August 4, 1997:

There were about twenty people who showed up to see the CoC document that Sprague and Shonkwiler had created, including three city staff members and a newspaper reporter.

The group was informed that the document for the Council had been completed, basically finished. Modifying it was out of the question. It was only regarded as a draft in terms of not having been finally approved by the Council.

The only programs recommended for funding were the three offering permanent supportive housing and transitional shelter for families with children: Home Start, Placer Women's Center and PEACE for Families.

Sprague and Shonkwiler tried to justify railroading their "draft" version of the CoC through the City Council process by alleging that the city was under "a tight time constraint." They insisted that data from past meetings and forums was still relevant and valid, making more input from the community unnecessary.

When the press asked us for comments after the meeting, Jim Bush was the most vocal: "You're only dealing with women and not with the single males who may be sick or mentally ill and need services as much as the women do."

St. Vincent's Dave Sorensen was critical of Sprague's claim that the city took shortcuts because it was up against the clock in preparing the document. He also bashed the city for the low priority placed on the need for services to homeless single males.

I followed by calling out city staff for misusing statistics in its "gaps in services analysis" to legitimize the phony ranking of projects. That effectively eliminated any funding for services to the homeless single population, male or female. Sherry Schiele summed it up, adding, "The whole thing is a sham."

Several of us decided to formulate a letter to the Council asking that approval of the document be delayed. We wanted time to put together funding proposals for aid to single men.

Given that Schiele's agency, Home Start, was fortunate enough to be listed for funding in the city's final CoC document, it might seem strange that she would criticize the city for its tricky handling of the process. That was just Schiele's way. It was the right thing to do.

In fact, her concern did not end with a couple of terse and insightful comments. She decided to hold the city accountable by carrying her complaint forward to HUD. She asked the feds not to accept the city's CoC Plan until the city "involves more than just city officials" in the process, and until the plan "includes adequate services for single homeless men."

August 7, 1997:

John Sprague was on defense. He wrote to the *Bee*, detailing all of the programs and activities Roseville had been engaged in over the years that provided housing and shelter to resident families. He also brought up how the city helped support the National Guard Armory emergency winter shelter for six seasons until the winter of 1994.

However, what he did not say was more memorable. He failed to share the details as to why there had been no publicly sponsored shelter since.

Instead he sermonized, "The Roseville Community...expects all residents and visitors to behave responsibly and obey the law...When irresponsible behavior means residents can't enjoy their homes...and merchants can't earn a livelihood, then the community has a right to act. (Their) legal action was in response to constantly inappropriate behavior...by homeless men."

The Roseville and Union Pacific police had Sprague's unconditional support to continue their tactics.

August 13, 1997:

HUD investigator David Philipson let me know that his agency's review was complete and had been sent to San Francisco and Washington D.C. for approval. He said there was lively interest in the results, commenting that he was contacted almost daily by both offices with questions and comments about the disposition of the case. Final letters to both the city and me would come from the San Francisco office.

August 20, 1997:

When Bill Lesh and I were finally able to get some answers from the Roseville Police Department about the COPS grants, spokeswoman Dee Dee Gunther and Captain John Barrow assured us that the focus of the grants was to discover how to revitalize downtown, not to be used to single out or blame homeless men for the district's economic problems.

We were told that the city had contracted with a homeless consultant for the COPS grants project, Lynette Lee-Sammons, a professor of Criminal Justice at California State University, Sacramento.

August 21, 1997:

City Manager Al Johnson was quick to follow up with HUD after hearing that Schiele had complained to the federal agency about the 1997 CoC process. He sent a letter of his own to HUD, defending the city.

August 25, 1997:

Schiele introduced me to Joe Esparza. He was her first choice to be the new face of the provider community seeking a shelter solution. He was a local resident, regional insurance broker and Chair of the Home Start Board of Directors. She was wise enough to know neither she nor I could make a public request. The City Council would absolutely kill any project that even looked like it had our fingerprints on it.

Schiele thought Esparza was a great choice, hoping his fresh face and compassionate message would do the trick.

September 9, 1997:

In one of our parking lot meetings, Schiele wanted to talk about a timeline for incorporating What Would Jesus Do? (WWJD?). I mentioned that St. Rose Parish still had The Placer Community Care Center shell corporation, a 501(c)3 nonprofit that was ready to be matched with a homeless shelter project if one came on the scene. I asked her if she wanted to use it. All she had to do was change the name. Schiele was all for it.

I called Father Dan to see what he thought. He said it was a great idea, giving us the green light to make the transfer.

Schiele amazed me. She was an eternally optimistic idealist with the power of faith that made her indomitably positive about all things human because she saw each person as rooted in divinity.

The idea of truly helping the area's homeless folks was something that had been part of her consciousness for as long as I had known her. Even after the year-long Home Start ordeal with the city in 1995–96, she had not given up on housing for homeless single men and establishing a permanent program to serve their needs.

Schiele saw that all of the pieces were coming together for her. She would give the WWJD? name to the 501(c)3 corporation, and she had a plan and the perfect place for the housing, just around the block from Home Start.

She had been negotiating to acquire the B Street Apartments from the owner Patricia Holden of Fair Oaks. She believed she could raise funds for a down payment on the property and put together an application for operational funding through the 1998 CoC process. After all, she would already be applying on Home Start's behalf. Creating two similar proposals at the same time couldn't be that much more difficult.

September 17, 1997:
The City Council approved the staff's CoC package. The recommendations of our provider group were totally ignored.

The Council also adopted changes that expanded its homeless voucher program from operating just during the winter months to year round, including limited aid to single adults who were residents. At the same time, the Council majority kept the rules so tight that only established locals in need of temporary help for utilities, rent or emergency shelter could qualify. It looked like applying for the help required more backup paperwork than filing an income tax return.

Council members Crabb and Gray were absent from the meeting.

September 23, 1997:
HUD's Deputy Director of Community and Planning, Jimmy Prater, replied to City Manager Al Johnson:

"This is in response to your August 21, 1997, letter...Since the plan is still in its draft stage, there should be sufficient time to allow for additional comment and input into the plan, and additional meetings and/or public hearings."

Prater went on to say "...we are confident that city staff and the homeless providers in the area can reach some consensus on the issue. Our HUD staff remains available and willing to provide whatever assistance we can to help reach this consensus."

The federal agency acknowledged that Schiele's complaint had merit. But locally, there was no way for the Council to back off its September 17th decision without losing face.

Instead, city staff ran to the Council's rescue by urging the members to get a jump forward to develop the 1998 CoC document, using a process that would "create that respectable appearance" of transparency and inclusiveness.

September 26, 1997:

Home Start Board Chair Joe Esparza sent a letter to area pastors inviting them to a meeting at the Presbyterian Church on Sunrise Avenue to discuss how to approach the City Council about a homeless shelter for the upcoming winter.

October 10, 1997:

The Council approved an agreement with the Salvation Army to administer the Roseville Homeless Voucher Program adopted on September 17th. The agreement included very strict reimbursement guidelines, providing that if the Army didn't meet the city's complex rules, the city would deny its fifty percent reimbursement.

October 24, 1997:

In a comprehensive memo to the Council authored by Housing and Redevelopment Manager Sprague, the city administration presented its take on the past year's failed CoC process.

Sprague's depiction of events fancifully implied that he had gone to great lengths to stir up community interest while preparing the document, only to be disappointed that a mere handful of people came forward with input: "Thirty or less persons participated in the 1997 CoC development effort even though one hundred twenty citizens and organizations were noticed by mail and public notices appeared in the newspaper (in May)."

No one in the provider community could recall receiving such a letter. His comments appeared to be a flight of the imagination, an attempt to rewrite the record.

As far as preparing for the next year's CoC process, the city players were well aware of HUD's concern that provider agency participation had to be a key part of the process. Sprague recommended that to avoid that pitfall, the City Council authorize staff to recruit candidates from the public and provider community to serve on a CoC Review Committee for 1998.

October 28, 1997:
The city received HUD's findings on the complaint I had initiated in June 1996.

October 31, 1997:
When HUD let me know that the monitoring investigation had been completed, all I got was a notice letter. What a letdown! Where was my copy of the actual report?

I scrambled to get the documents. When I called the HUD office for copies, David Philipson told me that I had to file a FOIA (Freedom of Information Act) request to get them and any other papers related to the investigation.

November 1997:
There was a sudden change in leadership at St. Rose. In a very disconcerting turn of events, Bishop Weigand directed Father Mike McKeon to take the reins from Father Dan.

November 5, 1997:
The Council accepted Sprague's October 24th recommendation to recruit members of the public and provider community to serve on a seven member CoC Committee. The group would recommend the priority of the projects for the 1998 document.

November 13, 1997:
The likelihood of not having a winter shelter for Roseville's homeless population weighed heavily on the collective conscience of the providers and churches who had recently met at the Presbyterian Church on Sunrise. The group's leader, Joe Esparza, drafted a letter to the city clerk asking the City Council to pass a resolution to provide temporary housing for homeless adults from December 15th to March 15th.

The *Press Tribune's* Jim Janssen reported that Esparza's request was put on the City Council's December 17th agenda for members to determine whether it would be slated for a hearing and vote in the future. That meant that if a hearing on Esparza's request was scheduled, it would probably be no sooner than mid-January, a third of the way into the shelter season.

The city manager could have simply added the matter to a late November or early December Council agenda for a full hearing, but instead put the onus on the Council to decide whether to hold a hearing at all. That move took the heat off of city staff and delayed any process for making a final Council decision.

The city's stalling was a signal to both Schiele and me that we should move ahead to intensify our efforts to help homeless single adults as we had planned in August:

- St. Vincent's would give free pup tents to singles and motel vouchers to families on the waiting list for the Home Start program. The agency would also provide utility assistance and rent for families and ill adults.
- Home Start, where up to thirty families were housed at a time, would take in as many families as possible at its Riverside location.
- St. Rose would double its monthly stipends to two thousand dollars to each agency on a year-round basis.
- Schiele's new morning WWJD? services and breakfasts for homeless men and women would increase the number of days of operation. She would begin venturing out into the cold, damp winter dawn on an almost daily basis before going to her regular job as executive director at Home Start.
- Her Blanket Brigade program, which she had begun the previous winter, would be expanded by recruiting more church congregations to collect blankets to distribute to the folks she encountered during her WWJD? rounds.

Schiele's WWJD? morning routine involved loading blankets, sandwiches and donated snacks into the back seat of her red two-door Nissan sedan and putting a big pot of hot coffee in the trunk. Then, as she drove around Roseville, she would stop wherever she came across someone she thought was in need. Sometimes it was one person. Other times, it was a group.

The number of people didn't make a difference to her. She was not afraid and never seemed threatened by anyone she was trying to help. She had an uncanny knack for unlocking the deep, dark secrets of the hurt these folks had suffered.

Schiele also possessed a thorough knowledge of social services and medical options in the area and had loads of personal experience accessing them. She had several backchannel connections she maintained with county and hospital staff members who tried to help her and her friends – the ones she met on the streets.

On most days, Schiele would make her rounds just in the mornings. When the weather was the worst – while most of us were warm and secure in our homes, she would make a second trip after dark.

Schiele called her new service to homeless people "seeking." She did not wait for them to come to her. She literally sought them out. She was a warrior.

Mid-November 1997:

I finally got the HUD investigation documents. The material indicated that HUD planned a three-step process to help resolve the city's differences with the providers:

- Have the city first respond to the allegations;
- Have the city meet with HUD representatives to work on possible compromises; and
- Ask that the city and service providers sit down to resolve the problem areas HUD had identified.

If that failed to work, HUD was prepared to submit the matter to the Department of Justice for action.

The documents criticized city housing policies and practices toward homeless single adults in four specific areas:

- The city's Consolidated Plan: The HUD probe concluded, "We note that the city has given a low priority in its Consolidated Plan to the needs of homeless individuals with respect to outreach, provision of emergency shelters , provision of permanent supportive housing and provision of permanent housing... .We are concerned that the city policy...may discourage service providers from applying for funding to assist transient homeless adults."

- The city's attack on Home Start: The report stated, "We also understand that the city, in 1996, refused to provide a letter in support of an application...for Federal Emergency Shelter Grant funding submitted by Home Start until the organization formally agreed to cease providing temporary shelter to transient

homeless persons."
- The administration of the Community Development Block Grant Program: HUD concluded, "To the extent that the city has funded, supported, or permitted any homeless population to be housed or served, it has not been single adults. Because of the gender and disability – based differences between...single men and women with children, we are particularly concerned that the city is administering its CDBG program in a manner that may discriminate on the basis of gender and disability."
- Roseville's Congregate Residence Ordinance: The review found that "On its face, this zoning ordinance may violate the fair housing rights of disabled persons by denying them the ability to live in congregate housing in residential neighborhoods. Numerous Federal and state court decisions have invalidated similar statutes."

One California court decision published on June 17th, 1997, found that the plan in the City of San Diego's housing element for the development of homeless shelters and transitional housing was unrealistic. The court ruled that San Diego's "good intentions" to provide adequate housing and shelter for its homeless population were meaningless in light of its restrictive ordinance, which for all practical purposes "substantially constrains" the possibility of locating or building any such facilities.

Roseville's ordinance was similar to San Diego's in intent. Both effectively made it nearly impossible to develop or expand shelter and housing opportunities for homeless persons. However, I saw that Roseville's was different: it seemed much less sophisticated and more brutal.

This was borne out in HUD's report, which stated, "Essentially, the city's policy and practice vis-à-vis its transient homeless population appears to have a disparate impact on males and people with disabilities, and may have a chilling effect on housing providers whose clients are or may be transient homeless persons."

In effect, the document was a shot across Roseville's bow, making city officials sit up and recognize that their Congregate Residence Ordinance had to be overhauled to conform to current state and federal court rulings. The admonition included a reminder that "the Fair Housing Act requires HUD to refer zoning issues such as this to the Department of Justice."

While the city regulation had been designed by staff to serve as a catch-all to empower the Council to control and ultimately derail any shelter plan of any type, HUD regarded it as evidence of discrimination and an overreach in governmental authority to restrict the development or expansion of homeless shelters.

The law was the city's one fatal mistake in fighting against our efforts, its blunder of the decade. It was the principal act that put Roseville in the crosshairs of HUD's Office of Fair Housing and Equal Opportunity Enforcement Division. The very ordinance intended to stop the providers had become a trap for the city.

The HUD material also made mention of the city's perversion of the development of the city's 1997 CoC Plan. It pointed out that the CoC process was to be a collaborative tool for the city and service providers to assist the city and HUD determine which homeless programs should receive federal McKinney-Vento Act Homeless Assistance support. HUD guidelines were explicit that the CoC was a community plan "...to meet the specific needs of people who are homeless...to end homelessness and prevent a return to homelessness."

A community plan was defined by HUD as one which included the participation of "nonprofit organizations (including those representing persons with disabilities), government agencies, public housing authorities, faith-based and other community-based organizations and other homeless providers, housing developers and service providers, private businesses and business associations, law enforcement agencies, funding providers, and homeless or formerly homeless persons."

Within a couple of hours, I had the HUD package in the hands of reporters at the *Bee* and the *Press Tribune*. Then, I spoke with John Sprague. He said he was shocked by HUD's tone in the letter and report, particularly by the absence of HUD's usually diplomatic approach. It appeared that the language must have been so different from past correspondence that he found its frankness difficult to accept.

Sprague was uncharacteristically anxious. He seemed desperate to get to the bottom of the situation. There was immediacy in his demeanor, as if he needed to know that very day how HUD reached its conclusions.

As our conversation continued, he maintained that he had been wronged by the report's accusations and what he regarded as HUD's mistakes. For example, he told me that HUD's reprimands of city policies and procedures could have been avoided if HUD had covered those areas in its training.

I wondered if Sprague was parroting the city's position in their upcoming response to HUD's findings. Would the city attempt to shift blame for as much of its problem as possible back onto HUD – and even onto the service providers? In any event, the cordial and trusting relationship that the city had with the federal agency had become a memory. Sprague quickly submitted his own FOIA request for the particulars about the investigation.

November 20, 1997:

City government was in a tizzy. Sylvia Slade was recruited by the administration to appear on Sacramento's Channel 31. Before the TV crew could get to Roseville, Art Campos of the *Bee* had an article in that morning's paper, reporting that there was a possibility of losing "further (federal) funding" if Roseville "is not within the law..." in its treatment of homeless single men. Campos went on to say that HUD felt that "city policies had possibly inhibited (agencies that provide services to the homeless) from applying for block grant funding." Grant dollars totaling four hundred thirty-five thousand dollars were on the line for the city in the pending fiscal year.

November 21, 1997:

On Channel 10, Slade again defended the city's policies and actions, but this time, the *Press Tribune's* Jim Janssen kept things real. In his front page, above-the-fold article entitled "HUD says city ordinance may violate rights," he noted that "HUD wants to meet with Roseville before it refers the matter to the Department of Justice (for prosecution for civil rights violations)."

November 25, 1997:

A City Hall insider told me that the city planned to challenge HUD as being unfair in conducting the monitoring review. For example, the city would claim that HUD did not interview anyone from the public who supported the city's position – just those of us who reported city abuses.

Idealistically, I had told Janssen, a Roseville good-ole-boy, that I thought that HUD's presence might take Roseville politics out of the equation. I should have known better.

December 8, 1997:

The city had formulated its response to HUD. It was a political one, not signed by the city manager, even though the HUD letter had been addressed to him. Instead, the mayor herself, Claudia Gamar, did the honors. It was an unusual step to have her sign – a move that appeared to be intended to put the feds on notice that they were going to have a fight on their hands. The letter included a direct rejoinder to each of HUD's four allegations that made the city's comeback more than straightforward. It was blunt and confrontational. It had "City Attorney" written all over it.

The reply to the first HUD allegation that the low priority given to homeless singles in the city's Consolidated Plan discouraged service providers from applying for funds was "The city fails to understand how HUD can dictate the priorities assigned to the various groups. HUD needs to explain why these priorities are unreasonable and how HUD can recommend the city alter priorities."

To the second HUD concern that the city refused to support grant applications from Home Start until Home Start agreed to stop housing homeless single men, the response was: "The city questions HUD's authority to override the city's local approval process and dictate which programs the city must support. The city also questions HUD's authority to intercede and direct the city to terminate a contractual agreement between two private parties."

To the third point of disagreement between HUD and the city, that homeless service providers believed that requesting CDBG funds to help homeless single adults was a wasted effort because of city policies, Roseville retorted: "Apparently, the homeless providers have opted not to participate based on their disagreement with the priorities in the Consolidated Plan resulting from the 'Citizen Participation Process.'"

Yes! We opted out when we realized the "Citizen Participation Process" was rigged. No matter what objective data we provided to the city to help formulate any planning document that would direct how to use federal funds, the city always found a way to controvert the facts to build a case against helping homeless single adults.

And finally, to the fourth point of contention, the Congregate Residence Ordinance, the city blasted HUD for meddling in Roseville's business: "There is nothing on the face of the Congregate Residence Ordinance that violates the Fair Housing Act…City staff believes the Fair Housing Act complaint is completely without merit, and was submitted for the sole purpose of enlisting HUD's assistance in breaking a valid, preexisting contract between Home Start and the city. This interference in the city's contractual relationship violates State Law."

So much for diplomacy. Philipson had told me that his relationship with the city had become so acrimonious that city staff members accused him, rather than me, of releasing information to the press to deliberately undercut their credibility.

The defense plan that city authorities developed was a two-pronged strategy meant to defuse pressure from HUD. First, the Council planned to freshen its public face by modifying the city's homeless voucher policy to permit shelter aid to single Roseville residents.

The second part of the strategy was for city officials, especially City Attorney Mark Doane, to stave off HUD's intrusion into Roseville's affairs and to acquiesce to HUD's concerns only when necessary.

December 12, 1997:

The first formal face-to-face meeting between HUD and city staff to address HUD's concerns occurred just four days after Mayor Gamar had dispatched her blunt letter to HUD's regional office in San Francisco. The letter probably arrived too late to put the HUD staff on edge as they prepared for the meeting.

The conference went well despite Roseville's on-guard posture. The meeting concluded with HUD promising to provide a summary detailing the agreed upon points to resolve the issues raised in the Fair Housing monitoring report.

December 17, 1997:

With a heart filled with good intentions, Esparza prepared well for his Council request for a winter shelter. In the lead-up to the Council meeting, he told the *Press Tribune* that an alliance of volunteers from various churches and social service agencies was behind the effort. He went on to say "Greatness will not come (to a community) if the needs of all the community cannot be considered, especially the downtrodden...We need to provide for the downtrodden."

The Council denied Esparza's request to put the shelter matter on a future agenda. And what was their excuse?

As Council member Crabb said, "It takes a lot of planning to put something like that together."..."We're going to wait until after the new Continuum of Care committee gets done with its findings..."

The Council already had ten years' worth of findings, and winter was upon us. That same Council, on which Crabb sat in each instance, managed to wiggle off the hook. This time, Sherry Schiele, after learning that Esparza had failed in his request, doubled down with her own plan to get a shelter for singles ready as soon as possible. The program would be known as Starting Over operating under the umbrella of WWJD?.

She began serious negotiations with the B Street Apartments owner to cinch a deal calling for a one hundred thousand dollar down payment. Half of the apartments would be rented out to make the mortgage payments, while the balance of the twenty-seven units would house up to forty men participating in the program. Schiele said ten thousand dollars had been raised toward the down payment. In reality, the ten thousand dollars was personal savings that she and her husband had loaned to WWJD?. It was nearly the entire balance in their small savings account.

December 23, 1997:

HUD's recap letter of its December 12th meeting with the city optimistically conveyed the feeling that the differences between HUD and Roseville were about to be resolved. The HUD staffers had grounds to be hopeful, as detailed in these five points of agreement they documented in the correspondence:

1. A mutually acceptable plan "to continue to work toward resolving HUD's concerns"...would be developed;
2. The city agreed to "revise the Congregate Residence Ordinance and Zoning Ordinance language to satisfy both HUD and Roseville";
3. HUD staff agreed to be available to advise city staff as to how to revise its 1997 "Impediments to Fair Housing" document;
4. HUD would provide an overview of the CoC process to the new citizens' committee that would recommend and rank projects for the 1998 CoC proposal; and
5. The city asked "HUD staff set up a meeting with Sacramento Housing and Redevelopment Agency to explore the option of the city (Roseville) accessing the Mather Air Force Base Regional Homeless facilities" as shelter for Roseville's homeless population.

There was no mention of referring the Congregate Residence Ordinance to the Department of Justice.

Chapter 19:
Roseville Fends off HUD; Home Start Struggles
(Jan. 1998–Jul. 26, 1998)

January 21, 1998:

HUD kept close tabs on City Hall as Roseville began organizing its new Continuum of Care (CoC) Review Committee. The Council moved ahead with its plan to appoint the seven-member panel that would recommend projects for the city's 1998 CoC document. On the surface, it seemed that Roseville wanted the evaluation process to be as inclusive and transparent as possible.

Those selected for the committee were former police chief Greg Cowart, who was serving as California Attorney General Dan Lungren's Director of the California Department of Justice Division of Law Enforcement, Wendy Still of the State Department of Corrections, Betsy Donovan, a senior manager at Eskaton, Rev. Jerry Angove, Pastor of First Methodist Church, Curtis Banner, retired principal from the Roseville City School District, Machel Stokes of the Salvation Army and Robert Townley.

All were Roseville residents. Cowart, Still and Donovan were professionals in the field of aberrant human behavior. Angove and Stokes were from the church and service provider community, while Banner and Townley seemed to be plucked right out of the "Old Guard of Roseville Reserves."

The committee's makeup guaranteed that the two votes from Angove and Stokes would assuredly go for almost any proposal which came from the service providers, while Banner and Townley would cancel them out.

Wendy Still and Betsy Donovan were seen as steady professionals. Because I didn't know them, I assumed they could turn out to be wildcards.

Cowart, during his term as police chief, had encouraged progressive policing tactics and was politically astute. It was going to be an interesting few months.

And so it was. The city, in its attempt to avoid the pit it had fallen into with HUD on the previous CoC go round, managed to take on the appearance of transparency as it began its next effort. The seven-member citizen committee looked good on paper. The panel selection appeared to be a businesslike and a genuine attempt to ensure that the process got off on the right foot.

January 25, 1998:
The *Bee* published an article concerning a Sacramento County government survey, comparing the dollars other counties in the area spent on providing actual emergency beds for homeless persons with what Sacramento paid out. The data showed that jurisdictions in Placer, including Roseville, spent nothing on maintaining emergency shelter beds. The survey also laid out that more than forty percent of Sacramento County's shelter clients came from jurisdictions in Placer and El Dorado Counties.

The newspaper stated that the Sacramento Board of Supervisors chairwoman, Illa Collin, intended to meet with members of the boards of supervisors from surrounding counties to consider developing a

County spending on the homeless		
County	Expenditures	Per capita
Sacramento	$10.86 million	$9.78
Placer	$0	$0
Yolo	$500,000	$3.25
San Joaquin	$1.7 million	$3.18
El Dorado	$0	$0
Sutter	$0	$0

Source: Sacramento County Department of Human Assistance

regional plan for housing homeless people in the winter. Sacramento County was done taking care of the contiguous counties' homeless problems.

February 4, 1998:
City manager Al Johnson issued a letter to the feds giving his slant on what the city had agreed to at the December 12th HUD meeting. His account confirmed the correct nature of HUD"s memorandum as far as detailing the actions Roseville had volunteered to undertake to resolve code and certain technical issues.

However, beyond that, Johnson's depiction of the meeting appeared to be a fanciful interpretation of HUD"s concerns with city policies about the needs of homeless single males, as detailed in both

HUD's October 1997 letter and David Philipson's case notes of the meeting. Philipson cited discussions with the Roseville representatives about possible local actions to provide assistance, including overnight shelter for homeless single persons.

But Johnson's letter didn't mention a word about a local overnight shelter. Instead it focused on the technical assistance aspect with developing:

- "objectives and strategies in the Continuum of Care program"; and
- "efforts to address long-term assistance needs...".

Insofar as Roseville addressing short-term assistance needs, he wrote that "the city is only interested in regional efforts."

The letter appeared to be the city's latest attempt to distance itself from considering a local overnight shelter option for its homeless single male population. It went so far as to state that during the December 12th meeting, HUD staff suggested the city "consider a regional effort with Sacramento," when in fact according to Philipson's case notes and HUD's December 23rd memo, it was Roseville that asked "HUD staff set up a meeting with Sacramento Housing and Redevelopment Agency to explore the option of the city (Roseville) accessing the Mather Air Force Base Regional Homeless facilities" as shelter for Roseville's homeless population.

In a later critique of Johnson's letter, Philipson suggested that in light of Roseville's intended direction on the issue, it would be appropriate that "the city's proposals for short-term care may need to be revisited." Apparently, he wanted a much tougher approach on the issue than his superiors. Philipson seemed to feel strongly that HUD should not allow Roseville to walk away from the matter.

HUD management seemed to minimize Philipson's concerns and decided to set up an exploratory conference for Roseville staff members and their Sacramento counterparts later in the spring.

February 10, 1998:

Rosemarie Fernandez-Pifer, Director of HUD's Program Compliance Division, sent a confidential HUD internal nine-page memo to Bonnie Milstein, Director of the Program Operations and Compliance Center. Only two other staffers were copied on the document: Program Compliance Division's Paul Berg and David Philipson.

Both Fernandez-Pifer and Milstein were practicing attorneys with comprehensive experience dealing with discrimination issues like the one alleged in Roseville. Apparently, when Fernandez-Pifer determined that there was not enough evidence on hand to recommend the case to the U.S. Department of Justice (DOJ), she immediately raised her concerns so that HUD would take more time in building a case for prosecution.

The Fernandez-Pifer memorandum detailed the events of a January 22nd internal HUD meeting with Milstein, Berg and Philipson. She recounted how the four HUD officials had reviewed the possible ways fair housing laws could be used to "undo Roseville's Congregate Residence Ordinance."

Three of the four possible ways involved determining if there was a violation of the Fair Housing Act. Such a violation would be grounds for DOJ to get involved, if it was based on a complaint by a member of a protected class or a provider of services to that person. The complaint would have to show one of the following:

1. The city selectively enforced its congregate residence ordinance against a member of a protected class or a provider of services to a member of that class, denying the member shelter or housing.
2. The city used a law or ordinance which was neutral on its face, but which actually had a disproportionate negative impact on a member of a protected class or a provider, with the intention of denying the member shelter or housing. In order to prove this kind of discrimination, HUD had to show that there was both discriminatory effect and discriminatory intent by the city against either a member or a provider in enforcing some local law or ordinance against them. or
3. The city denied a request to accommodate the shelter and housing needs of a member of a protected class by refusing to provide an exemption from a city rule, policy, ordinance, practice or service.

The problem with applying any one of these methods to Roseville's situation was that there simply was no complaint by an aggrieved person or by a provider of services to that person. Unfortunately, none of us in the provider community were told that it was necessary for a member of a protected class or for an actual provider of services to a protected class to file a complaint in order to have HUD request a DOJ action. So far, only Home Start's 1996 complaint, which was withdrawn, would have qualified for DOJ intervention.

There was a fourth approach: The Secretary of Housing and Urban Development could authorize a second investigation of Roseville's

Congregate Residence Ordinance and other policies that impacted homeless single adult males to determine if they caused an injury to any members of the class. If the injury fell into one or more of the three categories mentioned above, the case could be referred to DOJ.

Fernandez-Pifer, Milstein, Berg and Philipson finally agreed that HUD should dig out more information from their internal files concerning the city's use of federal grant funds (Community Development Block Grant money) for planning and redevelopment activities. This would help them discover if funds were utilized to develop or enforce policies which kept Home Start from sheltering homeless single males.

The new information, if sufficient, could be used to start a compliance review or, at minimum, discussions with city officials to resolve HUD's current concerns. In addition, Philipson would continue to gather information in his meetings with the providers.

Even after I read and studied the February 10th memo, I remained puzzled why the contents of my PCCC complaint and all the information I had passed on to HUD about the new city ordinance, along with what I had recorded on City Council discussions, wasn't enough to trigger a DOJ investigation.

On the city side, John Sprague's office had the timeline well mapped out for completing the CoC document for 1998, with all of the committee meetings being held in the City Council chambers beginning mid-February and concluding mid-June. The final committee recommendations would be forwarded to the Council. All the committee meetings were to be televised on the city's Government Access Cable Television Channel.

March 5, 1998:

The Roseville CoC Review Committee met to highlight two HUD matters:

1. A review of HUD's letter notifying the city of the results of the monitoring investigation; and
2. An overview and presentation by HUD staffer Winston Moy on the CoC process, as requested by committee chair Greg Cowart and Roseville staff.

In addition, an ad hoc working subcommittee was formed, which could be co-chaired by any one of three CoC Review Committee members, depending on who was available: Greg Cowart, Wendy Still or Jerry Angove. Additional members of the senior committee were invited to participate, as were folks from neighborhood associations, governmental agencies and the provider community. I attended as the St. Rose Church representative.

March 6, 1998:

Sherry Schiele's world came crashing down. Her type-1 diabetes was totally out of control, leading her to make a colossal mistake. Schiele had completely forgotten about the final filing date for Home Start's application for the two-year one hundred seventy-eight thousand dollar Federal Emergency Shelter (FESG) Grant. It was the one grant that Home Start had relied on for life support during good times and bad.

It was only when the 5 p.m. deadline was upon her that she recalled that the application was due. Schiele told me that she just gave up. There was no way anyone could complete the paperwork on time.

When the Home Start Board of Directors learned of the mistake, they immediately put Schiele on the sidelines and took matters into their own hands. They asked the state agency that oversaw the FESG program in California, the Department of Housing and Redevelopment, for an extension to file the application.

March 15, 1998:

The request for the grant extension was denied; the Home Start Board members were certain of one thing: Schiele had to be removed as executive director, even though she almost singlehandedly had kept the agency alive since its birth twelve years prior.

Joe Esparza, who had become Board chair only a month before and who had joined the Board the previous fall, asked Schiele for her resignation.

According to HUD notes, Schiele realized she was not being terminated for just missing the grant deadline, but also because the Board saw her as a liability, albeit one with a heart full of compassion. She knew her blunt statements and challenges to the City Council and to the militant and vocal anti-homeless residents of Cherry Glen and Thieles neighborhoods made her board of directors uncomfortable. Missing the deadline just gave them the cover they needed for their action.

She didn't hide behind the flare-up of diabetes as an excuse for failing to meet the grant deadline, nor her firing as a tool of retribution. I thought her termination was discriminatory on its face. After all, type-

1 diabetes is a disability. She was disabled. Under the terms of the ADA, she could have called for special employment accommodations such as mandatory rest periods and excused time to consult with her doctor; but she never asked for any special treatment. Additionally, she didn't try to negotiate a severance package or threaten a lawsuit.

After Esparza gave her the news, she just packed up her personal supplies, including her computer, turned in her keys and left. I believe she would have donated her computer if she could have afforded another one. But she couldn't. She and her husband Lynn now had to rely on his salary as a press operator at the *Sacramento Bee* and the remainder of their modest savings account to get by.

She left the Home Start premises without a fuss, and to my knowledge, never considered filing for unemployment coverage. I never once heard Schiele backbite or complain about how her dismissal was handled.

Following her departure, the Board members quickly discovered how much she had loved and sacrificed for Home Start. For example, they were totally unaware that Home Start did not have a computer because the charity couldn't afford one. Schiele had used her own instead of burdening the organization with the cost.

March 19, 1998:
The principle item the Board members were acutely aware of was the importance of tapping into a source of funding if the program was going to keep its head above water into the next fiscal year. Joe Esparza and Home Start Treasurer Kristi Kinzel submitted a written request to the city for eighty-five thousand eight hundred dollars in financial aid from the HUD Community Development Block Grant (CDBG) program. They also wrote to churches, visited their pastors and congregations, applied for a grant from Roseville's Citizens' Benefit Fund, and contacted charitable foundations and philanthropists.

If Home Start's management was shaky before Schiele left, it became a total disaster after. The Board members desperately needed someone to take on the day-to-day operations. They opted for one of their own, Gregory Cirillo, who had joined the Home Start Board the previous September. He was among three possible candidates for the job.

The *Press Tribune* reported that Cirillo vowed to improve what he regarded as Home Start's "poor relationship with (its) neighbors and the city." He wanted to find common ground among all the players. "There is a place where we can all agree, and that's where I want to start," he said.

The neighbors were "pleased as punch" at Schiele's removal and embraced Cirillo. He was an immediate hit.

March 30, 1998:

During a conference call with city officials, HUD staff sketched out the requirements to conclude the investigation and follow-up. Simply put, city staffers were told that the books on the investigation could be closed if Roseville revamped its Congregate Residence Ordinance to comply with federal laws and also revised its Analysis of Impediments to Fair Housing document. The information was quickly relayed to the City Council members.

As far as the feds were concerned, the CoC portion of the complaint had been resolved with the appointment of the citizen committee and the adoption of what seemed to be an orderly and transparent process.

April 2, 1998:

The March 30th conference call wasn't enough to convince the Roseville gang that they might be off the hook. City attorney Mark Doane wrote to George Williams, Director of HUD's San Francisco Division of Fair Housing Administration asking for verification of what they thought they had heard.

April 27, 1998:

Roseville obtained the assurances it wanted in a written response from Williams, after which the demeanor of city officials toward the service providers markedly changed for the worse.

April 30, 1998:

On the advice of its working subcommittee, the CoC Review Committee adopted a list of priorities for services to homeless individuals, as well as families. The decision to include aid to individuals as a top priority was done in the absence of chairperson Greg Cowart, who had missed several meetings, including those of the working subcommittee.

May 4, 1998:

The first overt sign of the city's shift back to its hobophobic ways showed up in a brief and strangely worded General Information Memorandum from city attorney Mark Doane to the City Council shortly after he had received another letter from HUD. The memo's phrasing indicated Doane's excitement when he used what must have seemed to him a clever euphemism describing HUD's message as"...the bonfire has just about burned out."

HUD wasn't ready to give Roseville a free pass. The agency was still considering referring the matter to the Department of Justice for violations of the First Amendment, denying the providers and the sponsoring churches' religious rights.

A second clear sign of a hobophobic relapse came when Roseville representatives John Sprague and Carol Stuart met with Sacramento officials to discuss "Roseville's vision" of a regional solution. HUD representatives Jimmy Prater and David Philipson went along to facilitate, observe and take notes.

The wary Sacramento officials understood exactly what Sprague and Stuart were talking about: The Roseville reps were suggesting that Sacramento was the core attraction for homeless individuals in the region. Roseville was just an unfortunate victim of the overflow, implying that Sacramento should take responsibility for providing shelter regionally, possibly at its Mather homeless facility.

The Sacramento folks firmly stated without hesitation that they were tired of doing more than their fair share to address the region's homeless problem. Placer County, and Roseville in particular, had not picked up any of the load. The Sacramento reps pointed out that there were nearly eight hundred public emergency shelter beds in Sacramento provided by the county and private charities. Placer County had none. That marked the end of Roseville's outreach to Sacramento County.

May 12, 1998:

While new Home Start Executive Director Cirillo was busy overseeing the Home Start program and mending fences with the neighborhood groups and the city, Board Chair Joe Esparza tried tapping the religious and business communities for funding. I still have my notes of his impassioned plea to the members of the Ministerial Association at their monthly morning meeting at Carrows Restaurant.

Esparza quickly laid out the devastating reality facing the program. He foresaw that during the next two fiscal years, there would be a huge hole in Home Start's operating budget caused by the loss of FESG funding that the agency usually received. Unless other sources of income were found, the program might be forced to close its doors.

He stated that he hoped that the city would help Home Start by giving twenty-two thousand dollars of its CDBG funding toward filling the void. That was down from the eighty-five thousand dollar request he and Kristi Kinzel had made to the city in March. What Esparza and the rest of us at the meeting did not know was that all the CDBG funds that the city could grab were slated for its pet projects list.

More money could be especially effective in the Cherry Glen and Thieles areas, where the Council majority had used it as a deft political tool. They let the neighbors know that the money was earmarked to fund community park development, summer youth employment, low-income housing rehabilitation, a low-income paint program, a neighborhood cleanup program, sidewalk installation, handicap curb cuts, improved street lighting programs and additional police patrols. In exchange, it was hoped that the neighbors would vote to elect the Council candidates they most likely identified with, the hobophobic ones.

Esparza said he thought that the city was holding out the possibility of sharing the CDBG proceeds if Home Start signed a new memorandum of understanding that the agency would exclude single adults without children from its program. He had the impression that signing the new MOU would be a condition of being considered for any aid.

He also explained that in talks with Placer County Human Services representatives, it was their position that the county would only consider matching any city contribution if Home Start did what the city wanted. Esparza commented that he and several members of the Board clearly felt they were under duress to comply with the city's demands.

It was like the HUD monitoring experience never happened.

May 13, 1998:

The third indication that the city was still its old hobophobic self was the totally unexpected cancellation of a consent calendar status report on the CoC process at that night's Council meeting. Ordinarily, it should have been a very routine matter. But not this year!

Council member Gray motioned that the item be removed from the consent calendar and be relisted for a hearing at a later date. The vote was unanimous, with the record noting that Council member Crabb was absent from the meeting.

The report was pulled from the Council's consent calendar for a very strategic reason: It included the list of priorities (high, medium and low) for needed services for aiding families and individuals, as determined by the CoC Review Committee at its April 30th meeting. The priority need for services to homeless singles was shown as high.

It was also discovered that the parliamentary maneuver to remove the report had been carefully choreographed. City Clerk Carolyn Parkinson's work copy of her Council documents for the report showed her handwritten note that stated "(The status report of the CoC Review Committee) 5/13 /98 To be re-listed @ later date Info to be included for p(ublic) h(earing) July 8, 1998," indicating that she knew the item was being moved forward to the certain date of July 8th, even though there was no discussion about any specific date by the Council that night. The new date wasn't made public until the June 3rd Council meeting.

Parkinson apparently used her work copy of the agenda and related documents of City Council meetings to keep track of business.

Mid to Late May 1998:

Even as Home Start remained on life support in hand-to-mouth mode after the 1995–1996 city siege and the recent loss of FESG funds, the agency was faced with another financial shock. Executive Director Cirillo and the Board had to deal with results of an audit showing that during the 1995–96 city attack, Schiele had used city grant funds earmarked for a special Home Start project to pay for operational expenses, such as utilities and employee taxes.

It was the only way she knew to keep the program going and the resident families housed. When the audit results were revealed, the city called for immediate repayment of the money, something that the Board was in no financial position to do. City Hall eventually backed off of its bullying posture and agreed to a written repayment program signed by Home Start. Luckily, St. Rose parish had pledged a substantial stipend to the agency helping to pay social workers' salaries, rent, utilities and insurance.

Cirillo's job was a tough one. He quickly burned out. He told the *Press Tribune* that he worked fifteen hour days running the program and searching high and low for funding. He had sent out twenty-one grant applications to private foundations and several additional ones to federal agencies.

After two months on the job Cirillo quit, saying he was leaving because of differences with his Board.

It was lucky that someone was waiting in the wings to assume the job. His name was Dan Birks, a retired Salvation Army Major with a depth of experience operating shelters. He had worked with Home Start, helping Cirillo set up a chart of accounts and clarifying the organization's financial situation. Birks also had sat in for Cirillo during his recurring absences during his brief tenure. He went on to serve as interim executive director for over a year.

June 1998:

Schiele wasn't finished giving the city a hard time about its institutionalized hobophobia. Her departure from Home Start merely marked the end of one homeless advocacy enterprise and the beginning of another. She wrote this letter to the *Press Tribune* editor, making a public plea for financial help for her new Starting Over program.

Group will help homeless start over

Well, I've just read it for the umpteenth time how I, Sherry Schiele, the "late" (as in late for a grant deadline) director of Home Start, have earned nothing but mistrust from the neighbors, businesses and the City Council because I broke the memorandum of understanding that the city had with Home Start.

I would just like to tell everyone that it was because of a memorandum of understanding that I let single homeless adults stay at Home Start.

Long ago I "signed" a memorandum of understanding with Jesus Christ wherein I agreed to love my neighbor. Jesus did say, "Whatever you do to the least of my brethren, you do to me." He let us know that He takes it very personally what we do to others (even transients). Thank goodness, when we get to Heaven, the Lord is not going to ask us how well we pleased the neighbors, the businesses, or the City Council. He is going to say to us, "I was hungry and you fed Me, I was homeless and you took Me in."

There is a new non-profit corporation in town called W.W.J.D., Inc. (What Would Jesus Do? Inc.), of which I am the executive director. Its main purpose is to house homeless people, including single homeless adults regardless of their place of origin. We have a site where we are going to run a program called Starting Over, which is to help homeless single adults get back on their feet (or maybe get on their feet for the first time).

We will open as soon as we make a $100,000 down payment which we are in the process of trying to raise at this time. We plan to open in the fall. If anyone would like to help us in this endeavor, we would love to hear from you. My number is 725-6617.

Sherry Schiele
Roseville

The letter may have seemed perplexing to some because of its simple candor. Schiele always took full responsibility for her actions and spoke in such a forthright way that people often misread her.

Unfortunately, the letter wasn't complete. Schiele left out a critical piece of information regarding the 1992 "Memorandum of Understanding" required by the city and inked by St. Vincent's for Home Start. Its two-year term had expired before Home Start began sheltering homeless single adults in early 1995. Schiele had faithfully abided by the agreement while it was in force, despite the outcries of her foes to the contrary.

June 3, 1998:

At that night's Council meeting, the review of the "STATUS OF CONTINUUM OF CARE COMMITTEE," was again on the agenda, until John Sprague led another maneuver to postpone it. The Council and staff didn't like the fact that the committee had given a high priority to projects that would serve homeless single males. The status report had been postponed by the Council on May 13th for the same reason.

Although we knew in May that that status report would be put off until July 8th, Sprague "introduced a recommendation" from Housing and Redevelopment Supervisor Carol Stuart that the Council continue any action on the CoC priority list to the July meeting.

The Council and staffers knew if the priority list had been adopted, it would have become part of the official Council record. Thus, the higher-ranked shelter needs for single adult males would have been legitimized, something the city wanted to avoid at all costs.

That meant the effect of the high priority given to homeless singles had to be somehow mitigated before the July 8th meeting. Without missing a beat, Mayor Gamar formally and legally postponed the item to the same date the Council was scheduled to hear the entire CoC Review Committee's proposal, just as noted by City Clerk Carolyn Parkinson on her work copy of the May 13th agenda documents.

June 12, 1998:

Dave Sorensen, Greg Cowart, Fathers Mike McKeon and Mike Cormack, along with yours truly, met at St. Rose rectory to discuss how we could defend the CoC priority list before the City Council. During the discussion, Cowart mentioned that someone on the Council had called him in what he inferred was "a state of near panic," wanting something done to head off the St. Vincent's and WWJD? Starting Over CoC proposals for increased services to homeless single men.

Cowart relayed that the concern was that new services for single males had scored so high on the priority list that the committee was bound to recommend the two proposals that would provide those services.

June 18, 1998:

The meeting of the CoC Review Committee centered on a new recommendation made by Chairman Cowart. He proposed adding the following language to the CoC document: "Memorandums of Understanding will be executed between service providers and formal neighborhood groups regarding management of any housing facilities serving the homeless... ."

This new language seemed to catch some of the other committee members flatfooted; but it fit what I had already heard from a City Hall insider: The new MOU requirement introduced that late in the game would do just what someone on the Council wanted – throw a monkey wrench in the works for providers of services to homeless single males. This latest language would not affect providers of services to families. They had existing agreements on the books.

Schiele and I objected to the MOU move; but a majority of the committee went on to approve it.

July 8, 1998:

The Council meeting that evening was the first time any part of the CoC document was aired for public discussion.

As part of the CoC process, the city was required to determine the number of homeless people in Roseville. City staff reported that an average of sixty homeless single men and women were in town at any one time. Additionally, there were two hundred twenty individuals, including children, in homeless families.

If these family folks qualified and if there were enough beds, they were sheltered through programs operated by the Placer Women's Center, Home Start and the Salvation Army. Otherwise, they had to depend on St. Vincent's and the WWJD? street ministry.

It was noted that there had been seven public meetings of the CoC Review Committee in addition to several of the working subcommittee.

City staff suggested the Council approve the whole package, including the Committee's four recommended projects and the new MOU requirement that St. Vincent's and WWJD? hadn't complied with. The project rankings were:

1. Home Start;
2. St. Vincent de Paul's transitional living program for single men and women;
3. Placer Women's Center/PEACE For Families; and
4. What Would Jesus Do? Inc./ Starting Over program for singles.

Twelve members of the public addressed the Council about the CoC proposal and in particular Schiele's new Starting Over program. Eight were generally in favor of what the Committee proposed, except for the Starting Over program. Five of the eight people vehemently objected to it: Sally Bragg, Bill Schmidt, Sylvia Slade, Kristi Kinzel and Pete Stamas.

Three people spoke in favor of the Starting Over program: Schiele herself, one of her former employees, Pam Moyer and one of her Board members, Christine Crady. Much to Crady's credit, she spoke about the community's responsibility for helping its least fortunate members.

Al Saracini suggested more talks "to solve homeless issues".

Crady's remarks invited a slew of criticism. Cherry Glen residents KC Fuerstenberger and Betty Melligan lambasted her as an outsider in letters to the *Press Tribune* editor. The women said because Crady was from the Citrus Heights area, she did not understand the problems the two women had endured especially "the experience of living with transient males in our neighborhood for many years."

The hearing was continued to July 15th.

Before the meeting was over, the Council appointed Cowart to one of the three vacant seats on the city's planning commission.

July 15, 1998:

As the Council members prepared to accept public testimony, Mayor Gamar asked that anyone from the audience who had spoken at the previous week's hearing abstain from going to the podium again.

Apparently Sally Bragg and Sylvia Slade couldn't resist the temptation to do just the opposite. They jumped up to speak out against St. Vincent's and the "Starting Over" projects and to take personal jabs at both Schiele and me. Other audience members offered negative remarks as well. Only Linda Reno of St. Vincent's and Betsy Donovan of the CoC Review Committee spoke in favor of the St. Vincent's project.

When the public testimony session closed, Mayor Gamar, in a move that was obviously rehearsed, turned to Vice Mayor Crabb and gave him the floor. Crabb introduced the audience in the chamber and at home to a city-created video showing excerpts of the CoC Review Committee's June 18th meeting. The clip focused on testimony from both Schiele and me.

This is what the video showed:

After the Memorandum of Understanding topic had been introduced by Cowart, Schiele rushed to the podium. She objected, saying that the MOU requirement was just another thinly veiled attempt by the city to prohibit, block and forestall the development of any services for homeless single men.

She declared that the City of Roseville was "already in a heap of trouble" and that HUD's Bonny Milstein had "asked me to go out and locate a homeless person who had not been housed, and they (HUD) are going to start an action (against the city)."

When I had a chance to make my remarks, I said, "Our call goes beyond the law," that we felt it was a spiritual imperative to help people who were in need, even if giving them food, shelter or other aid violated local customs, rules, regulations, ordinances or laws. I also characterized the city's attempt to jam the MOU requirement down our throats as another desperate tactic to stymie us and which, like those in the past, would fail.

After Crabb's video concluded, some Council members engaged in a review of the CoC process, but not of the priority list. That was followed by sighs of exasperation, as they reflected on the history of city frustration in the tug-of-war with providers over the rights of "homeless single men" without ever using those three words.

Crabb then began slamming St. Vincent's: "Let's face it. St. Vincent de Paul can go out and buy two houses anywhere in town. They don't need an MOU. They can move six people into (each one) and we can't do diddly about it and neither can the neighbors. And that's the thing that bothers me so much about going forward with their request."

Council member Jim Gray jumped in, "Why should the city of Roseville be the only city in the county that is having this issue of dealing with the homeless?"

Crabb replied with something less than a complete and true statement of the facts: "They (the other cities) have turned their backs on us." He continued that Roseville had single-handedly helped its homeless population with over two hundred sixty thousand dollars in city funds for programs over the years. He failed to mention that St. Rose Church alone had donated at least that much in support of homeless initiatives at St. Vincent's, Home Start, Community Ministries, the Salvation Army and funding the Armory shelter in years past.

Finally, the Council reached the point of having to deal with tearing apart the CoC priority list. Members Roccucci and Graham began with a civil conversation, suggesting keeping the St. Vincent's proposal in the package at the number two spot. But Crabb and Gamar jumped in, adamant that it be pulled.

Both projects for homeless single adults were ultimately torn from the proposal. Neither had an MOU with their neighbors or the city. Only Home Start and Placer Women's Center/PEACE For Families – the two organizations serving families – were recommended for funding under the CoC.

Because the council majority and the neighbors simply did not like anything about Schiele, it was no shock to anybody that the project she proposed was rejected. As Harry Crabb publicly pronounced from the City Council dais, "We should have no part of any activity that Sherry Schiele is involved with."

July 26, 1998:

Father Mike McKeon had a more cynical take on the Council's actions. He wrote in a letter to the *Press Tribune*:

"The recommendations (of the CoC Review Committee) were formulated after months of consultation...City council members interfered in the process, exploiting the traditional rancor between service providers and representatives from the Cherry Glen and Thieles neighborhoods...The death blow to the process was choreographed by Councilman Harry Crabb...In the end, it was Harry's forum and he had his way."

There was no denying that as soon as HUD dialed down the heat on Roseville in its December 23, 1997, letter to City Manager Al Johnson, our programs became vulnerable once again. The result was that Roseville used the fresh opportunity to make its second CoC process just as phony and self-serving as its first.

———————————

Chapter 20:
Who Needs City Hall?
(Aug. 1998–Jan. 1999)

August 1998:

One HUD official tried to forewarn Roseville city staffers that the Council, by having its fingerprints all over the hatchet job it did on the 1998 Continuum of Care (CoC) document, further damaged the city's relationship with HUD. That person was Winston Moy, HUD's staff representative to Roseville.

He advised that all four of the CoC Review Committee's recommendations, which included the St. Vincent's transitional housing project and the WWJD?/Starting Over offering, be listed in the final HUD package. Moy pointed out that if the city followed his advice, HUD would do its job, making the final decision as to which of the CoC Review Committee's four recommendations might be funded, rather than not funding any of them.

Trying to manipulate the CoC outcomes caused some serious difficulties for the city, three of which directly and immediately involved HUD:

- HUD ramped up pressure on Roseville to revise its illegal 1995 Congregate Residence Ordinance or face penalties;
- HUD denied all of Roseville's 1998 CoC recommendations, including those of Home Start and Placer Women's Center/PEACE For Families, just as Moy had predicted; and
- HUD's Washington DC headquarters was considering referring its Roseville case to the Justice Department for prosecution, not as a fair housing violation, but as a breach of the First Amendment right of church members to freely minister to homeless persons as an expression of their religious beliefs.

The other three, all stirring up local controversy, erupted as a result of the Council's passage of the butchered CoC document:

- The first was Sherry Schiele's firing off of a new HUD civil rights complaint against the city.
- The second surfaced when both the *Sacramento Bee* and the *Roseville Press Tribune* ran opinion pieces in which the city was publicly chastised for twisting the truth about the development

of the 1998 CoC document.

- The third was a backlash from three of the seven CoC Review Committee members. Betsy Donovan, Machel Stokes and Wendy Still joined forces to implement their own transitional shelter program. It would be patterned after the St. Vincent's proposal – the one which had been stripped from the CoC recommendations by the City Council.

All six of these problems could have been avoided by city government if it had been more conciliatory with the majority of its CoC Review Committee and the providers.

Donovan started the ball rolling with a statement to the *Bee*: "For 10 years, the council has been appointing committees and forums to come up with solutions and yet it continues to not provide services for the individual homeless adults."

She followed up with a letter to the *Press Tribune*, in which she echoed the sentiments Father Mike had expressed in July. She said, "I would like to take this opportunity to express my disgust over the outcome of the Continuum of Care process. As a member of the Continuum of Care Committee...I really believed that the city council would do the right thing. I was wrong."

Her letter was not the end of the blowback against the Council's actions. In fact, it was just the beginning.

When I found out that Donovan had joined with fellow committee members Stokes and Still to probe for a way to resurrect the St. Vincent's CoC project, I got in touch with each of them and suggested that we set a group meeting at my home to plan our next move.

The St. Vincent's transitional living project had called for using regular housing in one of Roseville's neighborhoods to shelter six homeless people at a time to get them back on their feet. The idea was to begin with two homes – the first for men, the second for women.

For Sherry Schiele, the coming of August meant it was time to begin planning for the coming cold wet days and nights of winter. It was a familiar routine that many of us had gone through year after year: Step one was to ask the city and the county to sponsor using the Roseville Armory as an emergency shelter. Step two was to wait for their customary reply: "No."

A certain "no" never discouraged superwoman Schiele, not even after having her Starting Over program stripped from the CoC document. With the city and county rejection of the providers' request to open the Armory, she just immersed herself deeper into her WWJD?

street ministry and waited to hear back from HUD about her civil rights complaint. She had a vision of expanding WWJD? services into a daily year-round program, a huge undertaking for any one person, let alone for a type-1 diabetic with a disregard for her doctor's directives.

Schiele really wasn't alone in the effort. She had the four members of her board who could help, if she would have let them:

- Chris Crady, a Citrus Heights businesswoman who had met Schiele at a Toastmasters meeting;
- Pat Holden, owner of the B Street Apartments;
- Paul Kunz, owner of Citrus Heights Stained Glass at 328 Riverside in Roseville; and
- Jean Thompson, a Sacramento realtor.

The irony was that while Schiele had hand-picked each of them for several reasons, they had one characteristic in common: They all were completely occupied by their own business affairs. They were perfect for her Board. It was not her style to involve others in making decisions during the creative process. She regarded that as her job and hers alone. She would craft her vision to her own liking, lock the format in place, then inform her board of the list of things she had accomplished:

1. Qualifying WWJD? for assistance from The Placer Food Bank, enabling WWJD? to obtain a variety of surplus foods, including the canned goods and snacks she distributed;
2. Offering free transportation for homeless and low-income persons who needed a ride to the Employment Development Department, the Welfare and Social Security offices in Roseville, as well as to medical and mental health facilities in Auburn and Roseville;
3. Stepping up solicitations of cash, snacks, clean blankets, soap, razors, combs, clean socks and underwear, toothpaste and brushes from local churches and service clubs;
4. Providing first aid administered by volunteer nurses; and
5. Providing clean clothing and fresh blankets.

The community was eager to help. Mervyn's Department Store alone donated one hundred new blankets.

August 27, 1998:

Donovan, Still, Stokes and I met at my house to reaffirm that we were ready and willing to get the transitional housing initiative for adults off the ground. Together, the three women had the knowledge and skills necessary to make the program work. With Still's background in corrections management, Stokes' insights into how the local social service agency system worked and Donovan's administrative background with Eskaton, they would make a great team.

The four of us had one big, yet basic, problem; we were starting from square one. Our concept was nothing more than that – a concept in need of everything from a nonprofit corporate identity to a checking account with money in it. I offered to help by pulling the various pieces together to form the corporation and to make the necessary federal and state filings. Father Dan Casey had shown me the procedure when he had formed the Placer Community Care Center a few years before.

I mentioned to the women that Dr. Tom Stanko of the St. Vincent's Board, Father Mike McKeon and I had talked about reviving the St. Vincent's vision shortly after the City Council had axed it; but we were at a loss as to how to move ahead. That all changed once we heard of their interest.

Father Mike was so enthused that he went so far as to say that he would like to be part of the startup if someone else was ready to form a new organization. His commitment meant that St. Rose parish would be involved, bringing with it the moral and financial support of the Church.

Then the four of us talked about possible names for the project. I told them about how What Would Jesus Do? got its name. I wanted to underscore the importance of a basic point that Schiele was determined to make: that city actions against homeless single adults were in direct opposition to what Jesus taught.

It was important to me that our new organization be like Schiele's, and carry a name that proclaimed what we were doing was what Jesus wanted done, not what city cronies tried to legislate. We needed a name that meant something more than just what the new venture was about, or what it would do. The name should remind us of the common bond we share with Jesus who always stood with the truly poor. I focused on a name with biblical roots – The Lazarus Project.

I had mentioned the name to Father Mike in one of our earlier discussions. He was unimpressed. After I explained to him that the program's name was a reference to Lazarus the beggar in Jesus' parable in Luke's gospel, not to the Lazarus who was Jesus' friend in John's gospel, he seemed intrigued.

Having Lazarus the beggar as the face of this new outreach was significant because the poor Lazarus in Jesus' story was about as savory a figure to many in His audience as a tramp was to some of the folks in Roseville.

And of all the characters in Jesus' parables, Lazarus was the only one whom Jesus called by name – as if He may have known Lazarus as someone in his hometown of Nazareth or as a person He had met on the road.

This poorest of poor men, Lazarus, must have held a special place in Jesus' spiritual life, maybe even as a real person who Jesus saw suffering ridicule, hunger and rejection at the hands of the social elites of His day.

As our first meeting moved closer to its end, the four of us had an idea about an organization that remained without a name, but felt we had made genuine progress. We had a common vision to build on to make something meaningful from the wreck left by the CoC process.

However, before the meeting wound down, Stokes and Stills wanted to clarify an important point about their individual commitments. They felt they needed to state their intentions up front to avoid any confusion. Both would help get the new project off the ground, but could not commit to long-term support as corporate directors.

On the other hand, Betsy Donovan made it absolutely and unmistakably definite that she was all-in. She was there for the long haul.

We all agreed the next step to take was to arrange for Father Mike, Dr. Stanko and anyone else interested in the program to meet with us. A follow-up meeting was set for October 16th. In the meantime, each of us was to dig for possible funding and talk up the project with potential board members.

October 16, 1998:
Father Mike and I had dinner at the rectory to finalize how he wanted to proceed with formulating the transitional housing project. I could see that he was warming to the name of "The Lazarus Project." By the time we finished dinner, he was ready to set out for the meeting across the street at my house.

The agenda moved along smoothly with a step-by-step progression on the issues we needed to cover. When it came time to discuss what we should name the organization, Father Mike quickly suggested "The Lazarus Project." We all agreed.

I volunteered to check with the office of the California Secretary of State to see if the name was available. Donovan suggested that we ask the St. Vincent's Board if they would mind our group adopting the transitional living program they had proposed for the 1998 CoC document.

The consensus was that Donovan should make the contact since she was very involved in the program on the CoC Review Committee and was known to St. Vincent's as having a genuine interest in helping our homeless population.

It was also recommended that we ask St. Vincent's if we could funnel donations to our new project through their books until we obtained preliminary status as a tax-exempt corporation. This would enable our donors to receive tax deductions right away.

October 20, 1998:

After Donovan obtained the St. Vincent's Board's buy-in at their meeting, news of The Lazarus Project spread. Glenda Williams, manager of Auburn's Placer County's Office of Health and Human Services, faxed us a state Housing and Community Development Office notice about upcoming FESG funding and a registration form to get us on the mailing list. I signed us up.

At this point, we had pledges of real financial support from the following sources:

- St. Rose Church: twenty-five thousand dollars arranged by Father Mike;
- Placer County Dept. of Health and Human Services: twenty thousand dollars;
- St. Vincent's: five thousand dollars;
- Other religious groups: two thousand dollars; and
- SS. Peter & Paul Church: to be determined.

October 24, 1998:

At "The Lazarus Project" organizational meeting held at the St. Rose parish house, I reported that the name had been reserved with the California Secretary of State.

We went on to discuss the timeline for completing the formation and submitting our application for non-profit status to the IRS and the California Franchise Tax Board. I estimated that our submissions could be finished by the end of November.

The group voted to move ahead. Father Mike offered to have St. Rose cover the seven hundred dollars for filing fees in addition to the original pledge.

November 3, 1998:

City election results beefed up the Council with an even more vociferous anti-homeless majority. Claudia Gamar garnered the highest vote tally, ensuring that she would get another turn in the mayor's chair in two years.

The sympathetic ear of Pauline Roccucci was lost when she was sidelined by city charter requirements. Her tempering style was replaced by Earl Rush's hard-edged and tough-fisted rhetoric and politics.

Incumbents Crabb and Graham, with time left on their terms, sat out the campaign. But their colleague, Jim Gray, lost to Dan Goodhall. Goodhall had been appointed to the planning commission by the City Council.

November 16, 1998:

Harry Crabb was sworn in as Mayor. With the Council's politically tough-minded shift away from reconciliation, we thought it would be very difficult, if not impossible, to expand our services.

But we were determined.

November 28, 1998:

WWJD? and The Lazarus Project were two new bright spots that gave those of us in the provider community hope for the future. In fact, we were so pumped up about the prospects for making The Lazarus Project a reality that leasing a home for the program was not good enough. We decided to buy a house. We had no idea how we would pull it off; but that was our goal.

We also agreed this first home would be for men, and it would be located in the county, yet as close to Roseville as possible.

By placing the first home outside city limits, we would avoid giving Crabb, Gamar and the city bureaucracy an opportunity to stop us by using new restrictions or regulations that city staff might cook up. We would not have to deal with the city trying to keep our house off of the municipally owned utility system or rejecting our grant applications.

With that, we began the search for our first home. There were two built-up areas just outside of the Roseville city limits: the Livoti Tract and Annabelle Lane. The Livoti Tract was a wedge of land squeezed in between Roseville and Citrus Heights, lying east of Interstate 80 and Auburn Boulevard. Annabelle Lane was on the east edge of Roseville, west of Sierra College Boulevard between East Roseville Parkway on the north and the Sacramento County line on the south.

I had asked my son Paul, now a partner in the Keller Williams Real Estate brokerage, if he would put together a list of homes on the market that might meet our needs in those areas.

December 9, 1998:

During our board meeting, Paul sat down with us to review the list of homes he had found. The pickings were slim – just five houses in the Livoti Tract, the majority of them vacant, and none suitable on Annabelle Lane. Each home on the list was different from the others, all with different floor plans and yards, typical for houses outside the city limits.

We were so anxious to move ahead that we wanted to tour the unoccupied houses that night. Paul hesitated because he couldn't tell us which houses had the electric service turned on, meaning possibly no lights. It was after 7 p.m., long past dark, forcing us to resort to flashlights.

A drive past the two occupied homes told us that we weren't interested in them.

When we got to the other two houses, we found the electricity had been shut off. That didn't keep us from stumbling through each one, even if more often than not, the rooms were as black as windowless cells. It had been a Herculean challenge just to remain vertical, even with flashlights. The third vacant house we toured, on Whyte Avenue with utilities connected, held some promise. We decided to give it a second look in the daylight.

December 10, 1998:

That afternoon, we carefully rechecked the three vacant properties and decided to make an offer on the Whyte Avenue house.

December 12, 1998:

The sellers were interested enough to counter our offer, starting a two-week-long back and forth. The negotiations eventually collapsed. But we remained determined to soldier on, keeping our eyes on the prize – another opportunity.

Late December 1998:

Roseville decided not to participate in the 1999 CoC funding round.

Who Needs City Hall?

January 1999:

Paul located a new listing on Annabelle Lane for The Lazarus Project: a large house that could easily handle six clients at a time and also provide enough separate space for staff work and group meetings. The home had been beaten up over years of neglect. While it needed lots of TLC, it definitely had promise.

The Board decided to submit an offer – one that reflected the fixer-upper status of the property. We were surprised that eventually we were able to negotiate a deal. At the time, housing prices were skyrocketing due to low inventory, and because the Roseville area was growing by leaps and bounds, we counted ourselves lucky to have landed the property.

It was one thing to find a house that met our needs and another to finance its purchase. The Lazarus Project was a newly created corporation with no credit history. Every lender we approached turned us down. After struggling to find a lender willing to accept our untested financial capabilities, we finally admitted that we needed some help.

Father Mike took an extraordinary step, volunteering to ask the Bishop's office for a hand, which was extended.

What I witnessed with that occurrence seemed to be the second of two miracles: In just twelve months, Roseville had not one, but two new provider organizations for homeless singles, The Lazarus Project and the What Would Jesus Do? street ministry. Both were created in the face of the city's hard-hearted opposition.

The two new agencies were endowed with attributes that made them immune to Roseville's social service statutes, including its Congregate Residence ordinance. It was a state of affairs filled with irony, an unexpected turn of events for the city.

The Council's July 18th removal of the two proposals to assist homeless single males from the CoC document had backfired. City actions provided both the spark and the fuel for the blowback that would lead to the founding of the ministries.

Those of us in the provider community owed Council members Crabb, Gamar and their minions a gesture of thanks! Really, The Lazarus Project and Schiele's WWJD? ministry could not have taken hold in a year's time without them. Roseville did not have any means on the books capable of stopping these new enterprises – not one policy, ordinance, rule or law. Thank you City Hall. We couldn't have done it without you!

Chapter 21:
"Tribute paid to a visionary."*
(Feb. 1999–Dec. 1999)
Press Tribune December 29, 1999

February 1999:

Our two new programs, The Lazarus Project and WWJD?, continued to thrive. The Lazarus Project group was on target to begin providing transitional living for homeless single men beginning in the spring, and WWJD? expanded to a year-round effort.

The other big news item in the provider community was that HUD had initiated a second Roseville investigation because of Sherry Schiele's July 1998 complaint, adding to the ongoing probe opened in 1996 based on my grievance. The 1996 case was still active because the city hadn't reformed its illegal congregate residence ordinance as it had agreed to.

Schiele had started to formalize a complaint in 1997, focusing on Roseville's ramrodding of that year's Continuum of Care(CoC) document through the City Council without provider input; but she didn't follow through.

When the Council tried a variation of the same trick again in 1998, she couldn't restrain herself from giving the city both barrels. The city's mishandling of the CoC process two years in a row proved to yield Roseville nothing less than a pair of black eyes, one from the press and the other from HUD itself.

The dilemma Roseville faced in 1997 and 1998 was that if it wanted to access the federal homeless funds that were available, the city was required to use HUD's new CoC process. At the same time, it had to go it alone. There was no other jurisdiction in Placer County, including the county itself, prepared to file a CoC application, either alone or in conjunction with Roseville.

In any case, in 1997 and 1998, HUD did not encourage solo agency filings, like those of the city. Rather, it sought to facilitate collaboration among local governmental entities, including county government, urging them to join together to submit a consolidated CoC document. If Roseville had waited for other agencies to get up to speed so that they could come on board too, the city could have insulated itself from the embarrassment of the two failures.

Unfortunately, Roseville had to learn the hard way. When it came time for HUD's evaluation of Roseville's CoC documents for those years, they withered under the fed's scrutiny. Both of Roseville's applications garnered such mediocre scores that they were disqualified based on points alone, costing the city a loss of nearly two million dollars in federal funds.

Roseville took 1999 to prepare for the 2000 CoC funding cycle as a member of a regional group, "The Placer Greater Collaborative." The consolidated group would formulate one CoC document for all of Placer County and its incorporated cities.

Lost in all this news was the decision by WWJD?'s Sherry Schiele and her husband Lynn to donate ten thousand dollars to Starting Over by canceling the loan they had made for the cause.

Spring 1999:

To help with HUD's investigation, our provider group gave HUD a bundle of documents to support Schiele's complaint that Roseville had manipulated the 1998 CoC process. One example of the city's ongoing fabrications of truth came from a statement originally written in 1990. The city resurrected it, amended it to their satisfaction, and then included it as Attachment No. 1 to Roseville's 1998 CoC Proposal:

"Recommendations (of a Homeless Task Force appointed in 1989) presented to the Council in April 1990 focused on developing a transitional housing program for the homeless and hiring a homeless coordinator."

The city's recounting of the facts seemed innocuous enough. The problem was that it was only truthful by half. City officials only unearthed the parts of the 1990 Homeless Task Force recommendation that they could live with.

The other half that we revealed was that the Homeless Task Force had also recommended setting up a regional permanent emergency shelter and expanding transitional housing that included help for single adults. The original report proposed developing a center which would offer homeless services such as health care, mental health counseling, employment help, legal assistance and family counseling. In the end, the City Council rejected the entire Task force recommendation.

The city's pattern of presenting emblematic half-truths as fact was a constant tactic in Roseville's decade-long attempt to rewrite history and deny its hobophobia. It had to be stopped.

HUD officials concurred that a review and comparison of the actual statement in the 1990 policy document with the city staff's edited interpretation in the 1998 attachment provided one more piece of evidence to support the second investigation of city government.

The question this probe sought to answer was whether the Roseville City Council's refusal to endorse two of the programs recommended by the 1998 CoC Review Committee to the Council was an actual act of "disparate discrimination" as Schiele contended.

April 15, 1999:

Progress on development of The Lazarus Project continued. I prepared the IRS and State of California tax exempt documents for the corporation. Father Mike and Betsy Donovan met with Tom McNamara, the bishop's chief financial officer, and Lou Desmond, his attorney, to work out the details for the house purchase on Annabelle Lane. If St. Rose would donate sixty thousand dollars to The Lazarus Project for the down payment, the diocese would help to secure the loan for the balance of the price and hold a security interest in the property to guarantee repayment of any debt.

April 26, 1999:

Father Mike and Donovan gained the approval of the St. Rose Finance Committee, chaired by Mark Van Hook, to make the sixty thousand dollar donation to the Lazarus Project.

April 28, 1999:

Father Mike, Donovan and Van Hook met with George Howington, The Lazarus Project Board's volunteer accountant, to tie up loose ends. At the meeting's end, it was agreed that the purchase escrow for the Annabelle Lane house could be completed.

May 1, 1999:

The house officially became the first transitional living facility for homeless single men in Placer County. A mountain of work remained to be done before our first guests could walk through the door: building repairs including all the systems (heating, air conditioning, plumbing and electrical), painting, hauling trash and weeding.

We also had to find furniture and hustle donations of everything from pots and pans to towels and bedding. The whole process was basically overhauling the house and then outfitting it with necessities to make it a home. With some hard work, "Sierra House," as it came to be called, was quickly ready for guests.

Wade Jordahl, the organization's first executive director, did a great job working with the board members to get the new program operational and the Sierra House ready for guests. During the process, he also focused on building relationships with Placer County officials and staff. His efforts paid off quickly. Almost immediately, the county began directing state and federal grant funds and other financial aid to the new program.

July 2, 1999:

As Schiele continued her WWJD? street meet and greets, her activities finally popped up on the city's radar. The first pushback against her What Would Jesus Do? program surfaced.

Schiele was providing food to homeless men on Park Drive near Douglas Boulevard, which was about a hundred yards from several homeless camps, but also ironically on the doorsteps of a dozen or so stately homes belonging to Roseville old-timers. She should have known better.

She was approached by Roseville Police Officer Scott Jetter as she talked to her clients. Jetter told her the only way she could distribute food on any Roseville's street, let alone on Park Drive, was after she got both a city business license and a permit from Placer County Department of Health.

When Schiele raised questions about the requirements, the officer's response was, "Call the city attorney, licensing and county health department." With that, he retreated to his patrol car and sped off.

She knew it would be a fool's errand to call Mark Doane, the city attorney. She would never get a straight answer. Doane would only say what he wanted to tell her – to discontinue the WWJD? ministry because it lacked official approval.

Instead, Schiele contacted the city licensing department to see if their requirements for her new program had changed since the last time she applied for a business license for Home Start in 1995. The requirements were the same. All she had to do was go to the office, bring her corporate documents and fill out an application. There was no cost because WWJD? Inc. was a charity.

Schiele tracked me down to tell me what had happened. She remained concerned about the county health permit.

I said I would bet there would be no need for a permit from Placer County Health because the organization was not preparing any food for distribution other than peanut butter and jelly sandwiches. All the other food items were packaged or canned. I mentioned that the Director of County Health, Brad Banner, was a personal friend and that I would be glad to talk with him as soon as I could to get the question resolved.

I also suggested that Schiele obtain a city license before word got back to Doane that the police had made contact with her. All it would take for the licensing department to hold up her paperwork was his phone call. With that, she headed to the city offices.

Later that afternoon, she telephoned to say she had her business license in hand.

A few days later, she had a letter from Banner exempting WWJD? from any County Health Department permitting requirements.

Schiele also decided to move her ministry out of the public eye from the Park Avenue stop to Saugstad Park, a hundred yards or so from her previous location.

The encounter with Officer Jetter was the last recorded contact that Schiele had with the city regarding her mobile food and hot coffee program.

In addition to expanding the WWJD? ministry, Schiele remained hopeful about her HUD complaint. Immediately, her attitude lightened up when she learned her documentation had arrived at the San Francisco HUD office. I think she imagined that the city wouldn't escape federal prosecution this time around. Its repeated manipulation of the CoC process would reveal its bald-faced discrimination against a protected class of individuals.

September 1999:

Home Start caught a break on the financial front. It qualified for a Federal Emergency Shelter Grant (FESG) and a special seventeen thousand five hundred dollar grant from Roseville to help with overhead expenses. The new funds enabled Esparza and the Board to keep the organization going. Schiele was elated and fired up.

Everything was falling into place. Schiele recounted her in-depth conversation with Paul Smith of HUD's San Francisco office to me. Smith was in the process of writing up the official complaint document and wanted to get the particulars down as accurately as possible before he sent it on to HUD officials in Washington DC.

Schiele said that at the end of their discussion, Smith shared his take on the case. He figured there were two matters that would be addressed. The first was investigating the city for interference and coercion regarding homeless single males' rights to housing, whether emergency or otherwise. The second and less significant was having Dave Philipson conduct another programmatic investigation of the city, this one into its 1998 CoC process, to determine whether or not Roseville had conformed to HUD guidelines. She was thrilled!

I was happy for her, but told her I was concerned about her health. Her doctor had said that she needed to make some changes if she wanted to lead a long life. He warned her that if she didn't, it was just a matter of time before she ended up in the emergency room. Schiele was always polite when I shared my concerns; but after she listened to what I had to say, she treated me just like she would anyone else who got in her way: she respectfully dismissed my comments.

September 9, 1999:

After it became known that Smith was preparing to refer the Roseville matter to Washington for investigation, the city finally moved to replace its illegal congregate residence ordinance.

The planning commission held its first hearing on a new comprehensive social services ordinance that surprisingly covered food locker and dining room operations as well as what the city called "temporary resident shelters", previously known as "congregate residences". Typical of Roseville thinking, the replacement became the perfect vehicle to load up with provisions that were more restrictive, but legal, to control all of these social services.

City attorney Mark Doane and the planning department inserted wording to limit expanding existing activities that the old city ordinance was unable to control. Matters such as size, hours of operation, occupancy limits, parking requirements and other standards were more completely covered in the new law.

Members of our providers group quickly asked for a number of changes. Following the initial hearing, we held several meetings of our own to formalize a list of modifications we wanted incorporated into the proposed ordinance.

St. Vincent's president Richard Roccucci lobbied city Associate Planner Colleen McDuffee for the changes prior to the planning commission's second hearing.

Sherry Schiele's opinion of the whole process was that it was just one more example of the city's lack of good faith when dealing with the providers. She felt we had good reason to feel betrayed again. However, she was gratified and relieved that none of the proposed regulations affected her WWJD? ministry. That meant that she was spared having to attend meetings with city staff and the planning commission. Most of all, she was grateful that she didn't have to engage in another verbal exchange with the City Council.

The approval of the revised ordinance required a total of three additional public hearings: one more with the planning commission and two others with the City Council before it became etched in stone. Lots of heat could be generated over the course of the three months that the hearings would be held. There could be quite a bit of community controversy about the changes.

Fall 1999:

Schiele told me her WWJD? ministry had outgrown her small car: It didn't have enough space for the all the items she needed for just one of her rounds. To solve the problem, she said she needed a van, and coincidentally, she had located an old Ford Econoline that was just right. The van could carry enough supplies to complete her rounds without having to reload.

Fortunately, she had a new benefactor, an Episcopal priest, Father Malcolm McClenaghan. "Father Mac" had been making regular contributions to WWJD? and was not only a good listener, but also an understanding soul who had Schiele's best interests at heart.

I asked her more about the van: What kind of shape was it in? Did it run? Would it pass a smog test? Did she have to pay for it, or was it a gift? Did WWJD? have the money for insurance? She avoided answering me. Instead, she invited me to go with her and Father Mac to check it out.

Later that day, the three of us took a drive over to North Highlands to evaluate the prospect. The van was stored in a covered chain link enclosure on the backside of a closed TV store and repair shop.

First impressions are important. This one left me cold. The van was dingy, dirty and forsaken-looking, an early eighties model. A thick coat of dust enshrouded the vehicle like a blanket designed to hide any luster that might have remained in the paint. When I looked closely, I could see that the color was gray with the TV store's name in faded red lettering. The tires were nearly flat, and the hubcaps were missing.

The van had been sitting there for at least a year; the license had expired in 1997.

But, Schiele had no doubts about its potential. She saw it as a brilliant gem, just what she needed for her ministry. She had said it could be bought for just a few hundred dollars.

I understood why.

Father Mac, on the other hand, either because he had already decided he was going to help her get this van or because he actually understood its potential, said he was for the deal.

I gently tried to get them to change their minds, turning the conversation to what it would cost to get it on the road. Schiele said that with new tires and wiper blades, a tune-up and smog check, a paint job and an insurance policy, it would be ready to roll. I responded that I thought the mechanical work alone could be as much as two thousand five hundred dollars, if the engine and transmission actually worked. And we would have to have it towed to a shop just to find out.

Father Mac chimed in saying he would foot the entire repair and repainting bill, plus cover the cost of the van. I was shocked. I thought he was being a bit impulsive.

Thanks to Schiele's vision and Father Mac's generosity, within a month, the WWJD? van was rolling on Roseville's streets. It sported a paint job donated by J&J Body Shop in Roseville and new magnetic signs announcing a phone number for emergency help, 786-WWJD. With winter weather approaching, the van allowed Schiele to streamline her routine and help more people stranded in the cold.

Getting the van didn't make Schiele complacent. She never thought she had given enough of herself to help Roseville's homeless men and women. She went on to recruit The Lazarus Project, St. Rose Church, St. Vincent's and First United Methodist Church to jointly ask the Placer County Board of Supervisors to set aside the Roseville Armory as a winter shelter. The request followed Governor Davis' State Assembly Bill 612 that allocated over one million three hundred thousand dollars for the use of only fifteen armories statewide as emergency winter shelters, one of which was Roseville's.

The availability of the Armory, the allure of state funds to help pay for the cost of operations and the endorsement of the plan by the *Press Tribune* didn't entice the members of the Board of Supervisors one bit. As in years past, when our County Supervisor Bill Santucci refused to champion our request, the other Board members followed his lead and turned a deaf ear to the proposal.

As always, the Board's inaction didn't stop Schiele. She let me know that she had raised sufficient funds and had so many community connections that she felt assured she would be able to fund her WWJD? program into spring.

Schiele worked countless hours, but never seemed to fret that she went without pay for her hard work. When I asked her about it, she said that was an easy problem to solve. She planned to offset any shortage in income by turning her hobby of making holiday crafts into a paying proposition. She handled her personal financial realities just like she dealt with her health issues. She tended to ignore them.

October 28, 1999:

By the time of the second hearing by the planning commission of the city's proposed new social services ordinance, St. Vincent's president, Richard Roccucci, had been able to get the planning department to agree to modify two central provisions that could eventually negatively affect all social service programs in Roseville: the thirty-day closure rule and the requirement calling for renewing use permits annually. The thirty-day rule was changed to six months, and the annual use permit renewal was scrapped. City officials said the current code's provisions that provided for use permits to remain valid until revoked were adequate.

Late 1999:

Retired Salvation Army Major Dan Birks, who had come on board as interim executive director at Home Start in June 1998, stepped aside when Ann Engelbrecht was recruited and in place as permanent executive director.

December 12, 1999:

An erroneous statement attributed to the city attorney's office appeared in the *Neighbors* section of the Sunday *Bee,* suggesting that HUD had closed its books on Sherry Schiele's HUD complaint of city discrimination, when in fact the case remained alive and well.

Schiele paid little mind to what the Sunday *Bee* had said and went about her business. She informed me that the police had stepped up patrols in the park. She also said she had a client who lost all of his personal belongings, including his false teeth, during a police sweep on a recent rainy night.

Because Schiele, along with her new coworkers, Bea and Bob Young, knew that the people they encountered every day at Saugstad Park were feeling more pressure than usual because of the cops, the trio wanted to do something special for them. They decided to plan a Christmas dinner and provide gifts for everyone.

December 15, 1999:

The City Council adopted the new comprehensive social services ordinance incorporating the changes that Richard Roccucci had bargained for. Roseville thought they finally had a document that appeared to comply with HUD's 1997 directive.

Even with the modifications Roccucci was able to obtain, there were still provisions in the new ordinance governing facility expansion and location that were even more restrictive than the old code. For example, if a shelter provider wanted to add more beds, the entire operation was subject to all the requirements of the new law, including the issuance of a use permit. And if a provider intended to build a new facility, its operation, in addition to being subject to use permit restrictions, would be limited to certain parcels of land and locations in town as designated by the new ordinance. Many of those parcels were located in remote parts of the city that were inappropriate for homeless services.

We soon discovered that to make a case against the new ordinance for causing disparate impact discrimination toward homeless single men, we would first have to be stopped from implementing plans to expand or to build a new facility. The interference had to result from some formal city stricture, like a zoning code prohibition, constraint or refusal by the city to allow public utility hookups for the parcel or unreasonable requirements legislated by the City Council as a condition for issuing permits.

For example, if city officials denied us a use permit because the location we found was not allowed by the ordinance, even though common sense showed the property was suitable for serving homeless single males, we would have grounds for a bona fide HUD complaint.

Unfortunately, no one in the provider community had the resources to risk taking that huge step. It looked as if until we were ready to take the risk, the city prohibition would stand.

We could live with the ordinance's terms because the city was still prohibited from interfering with the existing services we operated.

December 22, 1999:

Despite the refusals of both the County Board of Supervisors and the Roseville City Council to support an emergency shelter for the winter, Annette and I somehow managed to finally get into the spirit of the season. I felt a bit more relaxed knowing that the ordinance issue had been put to bed and that it wasn't mistletoe hanging over the heads of city officials, but rather Sherry Schiele's pending HUD complaint.

Even with those good thoughts, Annette and I found we couldn't sleep for some unexplained reason. Around 3:00 a.m., instead of languishing in bed wide-awake, we decided to get an early start on our to-do lists, at least until we found we were ready to take another stab at snoozing.

We were in the kitchen when the phone rang. I was standing right next to it. Annette was close by. The ring startled both of us. A phone call at that hour could only mean something bad.

When I picked up the receiver, I heard the voice of Sherry Schiele's husband, Lynn. He was calling from Mercy San Juan Hospital, about four miles from their home in Citrus Heights. He was calm, as always, and apologized for calling us at that hour, but he felt compelled to tell us right away that Sherry had died.

He said that during the night, he woke up to the sound of her groaning in pain. When he checked, she was unconscious. After he gathered his wits, he picked her up, put her in the car and sped to the hospital, six or seven minutes away. But, it was too late. She had suffered a massive heart attack and the hospital staff couldn't bring her around.

Annette and I were stunned. Schiele was an irreplaceable friend and confidante whom we had both grown close to over the years. While most of my talks with Schiele had focused on helping her with strategy, coping with city harassment and developing her programs, Annette had a very close friend in Schiele, a source of mutual emotional support. Suddenly, she was gone.

For the rest of the day, I stayed in contact with Lynn. He was surprisingly resigned. One of the first things he did that morning was notify the *Sacramento Bee* about his wife's death. I was amazed at how quickly he made the final arrangements, including cremation and buying a plot at Sylvan Cemetery.

December 23, 1999:
Bee staff writer Steve Gibson picked up the story and wrote Schiele's obituary as a comprehensive featured article. He praised her as "a tireless and controversial advocate for homeless people in Rosevill...."

It was only after I had read the piece that it dawned on me that someone had to pick up where she had left off. I could see that her death would have a huge impact on the single adult members of the homeless community if no one stepped up to keep the WWJD? services going. All of Sherry's hard work could not be allowed to go down the drain.

I also had a hunch that among all the local social service providers, WWJD? would continue to be particularly vulnerable to attacks from the city for two reasons:

1. Even though Schiele left us a wonderful new cause, it had no organizational structure. She ran WWJD? in Lone Ranger mode. She did almost everything herself, from fundraising, buying supplies and doing her beloved "seeking," to visiting the homeless people who frequented Saugstad Park almost every day. Creating a sound operating structure was absolutely necessary if the nonprofit was going to be able to fend off the attacks.

2. Most of her work was conducted in Saugstad Park, a big investment of city dollars and a source of civic pride. Officials naturally wanted to protect that investment and its reputation as a safe place for family recreation. They felt threatened that their vision was being ruined by the presence of homeless adults who lounged under trees and used the barbeque pits to cook their afternoon meals. The city erroneously regarded WWJD? as the cause of their problem, even though the program operated for only an hour a day.

Schiele's "new baby," WWJD?, needed to be transformed from a one-person exercise in charity into a functioning organization with a structure ensuring that it would last for years.

After knowing her for so long, I had learned only too well that Schiele was able to get a project going just by sheer will. But she was not a person who would tie up loose ends or pay attention to details. I also knew that the people she asked to serve on her boards and advisory panels were there for show – to fill ceremonial slots to satisfy legal requirements or social protocols.

Because of the way Schiele had managed the program, I doubted anyone on the WWJD? Board of Directors knew what she had been doing day-to-day, or if any one of them understood how WWJD? actually operated. Even if they did, I was certain that they would not have the time to take on the extra responsibility.

Hobophobia

December 24, 1999:
When Lynn had asked me to handle the church arrangements for Sherry's funeral, I contacted St. Rose liturgy director Joy Robles and developed an outline for the service.

It was only then that it hit me – I would likely be dragged into the WWJD? mess. Someone needed to structure and manage the program if it was to survive. I was Sherry's friend and knew how to develop that structure. However, I couldn't take on the responsibility by myself. Developing a plan the WWJD? operation would have to be a team effort.

In addition, I knew that the nature of the ministry meant that the team would be volunteer-run. The work of WWJD? by design was the kind of help you don't pay someone to do. It was like the charitable work of Franciscan friars and nuns. It sprang from the heart and offered hope to all.

The big question for me at the time was how we could put the team together. None of the current Board members had time to devote to the job. They were already obligated to their own business and family situations.

My circumstances were similar. I was assigned to serve at St. Rose Church. When I resigned from St. Vincent's management in 1988, I firmly believed that I would no longer be tied down to overseeing any of Roseville's homeless charities as an executive director or president.

However, once I understood the consequences of Schiele's death for the WWJD? program, all that changed. Nothing would have pleased city officials more than the spectacle of that fragile program wilting away. That little thorn in their side would have been excised without any effort on their part.

I met with my boss, Father Mike McKeon, to settle on how we should proceed. I told him I thought I would be invited to become a WWJD? Board member in the near future, especially when the others realized that my membership would improve the chances of WWJD? gaining St. Rose support.

I got the green light to do whatever was necessary to build WWJD? into a viable volunteer organization. I agreed to be "the point person."

December 27 1999:
An evening scripture service in Schiele's memory was held at St. Rose.

December 28, 1999:

St. Rose Pastor Emeritus Father Mike Cormack, Episcopal Father Malcolm McClenaghan and I shared ministerial duties accompanied by Joy Robles' and Dona Gentile's music ministry to lead Schiele's funeral service. Many of Schiele's long time coworkers and friends, including Leandra Hackworth, who had been close to Schiele for thirty-three years, attended.

Other people came to share testimonials of Schiele's saving grace in their lives – how she had rescued them from the abyss of hopelessness and addiction, helping them regain their sanity.

Several spoke of her personal courage and the strength of her convictions. Schiele was brave, even in the face of a hostile crowd or before a dais filled with grim-faced politicians who acted as if nothing would make them happier than running her out of town.

All this was shared in Schiele's house of worship. Those who were well-dressed sat with those who were unwashed; together, they sang the praises of a lady whose time among us had been well-lived.

After the Mass and several eulogies, all gathered in the parish hall for a meal where talk of Schiele's goodness continued. Heartfelt tales about the seemingly unending giving that defined who she was were shared by those she had cared for.

More than three hundred people, including a group of homeless men, paid their respects at either the scripture service or the Mass.

December 29, 1999:

The *Press Tribune* summed up the events at Schiele's memorial with a feature multi-page news article beginning on page one with photos. The headline read "Tribute paid to a visionary." In addition to the news item, the opinion page carried a seven hundred-plus word editorial by staff writer Amy Yannello, saluting Schiele for her strength of character and dedication to her cause:

"It's rare the number of times you come across a person who does good work, for good work's sake...Does it with a politically incorrect issue such as homelessness.... That Schiele died so young...is a loss to her family and friends. That she died without having her dream realized – a transitional living shelter for single homeless men and women, is a loss for Roseville, although there are those who won't see it that way."

While Yannello was correct about who Schiele was, she mistook the nature of Schiele's unrealized dream at the time of her death. Her uncompleted vision was not about a transitional living program. That part of her dream had come alive with The Lazarus Project.

Many times, Schiele had told me she was troubled that Roseville didn't have a full array of services for homeless adults: It lacked a comprehensive shelter program. She was quick to add that she couldn't rest until that dream was a reality. With her passing, the torch that had lit her way was passed to her friends.

I called WWJD?'s president, Jean Thompson, to offer my services. We had met during the events following Schiele's passing. I told her about my experience setting up the St. Vincent's volunteer organization and said I would be glad to give WWJD? a hand. She welcomed my offer.

There were only a few other people I could rely on to continue providing limited services in the park until WWJD? got on its feet. Among them were the Youngs, who had helped Schiele over the years. When the Youngs heard that Schiele had passed away, they stepped right up and followed through with the plans for the Christmas party in the park for the homeless folks.

I arranged to pick up the WWJD? files and paperwork from Schiele's husband, and Bob Young moved the van to his house.

We would continue her work, but she would be sorely missed. She was such a unique and complex person, determined and thick-skinned, yet innovative and adaptable. Her no-nonsense and forthright manner at times hid her finer qualities of compassion and kindness. Most of all, Schiele was a woman who lived her faith. She was willing to take risks for the good of others.

Of course, because Schiele operated so differently than most, people sometimes couldn't recognize those qualities. It took a quarter of her lifetime – her final thirteen years – before even her friends were able to put together a realistic picture of who Sherry Schiele was.

For those final years, her work put her in the public eye, something she didn't like. While developing Roseville's first transitional homeless program, beginning with Project Home and then continuing with Home Start, she remained focused on her ministry, not her career. As Amy Yannello stated, "...without grandstanding and without a lot of self-publicity...", Schiele accomplished all this with little financial compensation.

Schiele never broke her word with anyone that I know of and

certainly did not with the city. She never cared what others thought of her personally. Rather, she lamented the thought that Roseville city government was so unbending and extreme in its dislike for homeless single men that it couldn't extricate itself from its hobophobia.

Overwork, exhaustion and her diabetes-related disability led to her death. The words "What Would Jesus Do?" have come to define her legacy. As Yannello's tribute pointed out, "(What Would Jesus Do?) seemed to embody the very principles that guided her decisions and her life."

Sherry Schiele remained faithful to those principles to the very end. Those words became her badge of honor.

Chapter 22:
The Third Millennium! What Changed?
(Jan. 2000–Dec. 2001)

January 2000:

The worldwide media frenzy surrounding "The New Millennium" had grabbed the imaginations of most of us, including me. As 1999 ended, I was fascinated by the possibilities of what might lie just over the horizon. The air was filled with prattle proposing wild-eyed opportunities and potential perils. It was called by many names. The one which I preferred was "the Y2K Phenomenon."

Both electronic and paper news sources flooded us with tales about the future. Time magazine reported that it had "a generator-powered 'war room' in the basement of the Time & Life Building, filled with computers and equipment ready to produce the magazine in case of a catastrophic breakdown of electricity and communications."

Some individuals also reacted in the extreme, storing food, medicine, guns and survival gear, hoping to survive the panic that they predicted would occur when the rest of us realized we were caught up in the apocalyptic end of time.

A more realistic fear that the press exploited was the chance that our computer networks wouldn't be able to withstand the shift. The big question was "Would the final second of 1999 or the first moment of 2000 bring a catastrophic end to our emerging technological life?"

Folks who regarded themselves as reasonably bright and sensible seriously considered the possibility that the worldwide web would crash. It is safe to say that right up to the final click of 1999, most of us remained at least a little apprehensive about what would happen.

When the clock did strike midnight, 2000 smoothly and quietly settled in. Those of us who had been skeptical about the future quickly found that we were once again buoyantly confident. I tried to save face as if I never doubted. I found myself wanting to tell others that I never took the whole Y2K thing seriously whenever the subject came up.

However "the 2000 conversation" had made me reflect on life. I was at a definite point of separation from the past. Without deserting lessons learned or denying queasiness about what the new millennium held, I wanted to walk into the future on a very different path. A growing dislike for the reactionary leadership style in our church, starting at the top with Pope John Paul II and reaching all the way down to our bishop, William Weigand, made me question my desire to follow them any longer. And I had less patience for Roseville' hobophobic politics.

January 18, 2000:

The WWJD? Board of Directors got word of a sad state of affairs. Volunteers Bob and Bea Young reported that during the previous night's storm, the police had rousted several homeless men from their camps, tossed their personal belongings into the rain-swollen creek and tore up one man's identification documents.

After their report, the Youngs left to meet the men at the laundromat on Folsom Road to help them clean and dry the clothes they had on and to give them a fresh change.

I officially accepted the Board's invitation to serve as a member.

January 19, 2000:

When I followed up on the Youngs' report on the police matter and spoke with Herb Whitaker to discuss what our response options to the raid were, I mentioned Schiele's account of a similar event in December.

Both of the raids occurred at night. Apparently, the cops felt that their tactics were more effective if they preyed on the men during the wet winter darkness.

Whitaker said that the whole issue boiled down to having a documented case that he could take to court. To do that, he needed at least one or two of our clients to cooperate with him as witnesses.

The one type of cooperation the men didn't like was having to commit to give testimony. They felt that being a party to a formal complaint left them unprotected and in the crosshairs of the police once their identities were revealed.

We couldn't get anyone to testify.

February 2000:

When the WWJD? van wasn't in use, it was stored at the Youngs' house on Whyte Avenue. The corporate files were kept in my office at St. Rose and the Board of Directors managed the checking account.

The program, in addition to relying on the Youngs, had the help of a new volunteer, Margo Ezell.

Ezell was recruited by Annette one Sunday after Mass. When she told Annette she recently retired from a job in the communications industry and felt at loose ends, looking for something worthwhile to do, Annette took the opportunity to tell her all about WWJD?.

Ezell and the Youngs formed the nucleus of the WWJD? van program. They saw to it that the van service continued to operate one hour a day, five days a week in Saugstad Park. They offered hot coffee and hot chocolate, food, clean clothing and friendship to the forty or so men, women and children who relied on the program to help get them get through the day. The organization was so dependent on Bob Young's dedication that when he took Tuesdays off to play golf and Saturdays to observe the Sabbath, WWJD? simply didn't have the people power to send the van out.

March 23, 2000:

The Placer Greater Collaborative conducted a homeless count as part of developing its CoC document. The census wasn't a scientifically controlled process of head counting in the field, which made it less than reliable from the get-go. Instead, it took the form of a mass mailing to four hundred eighty churches and organizations throughout the county, asking them to report the number of homeless individuals and families they assisted on one designated day.

Only homeless individuals and families who sought services on that one day were counted. Everyone else was left out of the census.

Additionally, if people sought services from two or three different agencies that same day, they were counted that many times. But what the final tally was remains a mystery. I haven't been able to uncover what the numbers were.

Spring 2000:

By winter's passing, I had managed to buttonhole enough volunteers to flesh out a couple more van teams to serve in the park. The WWJD? program was able to operate six days week, taking Saturdays off when the Salvation Army served a hot sit-down breakfast.

Before the new volunteers began their solo trips to the park, Bob Young showed them the ropes, demonstrating how to interact with the clients and what foods could be provided under County Health Department regulations.

I found that organizing the WWJD? operation was a struggle until Denise Sewart and Sharon Sullivan signed on as board members. They were particularly helpful when two members of the original WWJD?

Board, Paul Kunz and Pat Holden, resigned. Sewart, Sullivan and I were able to bring some needed order to the organization. Sullivan assumed the responsibility of corporate treasurer, and Sewart oversaw development of operational policies and procedures, as well as of volunteer rosters, schedules and reports. She also served as corporate secretary. Sewart had joined WWJD? with one caveat: She reminded me that her focus would remain on growing the social justice advocacy program she was involved with in Davis.

When simple new guidelines were developed and put into writing, volunteers exhibited a new confidence, enabling the program to take off. From that point forward, it seemed that nothing could hold us back. As new recruits became easier to find and train, the workload continued to spread out. The Youngs took responsibility for buying supplies and the food that was distributed from the WWJD? van. They also made sure that the big urns of coffee and hot water for each trip to the park were ready.

St. Rose parishioner and master craftsman, Vince Cukar, created a wooden assembly of bins that fit into the area just inside the double back doors of the van to keep the food and supplies from flying all over the place when the van was moving. When the crew opened the doors, the hot chocolate, oatmeal and Ramen packets were all where they should be, as were the canned goods and candy bars, ready to be distributed.

The Youngs often used their personal pickup truck as a mobile clothes closet, which included boots and sleeping bags. Ezell provided her own van to take over the transportation service that Schiele had provided the men and women.

We did have some logistical problems that had to be remedied. Storing the WWJD? van and all the necessary food and supplies at the Youngs' house made it difficult for the new volunteers to access them. We needed to streamline our setup, getting everything centrally located.

We got the go-ahead from St. Rose pastor Father Mike to store the van in the parish parking lot and to move the coffee and hot water pots close by to the former convent kitchen located at the west end of the St. Rose property. I set up a timer system so that the coffee and hot water were ready to be transferred into our new Cambro serving containers when the team arrived in the morning.

Extra food supplies were stored in my garage, a handy half-block from the parked van.

Fall 2000:

The WWJD? food storage problem continued to be a hassle throughout the summer. I grew more frustrated each time I drove the van to my house to load it with the supplies kept in our garage.

When I talked with Father Mike about having some storage space on the parish property, he said the parish was already overwhelmed providing storage for all of the parish and school organizations. I went on to ask him whether he would allow WWJD? to store enough groceries for a few days in a temporary, makeshift, but watertight, cabinet at an out-of-the-way location on the property. If WWJD? could do that, the volunteers could stock up the van themselves every day.

He rhetorically asked, "Is there such a place?" I told him of one I had found. It was under the eaves of the former convent complex.

He gave me a puzzled look and asked how I could keep the food dry and safe.

I explained that I had found a large watertight cabinet at Ace Hardware that would fit under the eaves on the lee side of the building.

He shot another puzzled look my way, but gave me the okay, saying if I thought I could do it, to go ahead and try.

A Rubbermaid outdoor toolshed did the job. It was a perfect fit. My garage on Fischer Court would only be used for overflow storage.

November 19, 2000:

As I had been doing just prior to the holiday season for the previous six years, I was preaching the homily at each Mass, asking for funds for the homeless programs that the parish supported. The response from the congregation was always generous, averaging over fifteen thousand dollars each year. The offering was added to other funds the parish had set aside to help St. Vincent's, WWJD?, Home Start and The Lazarus Project and would be divided and given to them as the Parish Finance Committee and Father Mike decided.

That year, as I prepared my message, I realized that each agency complemented the others by providing services tailored to meet the needs of a certain part of the homeless population. The four offered services that covered a broad spectrum of needs. But the agencies operated independently with separate boards and executive directors and had been created at different times, usually years apart when we saw an opportunity to initiate a new service without city interference.

I knew the operation of each one inside and out, and realized that each, on its own, was less efficient than it could be if it became part of a larger organization of the four. If they would join forces, especially when seeking funds, they could be much more effective.

It would be ideal to eventually bring the four into one agency. It would be a formidable team which could readily garner state and federal grants by presenting a unified front. The big question was how to overcome the natural resistance to change that would exist in each of the four organizations.

I thought the answer came after Mass that Sunday as I was standing outside the main exit from the church, greeting the parishioners as they left. As I was shaking hands and making small talk by the main doors, I noticed a distinguished looking man with a mustache and goatee in a wheelchair being pushed by a petite lady. They were coming around to the front from the church exit that had a ramp. Even though both were senior citizens, they emitted an amazing amount of energy. Surprising to me, they had me in their sights!

I had seen the couple in church that morning and on other occasions, but had never met them. It looked like I was finally going to get my chance.

As soon as I could, I focused on them and reached out to greet them both, shaking hands with the man and introducing myself. He responded that they were Jack and Mary Epling. He said they had just moved from Southern California to be close to their daughter, Kathleen Beiler, a teacher in the Roseville area. Both Jack and Mary were anxious to speak to me about a special idea.

The Eplings explained that he had spent years volunteering as a successful fundraiser for the Muscular Dystrophy Association. It was clear that he was a natural-born salesman, hooking me when he said "You need help, and we know how to give it."

He had my attention and continued saying that one of the best ways to raise funds for charitable projects was to promote a "wine tasting" event. Vintners would provide samples of their wines, while local restaurants would serve samples of their cuisine. The guests were offered a chance to enjoy not only the wine and food, but also acquire special deals through silent auction items and raffles. The evening would be capped with a live auction of items ranging from donated cases of wine to fabulous vacations.

Epling said an event like this was a draw for entrepreneurs because it provided them a unique platform to introduce their brand to customers they couldn't reach any other way.

He then explained that the big money for the charity was not made from the raffles, auctions and drawings, but from pre-selling admission tickets. For example, if the tickets cost forty-five dollars each and five hundred were pre-sold, the charity would earn a minimum of twenty-two thousand five hundred dollars .

He wanted to know if we could get the representatives from St. Vincent's, WWJD?, The Lazarus Project and Home Start together to present his idea to see if they would jointly sponsor such an event.

I didn't realize how long we had been talking. By the time we wound things up, the folks who had been visiting on the church plaza after the last Mass had disappeared, and the first ones for the next Mass had begun filing across the concrete and bricks and into the church.

Over the next few days, I was in touch with key people in each organization. After I had pitched the idea, two said they wanted Board approval before moving ahead. Another told me he wanted to think about it. Only WWJD? jumped in right away.

Epling was ready to organize the first event regardless of whether the other three committed to the project.

December 13, 2000:

Epling presided over "the meeting of the Wine and Food Committee" at St. Rose. All four charity organizations sent representatives to learn what this fundraising experiment was all about. I think they sensed that if they didn't have a spokesperson present, they might be left behind. Everyone agreed to meet again after the hubbub of Christmas had passed. Before the meeting adjourned, the Eplings invited everyone to attend their holiday open house.

December 16, 2000:

The party at Jack and Mary Epling's was not only a fun afternoon. It also proved to be an opportunity to experience what a wonderfully loving couple the Eplings were.

A few days after the open house, I began working on the federal IRS and state Franchise Tax applications for the new organization's non-profit status. I hoped that this new partnership among the four nonprofits would be the first step toward bringing them into one.

I threw a name on the fundraising group: The Placer Care Coalition Inc.(PCCI). Calling it a "Coalition" hopefully would encourage the four organizations to think about joining together.

Late December 2000:

After Christmas, Epling and I got together to review the tax exempt paperwork. He was all for what I had prepared. I asked him how he felt about beginning our public awareness program by asking for a meeting with County Supervisor Bill Santucci and County Health and Human Services Director Ray Merz. I told Epling that I knew both men well and believed they would support a merger. He agreed that we should at least bring them up to date. But he told me right off that he thought the merger was a long shot at best.

Either way, we had committed to raising funds and awareness about how the four programs changed lives for the better.

On Roseville's homeless front, St. Vincent's manager Charlotte Magennis told me that as lucky as the people were who entered the Home Start and The Lazarus Project programs, almost every day, her agency encountered other homeless families and individuals who had no prospects for improving their situations without the structure provided by a formal, yet flexible, transitional housing plan. Magennis felt that Roseville needed another player offering transitional housing and rehabilitation. She told me that she had been able to secure funding from St. Vincent's budget to lease six units in the B Street Apartments where she had started the transitional housing program "New Beginnings" for singles and families.

At the St. Rose parish house, the usually skeptical pastor, Father Mike McKeon seemed to have an extra boost of optimism. I wondered if it had anything to do with the arrival of the new millennium. He asked Denise Sewart and me to join him to discuss a proposal Sewart had made to form a social justice committee at St. Rose. He was so impressed by the comprehensive action plan Sewart had developed that he probably would have felt remiss if he didn't act on it.

When the three of us met, it was evident that this new program was a very important cause for the two of them. After listening to Father Mike's pitch, I knew I couldn't handle another project on top of my regular parish work, managing the WWJD? ministry, helping The Lazarus Project and beginning my commitment to what would become the PCCI.

I didn't say anything at the meeting about declining his invitation. I waited until the next day to tell him. However, I also let him know that I would make time to be supportive of the program and would attend meetings when I could. He settled for that. Sewart moved ahead with founding the St. Rose Social Justice Committee, which would eventually expand to SS. Peter & Paul parish in Rocklin, and become known as the Social Justice Advocates of Placer County.

January 3, 2001:

Epling chaired the first working meeting of The Wine and Food committee, kicking off the conversation by focusing on possible names for our event. The initial suggestions were either too corny or too tacky to take seriously. Just when I thought we would make a pretty hopeless bunch of advertising executives, we were saved when a soft voice came from the back of the room. It was the voice of someone who at the December 13th meeting had been as quiet as a church mouse: Shannon Jordahl, the wife of The Lazarus Project's executive director. She timidly asked "What about 'Raising Spirits'?"

Within a few minutes, the "Raising Spirits" name was adopted.

Next, we needed a date for the first event. Epling proposed it be on the last Sunday in April, a couple of weeks after Easter and a month or so before graduations and summer vacations. His recommendation was followed by a bit of hemming and hawing, but we eventually agreed.

Sunset Whiney Country Club had a banquet room available that day at a reasonable price. All concurred that should be the place we would hold Raising Spirits' premiere. Everything was falling into place.

Next, we formed committees to cover all aspects of the celebration: ticket sales, auction items, raffle prizes, entertainment, public relations and inviting restaurants and vintners to sponsor the event.

Towards the end of the meeting, I presented an update on forming the umbrella corporation for the new project. The group okayed filing the corporate name "The Placer Care Coalition Inc."

I also mentioned that Epling and I would ask county representatives for a meeting to discuss our plans for the PCCI to both be a fundraising instrument for the four organizations and also a means of eventually uniting them under one corporate banner. Some members seemed wary of the merger idea, but couldn't resist the lure of maybe having better access to government funds. The temptation of money was enough to get their okay for a meeting with the county.

Mid-January 2001:

It looked like Home Start was finally financially back on its feet. The organization was doing so well that the 2001 budget provided for nineteen thousand four hundred dollars to be put aside as savings for property purchase.

Then the Home Start Board got incredible news! The organization was to receive a once-in-a-lifetime gift. An anonymous donor had pledged four hundred thousand dollars for Home Start to the purchase the property it had been leasing for years.

St. Vincent's New Beginnings homeless program was doing well too, so much so that manager Charlotte Magennis wanted to expand the scope of services. She optimistically applied for City Council approval of a federal emergency shelter grant application to obtain help with apartment rental expenses, operational costs and administrative overhead for a case manager.

It didn't take the city long to turn down the request because St. Vincent's had forgotten to jump through the hoop of obtaining a Memorandum of Understanding with the Thieles Neighborhood Association. The MOU would have guaranteed to the city that St. Vincent's wouldn't house any transients in any of its B Street housing units. The loss of funding meant that the agency would be strapped for money again and would have to look elsewhere for support. The city had a long memory and showed no mercy on the program.

Even if the funding was denied, the effort wasn't a waste: We had documented proof that Roseville was still hobophobic.

Officials were also noticeably annoyed with WWJD?. They believed that the organization was frustrating their efforts to rid the park of the homeless folks who hung out there, going so far as to label the WWJD? one-hour van service as the reason the homeless men stayed in and around the park 24/7.

The police department also jumped in, doubling its efforts to move the men out of the park by increasing patrols and tapping into the fear factor among the members of the city's Neighborhood Watch programs. Officers were sent on several occasions to meet with members of the Hillcrest Neighborhood Association who lived to the east and south of the park. That was my neighborhood and I attended each of the meetings.

The police department's message was focused ostensibly on the broad-brush subject of neighborhood safety. The topic was so popular that it continued to crop up in neighborhood meetings over the next couple of months with euphemistic titles like "public safety," "home security" and "neighborhood watch."

However, the final meeting was a blunt discussion of the danger of transients in the neighborhood. No euphemisms there! The police then

331

successfully led the neighbors to make an effective nexus between their safety concerns about the dangers posed by the homeless men who frequented the park and the WWJD? service program. The politics of fear!

At that point, I had to reevaluate our chances of continuing the van operation in the park. Providing meals and services in the park six days a week would soon no longer be sustainable. I had to do something.

First, I thought we should invite neighborhood association members who were concerned to visit the van operation in the park to see what was really going on.

And second, we would attempt to move the van services out of the park on as many days as possible by relocating to other sites. I had a few locations in mind: St. Vincent's, the Salvation Army and the Methodist Church. If we could move services to their sites three days a week, we might be able to lower the hobophobia index in the Hillcrest area..

I soon discovered that even if I got permission to move the van to these locations, I would still face some tough opposition from Ezell and the Youngs. They let me know in no uncertain terms that they did not like the idea of moving to new locations because the men "were comfortable" in the park. Their objections didn't change the fact that circumstances were rapidly deteriorating and I had to act to avoid a conflict with the city.

The WWJD? Board of Directors continued to evolve and grow stronger in numbers. St. Rose parishioners Bob and June Bonnici joined. Bob served as a Board member and coordinated the van team members and van loaders, while June helped with administrative and clerical work. Bonnici, with his administrative background and management responsibilities with the State Board of Equalization, soon began overseeing all the organization's day-to-day operations.

Other active volunteers, Bob Collins, Pat Kumpf and Rich Fogarty, signed on to the WWJD? Board as well.

As Bonnici and I looked for new locations for the van food service, the Youngs raised another concern they felt needed to be addressed: The weather was making it difficult for the clients to enjoy their coffee and breakfast snacks. They were forced to stand in the cold and damp conditions in the open park environment. The Youngs suggested we move the van food service from the back of Saugstad Park towards Douglas Boulevard, close to the Sacramento commuter bus shelter in the front parking lot. The shelter could provide some protection when it was rainy or foggy.

After a long discussion, I reluctantly agreed to give it a try, in part to soften the Youngs' opposition to my plan to move the operation outside of the park on some days.

I soon discovered I had made a big mistake. It was a decision city officials did not like and quickly pounced on. WWJD? had become too visible at the front of the park. They must have thought we were trying to commandeer the bus shelter. Now city pressure was not only directed toward the men in the park, but also laser-focused on the WWJD? program.

On several different days while our van workers were giving out food near the bus shelter, they were approached, sometimes by "Dave," the park supervisor, and other times by the police, who always had the same message: Our clients were causing a nuisance by hanging around the shelter in the morning before the WWJD? van showed up.

I followed up on the accusation by contacting Lorraine Browning in the city transportation office. I had known her for years from my St. Rose parish work. I asked her if there had been any public complaints about our clients using the bus shelter.

She said there weren't any commuter complaints, but the park maintenance people were sure the men would eventually scare someone off. Lorraine also said that the commuter buses were done picking up passengers there by 7:30 a.m., an hour before our van arrived.

I decided that the way to be sure that there wouldn't be any commuter complaints would be to check the shelter before 7:30 a.m. for our clients. If any of them were sitting or lying on the benches, I'd ask them to leave and come back at 8:30 when the van arrived. The shelter was less than a five-minute drive from my house.

For two weeks on every morning when the van service visited the park, I made a daily trip to the site. I told anyone in the shelter who looked like one of our clients to leave and come back at 8:30 a.m.

Of the two or three clients who were there for my daily check, all were more than willing to oblige. Word spread fast: stay away from the shelter until the last commuter bus left. That was all I wanted.

Bonnici took on more of the organization's daily tasks as he became more familiar with the operation. That gave me some time to chat up the park workers, and to protest to police administration. I let them know that the cops didn't need to be aggressive with us. I hoped the dialog might buy us time to secure other sites.

I met with "Dave," the park supervisor, to tell him that we planned to shift service on some days to locations outside the park beginning in May.

He seemed surprised that we could move whenever we found another location without any government okay. Did the city folks think that by shutting down the WWJD? park operation, they were shutting down WWJD? My guess was they didn't realize that there wasn't a law or regulation on the books prohibiting us from opening for business in nearly any public spot we chose, even in the park. I could see that Dave couldn't fathom the idea.

He also couldn't understand that if we didn't find alternate sites, we would continue to serve in the park.

March 2001:

"The Placer Greater Collaborative" members voted to change the name of their group to "The Placer Collaborative Network" (PCN) and assembled a working sub-group composed of representatives from an array of organizations, including Placer County, Roseville, religious-based charities and other local agencies. The new ensemble of representatives was labeled the "Placer Consortium on Homelessness and Affordable Housing" (PCOH) and was charged with two tasks:

1. Prepare a ten-year plan to end homelessness in Placer County; and
2. Oversee the annual preparation of HUD required CoC materials.

March 30, 2001:

Home Start was hit with an eviction notice. Sacramento attorney Rick Peasley, representing the owners of the property Dinesh and Mukesh Patel of Cincinnati, Ohio, said that Home Start had failed to renew its lease in 1997 and didn't exercise an option agreement to purchase the property for five hundred twenty-five thousand dollars. The agency was then on a month-to-month tenancy that could be terminated on 30-days' notice.

Board Chair Joe Esparza reported that the organization was caught flatfooted by the notice. Apparently, it was not enough for the Patels to get their monthly rent on time. It looked like they decided to end the relationship, according to the picture Peasley painted.

Really? Did the Patels want to take over and operate their forty-five year old rundown motel again? Or could it be that the anonymous January benefactor had tried to discreetly initiate purchase negotiations with the Patels and discovered they needed "some softening up" before they could be dealt with?

If the Patels thought the mystery donor's interest was waning, did they get nervous, leading to the eviction notice, not so much to dislodge Home Start, but to light a fire under the donor to get a deal done?

Their strategy evidently failed. Instead, Roseville attorney Robert Sinclair was called in to represent Home Start in the eviction matter. The anonymous donor's January pledge of four hundred thousand dollars remained on the table for the Patels to grab.

Later that afternoon, I got some WWJD? news that I had to attend to: Bea Young came by the house to tell me that the volunteers experienced a new hassle with the city. Again, it was with "Dave," the park supervisor.

I drove to the park and went to the maintenance shop, looking for Dave. Another man named Gregg told me his boss had gone home that Friday afternoon. Calm and cool, Gregg said that Dave was stressed because the park was getting into its busy season.

Even though Bob Bonnici and I were constantly looking for alternate sites for WWJD?'s van program and I had told Dave that we planned to move to a few new locations in May, we still didn't have a single alternate site nailed down.

Spring 2001:

The Lazarus Project acquired its second home. This one was within Roseville's city limits and was designated to house a transitional living program for up to six single women.

The home was named Schiele House, and was purchased with one hundred thirty-two thousand dollars from Placer County as a portion of the eight hundred thousand dollars it received from Governor Gray Davis' Homeless Initiative, AB 2034, authored by Darrell Steinberg.

The city, true to character, did make one feeble attempt to stall the opening of Schiele House. When Executive Director Wade Jordahl asked City Hall to have the utilities put in the corporation's name, city staff balked. This was despite assurances contained in a city September 8th, 1999, letter, which I had in hand, and other recent pledges obtained from officials that any Lazarus Project house, whether for men or women with six or fewer residents, would be treated as a regular residential use.

It took phone calls from Father Mike and Betsy Donovan to remind the Roseville bureaucrats of their commitment. With that, they backed off. No special permits were required to connect utility services to

Schiele House. The precedent was set.

April 9, 2001:
The Lazarus Project's Schiele House began receiving guests. The program now had a home for men and another for women.

April 29, 2001:
The first Raising Spirits fundraising event proved a success. Proceeds provided each of the four charities with a bonus check for five thousand dollars, with an additional five thousand dollars in profits retained to cover start-up costs and seed money for next year.

May 2001:
WWJD? finally secured a couple of new sites for van stops:
- The First Methodist Church at Church Street and Washington Boulevard gave the organization permission to use their parking lot on Monday mornings for the van service. That was a nice fit, since the Methodists provided a hot dinner at noon on Mondays as part of the provider consortium's plan.
- A similar arrangement was made with St. Vincent's at the Bonita location for Sundays and Wednesdays. St. Vincent's gave us a couple of conditions if the service at the Bonita site was to be a long-term arrangement.
    o WWJD? volunteers would have to be sure the clients ate and visited inside the waiting area enclosure for the Dining Room and picked up their trash.
    o They were not to block the sidewalk on Bonita or hang out in the street.

The Sunday crew was made up of members of Denise's Sewart's social justice group from SS. Peter & Paul Parish in Rocklin, with her co-chair Denise Johnston coordinating that day. The group felt that volunteering to help WWJD? in its mission on Sundays added a new dimension to what it meant to be Christian.

June 2001:
A sub-committee of the PCOH, the Placer County Shelter Committee, was assembled with a task that was identical to all the previous city sponsored homeless shelter committees and forums: to search for a workable solution to the larger homeless problem: a year-round 24/7 shelter plan for all homeless people, including single adults.

July 2001:

On a very hot day, as Bob Bonnici and I were moving cases of canned goods and supplies for WWJD? from my garage to the storage unit, he asked a very logical question: Why didn't WWJD? have a week's supply of groceries at St. Rose so that the van could easily be restocked? I reminded him that we just recently got Father Mike to let us store the van in the church parking lot and have the coffee and hot water pots handy in the old convent. To push our luck too far might backfire.

Bonnici thought and then said, "That's not what I mean. What we need is a separate building – a good-sized storage shed so we could have plenty of stuff on hand all the time."

I knew he was right. But how would we pay for it, and where could we put it?

We ambled over to the Vine Avenue sidewalk in front of St. Rose to check out prospects for a site. I said that I thought there might be room at the west edge of the property. We walked down that direction to see.

Sure enough, if an eight-foot section of fence was taken out, there would be plenty of space for a shed as big as eight-by-twelve feet, plus a place in front of it to park the van! Bonnici seemed pleased. I was still worried about the cost.

I think he was just waiting for me to share my concern, because as soon as I did, he immediately suggested, "Would it be any easier if June and I paid for it?"

That clinched it. The next day, I asked Father Mike if we could locate a WWJD? storage unit, "like a Tuff Shed," at the west end of the property and park the van in front of it.

We walked down to the area. I had marked where the fence would be removed and where the shed would sit. I also had parked the van immediately in front of the area so that the project would be easier to visualize. After looking things over, he casually said, "Looks fine to me."

As soon as we got back to the parish office, I called Bonnici to give him the good news. Within a month, the shed was installed, solving our last operating problem. All the new building needed was a coat of paint.

The van service to the Methodist Church on Mondays and to St. Vincent's on Wednesdays and Sundays was running smoothly. The move had helped, but serving in the park on three days – Tuesdays, Thursdays and Fridays – was still too much.

I had hoped we could make an arrangement with the Salvation Army for Fridays. The Army, like the other social services providers, had found ways to expand its programs for homeless folks over the years. It continued to provide a free Friday noon dinner and a Saturday sit-down breakfast and had added a free shower program, including a clothing exchange run by Joyce and Don Sweely. The couple swapped freshly laundered clothes to replace soiled ones, and then washed and mended them if possible to offer to other needy souls.

With the Army's history of helping homeless persons, it felt odd when I discovered that the recent new leadership of the Roseville Corps was reluctant to cooperate openly with the other providers in town. Captain Kris Potter was unlike his Army predecessors, Kit Wetter, Jim Durel, and Randy Clark, who all were open to new ideas. He was apprehensive about allowing us to bring the WWJD? van to his facility Friday mornings, but couldn't come up with a plausible reason for his hesitation. When I learned about his pre-Salvation Army career as a private investigator, I understood.

August 2001:

HUD closed Sherry Schiele's complaint a year and a half after her death. The result of the struggle turned out to be neither a win nor a loss for the city. The feds admitted that they couldn't prove criminal intent, but pointed out that Roseville was "being bad." The upshot was that the city lost Brownie points and that HUD had officially documented Roseville's conduct.

The feds remained persistent in their attempt to hold the city accountable. The agency went so far as try to mediate a conciliation agreement between WWJD? and the city. Roseville continually rebuffed HUD's attempts. The city twisted and squirmed, using any excuse it could muster to avoid sitting down at the table to work out a compromise.

St. Vincent's New Beginnings homeless program had learned its lesson the previous year and entered into an MOU with the Thieles Neighborhood Association, allowing the agency to win approval for an eighty-five thousand dollar grant by the City Council.

September 2001:

So many well-qualified people wanted to donate their time to WWJD? that the organization grew to include sixty competent, reliable volunteers. Within the group there, were two volunteer registered nurses and a volunteer licensed physician's assistant who provided first aid, triage and referrals either to doctors or to local hospitals. We also had two volunteer social workers to help elderly and disabled clients connect with county services and housing agencies.

September 18, 2001:
A General Information Memorandum from the police department and city planning to the City Council identified "Transients" as a problem.

What a revelation!

But the memo had teeth.

Police chief John Barrow announced that he would ask the Council to replace the city's two parks and recreation department rangers with two sworn police officers who would be assigned to park patrol, enabling the city to better manage the transient problem.

From the beginning of Chief Barrow's crusade, the officers seemed to enjoy harassing not only homeless single adults in city parks, but also those who looked like transients walking down a street or riding a bicycle in a way that might violate city codes. The cops randomly stopped anyone carrying a pack, forcing the person to sit on the curb while they checked for outstanding warrants.

I received continuous reports from WWJD? volunteers, as well as from homeless persons, about what they regarded as police officers overstepping their authority. The cops would go through the clients' personal belongings and take money, prescribed medications, clothing and bedrolls, claiming it was all being booked as evidence to back up the citations they issued.

Whether or not they cited the homeless person, sometimes officers would put them into the patrol car and drive them up the I-80 freeway toward Auburn, usually at night. When they came to a remote section of the Interstate, the officers would kick them out of the patrol car and leave them stranded in the dark on the freeway, a good distance from any exit.

Fall 2001:
After months of phone calls and meetings, Salvation Army Captain Kris Potter finally gave WWJD? permission to bring the van to his site. The service at the Linda Drive curbside seemed to work well. Then, after our first visit, he tried to go back on his word. During a heart-to-heart talk about the situation, he finally confessed the reason for his apprehension: His dread that the van's presence would damage his relationship with the city. The Politics of Fear!

Despite Potter's efforts to dislodge us from the area, we stayed.

Late December 2001:

The negotiations for the purchase of the Home Start property by the agency's secret benefactor resumed. The sellers were ready to make a deal for four hundred fifty thousand dollars cash, providing the transaction was completed by Christmas. The generous donor put another fifty thousand dollars on the table, making sure the deal closed on time.

By the end of the year, the secret donor's identity had leaked out. The generous contribution was the gift of John and Laura Mourier, regional real estate developers, both born and raised in Roseville. The Mouriers told the *Press Tribune*, "This donation to Home Start gives something back (and) a hand up to these families that are striving for a better future for their children."

Chapter 23:
Finally, a Foundation for a Homeless Shelter
(Jan. 2002–Mar. 2004)

January 2002:

Joe DiPentino, Dorothy Robertson, Valerie Boughner, Cindy Lopes and Margaret Hutchinson joined the WWJD? Board.

Denise Sewart resigned her position as WWJD? corporate secretary, but continued on the Board. She was shifting her focus away from WWJD? management to developing an area-wide Social Justice Advocates group, which was not limited to St. Rose Parish, but also included SS. Peter & Paul in Rocklin.

With all the capable help, I also decided to completely sever ties with WWJD?. I wanted to spend more time working in St. Rose parish ministry.

February 2002:

A long-time friend, Karen Bocast, agreed to become the WWJD? corporate president. The position had been vacant since Jean Thompson had stepped down. Bocast could easily handle the position. She brought excellent leadership and administrative skills developed in the IT business. She said would only take the position if I remained on the Board as administrative vice president. With that, I rescinded my resignation.

March 2002:

The "Placer Consortium on Homelessness and Affordable Housing" (PCOH) members worked away on the annual Continuum of Care (CoC) document and held their first meeting on the next task the group was chartered to carry out: the development of a countywide ten-year plan to end homelessness.

A private consulting group, Sergei Shkurkin and Associates, was hired to conduct Placer County's first official homeless census. The census was promoted as fundamental to understanding what was necessary to develop an action plan to address homelessness in the county. Carried out during the last week of the month, the count yielded four hundred five homeless people.

Hobophobia

April 2002:
The Second Annual PCCI Raising Spirits event earned twenty-eight thousand dollars .

April 4, 2002:
WWJD?'s success in moving the van service to other locations apparently wasn't enough for the city. The Council, led by Mayor Claudia Gamar and Police Chief John Barrow, along with the city's economic and community services manager Jan Shellito, remained convinced that the presence of transients in the park and their camps in the creek bed was directly caused by the WWJD? van service. A new General Information Memo identified WWJD? as the culprit.

May 6, 2002:
In a conversation with city representative Jan Shonkwiler, I learned she was under a lot of pressure from Shellito to get what she called "the transient problem" resolved. When I reminded her that WWJD? had found other locations for its service, using the park site only two days a week, she was stunned! She admitted that was the first time she had heard that WWJD? had made any changes.

For my part, I was miffed by the casualness of her use of the word "transient." I guess I was just struck for the first time that the expression had not only become a euphemism replacing the harsher word "tramp," but also had degenerated into a "dog whistle" to describe the presence of any undesirable-looking lone adult, whether the person was from out of town or a local.

The earliest use of the term "transient" by city operatives that I found in my records was during an April 1985 Council meeting when Mayor Crabb and then police chief Jim Hall threw the word around as if the two men were just "good ole boys" who didn't know any better.

Here it was 2002 and nothing had changed.

Shonkwiler had another item on her agenda to talk to me about: She wanted to hold a meeting of unnamed city "officials" and WWJD? representatives in the next couple of days to discuss the serious "T" problem.

I said that on such short notice, it might be difficult to set up a meeting of any consequence on what she regarded as such an important subject.

She insisted that we meet. She had already reserved a conference room in the civic center.

May 8, 2002:

I did the best I could do to accommodate Shonkwiler's request. My friend Jack Willoughby and WWJD? Board member Pat Kumpf attended the meeting with me.

It turned out that Shonkwiler and Kevin Payne were the only two city representatives who showed up. Payne, the expert on the city's permits system, made a point that WWJD? would need a permit to continue its work.

Willoughby set the tone for our position by saying that we would like to find a solution for the city's concerns, but more importantly, WWJD? had a religious commitment and a right under the Constitution to do the ministry.

Shonkwiler presented the city's position, concluding by asking how WWJD? was going to change.

Payne said maybe there were ways of accomplishing a mutual goal without a permit. Then both Shonkwiler and Payne offered to prepare a list of alternatives, including locations, which didn't require a permit.

But the conversation didn't end there. The two of them circled back and persisted with their original line that WWJD? might need a permit to operate even if the ministry was started by Sherry Schiele before the current anti-free food ordinance was passed.

The meeting concluded after all agreed the next step was for Payne to notify me when he had the list of sites, a map, and an answer to the permit question.

June 27, 2002:

Payne's letter, complete with attachments, claimed that the WWJD? van had no right to be located in the park. The documents also made it clear that the city would require that at any new van site where free food was distributed, like at St. Vincent's, WWJD? would have to operate inside of the building, not at the curb or in the outside waiting area. Plus, the host site would have to get a conditional use permit.

Reading between the lines, I could see that the city could muscle the Methodist Church and The Salvation Army into obtaining conditional use permits for the days WWJD? operated at those locations. The conditional use permit route would result in closing WWJD? down.

The city offered another option, which was equally insidious: WWJD? could build or remodel a facility within certain zones, as long as it was not within one thousand feet of another social service provider and met all code requirements contained in what I always thought as the overreaching 1999 social services ordinance. If the site didn't meet the city's requirements as laid out in the code, a conditional use permit would also be required.

None of these alternatives were viable for the all-volunteer charity with an annual operating budget of forty thousand dollars, with three thousand eight hundred fifteen dollars of it restricted county money for winter motel vouchers received through the Auburn Salvation Army.

July 11, 2002:
I wrote Payne an innocuous reply to his June 27th letter to buy time as I tried lining up an attorney to intercede for WWJD?. Jack Willoughby had retired; but Herb Whitaker was still at Legal Services of Northern California. Both men offered their services, with Whitaker taking the lead.

August 2002:
Home Start Board member Scott Hightower told the *Press Tribune* that the Board was committed to looking for funding to refurbish the old motel buildings. They were in dire repair; but they were heaven for those families whose best alternative was living out of a car.

Pastor Brad Swope of Horizon Community Church had telephoned me, asking if we could get together sometime to discuss the "homeless situation in Roseville". We agreed to meet for morning coffee later in the month.

Before we ended our phone conversation, I reminded him that we had never met. He said I would recognize him by his goatee.

August 21, 2002:
Sure enough, Swope stood out in the crowd.

When we sat down to talk, it didn't take long to find out that we shared a common concern: the city's overbearing rules that attempted to control services to homeless people.

Swope told me about the commitment at his church to support the poorer folks in the area:

- His congregation had a crew that worked at the WWJD? van;
- The church had a community clothes closet run by volunteer Bea Young at the church's headquarters, the old Bank of Italy building at the corner of Main, Lincoln and Church Streets.
- The church provided emergency housing help; and

- The members hosted a free evening dinner for all comers once a month in its headquarters.

Swope referred to the dinner as "The Common Meal." I had heard stories about it. From what had been told, it was more like a banquet!

He said the dinner had been running smoothly month after month until Chris Burrows of the city planning department met with him over the possibility that the meal program might not be in conformance with the rules of the 1999 social services ordinance. Burrows capped off his visit by saying that if the church wanted to continue the practice, it would be required to get a zoning interpretation from Patty Dunn, the city development director.

The interpretation didn't come back the in the church's favor.

Swope recounted that he was not deterred by the ruling. He asked Pastor Jerry Angove at the Methodist Church, two blocks away, if the Common Meal could be served there, irrespective of what the city requirements were.

He told me that the Methodists, known for providing free meals for anyone seeking help, disregarded the ordinance's prohibition against expanding their existing meal schedule and welcomed him with open arms. The city never said a word about the change.

I got the impression that having his church serve The Common Meal at the Methodists wasn't enough to satisfy his concerns for homeless people. He seemed to be on a mission to get an overnight emergency shelter program started in Roseville.

I shared with him that I also had a current problem simmering with the city as it tried to dislodge WWJD?'s services from Saugstad Park. Our similar encounters with Roseville's rules gave us an excuse to commiserate with one another. We both knew city leaders would continue to create obstacles for our programs.

September 27, 2002:
Legal Services of Northern California's Herb Whitaker notified the city that he was formally representing WWJD? concerning the park issue.

November 2002:
Rocky Rockholm replaced the retiring Claudia Gamar as Roseville's mayor.

December 2002:

Home Start Executive Director Ann Engelbrecht announced that the organization had received assurances from the city that it would help fund the remodeling project of its premises at 410 Riverside.

April 2, 2003:

Under Rockholm's leadership, the city made good on its pledge to Home Start when the Council, acting as the Roseville Redevelopment Agency, allocated two hundred fifty thousand dollars toward rehabbing the old building. Everyone knew that the amount was just enough to get the project going. The finished product would probably require at least another seven hundred fifty thousand dollars.

This allocation of city money was the first notable positive Council move to help homeless people under our new mayor.

Mid-April 2003:

Raising Spirits earned five thousand eight hundred dollars for each organization.

June 2003:

The PCOH Shelter Committee managed to inch forward. Following numerous meetings, it held a lunch meeting for local pastors to present the results of the homeless census commissioned the year before, along with a list of ideas to address the needs of the area's homeless population.

Unfortunately, no one at the lunch articulated the one idea which should have topped the list of solutions for Placer County's homeless problem: the development of a year-round, twenty-four hour, seven day a week shelter.

With that impasse, there were only two items of consensus that emerged:

- Another consultant should be hired to help the consortium formulate the plan to "End homelessness in Placer County"; and
- A fundraising crusade should be conducted to pay for the cost of another consultant's fee.

Placer County, the City of Roseville, The Salvation Army, Roseville Joint Union High School District and more than twelve churches came up with the money.

The contract went to a San Francisco firm by the name of HomeBase/the Center for Common Concerns, whom the Shelter

Committee touted as "a nationally-recognized public policy firm specializing in homelessness."

December 15, 2003:
The negotiations between WWJD? and the city over the Saugstad Park issue seesawed back and forth, and then suddenly died away without any explanation. There was no change in the status quo. WWJD? continued providing services in the park without the city so much as issuing the charity a single citation.

Whitaker suggested that the battle was over and that the file should be closed.

The WWJD? Board agreed.

December 30, 2003, 2 p.m.:
A Placer County Health and Human Services employee in a county car transported a severely disabled elderly man from Placer County to the steps of Loaves and Fishes in Sacramento, where he was dumped.

This wasn't the first time that Placer County had done this. But, Tim Brown, the Executive Director of Loaves and Fishes, was determined that this was going to be the last time. He promptly informed the *Sacramento Bee*. Reporter Jocelyn Wiener got on the story immediately.

By four o'clock, Placer County officials had retrieved the man, taking him back up the hill to Auburn. But it was too late for Placer County to cover up its mistake. The cat was out of the bag.

January 1, 2004:
The *Sacramento Bee* ran a juicy story covering the incident. When the article came out, the reaction of most of us in the Roseville church and provider communities amounted to no more than a shrug of the shoulders. We should have been deeply shocked, but we weren't. Whenever we had seen this kind of county conduct before, we always hoped we would never see it again. But we knew better.

The one person who refused to be cynical and wouldn't let the issue slide was Pastor Brad Swope of Horizon Community Church. He put out a call to church leaders and providers asking them to come to a three-hour morning get-together towards the end of the month to discuss what might be a new way to offer shelter, even in the face of the 1999 city ordinance.

January 24, 2004:

Swope had prepared brilliantly for the meeting with the ministers and providers. He knew exactly what needed to be done. There were about twenty key players from local churches and providers in attendance.

His plan began to unfold when he had Pastor David George and Elder Ed Donohue of Valley Springs Presbyterian Church share what they had witnessed on a special a sixty-two mile trip they had taken to Fairfield with Swope. The men had gone to observe a thriving homeless shelter program named "Mission Solano."

That three hour meeting was chock-full of information and discussion, including a video. The three men were completely enamored with the Mission Solano program, giving me hope. I was finally hearing something that could break the stalemate that had existed for years with the city. There was a way for our churches and providers to skirt any government opposition to overcoming the "Roseville Problem."

I felt that if the Mission Solano program was all that Swope, George and Donohue cracked it up to be, it could be duplicated in Roseville without political opposition. The model managed to offer the Fairfield community security even as it provided safety for homeless people so they could rest and sleep at night. It could do the same in Roseville.

The best part was that this concept didn't require a shelter building. We all learned that the Mission Solano program was a "nomadic shelter": Local churches would take turns serving as temporary shelters, hosting the area's homeless population usually one night at a time according to a schedule. When a host church's turn came up, the congregation provided an evening meal, friendship and a safe place to sleep.

A different church could offer the shelter each night or it could be the same one serving for as long as two weeks at a time. Each church could commit to as many days as was appropriate for its particular pastoral situation.

The big thing that set bells ringing for me was that the Fairfield churches were at the heart of the Mission Solano program. The base of public support for the program came from the members of each participating church. The political support was built into the program.

I didn't even have to visit Mission Solano to understand that. Church members who were active in their own congregations were also usually engaged in civic affairs, such as voting. Local politicians and civil servants were loathe to tangle with a group of church congregations which had adopted a spiritually uplifting ministry, even one that invited homeless persons into their sanctuaries. And there was strength in numbers. A fight with a consortium of churches dedicated to such a mission could cost a local politician an election or a bureaucrat a promotion.

The only questions I had at the conclusion of the meeting were about the mechanics of the program. How did it operate day-to-day?

Even though I didn't have all the answers yet, I found it easy to get behind the Mission Solano model sight unseen. I was 100% for the concept simply because housing homeless people in a different church each night made the process politically possible. As such, it would be a shoo-in for Placer County.

Before Father Mike and I left the meeting, I made certain that Ed Donohue and David George knew how interested I was in bringing the program to Roseville. I assured them I would be in touch. I also picked up a copy of the sign-in sheet with email addresses from Swope.

From that moment on, I was focused and determined to get a Roseville program modeled on Mission Solano ready for the following winter.

January 25, 2004:
I emailed Donohue and George, asking them for a couple of hours sometime during the following week to learn more about the Mission Solano operation.

January 26, 2004:
WWJD? was in good financial shape and blessed with more than one hundred volunteers, including seven nurses: Jan Spangler, Pat Abbott, Kristine Abueg, Beatrice Meyers, Rita Petrella, Yvonne Ryan, Kathleen Waldman and nurse practitioner Angela DiGrandi. Jan Spangler was "the anchor" for the group, serving several days a week. The others took turns helping at the van locations as their busy schedules allowed.

We had held meetings for "Vision and Goal Planning," along with thank-you parties and potlucks for the volunteers who had done wonderful work growing the organization. The volunteers worked in teams with responsibilities varying from:

- serving and visiting with the clients to buying the groceries and supplies;
- dressing a wound to taking someone to the doctor; and

- editing, publishing and distributing the newsletter to answering the emergency service phone.

Together, these thousands of individual acts of kindness every month provided solace and healing to our local homeless folks, each built on the foundation that Schiele had provided.

There were entire families who together served on the van crews and others who contributed by taking turns cleaning and washing the van on Saturdays. In addition, our WWJD? mechanic, John Sorenson, kept the old van operating in good form.

January 27, 2004:

Father Mike agreed that St. Rose would pledge twelve thousand dollars to the new nomadic shelter program from the Homeless Fund collection that I preached for during each Advent season. He also committed the use of the parish hall for the shelter from Christmas through the first of the year. That made St. Rose the first church to join the shelter program.

He added that I could rely on receiving one thousand dollars as seed money to cover deposits necessary to set up a new 501(c)3 non-profit entity.

My next step was to ask Leo McFarland of Volunteers of America in Sacramento for help putting together a budget for the project. His years of experience overseeing shelter and housing programs for homeless folks would be invaluable as I moved ahead.

January 28, 2004:

Donohue and I met and decided we would make the trip to Fairfield to observe the Mission Solano program in action. He called ahead to the program's founder and executive director Ron Marlette, setting an appointment to meet him the following Sunday afternoon.

January 29, 2004:

I held a telephone conference with Leo and Eileen French about the plan to have a shelter service up and running in Placer County by the upcoming winter. They were elated and were on board.

The Frenches were my long-time heroes, always there when we needed them, but insisting that their family's good works be kept secret, something I did until after they both passed away.

Eileen was a regular at St. Vincent's Dining Room on Tuesdays, working with the Shepherd of the Sierra Presbyterian Church crew. She also usually came in on the one Saturday a month when the Placer Title Company employees brought and cooked fresh food for a great midday meal. Sometimes Leo would show up with them.

The couple had been long-time supporters of the Glide Memorial Church social outreach programs in San Francisco, well before they focused on Roseville. They were Catholic, but religion was never a consideration when doing charitable work. I will bet that besides the programs I heard they had helped, there were many others no one outside of the family would never know about.

One of my favorite stories about their kindness and generosity took place a few years before:

Every once in a while, Leo and I would run into one another. This time, it was in the St. Vincent's dining room on one of those Placer Title Company Saturdays. He had his apron on and was busy chopping vegetables. Leo was a big bear of a man, with a shaggy, stubbly beard and friendly eyes behind his glasses, which usually managed to slip down the bridge of his nose. He would immediately push them back up. Once his eyes caught you, you knew that you were in the presence of a good heart.

As always, when he saw a familiar face, Leo's attention honed in with an "A-OK smile" just for that person. That was Leo, the natural born public relations man at his best. His demeanor that Saturday was no different.

After we said our "hellos," he said he wanted to take a break and that I was as good an excuse as any for him to sit down for a while. We relaxed in one of the booths, sitting on opposite sides of the table to catch up on things. Our legs were stretched out on the seats with our feet dangling over the ends of the benches. We each had one arm resting on the table, the other over the back of the booth as we looked around the room.

He had been out of the state for some time. This was his first Saturday cooking in several months. It was the first time I had been in the dining room for quite a while, too. I wasn't part of St. Vincent's management then.

We were both shocked at how run-down the place was. The booth seats were torn, the bathroom plumbing was out of order, and the vinyl flooring was torn and dirty.

Spilled food coated the kitchen stove and the refrigerator shelves. The place had the odor of rancid grease that you pick up in a dirty restaurant. We both smelled it, and he commented on it.

I told him that I was ashamed to admit I had something to do with starting the place. We both remarked that it was terrible that the people who ate there had to put up with that kind of dirt.

Then he looked around the room and said, "A good cleaning, some paint, a new floor, a few plumbing repairs and decorations and this would be an okay place!"

I responded, "I don't think they (St. Vincent's) have the money for that."

He asked me how much I thought it would take to get it fixed up.

I looked around and then told him that the last time the place was done over, the cost was more than five thousand dollars.

I was just thinking out loud; but Leo never seemed to miss an opportunity to do good.

He said, "I'll talk to Eileen and be in touch. But when we give the money to St. Vincent's, will you oversee the work?"

"Sure!"

The next day, he called me from home to tell me that I could pick up a check at his office on Monday so the work could begin.

January 29, 2004:
WWJD? volunteer Margo Ezell and two clients were featured in a *Sacramento Bee* story after Ezell helped a black homeless couple who had been harassed by the police. The man, Maurice, had some mental disabilities. His wife, Alesya, was disposed to demonstrations of vocal outbursts (possibly Turret's Syndrome) and was wrongly cited for public drunkenness when we knew she was just stressed, something which exacerbated her condition.

In fact, Alesya had just been released from the hospital following surgery and was so unable to get around that WWJD? put her up in a motel for a week. The police clearly wanted the pair out of town. One officer told Maurice "We don't like your kind 'round here!" Then the cop demanded "What you doin' in my park?"

The situation was so hot that WWJD? President Karen Bocast arranged for the two of us to meet with Deputy City Manager Julia Burrows whom we both knew. Burrows, who had always been supportive of our cause, said she would take it up with our new police chief, Joel Neves.

Following our contact with Burrows, I asked Herb Whitaker for his help. When I told Whitaker that Alesya was willing to sign a civil rights complaint against the city, his demeanor went from his usual mellow self to excited in an instant. He realized that he finally had a homeless person who would help him make the case against Roseville. He said he was out of patience with the city and was ready to formalize his concerns.

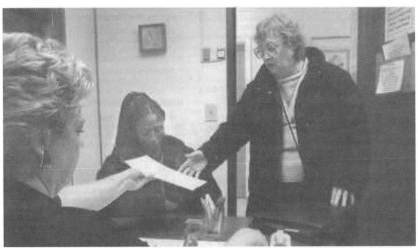

"Roseville WWJD? volunteer Margo Ezell, right, drove Alesya Ross, who is homeless, to a doctor's appointment in Auburn to get medical care. Christine Dottavio, left, of Placer County Health and Human Services helps with the paperwork."
Courtesy Sacramento Bee

Together, Whitaker and I outlined a simple strategy:

1. Whitaker would get approval from his Sacramento office to take Alesya on as a client.
2. He would file an action with Placer County to get Alesya the proper general assistance award that she had coming to her.

3.I would develop a simple incident report form that both our clients and volunteers would use when they believed a Roseville officer crossed the line.

4.Whitaker and I agreed that WWJD? would continue to put up Alesya in a motel for safety's sake until her complaint was resolved.

The WWJD? Board quickly endorsed Whitaker's involvement, authorized funds for Aleysa's motel costs and gave Ezell authority to hand out the incident report form. As soon as the forms hit the street, the police harassment evaporated.

February 1, 2004:

The momentum from the previous week helped make the Mission Solano tour an outstanding experience. Our enthusiastic and knowledgeable host, Ron Marlette, was ready to answer every and any question Donohue and I had. I was kept busy taking notes on how the program worked on a daily basis.

I also took a passel of pictures, showing the process in detail:

- The mid-afternoon process of checking in about forty guests
- The shower facilities
- The safe storage of guests' extra belongings
- The bus ride to the hosting church
- The members of the hosting church greeting guests, cooking and serving dinner
- The guests carrying the sleeping mats and their personal storage bags from a van into the sleeping area, and
- The recreation activity that was provided until it was time for lights out at 10 p.m.

The routine the following morning for the shelter guests had them getting up at 6 a.m. to:

- Take care of their personal needs;
- Have coffee and something simple to eat;
- Do their chores (clean the sleeping space, clean the bathrooms, pick up the sleeping mats, fold the blankets and put them into their personal storage bags, etc.);
- Load everything into the van; and
- Check to be sure they had all of their personal belongings before jumping onto the bus.

At first glance, the process looked easy enough. But then I started making a mental list of what we needed to set up the program in Roseville:

- A place for the guests to check in, take showers and safely store their belongings;
- A bus and drivers licensed to drive it;
- A day crew of two employees to check in and monitor the guests' behavior from the time they arrived that afternoon until midnight;
- A night crew of two more employees to monitor the guests' behavior until about 8 a.m. when they were returned by bus to where they checked in the afternoon before; and
- Some churches willing to support the program by cooking dinner for the guests and hosting them overnight.

There were even more fundamental ingredients necessary to grow such a program:

- MONEY;
- A nonprofit corporation to accept donations and to administer the program;
- An accounting system;
- Corporate bylaws and a board of directors;
- Various kinds of insurance – for the bus, the program, the host churches, the employees and the directors;
- A team of volunteer workers to help get the project underway by November;
- Health screening, including tuberculosis (TB) testing, of everybody involved in the program (the yet-to-come Executive Team members, employees and guests);
- Drug and alcohol screening of employees and guests;
- Background checks of all employees;
- Program policies and operational manuals;
- Etcetera ad nauseam...

Getting this endeavor up and running was not going to be so simple after all.

All the way home from Fairfield, Donohue quizzed me, as if he didn't believe that I was ready to tackle the project. He also clarified that if I undertook the job of organizing the winter shelter, the extent of his involvement would be as a representative of Valley Springs Presbyterian Church, and not as a coworker. He said that his job at Oracle and his obligations at church made deeper involvement impossible. To emphasize his point, Donahue said if I failed to bring the project together, my neck "would be in the noose," not his.

If I was supposed to flinch at his remark, he was disappointed. However, I was little miffed that he remained uncertain about my commitment. Donohue's next move was to cement my pledge, suggesting that we have lunch the next day with Jeff Chalfant and Tom Savage, fellow members of Valley Springs.

I thought it was worth jumping through the hoop and give the trio the opportunity to evaluate whether my commitment was truly serious before they committed their church to the project. They were not risk takers.

February 2, 2004:

Donohue introduced me to the other two men at the lunch. Chalfant was a teacher in the Roseville School District and Savage was Associate Pastor at the church. The lunch seemed more like an interview than a chance to work together.

I was asked questions from every angle. The three were doing Pastor George's bidding. They were looking for some kind of certainty that I could make this dream a reality. None of them wanted even to think about having egg on their faces.

Up to that point in the lunch, I hadn't revealed to them the hard assets I was bringing to the table:

- The twelve thousand dollars St. Rose pledge for the project;
- The use of the St. Rose parish hall for a solid week during the Christmas holidays; and
- The St. Rose funding of the up-front money needed to form a non-profit for the project.

As we ate our lunch and I fielded their questions, I remained mum. The stark truth for me was that I needed to be uncharacteristically patient and keep my cool.

It had taken over twenty years to get to this point, to have a real conversation about getting a permanent winter shelter up and running. Never before had the opportunity been so close. I was beyond excited; but because the goal had been so elusive for so long, I knew had to tread lightly. It was the one and only golden opportunity.

When their questioning seemed to peter out, I figured it was time to reveal my secrets. I told them about what St. Rose Church had committed to the project. They were dumbfounded. Apparently, money talks very loudly among Presbyterians, just like it does among Catholics.

There was an immediate change in their demeanor. Their eyes lit up and Donohue announced that he would like to schedule another meeting to include his pastor, David George, and my pastor, Mike McKeon, along with the four of us. At first, I thought I had passed whatever test they had laid out for me. But I was wrong.

Before we adjourned, Donohue revealed that at the next meeting he just wanted to verify in the presence of our respective "bosses" the validity of what I had just told them.

After checking everyone's schedules, it was settled. There would be a "summit" February 12th over lunch at Fresh Choice in the Rocky Ridge Town Center.

February 7, 2004:

Next on my to-do list was to gain the support of Denise Sewart and Denise Johnson, co-chairs of The Social Justice Advocates of Placer County, for the new ministry. I met with Denise Sewart to discuss the possibility of The Social Justice Advocates' helping to form an "Ad Hoc Homeless Outreach Committee" to oversee the preliminary "spade work" that needed to be done to ensure the project's success. She seemed interested and said she would have to take it up with her group.

February 12, 2004:

The noon "summit lunch" was my third evaluation by Valley Springs. As the conversation progressed, the Presbyterians had an epiphany: the Catholics were for real, and I was ready to put my reputation on the line.

Late in the course of the meeting, Valley Springs leadership finally decided to make a commitment to the program. The church would host the shelter project each Monday of the year and would look into the possibility of providing a bus for the program's use.

Then, when Elder Donohue and Pastor George strongly pushed for hiring a paid executive director and staff, I said that I thought it would be unwise to spend the money on employee costs that early in the game. Maybe such a move could be justified after the program was established.....

After Denise Sewart and Denise Johnson polled the members of the Social Justice Advocates by email and found that the group was interested in maybe helping out, they gave me agenda time to pitch my plan at their 7 p.m. monthly meeting.

My message was simple and direct: I can't put the program together by myself. Their help was the key to getting the project up and running.

At the conclusion of my plea, I was thanked and asked to step outside to allow the members to deliberate the proposal.

Within ten minutes, I was invited back in and told that the Justice Advocates were "putting skin in the game." They had voted to help form the Ad Hoc Homeless Outreach Committee.

I was so tired of being a one-man-band that just knowing that a team of such good people was with me provided a fresh boost of energy.

February 18, 2004:

I made my first contact with Adventure Church, meeting with Reverend Dave Doty, who headed up the compassion ministry. We discussed a possible role for the congregation in hosting the program. Doty indicated Adventure Church might have an interest.

February 26, 2004:

There was good progress at the first meeting of the Ad Hoc Committee. Twenty-nine people showed up. Denise Sewart and some of the members of the Social Justice Advocates volunteered to take on the development of a promotional package which would include presentation packets for church leaders and a PowerPoint presentation for viewing by congregations, pastoral councils and church boards.

Their help came in just the nick of time, and got me out of a jam. I needed professional-looking materials to present, something I couldn't create myself. Their help was critical to selling the nomadic shelter idea.

End of February 2004:

I had a new long list of detailed items to do and one key question for Ron Marlette : What made his Mission Solano operation run so smoothly?

Marlette and I had countless lengthy phone conversations, and I traveled to Fairfield several times to meet with him. Sometimes Ed Donohue rode along with me.

On one trip, as we were driving to Mission Solano, Donahue brought up the topic of health issues among our program's guests. At the top of his list was ensuring that none of them had active TB. I responded that I had already made TB screening one of the requirements for entering the program. I avoided telling him I had no idea how we could get that done. In any event, he seemed satisfied with my answer.

At our meeting with Marlette, he excitedly answered all of my questions, going to the extra effort of letting us know that he wanted to do everything he could to help us succeed. He shared the secrets of his own accomplishments: how he developed his fundraising techniques, how he wooed both the city and county into his camp, how he fine-tuned the operating details of his program and built relationships with potential host churches.

I had to learn from his experience to make a go of our effort.

March 1, 2004:

I met with SS. Peter & Paul parishioners Jim and Margaret Reilly to discuss funding possibilities for the project. Margaret had a great knack for writing successful grants for WWJD?.

After telling the couple about the shelter proposal, I got a surprise when they told me about their own experience with the nomadic model at St. Joseph's Parish in Cupertino. They had nothing but good things to say about it.

Then Margaret volunteered to write a grant application for our project to The United Auburn Indian Community, the tribe that operates Thunder Valley Casino Resort.

March 2, 2004:

VOA's Leo McFarland and his chief financial officer Joseph St. Angelo had put together a budget for the nomadic shelter project. Their estimate was a modest eighty-four thousand two hundred forty-eight dollars for four months of operation. They also offered to help recruit a program supervisor and employees to monitor the guests' conduct from check in to check out.

March 3, 2004:

I made a presentation to "the Social Concerns" group at St. Clare Church.

March 4, 2004:

Following my update report to the Social Justice Advocates of Placer County, the members continued with a lively discussion on the direction the program would be taking.

March 5, 2004:

Ron Marlette and I met at Mission Solano. I had a new list of questions and a fresh pad of paper to write down his answers.

March 8, 2004:

Things quieted down. During the week, I only had a few calls to make, some emails to send and two meetings to attend, one with Margaret Reilly to discuss the shelter grant she was working on and the other with the local ministers at their monthly breakfast to bring them up to speed on the shelter project.

March 13, 2004:

I met with WWJD? President Karen Bocast and later with the Social Justice Advocates co-chairs Sewart and Johnston to firm up the areas of responsibility that each organization would have in starting up the nomadic shelter venture:

- With the approval of Bocast's board, WWJD? would act as the 501(c) 3 fiduciary agency for the shelter project until the new operation gained IRS and California's Franchise Tax Board approval as a nonprofit corporation. WWJD?'s job would be to temporarily collect tax deductible donations and authorize expenditures for the shelter project.
- Denise Sewart took on the task of the forging a link with Placer County to develop a TB testing protocol for the shelter.
- I would work with the members of both the Social Justice Advocates and the Ad Hoc Committee to network with their friends to develop contacts in other churches and organizations.
- The Social Justice Advocates would:
  - ○ Complete the PowerPoint and presentation packets for congregations, pastoral councils and church boards;
  - ○ Update my old lists of donors, including the ninety churches in the south Placer area and the important contacts at each church; and
  - ○ Inventory the resources each church could provide including:
    - Space and cooking facilities;
    - Buses and drivers;
    - Volunteers to provide meals and services;
    - Volunteers to move shelter equipment from church to church;

- Pledges of financial support; and
- A current email contact list of persons interested in the project.

March 15, 2004:

On the road again! Yet another afternoon trip down Interstate 80 to Mission Solano to confer with Marlette. This time, I had St. Vincent's general manager Charlie Frost in tow.

I hoped that once Frost saw the program in action, he would get behind our effort and agree to ask the St. Vincent's Board if our project could use a portion of their campus for our intake site.

I also needed another meeting with Marlette to ask questions about a few issues the Roseville program would have to grapple with:

- How many churches with schools attached were involved in his program, and what advice did he have to calm the parents' concerns?
    - o Marlette said he had two churches like that. At night, the guests arrived after the children were gone, and in the morning, everything was back in shape before the kids were back.
- Did he think that having an advisory board that could later become the board of directors was a good idea?
    - o He thought it was a great idea.
- How did his program handle guests with special circumstances, such as:
    - o Pets?   No way to take care of them
    - o Bicycles?   Stored at intake site
    - o TB Tests?   Currently not given
    - o Hepatitis shots?   Only to staff
    - o Head lice?   Treat as needed
    - o Attendance Issues?   Miss a night and you're out

March 16 2004:

Pastor Swope said he thought we should call another meeting of the pastors and providers to firm up their commitment to the project. He asked me to make a presentation. After we talked for awhile, I told him that my pitch would be very simple, but heartfelt, something for each person to consider: "What will you do to help get the shelter project up and running?"

March 17, 2004:

First thing that morning, Deacon David Haproff showed up at the house with a gift for the project, a one thousand dollar check from both him and his wife Jane – a total surprise. I got a feeling that it was going to be a good day!

Next, Charlie Frost called to let me know that the St. Vincent's Board had met the night before. He asked me to meet him at his office at 139 Riverside after work. He didn't say anything else. That was it. I had to wait all day to find out what they had decided, if anything.

When I arrived, all of the office employees and volunteers had gone home. Frost was alone, sitting at his desk with his head down, working away on some papers.

After I sat in the chair in front of his desk, he looked up with a frown on his face. I wondered what I was in for!

As he began to speak, his grimace turned into a grin and his eyes lit up. He knew he had pulled one over on me.

We had a good laugh. Then, he began talking in a businesslike, but very friendly, way. His message was short: the St. Vincent's Board welcomed the shelter project!

Over the next hour or so, we agreed on four important items:

1. The shelter project employees would supervise and monitor the guests' behavior on St. Vincent's site, morning and evening.
2. The project would construct and pay for its own shed to be used for office space, checking in the guests and storing their belongings.
3. The project would cover any costs of relocating or altering any facilities such as fences, gates and doors on the St. Vincent's property for the project.
4. The two St. Vincent's public bathrooms would be available to the guests for toilet needs and showers.

Frost asked me to attend the Board's April 20th meeting to reinforce our agreement that any costs to accommodate the nomadic shelter project on St. Vincent's premises would be paid for by the program. He felt they needed my word before they would totally rest easy about the changes.

I told him that we would also provide liability insurance coverage to protect St. Vincent's from any loss due to any project-related incident on the property.

March 19, 2004:

Karen Bocast and Denise Sewart met with Father Dillon, the pastor of SS. Peter & Paul Church, to recruit the parish as a host church. They told me in separate conversations that it didn't take long for them know how he felt: After the program was explained to him, he had a just few questions, business ones like "What kind of insurance coverage would the project provide?" and then those that were more mundane such as "Would cleanup of the hall and the restrooms be done before the guests left?"

When he seemed satisfied with what he heard, Father simply said the parish would host the project one night a week. His vision called for different parish groups to cook and serve the meals and provide the hospitality. He told the two women that someone from our program should contact the Sacramento Diocese to get the details on the insurance coverage needed for the Catholic parishes to be involved.

He also wanted the program to coordinate with parishioner Bettye Nippert, who would manage the parish's end of the bargain.

Then, Dillon decided that hosting the program on Thursday nights would work best for the parish.

The news that the women had signed up the Rocklin parish would knock the socks off the ministers and providers at Swope's meeting. A report that three churches had committed to hosting the winter program, one of which had also offered substantial financial support, and that St. Vincent's would be the project's intake center fit right into my theme: "What will you do to help get the shelter project up and running?"

March 21, 2004:

Swope and I credited a lot of the success of the Sunday afternoon meeting to Denise Sewart's great work providing professionally prepared documents and visuals. The marketing materials were outstanding.

Included in the package was a brochure detailing the different aspects of Placer County's homeless population: age, mental health, substance abuse groupings, etc. There was also a list of services they needed, but which didn't exist in the county, the principle one being access to shelter services. With our program, the basic needs of food and shelter would be met, and hopefully other services like mental health counseling, permanent housing aid and triage services could be added quickly.

Elder Donohue had insisted that another component be added: "Our thirst for God's Word". I had a handout ready to satisfy his concerns, listing scriptural citations and quotations. It was entitled "Our Biblical Imperative."

The passages were Deuteronomy 15:7-11, Isaiah 58:5-12, Isaiah 61:1-5, Ezekiel 16:49-50, Luke 6:20, Matthew 25:31-46 and Galatians 2:9-10, all containing the theme that God has called us to attend to the needs of those among us who were homeless and hungry.

I think it was a home-run with the ministers.

St. Vincent's past president Richard Roccucci came over to talk with me after the meeting, saying that he was impressed by what he had heard because it gave him hope.

March 22, 2004:

At WWJD?'s monthly meeting, my report to the Board members about the shelter developments went over so well that without a lot of coaxing, they decided to make their agency the fiscal agent for the new program. They also accepted the preliminary cost estimate for the first winter's operations. I was more than surprised when they approved it without getting the jitters. The eighty-four thousand two hundred forty-eight dollars was nearly twice the amount of WWJD?'s own budget.

Next, I handed out an insurance worksheet estimating that the cost could be as much as two thousand dollars a year. I told the Board that we would provide each church in the program with a certificate of insurance.

At the end of my report, I anticipated questions from a couple of the members. Instead, I got something altogether different: They all seemed totally satisfied with what had been presented. What a good feeling!

March 23, 2004:

Sewart and I met with the Seventh-Day Adventist Church leaders to discuss the program. When we finished our presentation, we were thanked and told that they would be in touch.

WWJD? Volunteer and Adventist church deacon Bob Young was among the decision makers that night. He had also attended Swope's meetings along with his pastor Martin Weber. Both Young and Pastor Weber were strong advocates for the nomadic shelter.

He told me as we left the room that he and Weber would do their best to persuade the church governing board to give the program a try.

The board was ready to take the request under consideration.

Later that evening, I got calls from both Pastor Weber and Bob Young letting me know their board had unanimously agreed to host the program on Tuesday nights. With that, we had Mondays, Tuesdays, Thursdays and an entire week during the Christmas season covered.

March 24, 2004:

First thing that morning, I telephoned Swope and Donohue to bring them up to date.

Then I got a call from Bonnie Sarasin of Seventh Day Adventist Community Services. She told me that she would ask Deacon Young to pass along a donation check of one thousand dollars for the program. It seemed like help was flooding in from all directions.

March 25, 2004:

At a meeting that day with Tim Brown and Rebecca Hugo of Loaves and Fishes, WWJD? President Karen Bocast and I received moral support and their promise to conduct a fundraising mailing to their Placer County donors.

That night, we held the second meeting of the Ad Hoc Committee. Only fifteen people showed up. That was half the number who had attended the session in February. The shakeout of souls who had lost interest in the project was dramatic. But, it didn't matter. The people who needed to be there were there. After updating everyone and adjourning the meeting, Sewart, Bocast and I decided it was time to officially name our venture, to call it something other than "the program." We agreed to a time to get together to discuss possible names.

March 29, 2004:

The three of us met for lunch in Sacramento at a coffee house close to where Sewart worked. When Bocast and I arrived, I firmly believed that nothing creative would come out of the meeting, that none of us would have a unique idea of what to call the venture.

As we ate our lunch, our conversation danced around the subject. We floated unoriginal names like "The Placer Shelter Project" and "Mission Placer." Then Sewart said she had an idea she would like to offer: "What about a name based on the popular hymn 'Gather Us In'?"

The theme of the hymn is caught in these few words:

Hobophobia

"Here in this place, new light is streaming.
Now is the darkness vanished away…
Gather us in the lost and forsaken.
Gather us in the blind and the lame.
Call to us now, and we shall a-waken,
we shall a-rise at the sound of our name."
(© 1982 GIA Publications, Inc.)

She thought that the name "The Gathering Inn" would be a good fit because our local church communities would be "gathering in" God's homeless people into their spiritual homes. She added that congregations themselves would be "gathering" together in unity to serve, dissolving boundaries and differences in creeds. She finished by pointing out that the word "inn" conveyed warmth, hospitality and safety.

"The Gathering Inn" name caught my imagination right away. What a great choice! It would fit right in with our marketing and promotional tools. Plus, it would give pastors an inventive way to bring new life to their preaching, motivating their members to walk the talk and experience the joy of helping others. Their very own churches would become places of refuge for people who would otherwise probably be alone, hungry and homeless.

The other names paled in comparison. Our search was over. I asked Sewart to check with the California Secretary of State's office to see if the name was available for our use. If it was, she agreed to reserve it to protect our rights.

When she called to tell me that she had been successful, I got busy spreading the word about the proposed name and planned an impromptu lunch with some prominent faces in the PCOH and the county. All had excellent connections in county government: David Loya of The Lazarus Project, Kathie Denton and Tom Kurowski of Placer County Health and Human Services, Michelle Talbott of the Auburn Salvation Army Corps, Janice Critchlow, Placer County's CoC Coordinator, and WWJD?s Karen Bocast. All RSVP'd that they would be there.

March 30, 2004:

The lunch was a big step for the program. It was the first opportunity I had to lay out the vision for all these folks, to bring them up to speed about where we were in the start-up process. We were cruisin'!

I provided them with handouts about the program: our brochure, paper copies of our PowerPoint presentation telling the story of the beginnings of The Gathering Inn, its mission, vision, goals and progress to date, as well as copies of the important letters of support for Mission Solano from Fairfield's Assistant City Manager and the Director of Solano County Health and Human Services.

The personal responses I got from the group could not have been more positive. For example, Michelle Talbott immediately offered to arrange for the Auburn Salvation Army staff to register our guests from that area, provide storage for their spare gear and give each one a bus pass for transportation to the Roseville intake site. She also offered to spread the good news among the members of the Auburn Ministers Association.

I knew that what had been shared that day would be parroted back to Placer County's decision makers and probably help us get a hearing with higher-ups in the bureaucracy.

At this point, I felt that we had the base we needed to build on. I was convinced that The Gathering Inn was the program that would finally overcome the years of political opposition to the attempts of religious leaders and service providers to establish a shelter program.

There was a feeling in my bones that during the weeks and months ahead, we would continue to be blessed. I truly believed we could open The Gathering Inn program by mid-November. But I did keep my fingers crossed.

"Human progress requires...the tireless exertions and passionate concern of dedicated individuals."
(Martin Luther King Jr.)

Chapter 24:
The Gathering Inn:
The Political PATH to a Shelter Solution
(Apr. 2004–Mar. 2, 2005)

April 2004:

It finally struck home that I had lost the battle to bring St. Vincent's, Home Start, The Lazarus Project and WWJD? into one operational group. I felt that the self-interest of their leaders was apparently stronger than their desire to broaden funding opportunities and improve services for the region's homeless population. For four years, Jack Epling and I, along with representatives from these four entities, had met together with Ray Merz and his staff numerous times to lobby for the needs of the homeless folks in our area. In the process, I always held out the hope that the organizations would recognize the benefits of becoming one force, giving the Roseville providers a stronger voice in forging homeless policy and fund allocation.

I realized that I needed to let that dream go. Maybe someone else would pick up on the idea. The agencies' leaders seemed to regard any merger not in terms of benefitting the people they served, but as a threat their turf. Epling's initial instinct was right on. It was a big, if not impossible, undertaking for me.

I shifted my focus to strengthening the base of support for The Gathering Inn by recruiting new program partners from a pool of friendly organizations and institutions. Sewart, Bocast and I held one-on-one and group meetings with representatives from at least sixteen churches and agencies. Some of them were new connections, while others were old friends who had partnered in past efforts:

- Placer County Health and Human Services Director Ray Merz and his associate Dr. Rich Burton
- Former Auburn City Manager Paul Ogden
- Legal Services of Northern California lead attorney Herb Whitaker
- Placer County Health and Human Services branch manager Glenda Williams
- Bethlehem Lutheran Church of Auburn's Pastor Bruce Lundberg
- First Presbyterian Church of Roseville's Associate Pastor Dr.

The Gathering Inn: The Political PATH to a Shelter Solution

Bruce Ellithorpe

- St. Clare Catholic Church's Deacon Carl Kube
- St. Teresa of Avila Catholic Church of Auburn's Father Peter Bosque and Deacon Dave Morgado
- Foothill Community Church's Peter Carlson
- Housing Alliance of Placer President Paul Guisande
- Home Start Executive Director Ann Engelbrecht
- The Lazarus Project Executive Director David Loya
- First Methodist Church of Roseville's Pastor Jerry Angove and lay leader Jim Bush
- Horizon Community Church's Senior Pastor Brad Swope and
- The Salvation Army Auburn Corps' Michelle Talbott and Major Mick Sanders.

I got a kick out of Glenda Williams, who gave me some much-needed encouragement when she said, "I want to be more of a trouble-maker like you!"

There were other people like WWJD? Board member Joe DiPentino who helped out exactly at the right time. DiPentino came to the rescue when Sewart and I realized that using the St. Rose projector for our PowerPoint presentations wasn't going to work because parish groups had priority even if we had we reserved it ahead of time.

He arranged for his employer, Hewlett-Packard, to loan us one.

We tried to create a partnership with Bayside Church of Granite Bay pastors Jim Holt, Steve Lindner, Ross Thompson, Scott Brown, and Adam Smith. Unfortunately our timing was off. Bayside was on the verge of founding its own homeless program for at-risk mothers and children called "Acres of Hope." They were tapped out.

April 20, 2004:

The new projector from Hewlett-Packard put us on a roll. After Sewart and I got our foot in the door at the First Methodist Church, we made a very polished presentation to their board.

As soon as we finished, the church members jumped right in and discussed which night would be best to host the program. Pastor Angove and Jim Bush suggested that Sunday would be a good fit because the church also hosted a noon meal on every Monday. After a few more questions, the Board began deliberating the matter. They were concerned that they didn't have the membership numbers to muster a crew every Sunday.

After we saw that they had too many loose ends to tie up, we quickly thanked them and made a beeline for St. Vincent's on the other side of the tracks for our second presentation of the night. This one was extremely important because the Board would finalize the details of the March 17th agreement Charlie Frost and I had formalized covering the shelter's use of some of their space.

When we finished at St. Vincent's, the Board unanimously ratified the agreement. We had a site to work from.

April 21, 2004:

During a meeting at the Auburn Salvation Army facility, Michelle Talbott, Major Mick Sanders and homeless advocate Bev Anderson confirmed Talbott's March 30th offer that the Army would register our guests from the area, provide storage for their spare gear and give each one a bus pass for transportation to the Roseville intake site.

It was great news, but it didn't take long for the four of us to realize that adding an Auburn intake center would bring a whole new set of problems to the operation. When we began to explore the intake procedures and other logistical questions, we soon realized that the Roseville process wouldn't work in Auburn. On weekends the building was closed and Placer County Transit didn't operate on Sundays and holidays. The Auburn guests wouldn't have any way of storing and getting to their belongings or of getting to and from Roseville. We had some work to do on this one.

We moved on to the next item: Bev Anderson gave me a list of area pastors I should visit to talk up the host church program. She also said she would print up and mail The Gathering Inn brochure to the four hundred Auburn area contacts on her mailing list.

April 22, 2004:

As a follow-up to the mid-February "summit meeting" with David George and Ed Donohue of Valley Springs Presbyterian Church, the three of us met again, this time with Jeff Chalfant, Peter Burnett and Mission Solano's Ron Marlette. One of the reasons I had asked for the meeting was to see if we could wrangle a bus out of one of Marlette's Board members, who also was an executive of MV Transportation which was headquartered in Fairfield at the time.

At the end of the meeting, Marlette said he would ask the MVT executive to help us locate a bus. In addition, the Valley Springs men generously promised to provide The Gathering Inn with a backup bus and driver when the program's bus was out of commission. They also offered to supply someone to train our drivers to pass the California DMV exams.

We still had no bus of our own; but half a loaf was better than none!

Later that day, Sewart and I gave the PowerPoint presentation to our Ad Hoc Committee.

Afterwards, I brought the group up to date on the events since our last meeting, including asking for their approval of The Gathering Inn name, and their response to more than a dozen questions about possible policies for the operation, with dos and don'ts that would govern guest conduct at the top of the list.

I offered the policies as questions so that the members would feel free to mold them into policies they were satisfied with. For example, the question "What happens when a guest misses a night and then reapplies?" resulted in a policy the group developed that stated such a person goes to the bottom of the list and will be readmitted only after all other qualified guests have checked in.

After a lively discussion, the members approved both "The Gathering Inn" name and the new policies they created.

April 23, 2004:

Bocast and I finally had the opportunity we had been waiting for: to debut the shelter proposal to Placer County Health and Human Services Director Ray Merz and his associate Dr. Richard Burton. The presentation, along with endorsement letters of the Mission Solano program from both Solano County and the City of Fairfield, put The Gathering Inn over the top. Burton was so impressed, he remarked, "This is the most exciting thing I've seen since I began this job!"

April 25, 2004:

The annual Raising Spirits fundraiser was a big surprise, generating a net profit close to sixty thousand dollars.

April 26, 2004:

The WWJD? Board unanimously approved "The Gathering Inn" name for the shelter project when Sewart presented it for endorsement.

Then, Sewart and I asked for input and advice from the Board on guidelines and procedures for the new program. We drew on the same technique that I had used at the Ad Hoc Committee meeting on the 22nd: the question-and-answer format. We got great feedback that validated our selection of proposed policies, and gained the up-front support of the group.

After the close of the meeting, Mike Miller of the Social Justice Advocates and a WWJD? volunteer came over me and said he would like to do some preliminary research about how we might set up our own bus operation – a big step that could eventually lead us to independence. Prior to Miller offering to take on the job, all I had regarding a bus were the good intentions of our friends at Valley Springs and Mission Solano.

Miller's research on the bus situation quickly revealed its complexity, which meant that it needed to be resolved sooner rather than later if we were going to have our own bus operation. Luckily, the emerging multifaceted mess didn't deter Miller. Even though we were just getting to know one another, I could tell once he committed to do something, it was more than just words. He would make it happen.

Miller was the kind of person who was determined to do a job right. I soon asked him to join Sewart and me to form the Executive Team. When he accepted the offer, the Executive Team of Sewart, Miller and Boudier was complete, making the prospects for The Gathering Inn program all the more positive.

A few days after, Miller called to tell me that he had been in touch with Ron Marlette about the bus and bus driver training issues. Miller said that he wanted to begin training as a bus driver and recruiting other people for the job as well. He had visited the DMV to get an overview of what we had to do to operate our own bus and driver training program.

When the two of us got together to look over the DMV test booklets and the medical forms, I told him I wanted to be a licensed bus driver, too. Parallel parking a bus sounded like a kick!

April 29, 2004:
Pastor Swope of Horizon Church offered to help publicize The Gathering Inn. He said he would network with other pastors in the evangelical community and to have me speak to his congregation.

May 2004:
After a few days of working together, Sewart, Miller and I found we were a great fit for the tasks that lie ahead. The three of us as the

Executive Team had the kind of relationship that made our jobs as enjoyable as such an endeavor could be. We worked in concert with the smoothness of a well-oiled machine, picking off problems as they arose and completing the tasks on our timeline one by one. We were on the job nearly every day, and we weren't getting paid. We loved it!

One of the first problems the team had to resolve was a most delicate one. If it was left unchecked, it could undermine the program. Simply put, a few of the faith groups which committed to the program saw the presence of the homeless visitors housed in their churches as an opportunity to overtly convert and "save them," rather than treat them as genuine guests. These church leaders all had the best of intentions, but they continued to wrangle with us over what they saw as the imperative to save souls.

The Executive Team agreed that the hosting guidelines had to delineate parameters on how any spiritual message was shared at a host church. We decided the message, if offered, was to be only at the beginning of the evening and before dinner. It was to be presented only using skits, music and stories based on general biblical themes. There would be no form of preaching which might be seen as proselytizing.

May 2, 2004:

Bocast and I met with a group of about twenty members of Valley Springs Presbyterian Church interested in the program.

Elder Donohue told me that he had been in contact with Miller about the bus driver training, letting him know that it would take six to eight weeks to get a person prepared to pass the various DMV tests. That meant that we could begin our training program as early as mid-July.

When we mentioned to the group that The Gathering Inn needed an office and storage shed built at St. Vincent's, Ellis Cody volunteered to lead the construction crew with the help of the men in Valley Springs' "Tool Box Ministry."

The plan called for a one hundred eighty square foot shed, with storage shelves for our guests' bags, a "sign-up" window, and an inside counter for the monitors (paid staff members who supervised the guests overnight) to do their paperwork. The area would need to be equipped with electric lights and outlets. I assured Donohue that The Gathering Inn would pick up the cost of all the materials.

Following The Gathering Inn's first contact with the city – a building inspector concerning the shed – it dawned on me that we needed to bring the city's power players up to speed regarding the larger program before they heard about it through the rumor mill. While I felt we were on firm ground and beyond being stopped by the city, I still wanted us to be open about our plans and not be seen as trying to blindside anyone. I set up a meeting with City Council member John Allard, and booked one with Roseville's mayor Rocky Rockholm with the help of our friend Scott Peters. I also contacted John Sprague to put together a meeting with various department representatives.

May 4, 2004:

My contractor friend, Terry Saalfield, volunteered to modify St. Vincent's restroom facilities, which would double the number of showers available for The Gathering Inn's guests.

Soon after, Placer County's Dr. Richard Burton M.D. and Sutter Health physician Dr. Margaret Planta M.D. began developing the health protocol for admission to the program, including TB screening. Through her research, Dr. Planta had become keenly aware of the cost of homelessness to the community. Her study showed that Sutter Roseville alone had an annual three million dollar expense for uncompensated "indigent" healthcare expenditures. She focused on acquiring medical equipment and volunteer doctors to administer the test and to visit guests at evening host sites.

With Planta's involvement, Sewart was able to turn her focus and energy to fundraising with me. While the treasury only had about fifteen thousand dollars in cash and pledges, with a long way to go, we remained optimistic that we would be able to begin the program in mid-November.

People like Joan Nordine, a member of Shepherd of the Sierras Presbyterian Church, kept our spirits up. Because of her hard work, her church signed up to be a host and pledged to donate its proceeds from an annual CROP Walk fundraiser.

While Sewart and I were out meeting potential sources of financial support, Miller developed a bus operations plan and shopped for a used bus that would accommodate fifty adults. Our new bus budget allowed a maximum purchase price of sixteen thousand dollars, plus five thousand dollars annually for insurance and maintenance. He calculated that we should have at least fifteen regular volunteer drivers to fill the morning and evening schedules and a few others as subs. That meant we had to have the bus by July to train enough drivers by our opening date.

Two churches wanted to help Miller get the wheels turning on his project. The pastors at Abundant Life let him know they were available to show him their transportation and bus driver training programs. In the meantime, Ed Donohue thought that one of Valley Springs' drivers might be available to train our original seven candidates: Margo Ezell, John Raley, James Lyon, Ellis and Elinor Cody, Mike Miller and me. But we still needed a bus!

May 14, 2004:
I spoke by phone with County Supervisor Ted Gaines, whose district included a portion of Roseville. While we were setting up an appointment to discuss The Gathering Inn, I was surprised to hear him wonder aloud why one of the old buildings at DeWitt Center couldn't be used as a permanent winter shelter facility. That was the first time I had heard a supervisor suggest something like that. His idea would be seen as extremely radical by the Placer County establishment.

Gaines refocused and agreed to meet the following week.

May 17, 2004:
Pastor Tim Brooks of Hillcrest Alliance Church let me know that his congregation would be partnering with Pastor Ken Robilard of Bethel Christian Church to host The gathering Inn every Wednesday at Hillcrest. One week, the meal preparation and hospitality would be taken on by Hillcrest, and the next by Bethel Christian Church using Hillcrest's facilities.

May 18, 2004:
Methodist Pastor Angove's church board approved hosting The Gathering Inn on Sunday nights after I guaranteed that I would help recruit teams from other churches to provide hospitality and meals when their congregation needed a time-out from hosting the program.

At that point, we had churches signed up to host our guests Sundays through Thursdays during the seventeen weeks of planned operation. St. Rose's commitment to host for the eight straight days from Christmas to New Year's would give the regular host sites the week off to enjoy the season.

The three of us on The Gathering Inn Executive Team had developed our fundraising strategy. The first step was for me was to preach at St. Rose well before the project's start date, allowing other churches to follow suit. There was no better way to get something done than to lead by example. St. Rose was that example.

Father Dillon and Father Bosque soon calendared me for preaching in their parishes. There were six other pastors waiting in the wings, wanting someone to speak to their congregations during the summer about supporting and funding The Gathering Inn project.

May 21, 2004:

When Denise Sewart, Margaret Hutchinson and I met with Supervisor Gaines, he suggested that The Gathering Inn program might be eligible for county aid. He was careful not to say he would help us get it. My impression was that he was a cautious man and wouldn't venture beyond his comfort zone.

Gaines never uttered another word about using one of the old DeWitt Center buildings for a permanent winter shelter. However, he did suggest that there was an outside chance that one of the structures might be used as a Gathering Inn host site just one night a week, on Saturdays when county offices were closed. He liked our plan to screen the guests for TB and drug or alcohol abuse before being busing them in to the site.

May 24, 2004:

Kathy Kossick, Executive Director of the Sacramento Employment and Training Agency (SETA), joined the WWJD? Board. With SETA's huge annual budget and dynamic program, Kossick brought priceless experience and expertise to the charity. She took on the job of keeping an eye on WWJD?'s cash flow.

The WWJD? Board voted to give ten thousand dollars of its Raising Spirits proceeds to The Gathering Inn project. To date, we had twenty-seven thousand six hundred dollars in cash and pledges.

May 26, 2004:

We followed up the Gaines meeting with a presentation to Supervisor Bill Santucci. He was impressed by the program, and suggested that The Gathering Inn might be eligible to receive compensation for the savings it provided the county. The big holdup for him was that we didn't have the blessing of the Roseville City Council. He did not have the nerve to go after the money for us without Roseville's okay. Even after I emphasized that this was an activity involving at least twenty-five congregations from Roseville and Auburn, he was still gun-shy.

Santucci agreed with my assessment that it would be a mistake for Roseville City government to make The Gathering Inn operation an issue.

While we failed to get any direct help from the Supervisors, the faith community continued to grow more enthusiastic every day about the program.

May 31, 2004:

Fantastic news! My daughter, Michelle Raley, a teacher with the Eureka Union School District in Granite Bay, called to tell me that her district had a fifty-two-passenger bus it was retiring from its fleet, and that Bev Wilkinson in the district office told her we could purchase it for four hundred fifty dollars. That amount was just under what was allowed to sell the bus without school board involvement.

June 1, 2004:

Mike Miller and I drove out to the school district's bus yard to examine the vehicle and talk with chief mechanic Randy May. May said the bus was reliable and would easily pass the California Highway Patrol inspection. The district was selling it because it was the last manual shift bus in the fleet.

We went into the office and told Ms. Wilkinson that we would take it, and we would have the paperwork together after the next WWJD? board meeting at the end of June. When we asked if we could leave a deposit, she said that wasn't necessary. She had no problem holding the old rig for us.

June 7, 2004:

Ellis Cody and the other men from Valley Springs toolbox ministry began construction of The Gathering Inn office shed at St. Vincent's.

June 17, 2004:

Bocast and I made a presentation to Father Mike Kiernan's Catholic Charities group at the Pastoral center in Sacramento. We had hoped to receive a five thousand dollar grant for The Gathering Inn from the bishop's office.

June 18, 2004:

Karen Bocast, Herb Whitaker and I held a meeting with various city department representatives to explain the program's details. I had asked Whitaker to be on hand just in case the city tried to stop our momentum by laying out some phony rule or regulation as a stumbling block. We met with Dennis Matheson of the fire department, Gary Shonkwiler from the police department, Jan Shonkwiler of Economic and Community Development and Kevin Payne from planning and permits.

From the onset, the three of us emphasized that The Gathering Inn was a religious program, and we were not asking for government approval or funding.

The city folks, with the exception of Kevin Payne, were almost reticent in their remarks. Their concerns seemed pretty minor. They wanted guests who congregated at St. Vincent's to be on the bus and out of "the hood" by 6 p.m. We assured them that the guests would understand they couldn't show up for check-in and showers before 4 p.m. That was when The Gathering Inn employees started their shifts. While the guests waited for the bus, they would have to stay off the sidewalk and inside the compound and dining area. If they couldn't follow these two basic rules, they would be out of the program.

Payne was hesitant to say that churches could host the program without city permits. The other staffers only looked for our assurances that prior to the beginning of the season, the fire department would be called in to sign off on the safety for overnight sleeping at each host church. Of course, we agreed. It was the law.

And finally, they wanted both the police and fire departments to have same-day notice as to where the program was operating that night. We agreed. It would be a good safety policy for us to follow in every jurisdiction where a church hosted the program.

I was floored when I realized that the city people didn't want to contest whether or not the program was legal. Even Payne's reluctance to endorse the program seemed halfhearted. I wondered if Santucci had talked with city politicians and bureaucrats about the program, counseling them that it would be a big mistake if they tried to impede our opening plans in any way. It sure felt like that was what had happened, and I couldn't have been more thrilled or relieved. Instead of giving us the usual run-around, they concluded the meeting by recommending that we touch all the bases, officially presenting the program to the Roseville Coalition of Neighborhood Associations, and to the City Council at their meetings.

June 28, 2004:

The WWJD? Board authorized the school bus purchase. We had a bus!

June 29, 2004:

Bocast and I held meetings with the two strongest personalities on the Council, mayor Rockholm and Council member Allard. Surprisingly, both men openly supported the program. In fact, Allard volunteered to be a member of the Advisory Board.

Soon after the meetings, in a note to me, Allard wrote that the program "expresses the very best in faith-based leadership; one motivated by compassion and intent on meeting a longstanding community need." I concluded, based on these sentiments, that our appearance at a Council meeting wouldn't be necessary.

By the end of the month, Bocast, Sewart, and I had met with eleven Auburn churches, some for a second time, and contacted several others in the Roseville, Rocklin, and Loomis areas. Ad Hoc Committee member Jo Kellogg visited with Sister Sheila Browne of the Sisters of Mercy of Auburn, who indicated that the sisters were interested in learning more about The Gathering Inn.

July 6, 2004:

We took delivery of the bus after it had passed Highway Patrol inspection.

Valley Springs' lead driver Ross Lauger drove our "new prize" to St. Rose and parked it in the back lot, which would be its home until a CHP permanent "terminal," was nailed down.

Miller and I had already made it through some of the DMV hoops: record checks and two preliminary tests. We still needed to pass the bus driver and air brake tests and a physical exam before either of us could get our learner's permits. That meant our bus driving practice was restricted to the St. Rose parking lot. Just like the other four candidates, we resorted to practicing parallel parking, shifting, turning and backing the bus in that relatively small space. I think it made us better learners when we did drive on the streets with our instructor.

Miller lined up a licensed bus driver from the San Juan School District to give each of us six hours of supervised training. Miller and I continued to study the DMV test manuals and soon qualified for our permits. It didn't take long for us to begin driving the rig on the road with a licensed bus driver aboard.

It seemed like people were gawking at us – and not for the right reasons. Our bus needed a facelift. The old gal looked so drab in her faded yellow coat that Father Mike offered to pick up the tab for the "surgery."

Within a couple of weeks, we got her a new paint job in glossy robin's egg blue with black trim. She drove like she was twenty years younger.

Mid-July 2004:
Money started coming in. Margaret Reilly's grant writing skills paid off when ten thousand dollars in funds arrived from the Auburn Indian Community.

And then, my heroes came through again. Leo and Eileen French gave me two more personal checks totaling ten thousand dollars and another one thousand five hundred dollars from Placer Title executives Jim Johnston and Marsha Emmett. But then, I was jolted by their generosity when they told me they would be sending in an additional donation, a very substantial one of an undisclosed amount. The funds were from their trust and would be delivered before year's end. Their only stipulation they were going to make was that it would be delivered to me for the sole use of The Gathering Inn in any way I deemed fit. Wow! I had no conception of what the magnitude of the gift would be!

July 17, 2004:
The consulting firm, HomeBase/The Center for Common Concerns, which was hired during the summer of 2003 to formulate the plan to "End homelessness in Placer County," presented its report at a public countywide summit at Adventure Christian Church in Roseville. Over one hundred people attended.

HomeBase had held three preliminary meetings across the county in 2003 and early 2004 to develop this strategic plan as the blueprint to address "our homeless problems." Everyone had been invited to participate. One hundred four people from sixty-two different agencies and organizations had taken part in three sessions in Auburn, Roseville and North Lake Tahoe.

As the summit began, it was rumored that HomeBase had produced a proposal with everything needed to end homelessness in the area. The principle tool offered was the "Ten-Year Plan to End Homelessness in Placer County 2004–2014." According to those who had their hopes and dreams pinned on the project, the document really did contain "the ingredients essential to ending homelessness" in our county in just ten short years!

PATH was the acronym the consulting firm used to simplify the very complex problem. It was eagerly embraced by the committee members and somehow seemed to encapsulate their seemingly deep, but very unrealistic desire to find a way to cure homelessness.

P was for Prevention of homelessness;

A was for Access to housing and supportive services;

T was for Teamwork among community partners; and

H was for Housing for homeless people.

Before I saw the plan, I had high hopes. But, as soon as I laid eyes on it, I knew it was nothing more than a pipe dream, a PATH to nowhere. When I left the meeting, I was glad I had been focusing on The Gathering Inn.

Late July 2004:

Ellis Cody and the Valley Springs crew were well on their way to finishing our check-in and office shed at St. Vincent's, and contractor

Ellis Cody and the Valley Springs Crew putting the final touches on The Gathering Inn check-in and office shed, July 2004
Boudier Collection

Terry Saalfield had almost completed the shower project. Fence and gate alterations to accommodate our guests at St. Vincent's were done, and an additional concrete pad had been laid. The physical parts of the program started to come together.

As one task was completed, another popped up. The Executive Team still faced the challenge of developing the program's operational logistics (a euphemism for saying we had a hell of a lot of nuts-and-bolts paperwork to get behind us). Among the projects were:

- Implement the St. Rose and Valley Springs leadership agreement by launching the corporation for the project;
- Qualify The Gathering Inn Inc. for 501(c) 3 non-profit status with both IRS and the California Franchise Tax Board;
- Select and activate a board of directors;
- Develop employee handbooks, safety manuals and sexual conduct policies compliant with current federal and California law;
- Write daily operational guidelines and policies for employees, and create work related reporting forms and job descriptions for the program director, lead monitor and monitor positions;
- Select payroll materials and procedures;
- Complete the list of guest rules and regulations, including drug and alcohol testing and the TB testing protocol;
- Organize guest intake procedures, forms and policies, including those authorizing release of personal information to law enforcement and rules covering storage of belongings;
- Create a daily guest roster and a protocol for forwarding it to the local authorities every twenty-four-hour operational cycle;
- Negotiate with police departments on policies and procedures for performing warrant checks;
- Finalize host church and partner church calendars and procedural guidelines;
- Introduce the Advisory Council as a forum for host and partner churches to provide feedback for program improvement;
- Complete our own bus driver training;
- Recruit additional bus driver candidates;
- Initiate bus driver policies, reporting forms and rules and regulations in conformance with DMV, CHP and PUC regulations;
- Map bus routes to and from each individual host church;
- Delineate floor plans and sleeping area diagrams for each host church in conformance with state and local fire regulations for each jurisdiction where a host church was located;

- Establish a contact list of emergency first responders in each jurisdiction, and schedule fire marshal inspections of each host church's sleeping facility; and
- Get money rolling into the treasury to cover winter operational costs.

It was unnerving to realize that all of the jobs we had listed were just the ones we knew needed to be completed by October. We had no idea what other tasks awaited over the horizon. We began chipping away at the list.

Sewart filed the corporate papers with the California Secretary of State and headed up the formation of the 501(c)3 non-profit corporation. She had been through the process in 2003 when she helped incorporate a new regional program called "Care For God's Creation." She and a fellow group member who was an attorney crafted the documents for that startup and successfully walked them through the thicket with the IRS.

She also began coordinating relations with host and partner churches, implementing standardized procedures and guidelines, and finalizing employee manuals, safety manuals, and sexual conduct policy statements.

Miller oversaw refining and printing the corporation's operating policies and daily operational procedures, including those for bus management, program management, guest drug and alcohol testing, guest rules and regulations and program safety protocol procedures for employee interaction with host churches, as well as with fire and police agencies.

He also developed the employee operational reporting forms, focused on corporate insurance needs and served as our liaison with first responders in each community to assure our policies and operational protocols met their standards in case of emergency. Additionally, he worked with each congregation to ensure compliance with local fire department regulations, helping them calculate the maximum number of guests who could be permitted to stay overnight. He also created floor plans showing emergency exits and where the guests would sleep.

Other key tasks Miller assumed were recruitment, orientation, training, supervision and scheduling of our paid monitors and bus drivers and our volunteers who aspired to become bus drivers.

I was responsible for program development, oversight, overall corporate management, public relations, fundraising and forming our new Advisory Board, including vetting and offering invitations to selected community leaders to join.

While we made good progress on the program's operational issues, the outlook for finances had turned bleak once again. What had started at eighty-four thousand dollars for program set-up and operations for the four month season had grown to one hundred-five thousand dollars due to increased employee cost estimates. We were going to hire three paid part-time bus drivers who would work as many as four days per week until we had enough licensed volunteers to cover all shifts.

Another big unexpected expense came up when we were notified that our bus liability insurance limits had to be increased to at least three million five hundred thousand dollars, as required by the California Public Utility Commission. The increase would cost us a minimum of three thousand dollars a year.

There was a tremendous financial gap to fill if we were going to keep The Gathering Inn operating for its first full four-month season. Luckily, volunteers Steve Davis and John Sorenson signed on to help us minimize those bus overhead expenses. Davis committed to driver training, and Sorenson took on supervising bus maintenance and repairs.

To recruit paid drivers, Miller distributed fliers to several area school districts and to the Roseville transportation operators. Four licensed drivers from three different school districts responded. When we realized the paid drivers could only work weekends and evenings because of school schedules, it looked like Miller and I would be driving the morning shift until we could find others who could step in.

WWJD? Volunteer Margo Ezell joined the WWJD? Board and Pat Kumpf took over as corporate treasurer.

August 2004:

The provider community continued to rally around The Gathering Inn. The Placer Consortium on Homelessness (PCOH) gave its stamp of approval and acknowledged our program as a partner. There was no question about its value to the county.

And Sacramento's Loaves and Fishes came through on its fundraising pledge by printing and mailing over two thousand six hundred letters, donation envelopes and brochures to its Placer County supporters telling The Gathering Inn's story.

Offers to host The Gathering Inn and to cook meals were coming in from across the county. The Sisters of Mercy of Auburn decided to host two nights in December. The Unitarian Universalist Church in Auburn was ready to help with meals. Members of Granite Springs Church in Rocklin planned to cook meals at the Methodist Church in Roseville and would consider committing funds.

Pastors from four mainline Auburn churches, John Broad of Pioneer Methodist, First Congregational's Rick Kuykendail, Bethlehem Lutheran's Bruce Lundberg and Auburn Presbyterian's Ken Winter, expressed interest in having their congregations serve as host churches on Friday nights and possibly on Saturdays, as well. With their buy-in, all the nights for the first season could be covered. However, we had to temper our excitement: Each church had a governing board that would finalize the decision. Four evangelical churches in Auburn were also considering providing funds and meal assistance.

Much of the credit for recruiting all of the Auburn ministers goes to Bev Anderson, the one person who not only attended the monthly PCOH meetings, but also made it her cause to keep the problem of homelessness on the conscience of the larger community. As she diligently contacted local political and church leaders, she never gave them a chance to forget about the issue, gently reminding them of their responsibility to lead by example.

In Roseville, Adventure Church expressed a strong interest in hosting for two weeks, one in November and the other in February.

As the program developed, Miller and I saw that the safety of our guests, while always being important, could become more and more complex as the number of host churches increased. All could be serving on different nights of the week and in different jurisdictions, making it difficult for us to ensure that safety remained constant and consistent throughout the program.

We decided we would put a couple of additional measures in place to correct this:

- We would maintain our own twenty-four-hour emergency phone service to provide our employees and first responders with a direct line to The Gathering Inn office. I would be "the office."
- We would test our procedures with a trial run of the evening schedule. The timeline would be comprehensive, including all the steps the church would take to prepare for hosting, such as passing the fire marshal inspection. Of course, we asked Valley Springs if we could practice there. As always, they were willing to help.

At Valley Springs, we made our first floor plan of a church's dining and sleeping areas, showing where the sleeping mats could be best placed based on occupancy loads contained in the building code. At the end of the evening's test, we were able to start firming up operating guidelines for all the host churches and our staff.

The month went by quickly, and our financial prospects still looked pretty slim. There was only about thirty-six thousand dollars in pledges and cash in the kitty. I continued to beat the bushes and got invitations to make presentations to the Granite Bay Rotary and to the advisory board of St. Joseph's Catholic Church in Lincoln.

August 3, 2004:

I stepped down as the WWJD? representative to the PCCI so that I could focus on getting The Gathering Inn underway.

August 4, 2004:

Roseville city permits manager Kevin Paine telephoned as a follow-up to our June 18th meeting. He said the city regarded the program as "an incidental use of each church's property for religious purposes," meaning permits would not be required of host churches.

There would be no battle this time around. The Gathering Inn model left no room for criticism, only for goodwill.

Roseville's ruling set the precedent. Now as we continued to present the program to host churches in other jurisdictions in the county, we could spread the word that a permit was not required.

August 16, 2004:

County shelter advocates held the first of two follow-up meetings to the July 17th summit at the Auburn Salvation Army facility.

August 21, 2004:

Ellis Cody reported that his crew had completed our guest intake shed at St. Vincent's, electrical work and painting included!

A new opportunity for the program to connect with county services popped up when County Health and Human Services staff members Kathie Denton and Judy Canet showed up at our Ad Hoc meeting.

The women were there to determine if it was practical for a team of two county social workers to visit guests at a host church one evening a week. Their goal was to help the folks navigate through the maze of paperwork necessary to qualify for various county programs, like medical and mental health aid, financial and employment guidance, as well as housing assistance.

At the close of the meeting, Denton and Canet decided to move ahead by organizing and training county staff members for the project.

September 12–13, 2004:

The Gathering Inn fundraising campaign kicked off at St. Rose and marked the beginning of an improvement in our fiscal health. Amounts donated through second collections during weekend Masses were twelve thousand dollars from SS. Peter & Paul and ten thousand from St. Rose.

September 17, 2004:

I asked Ellis Cody if the Valley Springs' Toolbox Ministry would build shelving in the shed for the storage of the guests' extra belongings. Naturally, he said yes, promising that one way or another, the job would get done. The Toolbox Ministers nailed it!

September 21, 2004:

After passing four DMV tests and the bus driving road test, Miller received his license at the West Sacramento DMV, where commercial testing was done. The next day, he drove me to the facility for my tests. I also passed the exams, even the parallel parking!

Miller continued oversight and planning of transportation operations, including California Highway Patrol inspections, insurance needs, as well as training our new volunteer driver, Steve Davis.

For several weeks, Sewart had been working closely with county staff members to iron out the residual problems that were holding up establishing the TB screening protocol. The process was more complicated than any of us had imagined.

Finally, Dr. Burton was able to approve the guidelines and provide a letter verifying that the TB protocol met federal, state and county requirements for health screening for homeless persons. He also offered Placer County malpractice and liability coverage and reimbursement for medical supplies for any doctor or registered nurse who volunteered to help with screenings.

September 23, 2004:

The members of the Ad Hoc Committee voted to disband after acknowledging they had completed their task.

Bayside Church member Frank Calton and an anonymous local

developer provided funding for the Acres of Hope program, enabling the church to begin planning for the project for women and their children.

September 27, 2004:

The WWJD? Board voted to increase The Gathering Inn budget to one hundred twenty thousand dollars, even though we had only sixty thousand in cash and sixteen thousand two hundred ninety-five dollars in pledges. The additional program costs for set-up and the first season's operations were unavoidable. But the Board knew we had to go for it.

I obviously still had some hard work to do. No matter how much or how little cash we could raise, the three of us had resolved to keep the winter program going either until mid-March or until we went broke, whichever came first. I still had preaching gigs scheduled for St. Joseph's in Lincoln and St. Teresa's in Auburn. We hoped these two weekends would increase our cash position by at least fifteen thousand dollars. Each of us was focused, laser-like, on meeting our goals.

The WWJD? Board also authorized the hiring of employees for The Gathering Inn beginning November 1st.

Other Gathering Inn news that was reported:

- The first TB tests were administered to eighteen potential guests. Placer County authorized WWJD? nurses to give the test to its guests when the van was in the field. Five failed to complete the regimen, and three required follow-up x-ray exams.
- Sewart had completed most of the legal and procedural steps necessary to make The Gathering Inn a stand-alone entity and had developed the independent organization's logo and color scheme, the church hosting calendar (which showed which church was scheduled each night of the program's operation), and the nightly guest roster (a management tool used by the team, monitors, law enforcement and fire departments showing the number of guests hosted that night, who our guests were, and other relevant personal information).
- Miller was busy with the twenty-five host churches and their local fire departments to meet each agency's safety requirements for each site.

Bocast, Sewart and I continued to sign up new host churches, even if it meant scheduling them on nights that had been previously covered by other churches. We believed that the more churches took part, the lighter the burden would be for the others, especially for those that had made the huge commitment of serving one night each week throughout the season. The new churches would have a chance to host while the regulars would get some time off from what could become a weekly grind.

October 1, 2004:

The Gathering Inn's new Advisory Board held its first meeting at Valley Springs Presbyterian Church. The group included John Allard, Brooke Allison, Rev. Jerry Angove, Rev. Pam Cummings, Frank Calton, Elder Ed Donohue, Rebecca Hugo, Lisa Lloyd, Sister Bridget McCarthy RSM, Mike Miller, Denise Sewart, Pastor Brad Swope, Michelle Talbott, Herb Whitaker, Karen Bocast and yours truly.

The members selected an executive committee to serve as an interim board of directors until The Gathering Inn became a stand-alone corporation, after which it would be the agency's permanent governing board. I was asked to serve as board chair and president, Pastor Jerry Angove as vice president, Denise Sewart as secretary and Rebecca Hugo as treasurer. The old "Executive Team" of Denise Sewart, Mike Miller and me would continue to oversee program operations.

My good friend George Howington agreed to set up a chart of accounts for the organization and to churn out our monthly and yearly financial statements.

The consensus was that the Advisory Board would make a decision on November 5th whether and when The Gathering Inn would separate from WWJD?

The meeting's focus then turned to reviewing plans for the program's startup on November 15th. We had recruited a powerhouse of host and partner churches:

- Auburn: Auburn Presbyterian Church, Bethlehem Lutheran Church, First Congregational Church, Pioneer United Methodist Church, St. Teresa's Catholic Church, Sisters of Mercy of Auburn and the Sierra Foothills Unitarian Universalists
- Lincoln: Granite Springs Community and St. Joseph Catholic Church
- Loomis: United Methodist Church and Shepherd of the Sierra Presbyterian Church
- Rocklin: Cornerstone Community Methodist Church and SS. Peter & Paul Catholic Church

- Roseville: Adventure Christian Church, Calvary Chapel, East Parkway Bible Church, First United Methodist Church, Hillcrest Alliance Church, Horizon Church, Seventh-Day Adventist Church, St. Clare Catholic Church, St. Rose Catholic Church and Valley Springs Presbyterian Church.

Denise Sewart and Margaret Reilly took on the details of developing a dedication ceremony at Roseville's First Methodist Church to initiate The Gathering Inn program. Everyone was welcome.

October 6, 2004:
In a letter to Salvation Army Captain Kris Potter, I asked if he would provide the program with some of the new blankets he had on hand.

October 14, 2004:
Potter delivered one hundred thirty-eight new blankets. When I was told about the generous gift, I immediately thanked him with a phone call and asked if he would attend the dedication.

These blankets were in addition to the one hundred donated by Mervyn's Department Store and another fifty which came from individuals.

October 15, 2004:
I contacted the California Department of Justice and spoke with Retha Godbold to set up a "Live Scan" account for checking the backgrounds of all of our job applicants against federal, state and local fingerprint records.

October 22, 2004:
The provider community and churches held the dedication ceremony to celebrate the start of The Gathering Inn program. The service came off smoothly, with just one hitch: Sacramento Catholic Auxiliary Bishop Garcia, who had committed to attend, didn't show up. Instead, he sent Fr. Mike Kiernan of Sacramento Catholic Charities.

About this same time, Placer County shelter advocates held a second follow-up meeting on their Ten Year Plan to End Homelessness.

October 25, 2004:
I informed the WWJD? Board that the team was on schedule to recruit staff. Miller had sifted through the applications, conducted preliminary interviews and had initiated background checks.

That was followed by a report on The Gathering Inn Advisory Board's discussion of separating from WWJD?

With this new development, the WWJD? Board members discussed whether WWJD? should withdraw its May 2004 pledge of ten thousand dollars to help start The Gathering Inn project. They put a decision off until December.

The next order of business was my resignation from the WWJD? Board.

That was followed by a motion for an up or down vote by the WWJD? Board to separate The Gathering Inn from WWJD? effective when the new organization received IRS approval of its 501(c)3 status.

WWJD? decided to cut The Gathering Inn loose.

November 5, 2004:

The Gathering Inn Advisory Board members held their second meeting and acknowledged that the ten thousand dollar WWJD? pledge was a lost cause. They decided that I should send WWJD? a note of thanks acknowledging that while the money would be missed, the WWJD? Board's original intentions were appreciated.

The members then voted unanimously to split The Gathering Inn from WWJD? and have the new board of directors assume fiscal management as soon as the corporation received its IRS 501(c)3 status, but no later than December 30th, 2004.

Following that, the budget was increased from one hundred twenty thousand dollars to one hundred thirty thousand due to additional transportation costs.

With the financial decisions worked out, I suggested that the next order of business should be to adopt a policy that the program would not be limited to Placer County residents. One of the first lessons I learned working with homeless singles was that their highest priority was the same as the rest of us – personal survival. I came to realize that they would give me any answer I wanted to hear that would guarantee that end. Most just "self-reported" their personal information, didn't have any personal ID and fabricated any yarn to suit the situation.

I knew that when homeless adults were asked to report without any verification where "home" was, most were very adept at coming up with some connection to Placer County, with tales ranging from Placer was where they were raised to they had been living here with someone who had thrown them out. I never condemned anyone for that. I could see most of them were at war with either some form mental illness or addiction.

I also felt that it would be wrong to bar people who honestly said that they were from somewhere other than Placer County. These folks would probably the best candidates for our program because of their truthfulness and were most likely to be serious about looking for help to overcome their personal demons.

November 8, 2004:

The Gathering Inn new hires got their first real job experience by accepting guest applications from those who had completed their drug, alcohol and TB tests. The successful candidates were given spots on the opening night roster.

November 15, 2004:

With our employees in place, the bus ready to roll, and about eighty sleeping mats on hand along with two hundred eighty blankets, the program got underway on schedule. Valley Springs Presbyterian Church hosted the first night.

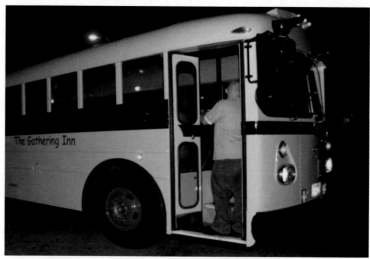

Big Blue's Maiden Voyage – November 15, 2004
A passerby checks it out.
Boudier Collection

Miller and I were on deck to make sure everything went well. It was a smooth opening, just as we had hoped for, no foul-ups and no problems. About thirty-five guests enjoyed a hot meal, music and a chance to get a free haircut or styling before they laid their heads to rest in a warm, safe place that winter night. The church members found themselves, as one said, "grace-filled" by the experience.

November 18, 2004:

The members of Board of Directors held their first meeting a week before The Gathering Inn received its 501(c)3 status. The Board was made up of members who had been part of the old Advisory Board and had volunteered to serve on the Board of Directors. The six were John Allard, Rev. Jerry Angove, Rev. Pat Cummings, Rebecca Hugo , Denise Sewart and yours truly. Guests Mike Miller and Bob Tomasini were present as prospective members. Miller had modestly and repeatedly declined my invitations to join the Board. Tomasini, a retired Superintendent of the Roseville Joint Union High School District, seemed very interested in signing up.

November 24, 2004:

The IRS granted 501(c)3 status to The Gathering Inn, allowing the program to officially split from WWJD?.

Donations continued to flow in like never before. It started with generous contributions from Jim Johnston, Marsha Emmett and other Placer Title Company executives. Then, Leo and Eileen French informed me of the particulars concerning "the substantial donation" they were planning to make before the end of the year. It would be a game-changing gift of more than two hundred thousand dollars!

When the funds came in, I earmarked them for a special project yet to be determined and deposited them in a separate Gathering Inn account.

December 8, 2004:

New donations from Roseville's St. Clare's and St. Joseph's in Lincoln, as well as many generous individual gifts of cash, had erased our operating deficit. We decided to expand our horizons by taking a shot at raising enough new money to stay open for another thirty-one days, into the middle of April.

When Adventure Church Compassion Ministries pastors Don Brewster and Richard Matthews heard that we wanted extend the program for a month, they let us know that the church would not only serve as a host for one of the weeks, but also make a donation adequate to pay for our employee and transportation overhead for that time.

The support was overwhelming. Someone who insisted on remaining anonymous walked up to me and handed me a check for forty thousand dollars "to cover operating costs for that month."

WOW! Our cup was running over!

Then we learned that the First Baptist Church of Rocklin and Auburn's St. Luke's Episcopal wanted to join up as host churches. With all of the good fortune, we comfortably added the thirty-one-day extension to the schedule.

Mid-December 2004:

The team attempted to partner The Gathering Inn with Home Start and The Lazarus Project.

The reason we tried to work with Home Start was we had noticed that during the cold and rainy winter weather, the program's families had to walk two blocks from their rooms to St. Vincent's five nights a week to have their supper.

We repeatedly contacted Home Start management to offer free transportation for its families on our empty bus as it made its way to St. Vincent's to pick up our guests. Home Start officials never responded. Even in the face of that silence, our bus stopped at their facility every night a supper was served for the first thirty days of our season. Not one family boarded the bus.

A similar failure to cooperate came from The Lazarus Project. The Gathering Inn offered The Lazarus Project the opportunity to shelter the adults stuck on its waiting list until it had beds available for them. The Lazarus Project declined the offer.

January 7, 2005:

The members of the old Advisory Board voted not schedule any future meetings, allowing the Board of Directors to assume all oversight of corporate business.

January 18, 2005:

The Gathering Inn's Board of Directors was rounded out with the addition of both Bob Tomasini and Executive Team Member Mike Miller.

The Board continued to focus on the future by adopting a budget of one hundred forty-nine thousand dollars for a six-month second season beginning October 17, 2005 and ending April 16, 2006.

January 2005:

The Placer County Homeless Survey was tallied, showing that four hundred eighty-three individuals were without shelter. One in three persons was a child or teen, and four out ten were female.

The Gathering Inn's operations and fundraising were going so well that I finally had a chance to focus on a new part of the program, the Advisory Council. The plan was for the host and partner church coordinators to meet with the team and our staff leaders to give feedback and make suggestions on everything from guest problems to dinner menus. The Council meetings would be held at a different church each time.

The blueprint for the Advisory Council came from Michelle Talbott of the Salvation Army's Auburn Corps.

February 4, 2005:

The first Advisory Council meeting was fantastic, with the format a hit with both the team and the churches. The productive conversation added to the program's viability and cemented our common bond as we continued our work.

One of the first items the new Council members considered was a program survey that asked each church to give feedback at the end of the first season's operations. The survey contained nine questions that could be boiled down to three basic themes:

1. Has The Gathering Inn program been spiritually beneficial to them and their church congregations?
2. Should the program be continued on a year-round basis?
3. Should the program operate with one paid monitor and one trained volunteer monitor on each shift, rather than with two paid monitors?

March 2, 2005:

Of the twenty-five churches that received survey questionnaires, twelve responded with written comments. Others contacted us to say how grace-filled being a participating church was. They all reported that the number of volunteers continued to grow as word got out about how rewarding this new ministry had been.

As I reviewed the comments, I was reminded of an old Spanish saying that summed up the spirit of this movement, "Mi casa es su casa" ("My home is your home").

That spirit of hospitality was renewed each evening when The

Hobophobia

Gathering Inn brought a bus load of homeless people to the door of one of the churches in the program. These folks were not treated as strangers, but were embraced as sisters and brothers. All were offered physical sustenance, sanctuary and warmth from the darkness of the night.

The Gathering Inn had become something more than just a program. It had grown to be a manifestation of goodness, the only medicine that could keep hobophobia cornered.

_____

Chapter 25:
The Gathering Inn Finds a Home
(Mar. 13, 2005–Mar. 2006)

March 13, 2005:

Sewart and I stopped for Sunday dinner at a Sacramento coffee shop on our way to Roseville. While we waited for our order, we began reading the Sunday *Bee*. As was my habit, I turned to the real estate section first. I always checked the commercial classified ads for interesting deals.

That Sunday, one ad caught my eye. It was for an eight thousand square foot commercial building in Roseville with off-street parking that was currently being used as a house of worship and for sale by owner. There wasn't anything too special about that, until I continued to read on that it was located in Old Roseville. Bells and whistles went off!

I knew exactly where it was, right off of Main Street, just west of Washington Boulevard. It was the old Church of the Nazarene facility, now a Sikh house of worship and social center. Immediately, I thought about Leo and Eileen and their two hundred thousand dollar "special project fund."

We thought the building was too large for just The Gathering Inn's intake center, but was the perfect size to serve as a multiservice center for all the Roseville nonprofits providing homeless services. Office space could be offered at no charge to the other agencies, giving them ready access to Roseville's homeless population. I asked Sewart what she thought of the idea. She said "Why not?!"

With that, I called the number in the ad to make an appointment.

When a man with an accent answered, I responded that I was inquiring about the property for sale. He explained it was his, told me where it was and how much he was asking for it. I just listened. Finally, he asked if I would like to see it. He said he was at the property and that he would wait for me even though it was getting into the evening hours. I did my best to mask my enthusiasm and responded with a reluctant-sounding "Okay." He proceeded to give me directions from the coffee shop. I repeated the directions back to him, even though I knew exactly how to get there.

After we finished our meals, we made the fifteen-mile journey to

Roseville and traveled through the labyrinth of its downtown streets to get to 201 Berkeley Avenue.

When Sewart and I pulled into the parking lot, we were both shocked by how shabby the property looked. A smiling man, wearing a Sikh headscarf, which I later learned is called a "dastar," was waiting for us. He introduced himself by a name I could not understand at first. Later, after hearing him say his name many more times, I learned it was Hardev Shergill, which I was able to pronounce, but had no idea how to spell.

He showed us around the property and confirmed that he owned it, even though it was being used as a Sikh house of worship and social center. I got the very distinct impression that he was very anxious to get it off his hands.

In addition to the building complex and its sixteen or so on-site parking spaces, the property Shergill was selling included a separate parcel of land across an alley, a fenced parking lot that would fit forty cars. He was asking one million two hundred thousand dollars for both; it was a package deal. We were very interested in the building, but not the extra parking. I called Miller to see if he could meet us the next day at property for a self conducted tour of the property.

March 14, 2005:
After the tour, the three of us sat down and quickly agreed that the main property would ideal for our use.

However, it had some major challenges. In broad daylight, we could see it was in even worse shape than we had first thought. Its scars and bruises were made all the more evident by a series of recent rainstorms:

- Most rooms had serious water damage;
- The buildings' main parking lot and the central court yard had draining issues;
- The buildings' rain gutters were missing or rusting away;
- There were two sets of public restrooms – one had no roof or flooring at all, and the second had broken fixtures and missing plumbing;
- Window coverings were either water-stained or non-existent;
- The landscaping had gone wild;
- The irrigation systems needed replacing;
- The heating and air conditioning units failed to respond;

- Several large panes of glass were broken;
- Twenty-one warped and rotting exterior doors needed to be replaced with commercial-grade steel doors and locksets;
- The whole complex needed reroofing; and
- The place needed a thorough cleaning before it got a much needed paint job, inside and out, along with new flooring.

Even though everything we saw was run-down and seemed too big for The Gathering Inn program, there was a positive side: we couldn't stop ourselves from exploring ideas on how the place could be used to empower Roseville's homeless population. I offered my thoughts from yesterday: that we offer rent-free on-site offices to the providers of homeless services. That would mean that local providers would be brought under one roof in a mini multiservice center, patterned after the enormously successful PATH Mall in Los Angeles which, for some time, had given homeless persons access to more than twelve service providers at one location. The PATH Mall model allowed those in need to find help in one spot, rather than having to wander over all over the city to find the right agency.

Sewart thought the site could be called "The Gateway". Just as the PATH Mall provided a single place for homeless people to access services, the Gateway could do the same. It could help Placer County meet its own recommendation for a multiservice center as provided for in the Ten Year Plan to End Homelessness.

Or the property could be used in ways to expand services to our own guests, instead of farming them out to other providers. The meeting hall and commercial kitchen could be used as a culinary institute where guests could receive training and work experience to prep them for jobs in the restaurant industry. Students of the institute could prepare and serve lunchtime meals to paying customers.

We continued to brainstorm how the site could be used to further develop the program. Sewart suggested that we set up a medical clinic for Medi-Cal patients in a suite of the rooms. The clinic could be staffed by volunteer doctors, nurse practitioners, physician assistants and nurses from both the Kaiser Permanente and the Sutter Health Groups. There was also a six hundred square foot on-site two-bedroom apartment that could be used as the program's offices and meeting rooms, or could be leased to The Lazarus Project or to Placer County Health and Human Services to house up to four men from one of their transitional housing programs.

If those ideas weren't financially feasible, we could create an income stream by leasing out a number of the meeting rooms for office space or other uses. The main meeting hall and the commercial kitchen could also be rented out for weddings, meetings and receptions, or to a church.

For every problem we saw with the property, we had an idea about how it could be used to uniquely help homeless people. The one space we could not justify was the second parking lot.

March 15, 2005:

The three of us decided to move ahead with an offer to purchase only the main property, offering eight hundred twenty-five thousand dollars, using one hundred thousand dollars of the "special project fund" given by the French family as the down payment. We tried to sweeten the pot for Shergill by buying the property in "as-is" condition. We also proposed taking an option to purchase the parking lot property at some point within the following five years for three hundred thousand dollars, with no out-of-pocket costs until that purchase was completed.

March 17, 2005:

We presented our offer to Shergill. To an outsider, we might have seemed crazy. Who would make an offer like that? It would take more than the remaining one hundred thousand dollars in the special project fund to rehabilitate the property. And we had not asked for permission from The Gathering Inn Board to make any kind of offer. We did act rashly, hoping to redeem ourselves by coming out with a good deal.

A couple of days later, the curtain was pulled back a little for our Board members when we notified them that we had made an unbinding offer to purchase an improved parcel of land in Old Roseville for The Gathering Inn's intake center and offices. We shared our plan to make the down payment on the purchase using a portion of the dedicated special project fund. We were sure to emphasize that any final agreement would require Board ratification before it would be binding.

March 20, 2005:

Shergill countered our offer. He didn't quibble about the down payment or the other general terms such as the interest rate on the unpaid balance, the monthly payment amount or even having to gain the approval of both our Board of Directors and Roseville's planning department. Nor was he concerned that it would take time to approve all of the relevant pre-purchase inspections and surveys before escrow could be closed. But he was insistent that we buy both the main property and the extra parking lot for a total adjusted price of one million one hundred thousand dollars.

March 23, 2005:

Our counter to his counteroffer was delivered. This time, we offered to pay one hundred dollars per month for the option to purchase the parking lot for two hundred seventy-five thousand dollars within the next five years. Our proposal to shell out eight hundred twenty-five thousand dollars for the main property remained unchanged.

When I brought our counteroffer to Shergill that morning, I asked that the two of us sit down and have a heart-to-heart talk about the ongoing deterioration of his buildings. As we concluded our conversation, I reminded him that he had until that afternoon to decide whether to accept our final offer.

I told him that later that evening, our Board members would be holding their regularly scheduled monthly meeting and would be looking for a solid deal to vote on. If there was no deal, there was no way I could keep their interest alive. He had to decide what he wanted to do.

He accepted our terms.

The team was then in a strong position to ask for an up or down Board vote on the deal in a closed session that night. During that session, I explained the nitty-gritty of the transaction, with Sewart reinforcing the message with a PowerPoint presentation. The Board agreed with the purchase terms: The cost for the Berkeley property was eight hundred twenty-five thousand dollars, with one hundred thousand dollars down and a six percent interest-only loan carried by Shergill for five years, which could be renewed for five more years with another interest-only loan at a rate equivalent to prime plus 2% with a maximum of 9% and a low of 7%. The High Street parking lot option would cost us one hundred dollars per month to hold, with the lot having a price tag of two hundred seventy five thousand dollars whenever we decided to purchase it.

Monthly payments on the main property would be about three thousand six hundred twenty-five dollars. I reminded the Board that the payment cost would be offset by a written letter of intent we had just received from Pastor Brad Swope of Horizon Church which offered to lease three rooms at $1.10 per square foot for its children's programs. That amounted to two thousand three hundred sixty-one dollars per month (before including utilities). The base rent was almost two-thirds of our potential note payments.

Horizon's offer left us with more than 5,000 square feet for our own operations and plenty of room for St. Vincent's and The Lazarus Project offices.

In fact, we could rent the apartment as transitional housing via a cooperative agreement with an agency such as The Lazarus Project or Placer County. That would mean that pegging the apartment rent at a below market rate of say, seven hundred dollars a month (before including utilities), our net monthly occupancy cost could be as low as seven hundred dollars plus utilities, maintenance and insurance.

The Gathering Inn Board voted that night to endorse the project, subject to their approval of what they saw during a walkthrough of the facility scheduled for the following Saturday morning.

March 26, 2005:

The Board of Directors' meeting and visit to the site went well. I was authorized to move ahead with the terms of our agreement and get all "needed inspections and cost estimates." Before our first season had ended, we knew that we would have a permanent home for The Gathering Inn program by the time we opened for round two in the fall!

April 17, 2005:

The Gathering Inn's first season ended on a very positive note, with very few problems over the five month period. The emergency telephone line was a great safety mechanism, coming in handy in the middle of the night. The few calls I received were from a lead monitor asking for approval to expel an uncooperative guest from that night's program.

I always authorized the move, and the person was held outside the church building until a cab showed up to drive the guest to any point in either central Roseville or Auburn, whichever was closer.

We had much to be thankful for:
- Funds raised by the end of the season amounted to about four hundred thirty thousand dollars, of which two hundred eighty thousand had been earmarked for the down payment and rehab of the Berkeley Avenue property;
- More than thirty churches had signed up to participate in The

Gathering Inn program, bringing with them thousands of volunteers from their congregations;

- Adventure Christian Church's Compassion Ministry Pastor Richard Matthews arranged for his congregation to tithe one thousand dollars a month toward The Gathering Inn operations budget;
- Nearly six thousand bed nights and meals had been provided to two hundred twenty-four different guests, a third of whom were female, for an average cost of just twenty-eight dollars per night per guest, including our program start-up costs;
- One in four guests had moved into either transitional or permanent housing;
- Seven thousand five hundred copies of our recent newsletter had been published and distributed to our participating churches, raising an estimated twelve thousand dollars; and
- A Muslim group using a room in the Berkeley Avenue complex under Shergill's ownership for Friday prayer had been invited to stay under The Gathering Inn's ownership.

In the face of all of these blessings, we encountered three significant problems, the most crucial being our failure to have an adequate system for serving homeless people in Auburn. While one in ten nights of the program were hosted by Auburn churches and one dollar out of every ten donated by individuals came from Auburn, only a handful of guests from the area were able to access the program. The Auburn Salvation Army had been very generous, serving as the check-in center; but that arrangement fell short in three important areas we had recognized last April:

1. Because the Army's office was closed on weekends, the Auburn guests had no way to access or store their extra belongings.
2. The Auburn people who did use The Gathering Inn had to travel to Roseville every day for showers and transportation to the host church, whether that was in Auburn, Roseville or some other location.
3. On Sundays and holidays, there was no public transportation to get to Roseville for check-in.

The second problem arose when Horizon Church cancelled its letter of intent to lease.

The third occurred when The Lazarus Project declined to lease the apartment for its transitional living program. Without Horizon and

Lazarus, the burden of the entire monthly mortgage payment of three thousand six hundred twenty-five dollars and cost of utilities remained on the shoulders of The Gathering Inn. We had made it through the first year and were confident we could do it again, even with the increased overhead.

The Auburn intake center problem looked like it could be resolved in time for the beginning of the second season, thanks to Bev Anderson. After she had introduced Miller and me to a new church leader, Pastor David Harris of Parkside Nazarene, we were able to meet with him several times during March, looking for the possibility that his church would participate as the program's Auburn intake center.

The facility he had was ideal. It was separated from the church sanctuary and could provide a site complete with an enclosed waiting area, showers and storage for guests' belongings. Pastor Harris grew to feel that the arrangement was positive for his congregation and agreed to seek the approval of his church governing board. Dr. Rich Burton, Director of Placer County Health and Human Services, was also working to secure a second stop in Auburn at the DeWitt Center.

April 27, 2005:
Adventure Church's Compassion Ministry Pastor, Richard Matthews, was elected to The Gathering Inn Board of Directors.

May 2005:
The team began working on repurposing the Berkeley Avenue site as "The Gateway," our new multiservice center to serve the homeless population in Roseville.

June 2005:
We successfully negotiated an important agreement just in time that let us participate in the City of Roseville's grant process for 2005: The Gathering Inn entered into a Memorandum of Understanding with the Roseville Heights Neighborhood Association.

In addition, the Parkside Church of the Nazarene Board invited The Gathering Inn to use its facility as the program's primary Auburn intake site. That generous move resolved a problem which could have handicapped our efforts in the Auburn area for years.

July 13, 2005:
Placer County Health and Human Services had expressed an

interest in leasing space at The Gateway. Denise Sewart and County HHS representatives Kathie Denton, Judy Canet and Mickey Richie met to nail down the details of the department's lease. The added cash flow was welcome help that went to cover our overhead.

Courtesy The Auburn Journal June 22, 2005

August 2005:

That was all topped off by the efforts led by Denise Sewart to successfully obtain grant funds for several projects:

- A solar panel and hot water containment tank system for our guests' showers;
- A solar-photovoltaic system to generate on-site electric power;
- A new washer and dryer obtained through the Roseville Employees' REACH program; and
- A near-new nine-passenger van through Roseville's Citizens' Benefit Fund. The van would be used to transport our Auburn guests and to move our program supplies from one church to the other.

The program also partnered with the Roseville Home Depot's "Orange Team" of volunteers. My son-in-law and long-time Home Depot employee Dan Raley secured a five hundred dollar donation for materials and recruited a volunteer crew of about fifteen employees to landscape The Gateway's yard. One Orange Team member, master craftsman Ben Steinle, even built three beautiful and sturdy benches in his home woodshop to finish the garden's project.

Homeless advocate Bea Young organized a needed clothing center at the Gateway, providing new guests with fresh duds after a shower.

Our good fortune continued that summer. We were able to sell our option on the High Street lot for twenty-five thousand dollars cash to Old Town investor Mike Rapport. There would be no more monthly option payments of one hundred dollars a month or liability insurance costs, and we got a quick and substantial profit.

Late August 2005:
The new Gateway facility was just about ready for the opening of our second season when Auburn businessman Rich Mussetter, the Miller beer distributor for Placer and Nevada Counties, offered his property on Bowman Road for the region's homeless shelter.

Our Auburn hero, Bev Anderson, and the Auburn Salvation Army's Board chair, Ken Takutomi, put the issue of the Bowman site to rest. The pair pointed out in an *Auburn Journal* article that the south Placer churches, the Placer Coalition on Homelessness and Placer County were behind The Gathering Inn effort. Bev told the *Journal* that Mussetter's offer sounded "wonderful, but when you look a gift horse in the mouth, it sometimes isn't as wonderful."

September 21, 2005:
The Gathering Inn hosted the Roseville Chamber of Commerce for the ribbon cutting ceremony for The Gateway facility.

October 16, 2005:
The Gathering Inn invited the community to an Open House.

October 17, 2005:
The program began its second season of operations with a full calendar of host and partner churches.

The team decided that a salaried Executive Director should take over. I had severely injured my back in a fall during the summer and realized that I'd probably never regain a proper sense of balance or sure footing . Neither Sewart, with a teenager at home and working full-time, nor Miller, who had his hands full with program operations and family responsibilities, felt that they could add my portion of the team's tasks to theirs for any length of time. A paid Executive Director needed to be hired soon.

October 25, 2005:

Linda Gordon of Gordon & Gordon Advertising was invited to join the Board.

With increased personnel costs, our focus turned again to bringing in more resources for day-to-day operations. Ron Marlette of Mission Solano led our board in a retreat to help the members develop a spirit of teamwork and to synthesize goals and fundraising strategies for the program.

For the balance of the year, fundraising was at the center of our work. The congregations of St. Rose Church, Rocklin's SS. Peter & Paul Church, St. Clare's Church, St. Teresa's Church in Auburn and St. Joseph's Church in Lincoln were very generous in their response to the homilies of Deacons David Haproff, Ken Boone and Mark Van Hook.

Denise Sewart coordinated a fundraising event at the Westfield Galleria called "Home for the Holidays," an auction of donated decorated trees and Christmas presents, as well as a wine and food tasting party held after Mall operating hours. The evening netted about twenty-seven thousand dollars.

December 14, 2005:

Sue McCabe, who had been managing the renting and operation of The Gateway's multipurpose room, Harmony Hall, was elected to The Gathering Inn Board of Directors and asked to be corporate secretary.

I decided that I couldn't continue as Board Chair and President because of my back issues, which would require another surgery. The directors asked Denise Sewart to take over both positions.

Late March 2006:

When I told Sewart and Miller that my health had deteriorated the point where I couldn't stay on as executive director until the end of the season, they stepped up right away.

Then, after a few days of rest, I experienced something very unusual. It wasn't anything physical. It was more spiritual: a part of me which had been buried by all the busyness of the last two years, managed to make its way to the surface. For the first time, I grasped the significance of the events that had made The Gathering Inn so vibrant with life. They were nothing less than miraculous:

- By November 15, 2004, less than eleven months after its

inception, the program had been organized, incorporated and funded with no government money.

- By April 17, 2005, in less than sixteen months, the program had found its own permanent home and had concluded its first season of five months.
- During its second season of six months ending April 16th, 2006, The Gathering Inn had provided nearly seven thousand one hundred bed nights of shelter to two hundred sixty-one different individuals.
- And something very special: At least forty south Placer County houses of worship, despite their doctrinal differences, had banded together to help homeless people.

Epilogue
(Apr. 2006–Jul. 2017)

April 2006:

Following the conclusion of Gathering Inn's second season, Board Chair and Executive Director Denise Sewart began efforts to grow the program to the next level. At the top of her agenda was the formation of a search committee to recruit The Gathering Inn's first salaried executive director. The committee consisted of Board members Bob Tomasini, Rev. Jerry Angove, Bonnie Marx, consultant Ruth Burgess, Sewart and yours truly.

Summer 2006:

St. Vincent's came into some money when it obtained a grant for its budding "New Beginnings" transitional living program, a place for individuals and families to grow and recover from homelessness.

The agency also received notice of a generous bequest from the estate of deceased St. Vincent's volunteer, Ed Lester. A portion of his gift was put to work in the transitional living program.

September 2006:

The Gathering Inn search committee had completed its task when the Directors accepted the recommendation that Suzi deFosset be selected for the position of executive director. She signed on just in time to oversee the opening of the 2006–2007 season.

The Frenches made another generous two hundred thousand dollar donation in response to Board Chair Sewart's request to help fund not only deFosset's compensation plan and overhead costs, but also the salaries of an office manager and a full-time social service caseworker, along with the extension of the season from six to eight months. There was enough left over to provide a good cushion to begin a year-round shelter program in the fall of 2007.

December 2006:

Sewart, during the previous six months, in addition to her program expansion achievements, had overseen the completion of the solar panel and hot water containment tank system, as well as the solar-

Leo and Eileen French in "Their Dancing Days"
Courtesy Placer Title Company

photovoltaic on-site electric power generating equipment.

She also put together a successful fifty thousand dollar grant application to replace The Gathering Inn's old diesel "Big Blue" bus polluter with a newer and more environmentally friendly model. And once again, she qualified the organization for financial support of the city's Citizen's Benefit Fund.

During the year, The Lazarus Project, under the leadership of Board Chair Betsy Donovan and Executive Director David Loya, added a third transitional living home, accommodating six more clients.

Spring 2007:
The Gathering Inn's 2006–2007 season ended up providing more than nine thousand bed nights of shelter.

Fall 2007:
As planned, The Gathering Inn launched its year-round shelter program.

By that time, the Frenches had funded The Gathering Inn with nearly six hundred thousand dollars in total donations for program operations and for the purchase and refurbishing of the Gateway site. They were the reason the program could commence year-round operations. Without them, this dream of dreams would not have become a reality.

January 1, 2008:
California Senate Bill 2 went into effect, requiring all cities and counties to set aside land for homeless shelters using "by-right zoning", and prohibiting governments from rejecting homeless shelter applications "unless specified findings are made".

May 8, 2008:
Retired county supervisor, former Roseville mayor and council-member Bill Santucci passed away.

A month later, as a reflection of the importance of his civic work, the county dedicated its new expansive court and justice center in Roseville as "The Bill Santucci Justice Center." Even though he was a local hero, at times when he was on the Roseville Council and after he became a county supervisor, he failed to stand up for homeless folks on a variety of issues that kept Roseville and Placer County far behind the curve in managing their homeless problems.

2009:
The Gathering Inn's Suzi deFosset announced the opening of an interim care home for homeless patients needing recovery time following discharge from one of Placer County's hospitals. The home accommodates up to four persons at a time and is funded by grants from both Sutter Roseville and Kaiser hospitals. Previously, homeless patients were released to the street after they no longer needed in-

hospital care.

The Gathering Inn also initiated its Access to Recovery initiative, an outpatient substance abuse treatment program and a triage medical facility open to the public.

St. Vincent's New Beginnings continued its expansion with the help of an endowment from the estate of the late Virgil Harrigan, a well-known local realtor with Roseville roots going back seventy years. The program eventually grew to accommodate up to twenty households of both individuals and families at one time.

2010:

The U.S. Census showed that Roseville's population was nearing one hundred eighteen thousand.

The Gathering Inn began partnering with two new agencies:

1. "Health Express," which enabled it to offer transportation to any person needing a ride from Roseville to Placer County offices in Auburn for a medical appointment; and
2. The Office of Emergency Services-Extreme Weather Shelters, so that on nights of freezing weather, a warm meal and safe place to sleep was provided for not only for its regular guests, but also for anyone without protection from the elements.

December 1, 2010:

The city finally abided by the provisions of 2008's SB 2 by amending its zoning ordinance

- to set aside land in certain locations for homeless shelters with "by-right zoning", and
- to acknowledge that it couldn't reject homeless shelter applications out of hand.

Several parcels were set aside, some along Kenroy Lane and Riverside Avenue opposite Kenroy Lane and others in the Taylor Road area close to the Highway 65 overpass.

2011:

With the help of the Mercy Foundation, The Gathering Inn converted the large building at the Gateway known as "Harmony Hall" to "The Community Resource Center." The Center began providing guests and other folks with free access to computers, workshops on parenting skills and anger management and referrals to Placer County Health and Human Services. The Community Resource Center is open seven days a week from 8 a.m. to 3 p.m. Folks have easy access to restrooms, coffee and snacks, a warm place to stay in the winter and a spot to cool off during hot summer days.

2012:
The St. Vincent's Board of Directors voted to discontinue its New Beginnings program so that the organization could focus its resources on the primary goal of providing for the basic health and nutritional needs of poor and homeless people in south Placer County. Both the St. Vincent's Dining Room and Food Locker, in addition to the free medical clinics at its facility on Giuseppe Court and at The Gathering Inn's Gateway, were regarded as central by the charity as its work.

One hundred sixty-six families and individuals had participated in New Beginnings, with ninety-three of them graduating into permanent housing and remaining there with ongoing guidance and counseling.

2014:
The Lazarus Project added a fourth location.

Over time, expanding the program had proven to be a capital-intensive proposition, especially in Placer County. With the purchase of each new house, the Lazarus Project had to invest several hundred thousand dollars to provide just six new beds, the maximum per house allowed by law.

A shift by Lazarus to the model that has been used by Volunteers of America at the Mather Community Campus in Rancho Cordova would decrease housing costs per client and increase the number of available transitional housing beds for singles. But such a dramatic change in Roseville or south Placer County would require the onerous conditional use permit process as part of local government consent.

April 24, 2014:
About a half hour prior to the arrival of the WWJD? meal program at Saugstad Park on a Thursday morning, a homeless man was severely beaten. He died of his injuries the following Sunday. The press coverage of the incident throughout the Sacramento region caused a sensation.

Early summer 2014:
With the smell of public fear in the air, compounded by the rumors of violence surrounding the homeless man's death, Roseville officials sensed an opportunity to finally gain the upper hand over WWJD?. They

stepped up their campaign of intimidation to force the WWJD? operation out of the park once and for all.

City staff used the ruse of warning letters, telling the WWJD? Board that the organization had proven itself to be an unsafe presence in the park and had no right to operate there without a permit. As an enticement to get WWJD? to move on, they also offered the charity an alternate site at the intersection of Denio Loop and Atkinson Street.

The WWJD? Board rejected the permit requirement after officials could not cite chapter and verse in city regulations where a permit was required. The Board members also declined to move to the alternate site because of the dangerous and "burdensome conditions" involved, including traffic and exposure to the weather.

Instead, in what I believe was an unnecessary and close to disastrous step, WWJD? retreated to a site on the campus of Abundant Life Church on Atlantic Street. The move set the clock ticking toward the six months needed for the city to declare that WWJD? had abandoned its right to operate in Saugstad Park.

September 2014:

Placer County's commitment to support programs to help homeless individuals looked like it was taking a turn for the better when the Board of Supervisors commissioned consultant Dr. Robert Marbut to carry out a fifty thousand dollars study of homelessness in the county. However, that was the last Board action taken to address the needs of chronic homeless single adults in 2014.

Early winter 2014:

WWJD?'s meal program returned to Saugstad Park on Sunday mornings after Abundant Life Church announced it didn't want homeless people at its location during church services. The change in venue happened just in time to stop the city's six-month clock from running out on WWJD?'s "grandfathered right" to operate in Saugstad.

When WWJD? resumed operations in the park, the city had to turn once again to its carrot-and-stick approach, applying pressure along with offering a new inducement to move to an alternate site for Sunday use only. The carrot was a small portion of a dumpy lot at the corner of Reserve Drive and Berry Street, with no amenities except for a pad constructed of cold-patch asphalt that was just big enough to accommodate the WWJD? van and a few clients. It is a very difficult location for someone on foot to get to from the downtown area. Plus, the city didn't offer to provide any protection from winter cold, storms or wind, not even an old bus shelter.

December 9, 2014:

During a month of record bad weather and rainfall, a concerned citizens group named Right Hand Auburn, along with Volunteers of America, came to the Board of Supervisors with a proposal to operate a shelter in a couple of vacant barracks buildings at the County owned DeWitt Center. It was then that the Placer County Grand Jury apparently became aware of community support for the move.

January 22, 2015:

After Right Hand Auburn wasn't able to get the shelter issue before the Board of Supervisors' first 2015 meeting, the Grand Jury launched a full-fledged investigation into what was going on. With the Grand Jury breathing down their collective necks, the Supervisors called for a special meeting to address the problem.

February 3, 2015:

The Board of Supervisors approved the use of the DeWitt campus barracks as a temporary emergency shelter.

April 7, 2015:

The Marbut Report's findings were presented to the Board of Supervisors. Dr. Marbut's assessment of Roseville's shelter program was that "its 'operational model' for single adults experiencing homelessness is no longer a national best practice and needs major operational changes as soon as possible."

While Marbut's conclusion might have been technically correct, his study failed to take into account the stranglehold Placer County politics had on preventing services to homeless single adults, going back multiple generations.

Fortunately, the full-blown Grand Jury investigation into the problem marked the beginning of the end of these negative political forces. It is doubtful that Dr. Marbut's report alone could have delivered the knockout punch needed to jar local government into making the change, any more than the 2004 Ten Year Plan to End Homelessness did.

Winter 2015:

WWJD? had held its ground on its use of Saugstad Park for Sunday mornings. But as the city's threats got to be more than the Board members could bear, they finally waffled and signed a "licensing agreement" for Sunday use of the tiny pad at the corner of Reserve Drive and Berry Street.

It was only after the document had been dictated by city staff and pre-approved by the City Council at its October 21, 2015, meeting that it was presented to WWJD? for signature. It amounted to an unconditional surrender.

After sixteen years of pushing and prodding, the city succeeded in ending WWJD?'s charitable works in Saugstad Park. All it took was a decade and a half of huffing and puffing, along with a lot of bluster and bullying, to pull it off.

Summer 2016:

Placer County's Supervisors took what they wanted to appear as another step forward in their effort to provide emergency services for Placer County's homeless population. The Board funded a site feasibility study on behalf of Placer Rescue Mission, Inc. for a shelter to serve south Placer County. The study carried a maximum forty-four thousand dollar price tag and focused on just one property: a piece of county-owned land at the south end of Cincinnati Avenue in the Sunset Industrial Park between the city limits of Roseville, Rocklin and Lincoln.

The land had been used until 1994 as the county's dumping ground for Sunset Industrial Park's sewage and had been declared contaminated.

July 7, 2016:

Comments by Brooke Stephens, Placer Rescue Mission Board President, to the *Press Tribune* indicated a heartfelt belief that what her group and Placer County propose is the ideal solution for the lack of a brick-and-mortar homeless shelter in south Placer County: "PRM has created a vision to solve the root causes of homelessness in an environment of respect and dignity for each and every individual."

June 23, 2017:

The Placer County Grand Jury released its annual report, stating that the county had failed to make any substantial progress in overcoming its homeless problem. The Grand Jury went on to say that county officials should settle on at least one of the two sites for the permanent shelters recommended by the 2015 Marbut Report.

June 2017:

The Gathering Inn had successfully operated its year-round nomadic shelter program for ten years, first under CEO Suzi deFosset, and then since 2015, under the stewardship of CEO Keith Diederich. The program remains the only south Placer provider of comprehensive year-round shelter services for homeless folks whether they be male or female, child or adult.

Diederich has built on deFosset's successes, further strengthening community relations and expanding services at The Gateway Resource Center. The Gathering Inn Gateway facility has become the place for accessing homeless services in Roseville, with the Board of the Homeless Resource Council of the Sierras (HRCS) calling it "our HUB", stressing "... that the more services that are directed to that centralized location the better...".

The Center continues to evolve into a multiservice operation, much like a mini version of the PATH Mall in Los Angeles, recently adding these services:

- Intake and screening for The Lazarus Project;
- Veterans' assistance;
- Placer County Health and Human Services aid;
- Advocates for Mentally Ill Housing aid;
- Cooperation and office accommodations for
  - o Volunteers of America representatives;
  - o Roseville Police Department Social Services Unit's problem-oriented police (POP) officers; and
  - o Placer County probation officials.

Diederich told the HRCS Board in June that:

- The Gathering Inn had obtained "a forty thousand dollar grant from Kaiser for a nurse practitioner (for) psychiatric and on-site medication management."
- In 2016, forty-nine percent of the guests who stayed with the program ten days or more had entered permanent housing.
- The cities of Lincoln and Rocklin now provide financial support to the agency.
- And as part of The Gathering Inn's community outreach effort, it has stepped up networking with Roseville police, as well as with the Placer County's Ready to Rent program and California's

Whole Person Care pilot program.

The charity also has joined the Roseville Downtown Partnership to establish a day porter program for the downtown area. The two porters, seasoned guests of The Gathering Inn, were hired by the Partnership to walk the main commercial area, helping folks with driving directions or other information, keeping the streets clean and noting problems such as burned-out lights, plugged storm drains and filled waste cans.

To show that The Gathering Inn continues its good neighbor policy, Diederich has created teams of the program's guests to clean the Gateway's neighboring Weber Park every Monday and the littered areas in the Washington Boulevard Seawell Underpass every Thursday.

A Final Look-Back:

As I researched and wrote this book over the last six years, I had anticipated with ever-growing, but mistaken, hope that hobophobia had been licked. Instead, I found that hobophobia remains alive in Roseville and Placer County, merely mutating and manifesting itself in ways which are ever more nuanced. It has merely cloaked itself in nice-sounding words of good intent such as "respect and dignity for each and every individual," even as some business interests, residents and government officials remain determined to shove our homeless men and women far away from our parks and population centers and into places so removed from the rest of us that we don't have to deal with them.

Even after encountering this new strain of hobophobia, I'm optimistic that the good work of the people of the south Placer County area, since the founding of St. Vincent's in 1983 and continuing all the way into this thirteenth year of The Gathering Inn, has made a difference for the betterment of our communities. Their efforts to alleviate some portion of the burden and pain borne by the thousands of homeless persons they have encountered has hopefully had some meaningful impact on their guests, as well as on them.

"If you can look into the seeds of time and say which grain
will grow and which will not, speak then to me."
(Shakespeare's *Macbeth*: Act 1, Scene 3)

Bibliography–Sources of Information*
HOBOPHOBIA:
THE POLITICS OF FEAR
*The materials listed below, with the exception of St. Vincent DePaul minutes, emails, cited published books and personal appointment books, are in the possession of and the property of the Roseville, California, Public Library, Local History Collection. Abbreviations: SB: Sacramento Bee; PT: Roseville Press Tribune; SVDP: St. Vincent DePaul; HUD: U.S. Dept. of Housing and Urban Development; LSNC: Legal Services of Northern California

Bibliography–Sources of Information

Chapter 1
1857–1983
The Grapes of Wrath, John Steinbeck 1939, The Viking Press; *History of Roseville* by Leonard "Duke" Davis www.roseville.ca.us./ visit roseville; Dictionary of American History; encyclopedia.com: Railroads; Roseville Historical Society; City of Roseville maps; Roseville, CA Wikipedia: *All-America City Award*; Wikipedia: Central Pacific Railroad; Wikipedia: History of the PFE; Wikipedia: The Long Depression, The Panics of 1873, 1893 and 1896; Oct 13, 1857, deed from Tobias and Eleanor Grider to Sacramento Valley Rail Road; Nov 9, 1859, conveyance from Tobias and Eleanor Grider to Tabb Mitchell and George Anderson; 1860 US Census; Sept 2, 1861, letter from Theodore Judah to Dr. Daniel Strong; Oct 1, 1863, deed from Tabb Mitchell and George Anderson to O.D. Lambard; Aug 13, 1864, plan for the town of Roseville, Placer County Recorder; 1868 Sacramento City Directory; *History of Placer County California, 1882* Thompson and West, Oakland, CA; 1888 US Senate Executive Documents, First Session of the Fiftieth Congress, Pacific Railway Commission No. 50 Vol. 2–6; Placer Herald Aug 4, 1894; *History of Sacramento County* by G. Walter Reed, 1922; E.W. Boudier purchase documents, 1941 Ford two-door sedan from Saugstad Ford 1941; 1976 US Bicentennial Rocklin History Article by Roy Ruhkala, Rocklin CA; LA Times Mar 18, 1988, obituary of Harold T. (Bizz) Johnson; 1998 California's Geographic Names: A Gazetteer of Historic and Modern Names of the State by David L. Durham; PT Jan 27, 2002; PT Apr 12, 2013, obituary of John Piches; *Gilded-Age Entrepreneurs and Local Notables: The Case of the*

California "Big Four," 1861–1877, Evelyne Payen-Variéras, Transatlantica, Jan 2013; Rocklin's Roundhouse 1867-1908, Rocklin and Roseville Today, Mar 15, 2015, by Gary Day; SB Jul 25, 2016; City of Roseville Population Statistics; City of Roseville Library on Line Collection, waymarking.com; personal notes, photos and records.

Chapter 2
Jun '83–Dec '83
Aug 22, 1983, SVDP minutes; Nov 15, 1983, SVDP minutes; City general information memo, SVDP 1983 and 1984 business licenses; Oct 30, 1996, conversation with Jessie Chambers, SVDP Food Locker founder Jan 31, 2012; deed, personal business and income tax records; chronology from personal notes, appointment books and records.

Chapter 3
Jan '84–Mar '87
Roseville City Clerk's Records; Placer County Recorder Deeds; History of Roseville by Duke Davis, Roseville's local historian, http://www.roseville.ca.us/visit_roseville/history_of_roseville/; Project Home chronology from personal files; SVDP 1983 and 1984 business licenses; Community Ministries chronology 1984 to 1986 from personal files; Feb 22, 1984, SVDP minutes; Catholic Herald – Jul, 1984; Nov 28, 1984, SVDP minutes; Jul 24, 1985, SVDP minutes; PT Aug 15, 1985, Harry Crabb comments; PT Aug 20, 1985; Sept 25, 1985, SVDP minutes; Oct 23, 1985, SVDP minutes; PT Nov 12, 1985; St. Rose bulletin Jul 1986; Jul 1986 SVDP meeting notes; SVDP annual report; SVDP Community Service News, St. Rose bulletin Jul 1986; SB

Nov 5, 1986; May 3, 1987; Catholic Herald, Jun 8, 1987; Aug 1, 1987, SVDP Board minutes; Sept 5, 1987, SVDP Board minutes; Sept 8, 1987, letter to City Manager Bob Hutchison; Dec 18, 1987, SVDP Dining Room Committee meeting minutes; St. Rose Parish bulletin, Dec 11, 1988; City general information memo, Oct 30, 1996; Oct 6, 2011, conversation with Rev. Tim Brooks, Oct conversations with Jessie Chambers, SVDP Food Locker founder, Jan 31, 2012, and Oct 1, 2015; chronology from personal notes and files; personal business income tax records; personal notes, appointment books and records.

Chapter 4
Apr '87–Oct '87
Roseville City Clerk's records; City of Roseville Archives; additional city archives and files copied Feb 18, 2006; 1987 City Fire Dept. report; 1987

County Health Dept. records; 1987 County Health Dept. meeting notes; SVDP records; PT Jun or Jul, 1987; Sherry Schiele Jun 26, 1987, report; City of Roseville Jun 30, 1987, letter; Jul 9, 1987, incident report by Janette Sanders; my Jul 13, 1987, letter to City Manager Bob Hutchison; Jul 29, 1987, letter from John Miners to Thom Carmichael; Aug 11, 1987, entry from personal chronology; my Aug 13, 1987, letter to City Manager Bob Hutchison; PT Aug 15, 1987; Aug 25, 1987, prop owners' letter; Sept 5, 1987, SVDP Board minutes; my Sept 8, 1987 letters to Mayor Ozenick, City Manager Bob Hutchison and City Planning Director Steve Dillon; City Planning Dept. letter released Oct 16, 1987; Oct 26, 1987, SVDP minutes; Oct 30, 1996, city general information memo; Nov 6, 1987, entry

in personal chronology; Nov 11, 1987, Ministerial Association "open letter"; personal notes, appointment books and records.

Chapter 5
Nov '87–Oct '89
Roseville City Clerk's records; Jack Willoughby Nov 13, 1987, letter to Bill Santucci; Nov 20, 1987, SVDP letter to pastors; Dec 1987 SVDP letter; Dec 4, 1987, SVDP Dining Room committee meeting notes; Dec 5, 1987, SVDP Board minutes; Dec 5, 1987, letter from Ed Tiedemann to Mayor Santucci; PT Dec 16, 1987; PT Dec 17, 1987; Dec 18, 1987, SVDP Dining Room committee meeting minutes; Jan 2, 1988, SVDP Board minutes; Feb 6, 1988, SVDP Board minutes; SB Feb 6, 1988; SB Feb 7, 1988; Feb 24, 1988, SVDP minutes; PT Mar 3, 1988; Mar 23, 1988, SVDP minutes; PT Apr 1988; Apr 2, 1988, SVDP Board

minutes; Apr 27, 1988, SVDP minutes; May 7, 1988, SVDP Board minutes; May 13, 1988, Blue Ribbon Committee report; May 18, 1988, SVDP memos; PT Jun 7, 1988; Jun 8, 1988, letter to City of Roseville; Jun 10, 1988, SVDP Board minutes; Jul 9, 1988, SVDP Board minutes; Jul 26, 1988, SVDP letter to Project Home organizers; Jul 27, 1988, SVDP minutes; PT Aug 9, 1988; SB Aug 10, 1988; PT Aug 11, 1988; SB Aug 11, 1988; SB Neighbors Aug 14, 1988; PT Aug 15, 1988; Aug 24, 1988, SVDP minutes; LA Times Nov 28, 1988; St. Rose Parish Bulletin, Dec 11, 1988; PT Dec 14, 1988, editorial; Dec 14, 1988, Ministerial Association Letter of Petition; PT Dec 20, 1988; letter of Dec 23, 1988; Dec 29, 1988 Blue Ribbon Committee report; PT Jan 10, 1989; PT Jan 4, 1989; PT Jan 10, 1989; PT Jan 23,

1989; SB Mar 26, 1989; Apr 1989 PT letter to editor from Marcia Fernaays; Jul 8, 1989, SVDP Board minutes; PT Aug 17, 1989, Committee on Homelessness Roster; Aug 23, 1989, SVDP monthly meeting minutes; PT Sept 3, 1989; PT Sept 24, 1989; PT editorial Nov 1989, PT Nov 23, 1989; San Mateo B of S Res. Jan 28, 2003; Placer County Request for Proposals 6485; Roseville City Council communication 8740; Gayle Smithson, Roseville PD; Sept 14, 2011; personal chronology of events; personal notes, appointment books and records.

Chapter 6
Nov '89–Jun 15, '92
Roseville City Clerk's records; PT Jan 31, 1990; end of season 1990 Armory Shelter Report; Apr 18, 1990, Homeless Task Force report; SB Neighbors Apr 26, 1990; Jun 27, 1990, SVDP monthly meeting minutes; PT

Aug 16, 1990; SB Neighbors Oct 18, 1990; Oct 24, 1990, SVDP minutes; PT Jan 17, 1991; SB Neighbors Dec 12, 1991; PT Dec 15, 1991; PT Feb 27, 1992; PT Feb 28, 1992; PT Mar 2, 1992; Mar 3, 1992, council communication, Summary Regional Homeless Program; PT Mar 5, 1992; Mar 24, 1992, SVDP monthly minutes; Mar 24, 1992, council communication; City of Roseville meeting notice; Mar 29, 1992, letter from Pauline Tomlinson; City of Roseville Apr 1, 1992, Agenda Item 18; PT Apr 1, 1992; SB Apr 1, 1992; SB Neighbors Apr 12, 1992; LSNC May 1, 1992, city memo; Legal Services of Northern California May 1, 1992; May 6, 1992 Roseville City Council video; PT May 7, 1992; May 14, 1992, memo from City Hall meeting; May 18, 1992, letter to City from Rev. Tim

Brooks, President, The Roseville Ministerial Association; PT May 27, 1992; my May 29, 1992, Pauline Roccucci meeting notes; Jun 10, 1992, Roseville City Council video; SB Jun 11, 1992; LA Times Jun 12, 1992; PT Jun 15, 1992; PT Jun 15, 1992, editorial; SB Jun 15, 1992; Attachment #1, City of Roseville 1998 Continuum of Care Proposal; 1998 Roseville Application for federal government McKinney Act funds; Gayle Smithson, Roseville PD, Sept 14, 2011; personal notes, appointment books and records

Chapter 7
Late Jun '92–Dec '92
Roseville City Clerk's records; St. Vincent de Paul Society, Roseville Area Conference history, undated; St. Rose Parish pastor Father Mike Cormack's notes; Sherry Schiele biographical information; Placer County Welfare

Dept. records; Jun 10, 1992, Roseville City Council video; SB Jun 11, 1992; PT Jun 15, 1992, editorial; SB Jun 15, 1992; Jun 1992 city budget hearings; PT Jul 2, 1992; Jul 22, 1992, SVDP minutes; PT Aug 6, 1992; Aug 10, 1992, SVDP letter to Thieles and Cherry Glen residents, businesses and property owners; Aug 26, 1992, SVDP minutes; PT Sept 3, 1992; PT Nov 5, 1992; Nov 10, 1992, letter to St. Rose Church from City Planning Director Patty Dunn; Nov 13, 1992, memo from Police Chief Tom Simms to City Manager Al Johnson; PT Nov 15, 1992; Nov 15, 1992, Harry and Jeanette Crabb neighborhood flier; Nov 16, 1992, Kevin Valine letter to St. Rose Church; Nov 16, 1992, Father Mike Cormack letter and remarks to the Roseville City Council; PT Nov 17, 1992; Dan McGrath column SB, Nov 18,

1992; SB Neighbors Nov 19, 1992; PT Nov 19, 1992; Joint Statement from the City of Roseville and St. Rose Church; PT Nov 20, 1992; SB Nov 20, 1992; PT Nov 22, 1992; SB Nov 22, 1992; SB Neighbors Nov 22, 1992; Catholic liturgical calendar for Nov 22, 1992; Nov 23, 1992, SVDP minutes. Nov 23, 1992, SVDP minutes; Catholic Herald Nov 25, 1992; PT Nov 25, 1992; Nov 27, 1992, Ministerial Association letter; PT Dec 1, 1992; PT Dec 3, 1992; SB Neighbors Dec 3, 1992; PT Dec 14, 1992; SB Dec 17, 1992; SB Neighbors Dec 17, 1992; SB Dec 24, 1992; SB Neighbors Dec 24, 1992; Nov 15, 2011, conversation with Fr. Mike Cormack; Dec 7, 2011, telephone conversation with Jack Willoughby; personal notes, appointment books and records.

Chapter 8
Jan '93–Sept 15, '93
Roseville City Clerk's records; my notes of conversations with Bill Santucci; St. Vincent de Paul Society, Inc. Roseville Area Conference history, undated; PT Jan 3, 1993; PT Jan 27, 1993; Feb 1, 1993, Roseville Shelter Committee Proposal; SB Neighbors Feb 4, 1993; Feb 24, 1993, SVDP minutes; Feb 25, 1993, Shelter Committee letter; Feb 25, 1993, Jack Willoughby letter to Roseville's city attorney; SB Neighbors Feb 28, 1993; Mar 3, 1993, Fr. Mike Cormack letter to Council members Crabb and Hamel; PT Mar 15, 1993; SB Neighbors Mar 21, 1993; PT Mar 1993; Mar 26, 1993, Roseville Shelter Committee proposal; my notes of Mar 30, 1993, meeting; Mar 31, 1993, John Haluck letter to city attorney; Homeless Program Project Development

endorsement letter for Santucci campaign; personal letter; PT Nov 11, 1994; Auburn Journal Nov 30, 1994; my Nov 30, 1994, letter to SVDP; Dec 1, 1994, SB Neighbors; PT Dec 2, 1994; SB Dec 7, 1994; PT Dec 9, 1994; SB Dec 9, 1994; SB Dec 10, 1994; Mel Hamel Dec 10, 1994, KXTV Channel 10 Interview; Phil Ozenick campaign mailer; personal notes, appointment books and records.

Chapter 11
Dec 11, '94–Dec 23, '94
Roseville City Clerk's records; Catholic Diocese of Sacramento website; Dec 11, 1994–Dec 23, 1994; Mel Hamel Dec 10, 1994, KXTV Channel 10 interview; PT Dec 13, 1994; Juan Lara Dec 20, 1994, KCRA Channel 3 interview; Dec 21, 1994, Roseville City Council video; Dec 22, 1994, Roseville Emergency Shelter Project flier; SB Dec

22, 1994; PT Dec 23, 1994; SB Dec 23, 1994; Auburn Journal Dec 23, 1994; PT Dec 27, 1994; Jan 16, 2012, conversation with Deacon Dave Sorensen; personal notes, appointment books and records.

Chapter 12
Dec 29, '94–Apr 6, '95
Roseville City Clerk's records; Dec 23, 1994, Bishop William Weigand letter to Mayor Mel Hamel; SB Dec 29, 1994; Jan 4, 1995, Roseville City Council video; Jan 4, 1995, KCRA TV; PT Jan 4, 1995; PT Jan 6, 1995; SB Jan 8, 1995; Jan 18, 1995, Roseville City Council video; SB Neighbors Jan 25, 1995; Feb 9, 1995, letter from Sherry Schiele to the Community Services Planning Council; PT Feb 20, 1995; PT Feb 26, 1995; PT Feb 28, 1995; audio tape Mar 8, 1995, Roseville City Council meeting; Mar 8, 1995, Roseville City

Council video; PT Mar 28, 1995; Mar 31, 1995, Roseville Emergency Shelter Program report; personal notes, appointment books and records

Chapter 13
Apr 11, '95–May 19, '96
Roseville City Clerk's records; 1995 City of Roseville Comprehensive Housing Strategy Annual Affordability Performance Report; 1995–96 Winter Shelter Program report; "Consolidated Planning Process" 2014 by Ed Gramlich, Director of Regulatory Affairs, National Low Income Housing Coalition; 1996 Roseville Municipal Code; Caltrans 1995 auction fliers; Apr 11, 1995, City general information memo to the City Council; Apr 20, 1995, Neighborhood Association letter to the City Council; Apr 25, 1995, City general information memo to The City

Council; SB Apr 27, 1995; my May 5, 1995, letter to SVDP; PT May 7, 1995; May 8, 1995, John Sprague memo; May 11, 1995, Provider Group Draft shelter straw design; my May 15, 1995, letter to Roseville Housing and Redevelopment Office; May 17, 1995 Roseville City Council video; May 18, 1995, SVDP letter to me; SB May 19, 1995; my May 20, 1995, letter to City Manager Al Johnson; PT May 21, 1995; Council Agenda Item #26 May 24, 1995; council communication, Agenda Item #30 May 31, 1995, pg. 71 of the Consolidated Plan; my memo-to-file given to David Philipson on Jun 1, 1995; PT Jun 6, 1995; SB Jun 6, 1995; SB Jun 8, 1995; SB Jun 11, PT Jul 21, 1995; SB Jun 11, 1995; Jun 13, 1995, audio tapes; SB Jun 14, 1995; PT Jun 23, 1995; Jul 11, 1995, HUD letter to

Roseville; PT Jul 16, 1995; PT Jul 21, 1995; Jul 25, 1995, Terry Anderson report; PT Aug 1, 1995; faxed Aug 2, 1995, letter to Michael and V.M. Patel from Central Roseville Revitalization Project; Aug 10, 1995, letter to Michael and V.M. Patel from Central Roseville Revitalization Project; Aug 11, 1995, City general information memo; Aug 22, 1995, HUD letter to Roseville; SB Aug 22, 1995; Aug 29, 1995, conversation with Caltrans' Susan Sears; PT Sept 3, 1995; Sept 25, 1995, Steve Barber memo; Sept 28, 1995, City of Roseville Building Division letter to Home Start; Oct 9, 1995, Placer Women's Center letter to Home Start; PT Nov 3, 1995; PT Nov 10, 1995; my comments on Nov 29, 1995, telephone conversation notes; Dec 8, 1995, letter to Steve Barber; Dec

12, 1995, personal notes; PT Dec 8, 1995; Auburn Journal Dec 25, 1995; SB Neighbors Dec 28, 1995; Jan 3, 4 and 5, 1996, telephone and meeting notes; SB Jan 8, 1996; PT Jan 9, 1996; Jan 23, 1996, Mark Doane letter and Building Division correspondence; Jan 29, 1996, Sherry Schiele letter to Rev. Paul Carlson; Feb 13, 1996, Home Start Board minutes; Feb 1996 Home Start income statements; PT editorial Feb 18, 1996; SB Feb 19, 1996; Mar 1996, Home Start income statements; Mar 12, 1996, Home Start unofficial meeting minutes; Mar 26, 1996, Board minutes; Apr 2, 1996, letter to HUD's Andrew Quint; Apr 3, 1996, Home Start Board minutes; PT Apr 9, 1996; Apr 16, 1996, Home Start Board minutes; Apr 19 letter to HUD's Andrew Quint; Apr 22, 1996, telephone

Bibliography- Sources of Information

message from
Andrew Quint;
Roseville's Analysis
of Impediments to
Fair Housing report
Apr 1996; May 14,
1996, Home Start
Board minutes; May
19, 1996, Paul
Carlson letter to
HUD; my May 28
and 29, 1996,
telephone notes;
Sherry Schiele Dec
1995 Home Start
grant report; A
Short History of
Roseville Home
Start, Inc. by
Corporate Secretary
Rexine Brewer,
undated; Sherry
Schiele notes;
personal notes,
appointment books
and records.

Chapter 14
May 28, '96–Aug
'13, 96
Roseville City Clerk's
records; Notes and
attachment to 1996
U.S. Department of
Housing and Urban
Development (HUD)
complaint; HUD
investigator David
Philipson's notes;
May 20, 1996, John
Sprague memo; my
May 28 and 29,
1996, telephone
notes; May 29,

1996, John Sprague
memo; PT Jun 7,
1996; Jun 11, 1996,
Home Start Board
minutes; my Jun 26,
1996, presentation
to City Council and
notes; Jun 26, 1996,
City Council video;
Jul 9, 1996 letter
from HUD; Jul 10,
1996, City Council
video; PT Aug 13,
1996; SB Aug 14,
1996; my notes
from Homeless
Forum meetings;
notes from
conversations with
LSNC Herb Whitaker
and Dave Sorensen;
Ministerial
Association letter to
Roseville City
Council; Sacramento
Business Journal,
Mar 29, 1998;
personal notes,
appointment books
and records.

Chapter 15
Aug 14, '96–Aug 31,
'96
Aug 14, 1996,
Home Start Board
minutes; SB Aug
14, 1996; Sally
Bragg and Silva
Slade letter to me;
my Aug 16, 1996,
letter to Silva Slade
and Sally Bragg;
Aug 16, 1996,

Archie Mull and
Herb Whitaker
faxes; my Aug 16,
1996, letter to
SVDP Board; PT
Aug 16, 1996; Aug
20, 1996, letter
from Silvia Slade
and Sally Bragg;
audio recording of
Aug 26, 1996,
meeting at
Chamber of
Commerce with
neighbors; Aug 26,
1996, draft of our
Superior Court suit;
my Aug 27, 1996,
telephone
conversation with
Rudy Martinez; my
Aug 28, 1996, letter
to Silvia Slade and
Sally Bragg; Aug 29,
1996, Telephone
Roadmap For
Homeless Forum
Representatives,
after Jun 6, 1996,
Homeless Forum
meeting; Aug 31,
1996, SVDP
corporate
resolution; Jan 16,
2012, conversation
with Deacon Dave
Sorensen;
personal notes,
appointment books
and records.

Jeff Steele notes; LA Times Mar 4, 1997; SB Mar 4, 1997; Mar 10, 1997, Sally Bragg letter to City Council; Jeff Steele's Points and Authorities in Support of Demurrer filed Mar 14, 1997; Mar 24, 1997, my notes of conversation with Chamber of Commerce office staff; Mar 26, 1997, Jeff Steele letter; SB Neighbors Mar 27, 1997; Mar 31, 1997, letter to David Philipson; Apr 16, 1997, my notes of conversation with Pam Harlan; Apr 18 and 25, 1997, Sally Bragg letters; my notes of May 5, 1997, conversation with Jeff Steele; Minute Order of Court, May 5, 1997; my notes of May 23, 1997, telephone conversation with City Clerk Carolyn Parkinson; Sally Bragg case management memo filed with court May 25, 1997; SB Neighbors May 25, 1997; SB Neighbors May 29, 1997; PT May 29, 1997; PT

Jun 11, 1997; Sally Bragg's Jun 13, 1997, dismissal without prejudice; Hoffmaster V City of San Diego, No. D025961, Court of Appeal, Fourth District Division 1, California, Jun 17, 1997; PT Jun 18, 1997; PT Jun 22, 1997; Placer County Superior Court Judge Roeder's Jul 1, 1997, ruling; St. Rose Office notes; personal notes, appointment books and records.

Chapter 18
Jul 9, '97–Dec '97

Roseville City Clerk's records; 1996 HUD Pre-Complaint Questionnaire; 1996 Roseville Municipal Code; Placer County Planning Dept. records; city-county MOU's Jul 9, 1997, and Jan 5, 2000; NY Times Jul 4, 1997; PT Jul 11, 1997, SB Jul 13, 1997; SB Jul 18, 1997; SB Jul 22, 1997; SB Aug 7, 1997; PT Aug 10, 1997; SB Neighbors Aug 10, 1997; Aug 11, 1997, City of Roseville Staff report and Council

communication 1703; Aug 13, 1997, telephone discussion with David Philipson; Aug 20, 1997, meeting notes; SB Aug 21, 1997; Council communication from Assistant City Manager Craig Robinson, dated Sept 5, 1997; my notes of Sept 9, 1997 telephone conversation with Fr. Dan Casey; Sept 23, 1997, letter from HUD's Jimmy Prater to City Manager Al Johnson; Sept 26, 1997, Joe Esparza letter to area pastors; my Oct 3, 1997, conversation with John Sprague; Oct 3, 1997, telephone conversation with David Philipson; PT Oct 6, 1997; Oct 24, 1997, Council communication and introductory memo from John Sprague to the City Council; Oct 28, 1997, HUD letter and HUD Monitoring report to Allen Johnson, Roseville City Manager; Oct 31, 1997, HUD letter to me; Nov 4, 1997, telephone conversation with Police Chief John Barrow; Nov 5, 1997 City Council Minutes; Nov 10, 1997, meeting with Fr. Deibel; Nov 13, 1997, Joe Esparza letter to Roseville City Clerk; Nov 17, 1997, conversation with John Sprague; SB Nov 20, 1997; PT Nov 21, 1997; notes of Nov 24, 1997, my telephone conversation with David Philipson; Dec 8, 1997, mayor's letter to HUD; PT Dec 17, 1997; HUD Dec 23, 1997, letter to Roseville; Dec 24, 1997, my notes of conversation with Jim Bush; HUD Notice: CPD-03–14 Dec 29, 2003; HUD Guide to Continuum of Care Planning and Implementation; DOJ COPS Quick Facts for California, Jan 4, 2010, pg. 187; Dec 30, 2013, www.downtownros eville.com/history#1 980n; HUD investigator David Philipson's notes of interview with Steve

Barber; *A Short History of Roseville Home Start, Inc.* by Corporate Secretary Rexine Brewer, undated; *A Brief History of PEACE for Families,* undated; personal notes, appointment books and records.

Chapter 19
Jan '98–Jul 26, '98
Roseville City Clerk's records; 1996 Roseville Municipal Code; HUD 1997–98 Roseville Consolidated Annual Performance Evaluation Public Review and Comments; Jan 21, 1998, City Council minutes; SB Jan 25, 1998; Feb 4, 1998, Al Johnson letter to HUD; David Philipson's notes on Johnson's Feb 4, 1998, letter to Paul T. Berg, HUD, San Francisco office; Feb 10, 1998, HUD internal memo from HUD's Rosemarie Fernandez-Pifer to HUD's Bonnie Milstein; PT Feb 22, 1998; PT Mar 5, 1998; SB Mar 17, 1998; Mar 19, 1998, Home Start letter to

City of Roseville; Home and Start Business Plan attachment; PT editorial Mar 20, 1998; PT Mar 25, 1998; Sacramento Business Journal Mar 29, 1998; HUD-City Mar 30, 1998, telephone conference call meeting notes; City Attorney Mark Doane Apr 2, 1998, letter to George Williams Director of HUD's Fair Housing Division; Apr 27, 1998, HUD letter to City of Roseville; David Philipson's Apr 27, 1998, meeting notes; May 4, 1998, City general information memo; May 5, 1998, WWJD? promissory note to Lynn and Sherry Schiele; May 11, 1998, Council communication; my notes of May 12, 1998, of minister's meeting; Roseville City Clerk's work copy of May 13, 1998, Council meeting Agenda Item #34; Greg Cowart's May 20, 1998, memo to the Continuum of Care Committee; PT May

22, 1998; my notes from May 26, 1998, telephone conversation with David Philipson; Jun 3, 1998, City Council minutes; my notes of Greg Cowart's Jun 12, 1998, memo to the Continuum of Care Committee; Greg Cowart's comments at the Jun 12, 1998, St. Rose rectory; video recording Jun 18, 1998, Continuum of Care Committee meeting; Jun 29, 1998, Draft Continuum of Care Document; SB Jul 5, 1998; SB Jul 7, 1998; Jul 8, 1998, City Council meeting video recording; Roseville City Clerk's minutes of Jul 8, 1998, City Council meeting; PT Jul 10, 1998; Jul 15, 1998, City Council meeting video recording; PT Jul 17, 1998; PT Jul 19, 1998; Jul 21, 1998, St. Rose letter to George Williams; SB Jul 22, 1998; McKeon letter to the PT editor Jul 24, 1998; PT Jul 26, 1998; Jul 31, 1998, Final Continuum of Care document;

Continuum of Care Committee Agenda; Starting Over brochure; Jun 17, 2014, and Aug 31, 2015 conversations with Joe Esparza; personal notes, appointment books and records.

Chapter 20
Aug 1998 –Jan 1999
Roseville City Clerk's records; Placer County Planning Dept. records; homestart.org; May 5, 1998, WWJD? promissory note to Lynn and Sherry Schiele; Jun 24, 1998, Schiele letter to the PT editor; PT Jul 28, 1999; Jul 31, 1998, Final Continuum of Care document; Aug 4, 1998, HUD notes; SB Aug 11, 1998; PT Aug 12, 1998; Sept 11, 1998, California Housing and Community Development Office notice; Oct 20, 1998, SVDP Board minutes; my notes of Oct 24, 1998, Lazarus Project organizational meeting; PT Nov 6, 1998; PT Nov 20, 1998; my Dec 8,

1998, FOIA request to HUD; HUD Final Analysis of Investigative Report WWJD? vs. City of Roseville, Aug 15, 2001; PT Jun 27, 2008; 2013 HHS and HUD PATH annual report; Jun 17, 2014 conversation with Joe Esparza; SB Jan 19, 2015; Mar 10, 2015, meeting with Dr. Tom Stanko; Feb 16, 2015, conversations with to George Howington; personal notes, appointment books and records.

Chapter 21
Feb '99–Dec '99
SB Jan 2, 1999; PT Jan 5, 1999; PT Jan 15, 1999; Jan 26, 1999, HUD's Lettie Barber notes of conversation with Jan Shonkwiler; PT Feb 14, 1999; Feb 18, 1999, WWJD? donation letter to Lynn and Sherry Schiele; Mar 9, 1999, Council communication 2753; SB Mar 16, 1999; Mar 17, 1999, City Council minutes; SB Mar 18, 1999; Mar 30, 1999,

Community Development Block Grant application; Sherry Schiele Jul 2, 1999, notes; Jul 8, 1999, Placer County Health Dept. letter; SB Jul 23, 1999; my notes of Sept 9, 1999, conversation with Sherry Schiele; Sept 9, 1999, letter from Betsy Donovan to the City of Roseville Planning Commission; my Sept 9, 1999, Planning Commission meeting notes; Richard Roccucci notes Sept 29, 1999, Providers' meeting; Richard Roccucci's Oct 7, 1999, list of issues to the City Planning Dept.; Providers' letter to County Board of Supervisors Oct 26, 1999; City Planning Dept. staff report, Oct 28, 1999; PT Nov 14, 1999; PT Nov 17, 1999; Nov 18, 1999, Council communication 3454 and Map, Attach 3; SB Neighbors Dec 12, 1999; Dec 17, 1999, City Council minutes; SB Dec 23, 1999; Amy Yannello,

PT Dec 29, 1999; personal notes, appointment books and records.

Chapter 22
Jan 2000–Dec 2001
Y2K the Movie, 1999; Time Magazine Jan 1, 2000, commemorative issue; St. Rose Parish Bulletins, 1994–2004; timeanddate.com/ millennium; my 2001–2002 Salvation Army file; 2001 Home Start budget; New York Daily News Dec 30, 2014; Time Magazine, Dec 31, 2014; my Jan 18, 2000, WWJD? meeting notes; Mar 16, 2000, Placer greater collaborative memo from Co-Chairs Jan Shonkwiler and Bud Bautista; Sacramento Business Journal Mar 26, 2000; SB Neighbors Apr 2, 2000; Sept 26, 2000, WWJD? conciliation proposal; PT Dec 31, 2000; Jan 7, 2001, St. Rose bulletin; PT Jan 14, 2001; The Catholic Herald, Mar

3, 2001; SB Apr 4, 2001; Apr 5, 2001, email from Jan Shonkwiler to PCOH members; PT Apr 8, 2001; Apr 9, 2001, calendar entry; Apr 24, 2001, Lazarus Project meeting minutes; SB Neighbors Apr 27, 2001; May 16, 2001, First Methodist Church Council meeting letter; my Jun 13, 2001, notes re: meeting with Wanda Patrick, Placer County Sanitarian; PT Aug 15, 2001; Aug 15, 2001, HUD Final Analysis Investigative Report WWJD? vs. City of Roseville; Aug 16, 2001 HUD Final Determination; Sept 18, 2001, City general information memo; SB Dec 15, 2001; PT Dec 16, 2001; WWJD?; 2001 annual report; SB Neighbors Feb 6, 2005; Sept 10, 2014, email from Janice Critchlow; my Feb 16, 2015, telephone conversation with George Howington; Apr 21, 2015, email from Janice Critchlow; my Aug

14, 2015, conversation with Joe Esparza; my Jun 30, 2017, conversation with Denise Sewart; Sacramento Diocese Archives, Vol. 1, No. 13 by Fr. John Boll; personal notes, appointment books and records.

Chapter 23
Jan 2002–Mar 2004
California Sec of State's records; Roseville City Clerk's records; Karen Bocast LinkedIn bio; my 2001–2002 Salvation Army file; my Jan 5, 2002, resignation letter to WWJD? Board; PT Jan 30, 2002; PT Feb 2, 2002; PT Feb 8, 2002; SB Neighbors Mar 21, 2002; PT Apr 3, 2002; Apr 4, 2002, City general information memo; PT Apr 14, 2002; PT May 1, 2002; Council communication 7150 for May 1, 2002, City Council meeting; May 6, 2002, conversation with Jan Shonkwiler; May 8, 2002, City meeting notes; Jun 27, 2002, letter

from Kevin Payne; Jul 11, 2002, my letter to Kevin Payne; my notes of Aug 21, 2002, meeting with Pastor Brad Swope; PT Aug 24, 2002; Sept 30, 2002, WWJD? meeting minutes; SB Nov 10, 2002; PT Nov 30, 2002; congressional record Jan 7, 2003; SB Apr 17, 2003; PT May 7, 2003; WWJD? Sept 2003 newsletter; Dec 9, 2003, email from Michelle Talbott of Auburn Salvation Army; Dec 15, 2003, WWJD? letter to Herb Whitaker, LSNC; WWJD? 2003 Christmas letter to donors; 2004–2005 Gathering Inn diary; SB Jan 1, 2004; my Jan 25, 2004, emails to Ed Donohue and David George; Jan 26, 2004, WWJD? minutes; SB Neighbors Jan 29, 2004; Feb 10, 2004, Brad Swope letter; Feb 26, 2004, Ad Hoc Homeless Outreach Committee minutes; Feb 26, 2004, Ad Hoc Homeless Outreach

Committee roster and tasks list; March 21, 2004, "United in Mission March 21, 2004" agenda; Mar 21, 2004, conversation with City Hall insider; Mar 22, 2004, WWJD? Board minutes; Mar 25, 2004, Ad Hoc Homeless Outreach Committee minutes; Mar 26, 2004, LSNC Authorization For Release of Information; PT Mar 18, 2006; Placer Herald Jan 10, 2009; Auburn Journal Jan 14, 2009, Jack Epling obituary; Feb 16, 2015, telephone conversation with George Howington; my notes of Apr 27, 2015, conversation with John Sorenson, WWJD? volunteer mechanic; my notes of Sept 1, 2015, conversation with Paul Boudier; my notes of Sept 9, 2015, conversation with Dr. Tom Stanko, MD; personal notes, appointment books and records.

Howington, TGI accountant re: WWJD? accounting; Feb 4, 2005, The Gathering Inn Advisory Council minutes; Feb 9, 2005, The Gathering Inn (TGI) Board of Directors minutes; 2004–2005 WWJD? operating statement; The Gathering Innspiration Holiday 2005 issue; PT Jun 10, 2006; PT Jan 24, 2007; Sept 2007 Historical Reflections by Denise Sewart; Jun 2009 HUD "Continuum of Care 101"; my May 23, 2013, telephone conversation with Herb Whitaker, LSNC; May 23, 2013, Home Base bulletin; Sept 10, 2014, and Sept 17, 2014, emails from Janice Critchlow; The 2014 Annual Homeless Assessment report to Congress, Oct 2014; Dec 19, 2014, letter to Roseville City Manager Rob Jenson; Apr 7, 2015, memo from Placer Co. Health and Human Services Director Jeffrey S. Brown to the Board of Supervisors Apr 27, 2015, conversation with John Sorenson, WWJD? volunteer mechanic; Jul 4, 2015, cconversation with

Denise Sewart; Jul 15, 2015, conversation with Bob and June Bonnici; Jul 16, 2015, conversation with WWJD? volunteer Margo Ezell; comments of David Loya at Sept 30, 2015, Homeless Shelter and Services Center meeting; Jul 24, 2015, conversation with WWJD? volunteer Bea Young; Sept 23, 2015, conversation with WWJD? volunteer Margo Ezell; Jan 16, 2016, conversation with WWJD? Volunteer Margo Ezell; Feb 7, 2016, conversation with Denise Sewart; Mar 8, 2016, Placer County Board of Supervisors minutes; Mar 29, 2016, conversation with Susan Farrington; Apr 3, 2016, conversation with Denise Sewart; Apr 4, 2016, conversation with Brad Swope; "Acres of Hope" website, Aug 16, 2016; personal notes, appointment books and records.

Chapter 25
Mar 13, 2005–Mar 2006
Roseville City Clerk's Records; The Gathering Inn diary; Feb 2005

Host Church program survey; Mar 2, 2005, survey report; Mar 17, 2005, email notice to Board Land and Building Available; Mar 17, 2005, Berkeley Ave. purchase offer and High St. option offer; Mar 20, 2005, Shergill's counter offer to sell Berkeley Ave. and High St. property; Mar 20, 2005, counter offer to purchase Berkeley Ave property and to option High St. property; Mar 23, 2005, final purchase agreement re: Berkeley Ave Property; Mar 23, 2005, The Gathering Inn Board of Directors closed meeting minutes; Mar 26, 2005, The Gathering Inn Board of Directors minutes; Apr 1, 2005, The Gathering Inn Advisory Council minutes; Apr 2005 The Gathering Innformer; my Apr 4, 2005, letter to Kevin Payne, Roseville Assistant Planning and Redevelopment Director; Apr 10, 2005, TGI Board of Directors special meeting minutes; Apr 27, 2005, TGI Board of Directors minutes; Apr 2005 recap and pie chart of 2004–2005 season;

May 24, 2005, TGI Board of Directors minutes; my May 26, 2005, thank you letter to Leo and Eileen French; Auburn Journal Jun 22, 2005; Jun 28, 2005, The Gathering Inn Board of Directors minutes; Jul 5, 2005, The Gathering Inn Board of Directors minutes; Jul 26, 2005, The Gathering Inn Board of Directors minutes; Aug 23, 2005, The Gathering Inn Board of Directors minutes; Sept 14, 2005, Denise Sewart email to the Advisory Council; Sept 27, 2005, TGI Board of Directors minutes; Oct 25, 2005, TGI Board of Directors minutes; my Dec 13, 2005, letter of resignation as CEO and TGI Board President for health reasons; Dec 13, 2005, TGI Board of Directors minutes; Jan 24, 2006, TGI Board of Directors minutes; Feb 9, 2006, TGI Advisory Council summary; Feb 28, 2006, TGI Board of Directors minutes; Mar 3, 2006, TGI Advisory Council summary; PT Mar 18, 2006; TGI 2004–2005 personal notes, appointment books and records.

Epilogue
(Apr 2006–July 2017)
City Clerk's Records; US Census records: Shakespeare's *Macbeth*; https://www.hudexchangeinfo; Social Security Death Index; Aug 14, 2006, The Gathering Inn (TGI) thank you letter to Frenches ; Auburn Journal Sept 20, 2006; Denise Sewart Jul 16, 2007, email to TGI Board of Directors; Jul 27, 2007, email from Denise Sewart; May 7, 2008 letter from C.R. Creswell, Calif Div of Housing Policy Development; Auburn Journal May 8, 2008; my letter of Dec 16, 2009; PT Jan 31, 2014; PT May 1, 2014; March 30, 2015, Marbut Report; Placer County Grand Jury 2014–2015 Final Report; 2016 accounting of French Family donations; May 2016 Denise Sewart's Recollections of TGI Development; Jun 6 & 7, 2016, Mike Miller emails; Jun 28, 2016, Downtown Partnership news release; my Jul 27, 2016, conversation with Denise Sewart; PT July 8, 2016; my Jul 27, 2016, conversation with Denise

Sewart; my Aug 7, 2016, conversation with Denise Sewart; TGI Gateway webpage Aug 26, 2016; Mar 15, 2017, email from TGI CEO Keith Diederich; Jun, 2017 H R C S Board meeting minutes; Jun 23,2017 Placer County Grand Jury Report; Jul 5, 2017, City Council meeting, Item #7.1; Jul. 11 & Oct. 18, 2017 comments by TGI CEO Keith Diederich; Advocates for Mentally Ill Housing, Inc. website Jul 13, 2017; TGI Facebook page Jul 13, 2017; Historical Reflections by Denise Sewart; personal notes, appointment books and records.

HOBOPHOBIA:
THE POLITICS OF FEAR
*Abbreviations: A: Acknowledgements; B: Bibliography (Sources of Information); D: Dedication; E: Epilogue; H: Hobophobia Page; T: Title Page

INDEX OF PERSONS

Index of Persons

Index of Persons

About the Author

Bill Boudier was born in Sacramento, California in 1941. He developed a strong sense of empathy for people in need as a youngster, learning from the example of his parents. He remembers them providing distressed families with bags and boxes of food during the holiday season. He also cherishes the memories of his dad helping homeless single men when he offered them steady jobs that provided security and dignity. These recollections became his inspiration as he shepherded the development of programs later in life to help homeless people in nearby Roseville, his adopted home town.

In 1962, Bill began his professional career with the State of California, where he became a resource writer and administrative analyst. In 1971, he left state employment to build his ownership in a chain of California fast food restaurants, Fosters Freeze. He soon became co-owner of the parent company, overseeing the operations of more than two hundred stores in California and Hawaii. In his late thirties, he moved from the fast food business and into banking, and then retired from business in 1982 at the age of forty-one.

Boudier returned to college and received a Bachelor of Arts degree in philosophy from California State University, Sacramento. During the same time period, he began his volunteer work by co-founding and organizing the Roseville St. Vincent de Paul Society to provide hot meals, free groceries, emergency shelter and other services to needy persons in the community. He and his wife at the time, Annette, anchored the Society's programs by purchasing several commercial buildings for its use beginning in late 1983. Bill served as the organization's president and CEO for five years. He went on to :

- Facilitate the launch of St. Vincent's Home Start, a transitional living program for families in 1986.

- Begin formal service to those in need and to the Catholic Church following ordination as a deacon by Sacramento Bishop Francis Quinn in 1988;
- Serve as Pastoral Associate at St. Rose Church, Roseville from 1988 to 2005;
- Serve for a year and a half on the Board of Directors of Roseville Home Start Inc. until November of 1996;
- Co-found The Lazarus Project, a local transitional living program for single adults in 1998, serving on its Board until 2001.
- Organize WWJD?, a ministry aiding homeless people living on the street, after the founder's death, serving as CEO, vice president, and board member from 2000 to 2004.
- Co-found and write the bylaws and nonprofit status application documents in 2001 for the Placer Care Coalition, Inc., a fundraising mechanism for the four charities he had invited to join: St. Vincent's, Home Start, The Lazarus Project and WWJD?, serving as a board member of the PCCI until 2004.
- Lead the founding and launch in 2004 of The Gathering Inn, a nomadic model emergency shelter program which provides services 24/7 to as many as ninety persons each day, including homeless single adults as well as families. He served as president and board chair until December 2005 and as CEO until March 2006, when he retired for health reasons.

Boudier remains an activist and advocate for Placer County's homeless men, women and children.